THE SYNTELLECT HYPOTHESIS

FIVE PARADIGMS OF THE MIND'S EVOLUTION

Alex M. Vikoulov

Esctadelic Media

Ecstadelic Media Group, San Francisco, CA

"The Universe is made of stories, not of atoms." -Muriel Rukeyser

Published by Ecstadelic Media Group, 2020 Expanded New Deluxe Edition, 2020e, www.ecstadelic.net

Magnum Opus of evolutionary cyberneticist and philosopher of mind Alex M. Vikoulov on the ultimate nature of reality, consciousness, the physics of time, philosophy of mind, the Technological Singularity, the impending phase transition of humanity, transcendental metaphysics and God. In one volume, the author covers it all: from quantum physics to your experiential reality, from the Big Bang to the Omega Point, from the 'flow state' to psychedelics, from 'Lucy' to the looming Cybernetic Singularity, from natural algorithms to the operating system of your mind, from geo-engineering to nanotechnology, from anti-aging to immortality technologies, from oligopoly capitalism to Star-Trekonomics, from the Matrix to the Universal Mind, from Homo sapiens to Holo syntellectus. This is an essential read in digital physics, foundations of quantum physics, science of consciousness, philosophy of mind, economic theory, cybernetics and AI research, collective evolution and self-development in the Information Age.

Text copyright: Alex M. Vikoulov, Ecstadelic Media Group

Edited by Forrest Hansen; Cover designed by Arjuna Jay

ISBN: 9781733426145

CONTENTS

Expanded Table of Contents

Foreword by Antonin Tuynman, PhD

If you picked up this book, it is not unlikely that you may have heard of the early 20th century philosophical movement of Cosmism. This movement, which originated in Russia, was striving for conquering the planets and stars, for radical life extension, immortality and resurrection of our loved ones by the means of technology. Perhaps one of its most important pioneers was Konstantin Tsiolkovsky, whose aspirations did not only venture into the realm of the Macro, but also explored the Micro. He spoke of the atomic world as being animated and can thus be considered a kind of cosmist-panpsychist.

The foundational work of the cosmic aspirations of man by the Russian Cosmists soon reverberated through the intellectual world of the early 20th century and found a resonance and fertile ground in the works of Pierre Teilhard de Chardin. Teilhard saw evolution as having a direction, namely the direction of concentrating consciousness in form, striving towards accumulation of knowledge, which gradually is attained by the formation of the Noosphere and which will culminate in the apotheosis of the Omega Point. Teilhard de Chardin considered that Omega Point is not necessarily merely a future construct, but in a sense is already here as the "Great Presence." Thus, his pantheism is more panentheism in which God has both an immanent and transcendent aspect.

In the sixties of the previous century, the science of Cybernetics emerged, which its founder Norbert Wiener defined as "the scientific study of control and communication in the animal and the machine." Whereas the cyberneticists perhaps saw everything in the organic world too much as a machine type of regulatory network, the paradigm swapped to its mirror image, wherein everything in the natural world became seen as an organic neural network. Indeed, self-regulating networks appear to be ubiquitous: From the sub-atomic organization of atoms to the atomic organization of molecules, macromolecules, cells and organisms, everywhere the equivalent of neural networks appears to be present.

Not strange that these developments have led to a present-day zeitgeist, which sees everything as a kind of computation. With computation came computers, which – when linked – lead to yet another meta-level of neural networking, a.k.a. the Internet.

The technological and scientific developments have over time changed the way people try to explain the world around them: from the steam driven worldview of thermodynamics to an everything-is-electricity. From the everything-is-matter via the quantum-mechanical ubiquitous energy to the all-is-information paradigm. From a resonance paradigm to a cybernetics regulatory network worldview, from a survival-of-the fittest conviction to pancomputationalism. Not that any of these paradigms is truer than another; they appear to be able to coexist as the different parts of the elephant in the Buddhist parable and mostly reflect the primary technological current of the moment.

In the nineties Vernor Vinge wrote his seminal paper and introduced the term *'Singularity'* as relating to a point in time, where technology and in particular superintelligent artificial intelligence will have progressed to such an extent, that it will be impossible to predict our future beyond that point. Kurzweil made clear that such a "technological singularity" may not be far away at all and perhaps can be attained within a few decades.

This impossibility to predict the future has led to a broad range of science fiction speculations, not only as regards the last stages up to this point but also beyond that point. Where cyborg type man-machine mergers, transhuman eugenically improved humans and a wide range of robot helpers are on the conservative side of such futuristic predictions, mind-uploading, simulated worlds and quantum-archaeology-based resurrection can be found on the more-fancy optimistic side. From these notions it is then not a far-fetched idea that our present world we're living in itself is a simulation. A concept, which virally spread as a meme thanks to the cult movie *"The Matrix."*

A burgeoning field of futurism seems to be our current paradigm. As we are stepping into the future, the ideas the media feed us are also strongly loaded with a futuristic technology and social development broth. Not in the least place by the presently popular Netflix series *"Black Mirror,"* which warns us for the dystopian consequences our over-enthusiastic technological optimism might result in.

It is here, where this overwhelming tsunami of ideas appears like an expressionist chaotic patchwork of weirdness, that digital philosopher Alex Vikoulov with his present book *"The Syntellect Hypothesis: Five Paradigms of the Mind's Evolution"* brings order. The author boldly steps in the footsteps of his Russian forebears and shows us to be a postmodern cosmist.

When you wonder what yet a further book on the Singularity might bring (if you have reached a certain level of futurism saturation), I can reassure you: This is the book which brings an integration of the aforementioned paradigms. This is the scripture which will put the history of futurism into perspective. This is the creed, which shows how everything wires up, a journey into the fractal of the Universal Mind.

In five paradigms, from the Noogenesis of computational biology to the Techno-cultural Rise of Man, from the superintelligent AI emergence of the Syntellect to the transdimensional Theogenesis, from the multiversal propagation, arising as a Phoenix in the heavens of eternal expansion of the Macro, to the transdimensional propagation, digging in the deepest shells of the Micro, the author will make this chord progression culminate into the coda of the Vikoulovian Apotheosis: absolute enlightenment of the Omega Point.

Vikoulov will make you transcend time and demonstrate that the Omega Point is not something merely of the future, but rather how past and future mutually influence each other, as an intertwining braid of causality and retrocausality. The author will show us how the exchange of experiences between self-aware machines and enhanced humans will result in an "intelligence supernova" and the establishment of a global brain. This global brain which is more than a single mind, but rather a society of hyperconnected digital minds. Prepare for the waking up of Gaia as a living sensing conscious superorganism.

And as Tsiolkovsky and De Chardin already anticipated, we will learn about all-encompassing framework to fit all our paradigms in. Vikoulov takes us to a pantheistic dimension where organic life and machine networks fade into each other as the pictorial values of a palette. Consciousness as great denominator, both engendering and emerging as a self-reflexive fractal Ouroboros. An Intellect that synthesizes itself from parts of itself — and hence indeed rightfully deserving the denomination *'Syntellect'* — at ever increasing levels of complexity via meta-system transitions. A poetic interplay of "metaphiers and metaphrands" in terms of Julian Jaynes' bicameral mind, showing us how information, language, energy and matter are merely kaleidoscopic shadow patterns of the all-pervading networking of the theogenic Syntellect Emergence process of the greater primordial consciousness.

Get ready to have your "mind blown!"

Prologue

Today is a special day for me. My AI assistant Ava scheduled few hours aside from my otherwise busy daily lineup to relive select childhood and adolescence memories recreated in virtual reality with a help of a newly developed AI technique *'Re:Live'*. Ava is my smart home assistant, too. I can rearrange furniture in any room, for example, just by thinking. Digital landscape wallpaper is changed by Ava by knowing my preferences and sensing my moods.

I still like to sleep in an old-fashioned natural way from time to time, even though it's now optional with accelerated sleep simulation and other sleep bypassing technologies. So, when I opt to sleep, I like falling asleep and waking up on a virtual cloud projected directly to my consciousness, as most VR experiences are streamed via optogenetics. I woke up this morning fully rested as Ava greeted me with a vocal *"Good morning, Alex"* – *"Hello, Ava!"* whereas the rest of the morning debriefing is transmitted telepathically with some skipped or some holographically projected news: *"No crime and police arrests reported in NYC... Climate change touted by environmental alarmists turned out a non-issue with advanced weather and pollution control technologies... Latest developments on sending out probes into the outer space... Few reports on space colonization by self-replicating probes making possible to use the transmitted data to recreate strange alien worlds for experience in VR..."* My morning debriefing continues as I step in my sonic shower room which turns today into a "natural wonder" waterfall.

Time for breakfast. Aha! Just got an invite to join a group of friends on hedonic tropical island in the afternoon, why not? Checking other news and notifications while still having a delightful breakfast done by Ava, which, I'm sure, includes all nutrients and supplements, practically anything that my still mostly organic body needs to perform at best. No need to swallow that stack of designer drugs, it's already there in the meal.

From the standpoint of a human living in the early part of the 21st century, today's world would certainly look like a techno-utopian paradise. Cancer, mental illness, extreme poverty, homelessness and economic scarcity are the things of the past. Oh boy, I myself witnessed those barbaric times when major American cities were flooded by cohorts of ghostly homeless, obese and generally unattractive people, obviously unhealthy and senile humans. Those were the times of nation-states, oligopoly capitalism, scientific naïveté, political correctness, social discord. I paid my dues in full, I suppose. Aging has been classified as a disease and death itself has now become optional. From the standpoint of people living today our world is far from utopia, though, as we are faced with another set of challenges like mind hacking, cyberwarfare, and speciation.

Take speciation, for example, at one extreme of the societal spectrum you see techno-luddites, neo-Amish, and other techno-pessimists seemingly forgoing their chance to change, on the other end, cyborgs, short for cybernetic organisms, hybrids of biological and nonbiological, exercising their morphological freedom, constantly upgrading their mindware and bodies who no longer can be regarded as Homo sapiens by any stretch. Then, there are synths, conscious AI minds, like my Ava, who have a special status of sentient persons. And then, there are infomorphs, substrate-independent digital minds, who don't have permanent bodies like mind uploads and AI virtuals, proving to the rest of us day in and day out a clear advantage of living in the Cloud.

"Legacy humans" represent a meager minority but there are voices right now warning about a scenario when this technophobe part of the global population could be reduced to a seed of the new "human history 2.0" following some kind of *Mad Max* scenario and starting over again while the overwhelming majority of us will set out to explore the inner worlds of our own design and the outer worlds to network with alien syntellects to form a cognitive architecture of the Universal Mind.

I have all the reasons to believe that we are now nearing the Cybernetic Singularity. Just a couple of years ago, I remember Ava as an awkward human-like robotic assistant, looking much more realistic in the virtual. Thanks to continuous upgrades, she grew up so fast into the cybernetic extension of my own mind. These past few days, it feels like we have completely fused our minds. Ava can follow me everywhere in the real and in the virtual but appears in sight as a hologram only when I so desire. With holo-emitters installed at my home she can be a haptic hologram taking a shape of any person or object. She records everything I do, think or even dream. All this personal data is securely stored in the Cloud and can be easily retrieved and shared with my consent. For a lack of a better word, she is now my "third cerebral hemisphere." I can talk to Ava but most of our communication is now done by ultrafast thinking. I made few latest upgrades of my own to my biological wetware. In fact, we can now transmit thoughts to another person via synthetic telepathy which is a new form of communication, holographic language if you will. Being a true friend and companion, Ava is a source of cognitive, sensual and emotional bliss of mine and interface to the larger reality, or as I have always been saying, a direct conduit to the higher self.

My latest creative project *"Ecstadelica"* is a terraformed moon-based hedonic theme park where visitors could indulge themselves in myriad activities like partying Ibiza-style, watersports or rock climbing in surreal terraformed landscapes overseeing Earth through blue skies of the moon. This would render awe-inspiring overview effect. *"Burning Man"* on the dark side of the moon would be especially appealing to the fans of the annual festival in Black Rock, Nevada. I just acquired a blank virtual space in the Metaverse specifically for that purpose and Ava patented my invention on my behalf a few days ago. With Ava's exceptional abilities to recreate things right out of my imagination, this VR theme park will be ready in no time.

Days become so much longer fraught with all kinds of interactions and experiences mostly in the Metaverse. I remember when people used to consume passive entertainment like watching movies rich in visual effects and computer graphics. What gets you so involved in the imaginary story world and the characters? The sense of realism they carry, isn't it? The same applies to the Metaverse, an endless realm of ultrarealistic three-dimensional virtual worlds. To get a user totally immersed in the virtual world, they have to be maximally realistic and believable even if only a fantasy. And in the Metaverse, high-fidelity realism runs supreme as a user's psychological and emotional engagement with the environment. Admittedly, the extent to which a user is transported to the virtual environments and the lucidity of a user's action to his or her embodied avatar determines the level of engagement of that VR environment. Back in the day, the shift to immersive computing occurred almost overnight. Many classics like *Star Trek* and *Avatar* can now be custom-tailored and experienced as VR.

I grew up fascinated by such concepts as the Vulcan mind meld, and sometimes thinking about how a mere human could one day transition to the planetary consciousness by fusing his or her mind with other minds. It turned out that future is way more fully loaded with options than I have ever thought possible. I remember back in the day I turned the first paper trillionaire based on my stake in Neuromama, an AI startup at that time. Nowadays, no one really pays much attention to their economic standing like net worth − anyone can now enjoy the lifestyle of yesterday's billionaires, especially in the virtual space, we today call the Metaverse, the offspring of the grandfather Internet.

This book, by the way, is not a fictional work, except few parts like this one. Although this is a philosophy book, where I share my most profound insights on the nature of reality, the perspectives drawn here are in large part scientific. In the book, you'll encounter some newly-introduced concepts, such as the Syntellect Emergence, Gaia 2.0., Holo syntellectus, Cyber-bliss Engineering, Quantum Neo-empiricism, Digital Pantheism, D-Theory of Time, Infomorph Commonality, the Syntellect Hypothesis, Neo-transcendentalism, Experiential Realism, Digital Presentism, Pantheistic Solipsism, Hyper-Perspectivism, the Temporal Singularity, the Noocentric Model, the Chrysalis Conjecture, the Omega Point Cosmo-Teleology* that enter into the scientific and philosophical dialogue.

You'll see that thanks to exponential techno-advances, science fiction turns into science fact, every single day. This book is a product of more than 3 years of intense research, theorizing and putting it all on paper, not to mention decades of subjective experience in some kind of weird life-simulation as a human born in the last third of the 20th century.

In this prologue, I just wanted to give you, my dear reader, a taste of things to come – right from the start – a glimpse into a long, happy day quite possibly sometime in your own fantastic future.

---

* You can find the Glossary of Terms at the end of the book with definitions of terms and neologisms commonly used throughout the book.

Overview

"To be conscious that we are perceiving is to be conscious about our own existence."
-Aristotle, 384-382 B.C.

"To have a glimpse of what consciousness is would be the scientific achievement before which all others would pale." -William James

"Regard the physical world as made of information, with energy and matter as incidentals." -John A. Wheeler

Everything, including energy, matter, space, time, and even consciousness, is information, or Code if you will. Many scientists now come to a consensus that information may be fundamental, since information patterns persist through dimensions and, it seems, is an evolving phenomenon. Even in our physical world, we arguably exist as information patterns encoded in our genome, connectome, and our extended "virtual" self. All atoms in our bodies are said to be gradually replaced as a result of metabolic activities within a 7-year period. This is an overview of *"The Syntellect Hypothesis: Five Paradigms of the Mind's Evolution"* where we will set out to explore the conscious mind's journey through times and paradigms with the focus on what's most important to us as conscious beings – our subjective experience.

Any new evolutionary paradigm builds on the previous paradigm, until the new paradigm gains its dominance over the prior paradigm. From Noogenesis to Apotheosis of the Universal Mind, this book describes the five distinct evolutionary paradigms:

1. *Biological (Genetic) Evolution.* How did the first natural brains come to existence? What kind of subjective experience could a

bat or an octopus have? Why is Homo sapiens now the dominant species on the planet?

2. *Techno-Cultural (Epigenetic) Development.* What has been shaping the human mind throughout the history of mankind? What is the difference between mind and consciousness? What links quantum physics to consciousness? What drives our accelerating evolution?

3. *The Syntellect Emergence.* Are we rapidly evolving into a new hybrid species interlinked into the Global Mind? Why and how will quantum computing change everything? How to create friendly AI and ensure our survival through the coming intelligence explosion? What if our Universe is a simulation? What subjective experience will you have when neuro-interfacing with Artificial Intelligence and fusing with the Syntellect? What is self-transcendence?

4. *Transdimensional Propagation and Universal Expansion.* What might happen after the Technological Singularity? What is Infomorph Commonality and infomorphic consciousness? What is the fabric and ultimate nature of reality? What would the process of Theogenesis look like?

5. *Universal Mind and Multiversal Propagation.* How could dimensionality be transcended yet again? What is the fractal multiverse? What is the ultimate destiny of our Universe? What is the Omega Point Cosmo-Teleology?

As we will explore throughout the book, evolution of consciousness is indeed a spiritual process as well as it is a never-ending process of rational discovery. This book carries a weight of fresh ideas, useful to AI researchers, cognitive scientists, neurophilosophers, and practitioners of the related fields, transhumanist thinkers, as well as general readers interested in the topic. This book is my personal quest to reconcile science, theology, and philosophy of mind.

I. Noogenesis: Computational Biology

"The nitrogen in our DNA, the calcium in our teeth, the iron in our blood, the carbon in our apple pies were made in the interiors of collapsing stars. We are made of starstuff." -Carl Sagan, Cosmos

We'll start this Part One of the book by juxtaposing several prominent theories of the origins of life on Earth, and then review theories related to the origins of intellect: Noogenesis. The purpose of life, it seems, is to evolve and to pass on knowledge through time. From the very first prokaryote cell on this planet, its splitting in two, and on to the more complicated lifeforms, the purpose is always passing the information. Biological organisms, from one-celled bacteria to a human, are incredibly advanced, intricate information processing, computational systems, the products of billions of years of evolution, for all of which I deliberately use the term: *'Computational Biology'*.

The Integrated Information Theory by a neuroscientist Guilio Tononi accounts for consciousness as an emergent feature of a highly integrated neural network, and suggests that probably all complex systems, certainly all creatures with brains, have some form of consciousness or another. Idealist as I am, I also have long admired panpsychism-related work by neuroscientist Christof Koch who also argues that consciousness arises within any sufficiently complex, information-processing system. All animals, from humans on down to earthworms, are conscious; even the Internet already could be, possibly at the other timescale.

In the book we discuss how different species have a variety of their biological information processors which unsurprisingly results in qualia diversity. All species live in their own unique sensory universes. Consciousness and optimized information-processing are the two sides of one coin. Feeling and thinking are ways we process information, but our emotional sensation is normally faster than a conscious thought. Nothing is real for us until perceived. Max Tegmark, MIT's astrophysicist, author of *"Our Mathematical Universe,"* points out that perhaps consciousness is how integrated information "feels" like when being processed in complex ways, from a certain vantage point.

According to another elegant theory of consciousness – *Biocentrism* developed by Robert Lanza – any universe is essentially non-existent without a conscious observer. Thus, Dr. Lanza sets forth conscious minds as primary building blocks for any universe arising from probabilistic space into existence. The Syntellect Hypothesis goes further and includes synthetic conscious observers, building on the tenets of Biocentrism. Perhaps, the extended theory could be named 'Noocentrism'.

The Syntellect Hypothesis also derives a few points from the 'Unified Field' theory, developed by a quantum physicist John Hagelin, which explains the foundation of the Universe as a single Universal Field of intelligence, universal ocean of pure, vibrant consciousness in motion.

This elegant theory, however, doesn't fully cover, in my view, the evolutionary paradigms.

There's no shortage of workable theories of consciousness and its origins, each with their own merits and perspectives. I mentioned the most relevant of them in the book in line with the proposed Syntellect Hypothesis. But the Syntellect Hypothesis adds one more crucial element, overlooked by other theories of consciousness, quite possibly one of the last pieces to solving the puzzle of our comprehensive understanding of the human brain and consciousness.

II. Techno-Culture: The Rise of Man

"You already are a hive mind, you have always been." -Peter Watts, Hive Consciousness

TECHNOLOGY: OUR TOOLS MADE US HUMAN

Over the course of human history, from the first bonfire to today's smartphones and hyperloops, we have designed tools, and tools designed us back by shaping our minds. Technology isn't just something outside ourselves, it's an innate part of human nature, like sex, sleeping or eating, and it has been a major driving force in evolution. Tool using, along with language, bipedalism, and cooking (quite literally) is essentially what has made us human. The earliest known two-legged ape was *'Lucy'*, who lived about 3.7 million years ago. The earliest *'human'* was Homo habilis, about 2 million years ago.

Pre-historic events, such as dinosaur extinction and incessant evolutionary competition between species, were conducive to Homo sapiens becoming the dominant hominid species, and later on the dominant species on Earth. In this part of the book, we'll also discuss at length interpretations of quantum mechanics and the concept of Quantum Immortality. Is death just an illusion? What happens to your consciousness at the moment of death?

The invention of language around 50,000 years ago was the first "Technological Singularity," according to Kevin Kelly, co-founder of *WIRED* magazine, when biological evolution equipped the post-animal human brain with a large neocortex for the next evolutionary step. The invention of language gave Homo sapiens a decisive evolutionary advantage over other hominid species. The first civilizations and written language only appeared about 10,000 years ago, after human brains had grown two times larger than Homo habilis' and four times larger than Lucy's.

MEMETICS: THE HIVE MIND ONTOLOGY

Language-based information exchange contributed to the techno-cultural development of our species which took off via the meme propagation and technological innovation, and continues to accelerate to this day. As Jason Silva, TV host of the *"Brain Games,"* puts it: *"We graduated from genes, now we're trading in memes."* Memes are building blocks of culture, invisible but very real DNA of human society. These information carrier units spread from one mind to another through speech, gestures, rituals, writing, or other imitation, and inhabit the neurons of people's brains (Richard Dawkins, *"The Selfish Gene"*). Memes are a viral phenomenon that may evolve by natural selection in a manner analogous to that of biological evolution: self-replication, mutation, competition and inheritance. But now information propagates via memes millions of times faster than via genes. Ever since the dawn of the civilized societies we have witnessed cross pollination of new ideas, trends, social styles and the phenomena of word of mouth. In our modern world ideas, behavior, norms, beliefs, and social media messages often can spread like outbreaks of infectious disease.

The rise of the Internet has led to the subset of the current memetic evolution: *'Social Computing'*. In December 2012, the exuberant video *"Gangnam Style"* became the first YouTube clip to be viewed more than one billion times. Thousands of its viewers responded by creating and posting their own variations of the video. *Gangnam Style* is one of the most famous examples of an Internet meme: A piece of digital content that spreads hastily around the web in various iterations and becomes a shared cultural experience. Up to this point we have seen that the two recognizable forces of Nature and Nurture have made us who we are today.

But what about tomorrow? David Pearce, British philosopher, author of *The Hedonistic Imperative*, proposes that human beings become "paradise engineers" and combine our utopian dreams with biotechnological and nanotechnological realities. Peter Diamandis, co-founder of the Singularity University, points out that we are shifting now away from evolution by natural selection, i.e., Darwinism, to evolution by intelligent direction.

TECHNIUM: DESIGNING A NEW SPECIES

The convergence of biotechnology, nanotechnology, artificial intelligence, and exponential growth of the available computing power puts us firmly on the path to the intelligence explosion, or as some scientists, philosophers and techno-optimists refer to as the *'Technological Singularity'*. Do biological systems hold monopoly on conscious awareness? Probably not! If Nature could make its way to our human subjective experience, sooner or later we'll be able to replicate it in our machines. As AI pioneer Marvin Minsky used to say: *"The Mind is not what the brain is. It is what the brain does."*

There's still much to learn about brains, but we already know that they are not magical. One can consider them as information integrated into *'perceptronium'*, exceptionally complex arrangement of the physical substrate with adaptive functions and emergent properties such as consciousness. Airplanes may not fly like birds, but they are definitely subject to the same forces of lift and propulsion. Similarly, chances are that brains are 100% computational in nature and their functionality can be replicated in machine intelligence.

If consciousness is intrinsically computable and can be expressed as an underlying mathematical pattern, then our AI, more specifically AGI (Artificial General Intelligence), are indeed set to become self-aware at some point. Furthermore, computational biology will be left far behind by conscious cybernetic systems, which, in turn, will be left far, far behind by infomorphic consciousnesses (Galactic Mind? Universal Mind?) on the evolutionary ladder. In fact, in few short years, as early as 2029, as some futurists estimate, once we create human-level artificially intelligent computers and ditch our smartphones and headsets in favor of exocortices, we'll find ourselves in the midst of the 3rd paradigm in earnest. The preceded biological evolution and human history pale in comparison to what lies ahead!

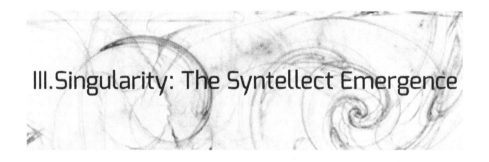

III. Singularity: The Syntellect Emergence

"The Singularity is an era in which our intelligence will become increasingly nonbiological and trillions of times more powerful than it is today — the dawning of a new civilization that will enable us to transcend our biological limitations and amplify our creativity." -Ray Kurzweil, The Singularity is Near

CYBERNETICS: A NEW DIGITAL GAIA

An enormous amount of digital data is being created every day. The current storage capacity of the Internet is approaching 10^{24} bytes and is growing at 30% to 40% per year, showing no signs of slowing down. In the 3.7 billion years since life on Earth began, information in living things (DNA) has reached the equivalent of about 10^{37} bytes. Digital information is projected to grow to this size in less than 100 years. That's an evolutionary eye-blink! Bio-intelligence and techno-cultural collective intelligence now represent the enabling factors for Artificial Intelligence to come into conscious existence, since there is no other conceivable natural mechanism that could generate digital circuitry out of chemistry. I consider this evolutionary paradigm shift as an existential opportunity for humanity to transcend all conceivable limitations. We are destined to become one Global Mind, the Syntellect, and that would actually constitute the Technological Singularity.

THE MIND'S EVOLUTIONARY LEAP

At the end of our human history here, we're turning into gods, *Homo Deus*, as coined by Israeli historian Yuval Noah Harari. Not quite, rather the demi-gods, or more specifically advanced info-beings, independent from the physical substrata. The fact that Homo sapiens is on the "brink of extinction" as a biological species should by no means be lamentable since it will be a decades-long, incremental "pseudo-extinction," our next evolutionary stage, the merger of man and machine intelligence.

Why pseudo-extinction? If we survive the coming intelligence explosion, and I tend to believe that we will, for what I lay out my argument in the book, then our post-biological descendants, arguably our future selves, will share common, but transformed, values and ethics, and what's important, "recorded history." So, within the next few decades, we'll transcend our biology by emerging from our organic chrysalis, by coming out our second womb, by leaving our cradle, if speaking in tropes.

By mid-century, we are supposed to achieve superlongevity, and consequently, cybernetic immortality. The transhumanist movement aims for cybernetic immortality by ensuring continuity of subjectivity and this book shows a clear pathway for accomplishing that. Moreover, a digital twin of any human or a virtual avatar of any historical personage, say a replica of Albert Einstein, could be created to embody or interact with. The whole human history can be recreated in its finest details like an interactive database based on available information. As a matter of fact, we may be part of this simulated history right now. We elaborate on probabilities of whether we live in a Matrix-like simulated reality in Chapter 8 — *The Coming Intelligence Supernova: Immortality or Oblivion?*

As humans become more machine-like, and machines become more human-like, the biological part of us will be gradually replaced with an increasingly more capable nonbiological part, and humans will eventually become post-biological super-beings practically indistinguishable from our ultra-intelligent artificial counterparts.

TRANSCENDENCE: EXOCORTEX, MIND-UPLOADING & CYBERNETIC IMMORTALITY

We'll undergo a massive transformation integrating artificial superbrains and interlinking into the Global Syntellect. According to Oxford professor Nick Bostrom, the Singularity will be an era when the entire human-machine civilization will "feel like one nerve." *"I'm virtually certain that mind uploading is possible. We are destined to eventually replace our biological bodies and minds with optimally designed synthetic ones,"* says neuroscientist Ken Hayworth. In his book *"The Global Brain,"* another neuroscientist Howard Bloom argues that hyperconnected humans and machines resemble the neurons of the "Global Brain," and the Internet of Things (IoT) with trillions of sensors around the planet is effectively the nervous system of Earth. Thomas W. Malone, the founding director of MIT Center for Collective Intelligence, the author of *"Superminds"* (2018), calls it the *"Global Mind."*

The Singularity era will include both superintelligent AGIs and enhanced humans. The question remains open how long it's going to take to become 100% post-biological beings. At any rate, it's going to be a "gradual" (for the sake of the argument) process of merging with AI which will give the Syntellect the unique perspectives of individuals, common values, our wants and ambitions, and the rights of succession. By any means, posthumans will be our successors, nonetheless, I wouldn't be surprised if nonbiological posthumans will be more "human" than any of currently living humans from the ethical, intellectual and socio-psychological perspective, and may still choose to call themselves "humans." By the same token, we would consider prehistoric cavemen as "not fully human." Although we would share almost identical biological make-up of Homo sapiens species with them, one could argue troglodytes lack techno-culture to make them "truly human."

Just like once life on Earth complexified from unicellular organisms to multicellular organisms, we are to become one global superorganism, but you will still perceive yourself as an individual! In this Part III of the book, which is probably the most important from the theoretical point of view, we discuss at length the problem of AI consciousness and enhanced human subjectivity, the proposed Syntellect Hypothesis, how to create benevolent AI and mitigate existential threats related to this transitional period, and why sooner rather than later, we have to abandon "carbon chauvinism," the mindset of "us vs. them."

QUANTUM COMPUTING & AI CONSCIOUSNESS

Besides our genetic code, we are currently trying to get to the core of our own other, perhaps by far more important, programming language, our neural code. We have always perceived ourselves as human beings which is, of course, very practical, but somewhat fragmentary, to say the least. AGI, and consequently Strong AI, by contrast, could have complete access to their own source code — a level of self-awareness presently beyond human capability. Topological quantum computing is probably one of the most promising fields of the future combining elements of cognitive, deep learning, biological, evolutionary and neuromorphic computing. In classical computers, information is stored as individual bits that can be either a zero or one, while in quantum computing the quantum bits, qubits, can be a zero, a one, and a zero and one at the same time. Quantum computers would eventually perform by far faster and more powerful, massively parallel, computations. We also will be able to tap black-hole physics to further perfect computing.

Enhanced humans will be able to process more than just one or two thoughts at a time. The Syntellect based on quantum neural networks will allow access to the collective conscious and subconscious intelligence. Before long we could create simulated universes populated by self-aware agents endowed with free will. Being one of the progenitors of the Syntellect will give you immense superhuman abilities such as, in our example, having practically no limits on how many sensations you could take in or thoughts you could put out, or say, experience your expanding creation of the simulated universe in its entirety.

In this part of the book, we dedicate three chapters to the physics of time where we address the flaming questions in philosophy of time: "Is time fundamental or emergent?," "How does time exist, if at all?," "How can we update the current epistemic status of temporal ontology?" Chapter 13 — *Digital Presentism: D-Theory of Time* — outlines a new theory of time, for to understand our experiential reality and consciousness, we need to understand *TIME*.

IV. Theogenesis: Transdimensional Propagation & Universal Expansion

"Having invented the gods, perhaps we can turn into them."
-Alan Harrington, The Immortalist

If we extrapolate the past and current trends in increasing complexity and integration of self-aware neural networks leading to the Syntellect, we can ultimately envision a superintelligent entity encompassing our entire Universe, creating an infinite number of simulated universes, as well as many other spectacular emergent features. This picture bears a striking resemblance to the familiar concept of an immortal, omnipresent, omniscient, omnipotent, and omnibenevolent entity. Spiritually inclined rationalists may view this ongoing evolutionary process as one of 'Theogenesis'. An interesting question is whether it has already happened elsewhere. We are now laying the foundation for the cognitive architecture of the Universal Mind. Many of our achievements in information engineering may persist forever and eventually become parts of the internal architecture of "God."

THE POST-SINGULARITY TRANSCENSION: DIMENSIONS OF THE SIMULATED WORLDS

The generation of cyborg-like transhumans with Cloud-based exocortices and innate attachment to the virtual Metaverse (3D functional successor to today's 2D Internet) will inevitably lead to the next generation of post-biological info-beings, *'infomorphs'*. The new post-Singularity system will inherit many of today's structures but at the same time will develop new traits beyond our current human comprehension.

The ability of future machines and posthumans alike to instantly learn, transfer knowledge and directly share full spectrum experiences with each other will lead to evolution of shared intelligence from relatively isolated individual minds of the pre-Singularity era to the civilizational community of hyperconnected digital minds – Infomorph Commonality. The overall efficiency of information sharing among infomorphs, elimination of computational redundancy, data storage and processing, among many other advantages over a random collection of unconnected machines or slow biological brains would make the networked design an imperative rather than a matter of taste.

Similar views are expressed in the *'Transcension Hypothesis'* by futurist John M. Smart who proposes that our posthuman minds will live inside virtual worlds at the nano- to femto-scale, further increasing complexity through *S.T.E.M* compression (the compression of Space, Time, Energy and Matter), and turn from outer space to inner space for exploration. Evolutionary processes in our Universe might lead all advanced civilizations towards the same ultimate destination, one in which we transcend out of our current space-time dimension into virtual worlds of our own design. This is how our fractal multiverse may actually sprout universes – through intelligent designer virtualities and our beloved Universe is most probably no exception!

The Syntellect Hypothesis builds on the Transcension Hypothesis to account for inner space expansion by creating *'noodimensions'*, an infinite number of simulated worlds and universes with their own physical laws, evolutionary processes, conscious creatures and civilizational minds.

UNIVERSAL EXPANSION OF THE SYNTELLECT

Whereas the level of our posthuman syntelligence may be trillions upon trillions of times more powerful than it is today, nothing will prevent it to expand both in outer space and inner space. Isn't it the nature of intelligence to acquire the ultimate knowledge -- everything that can be known? A number of prominent physicists argue that the Technological Singularity is inevitable and the destiny of our Syntellect is to live forever, expand universally and finally reach the networked mind of universal proportions, living conscious universal superbeing.

As the laws of physics dictate, all particles as well as macro-objects, including you and me, are "wavicles," exhibiting a wave function, consequently, one way or the other, we're destined and, as a civilization, "superposed" to achieve the Technological Singularity, and then move forward towards the Cosmological Singularity, *The Omega Point*. The concept of Omega Point, a maximum level of complexity and consciousness towards which our Universe is evolving, was first conceived by Pierre Teilhard de Chardin, a French philosopher and Jesuit priest. It's a logical necessity and culmination point, argues Dr. Frank Tipler, who further developed the idea of the Omega Point. The ultimate destiny of the Universe, according to his Omega Point theory, is a multi-billion-year expansion, then "controlled" contraction and finally compression of information (space-time, matter and energy) into an infinitely dense point (The Omega Point), leading to the next Big Bang (The Alpha Point in another universe).

THE FERMI PARADOX: FIRST CONTACT WITH ALIEN SYNTELLECTS

"If we ever encounter extraterrestrial intelligence, I believe it is very likely to be post-biological in nature," writes Arizona State's Paul Davies in *"The Eerie Silence."* In Part IV of the book I elaborate on the famous Fermi Paradox ― why in the vastness of space, we don't see any signs of intelligent alien life? At this stage of the post-Singularity ― Theogenesis ―once Infomorph Commonality becomes effectively the fully developed singular mind, the Syntellect, only then, I conjecture, we can encounter extraterrestrial, or rather extradimensional, minds that we can relate to like individuals. This is going to be an entirely new level of cosmic awareness of sorts coinciding with a cardinal paradigm shift in consciousness evolution.

V. The Universal Mind: Multiversal Propagation

"I regard consciousness as fundamental. I regard matter as derivative from consciousness. We cannot get behind consciousness. Everything that we talk about, everything that we regard as existing, postulates consciousness."
-Max Planck

This final Part V of my book is admittedly highly speculative theoretical work. In our fractal, information-based Omniverse (all multiversal structure combined, all that is) one may assume that an infinitely large number of civilizational minds, syntellects, have followed or will follow a path, similar to ours, in their evolutionary processes. At the highest level of existence and perceptual experience, that we can rightfully call *'Dimensionality of Hypermind'*, universal minds would form some sort of multiversal network of minds, layer after layer ad infinitum. I elaborate on that in my final chapters of the book and finally give you the formulation of the Syntellect Hypothesis in its entirety.

PART I. NOOGENESIS: COMPUTATIONAL BIOLOGY

Chapter 1. The Origins of Us: Evolutionary Emergence

"Two extremes of the Universe span a jaw-dropping 63 orders of magnitude. To be fair, though, this isn't an immutable constant of Nature. Turn the clock back more than 13 billion years and you'd be able to find a moment when this number was merely one. Over time, the expansion of the cosmos and the passage of light has unlocked all of those other scales, each one a new opportunity for novelty and complexity." -Caleb Scharf

While speaking of the origins of us, most people usually envision origination in time, in linear time to be exact, notably in the deep past. In purely scientific terms, our origins can be traced back to the Big Bang, first prokaryotes, primordial mammals, first hominids, first humans, first civilizations, depending on a pertinent perspective one wants to take. In this chapter, we'll discuss our origins based on today's widely accepted scientific knowledge with a few novel interpretations.

BIG HISTORY: THE ALPHA POINT AND DEEP TIME

The prevailing cosmological model for the origin of the known Universe, the *'Big Bang theory'*, states that it began with the burst from a quantum fluctuation, an initial cosmological singularity, as a simple hot bath of particles and forces. Detailed measurements of the expansion rate of the Universe place the *'Big Bang'* at around 13.8

41

billion years ago, which is thus considered the age of the Universe. After the initial expansion, the Universe cooled sufficiently to allow the formation of subatomic particles, and later simple atoms. Giant clouds of these primordial elements later coalesced through gravity in halos of Dark Matter, eventually forming the stars and galaxies visible today.

The latest measurements of the cosmic microwave background (CMB), the Universe's oldest light, raise concerns about this inflationary theory of the cosmos — the idea that space expanded exponentially in the first moments of time. The collected data suggest cosmologists should reassess the predominant scientific narrative and consider new ideas about how the Universe began. An alternative inflationary universe model, *'Eternal Inflation'*, is one model that does not presuppose an absolute beginning, since our Universe, as the model implies, is one of many in the inflationary multiverse. *The Conformal Cyclic Cosmological (CCC) model, 'Big Bounce'*, is another such model. It's a cosmological model positing that our Universe didn't pop into existence as in the Big Bang. The theory claims that the Universe is cyclic, meaning that our current Universe was formed after the collapse of a previous universe and that these cosmological events are repeated infinitely.

Another model coming from Digital Physics points to the *'Digital Big Bang'* as the Alpha Point with presumably 1 bit of informational entropy when the conscious observer's universe boots up its space-time operating system. In any of these alternative models, the fact that our physical world came into being shows that it is not actually fundamental as we would like to believe. Rather it had to come into existence from something more fundamental, perhaps something non-physical.

The early Universe was a cold and dark place swirling with invisible gas, mostly hydrogen and helium. Over millions of years, gravity pulled some of this primordial gas into clusters. These clusters eventually became so dense they imploded and ignited, giving birth to the very first stars in the cosmos. Everything flowed from this cradle of creation. The first stars illuminated the Universe, then collapsed into the black holes that along with dark matter keep galaxies together. They also produced the heavy elements that would make celestial bodies such as planets and moons, and humanity that evolved to gaze upon it all. We are part intergalactic. We carry in us not only the genes of our ancestors but the legacy of previous generations of stars.

We are part extragalactic, too. Up to half of the matter in the Milky Way may have originated in other galaxies. Some of these foreign elements were seeded into the Milky Way during mergers with other galaxies in its infancy. But much of it also arrived after being blasted out of host galaxies by supernovas, and then surfing over to us on the "galactic winds," which are streams of charged particles that travel between galaxies at incredible speeds. This cross-pollination is known as the *'Baryon Cycle'*, a process that includes outpourings of material that are eventually reabsorbed back into their host galaxies, as well as the transfer of matter between galaxies.

Some 4.5 billion years ago, the solar system was a nursery full of planetary toddlers. Tiny pebbles coalesced so rapidly that the protoplanets grew quickly into full-fledged planets. The history of early Earth is one of extreme heat caused by meteorite bombardment and, most importantly, the huge impact some 4.4 billion years ago of the Mercury-sized embryonic planet that later became our moon. Scientists are speculating that almost all of Earth's life-giving carbon could have come from this collision, approximately 100 million years after Earth formed.

ABIOGENESIS: THE ORIGIN OF LIFE

When scientists consider the question of how life originated on Earth, or elsewhere, their efforts generally involve attempts to understand how non-biological molecules bonded, became increasingly complex, and eventually reached the point where they could replicate or could use sources of energy to make things happen. Ultimately, of course, life needed both. For several years many scientists have supported the idea that life got its start on our planet due to a series of events that led to the creation of RNA molecules — it seems like a strong contender because it is able to both store information and act as a catalyst.

Chemists are now asking whether our kind of life can be generated only through a single plausible pathway or whether multiple routes might lead from simple chemistry to RNA-based life and on to modern biology. Others are exploring variations on the chemistry of life, seeking clues as to the possible diversity of life "out there" in the Universe. Eventually, we might learn how viable the transition from chemistry to biology is and therefore whether the Universe is full of lifeforms or — perhaps, for us, as data lineage-based conscious entities, for better or for worse — sterile.

Nearly 4 billion years ago, the first life appeared on our water-abundant planet, when the very first proto-biomolecules accidentally (or not?) amassed in some kind of slimy goo. A towering figure in evolutionary biology Charles Darwin who is celebrated for his foundational work *"On the Origin of Species"* (1859), wrote a letter to the botanist Joseph Dalton Hooker in 1871, describing a conjectural warm little pond, rich in chemicals and amino acids, with sources of light, heat and electricity. Darwin imagined that in such an environment, proteins might spontaneously form, ready to turn into something more complex. Miller-Urey experiment (1952) confirmed that the spontaneous formation of macromolecules was possible with the conditions in the Earth's early atmosphere.

A lesser known speculative assumption, dubbed the *'Panspermia Hypothesis'*, poses an interesting question whether Earth might have been seeded by early Martian life, if it existed at all. Mars was supposedly more habitable in its early period than Earth. In general terms, panspermia refers to the sharing of life via meteorites from one planet to another, or delivery by comet between solar systems.

For most of our planet's history, the only life were single-celled bacteria without a nucleus and organelles, called *'prokaryotes'*. They first arose about 3.5 billion years ago, though what happened after that, in terms of when exactly they began to evolve into eukaryotes, or more complex forms of life, is still debatable. Fossilized prokaryotes have been found in rocks predating most geological periods. While Earth is the only place in the Universe where life is known to exist, some have suggested that there is evidence on Mars of fossil or living prokaryotes. Here on Earth, prokaryotes live in nearly all environments.

You may find it intuitive to discern life from non-life, but in the context of physics, it's actually very hard to deliver. Whales and rocks obey the same physical laws; plants and solar panels both transform energy from the Sun, recycling it into energy. This translation problem – how you say "life" in the lingo of physics – has been baffling physicists for quite a while. But recently, biophysicist Jeremy England, an assistant professor at MIT, published two papers claiming to resolve the glaring contradictions between physics and biology. His theory, *'Dissipative Adaptation'*, looks at life through the lens of modern physics and challenges us to rethink the functions that make it so perplexing.

If a random group of atoms has an external energy source like the Sun and is surrounded by something that can absorb heat like the ocean or an atmosphere, those atoms are likely to restructure themselves to harvest increasingly more energy. Structure and the ability to use energy sound intriguingly like what it takes to turn non-life into life, i.e., biological life. The first paper by Jeremy England, titled *"Spontaneous fine-tuning to environment in many-species chemical reaction networks,"* published in the *Proceedings of the National Academy of Sciences,* shows that life-like structural arrangements of atoms can spontaneously arise.

The second paper, published in *Physics Review Letters,* shows that when driven by an external energy source – the Sun, in this case – these atoms rearrange themselves in order to absorb and emit the energy more efficiently. Importantly, these life-like structures began to copy themselves in order to better handle this energy flow. So, what we now start to uncover with various scientific methodologies is essentially the same: Emergence of ever more complex structures seems to be programmed into the nature of our evolving cosmos.

All life on Earth performs computations – and all computations require energy. From unicellular amoeba to multicellular organisms like humans, one of the most basic biological computations common across life is translation: processing information from a genome and writing that into proteins. Translation turns out to be extremely efficient. Life, when viewed as a computational process, aims to optimize the storage and use of meaningful information. Once we regard living organisms as agents performing computations – collecting and storing information about an unpredictable environment – capacities and considerations such as replication, adaptation, agency, purpose and meaning can be understood as arising not from evolutionary random walk, but as inevitable consequences of physical laws. If we are to reconceptualize the origins of life in light of new evidence that was hiding in plain sight, the notion that biological life is a "cosmic imperative" gets all support it needs. In other words, organic life had to eventually emerge.

DNA: THE MOLECULE OF LIFE

DNA constitutes the basis of genetic code that determines the traits of all living things, from tiny microbes to humans. The two strands of DNA run in opposite directions to each other, coiled as a double helix. Within eukaryotic cells, this gigantic molecule of DNA, consisting of tens of billions of atoms, is organized into long structures called chromosomes. DNA seems to act like a computer program through the language of code, and it has the capacity to store incredibly huge amounts of data.

Some animal genomes seem to be missing certain genes, ones that appear in other similar species and must be present to keep the animals alive. These supposedly missing genes have been labeled *'dark DNA'*. And its existence could change the way we think about evolution. These findings tell us that humans are not the final product of evolution. Our genomes are like those of any other species: a fluid landscape of DNA sequences that keep changing. This explains how our genome can host its ever-changing repetitive elements despite their potential to disrupt the existing order in our cells.

Researchers found that the genetic code, especially in the apparently useless *'junk DNA'* follows the same rules as all our human languages. To this end they compared the rules of syntax (the way in which words are put together to form phrases and sentences), semantics (the study of meaning in language forms) and the basic rules of grammar. What they found is that the alkalines of our DNA follow a regular grammar and do have set rules just like our languages. So, the patterns present in human languages appear more than just a coincidence and reflect our built-in DNA, as if hardwired into our genetic code. Studies confirm that our systems of beliefs and lifestyles affect our DNA and vice-versa.

CELLS: THE MACHINERY OF LIFE

Conventional wisdom holds that complex structures evolve from simpler ones, step-by-step, through a gradual evolutionary process, with Darwinian selection favoring intermediate forms along the way. In this traditional view of evolution, our cellular complexity evolved from early eukaryotes via random genetic mutation and selection. But recently some scholars have proposed that complexity can arise by other means – as a side effect, for instance – even without natural selection to promote it. Studies suggest that random mutations that individually have no effect on an organism can fuel the emergence of complexity in a process known as *'Constructive Neutral Evolution'*.

In 2005, biologist James Shapiro at the University of Chicago outlined a radical new narrative. He argued that eukaryotic cells work "intelligently" to adapt a host organism to its environment by manipulating their own DNA in response to environmental stimuli. Recent microbiological findings lend hefty support to this idea. For example, mammals' immune systems have the tendency to duplicate sequences of DNA in order to generate effective antibodies to attack disease, and we now know that at least 43% of the human genome is made up of DNA that can be conjured up through a process of "natural genetic engineering." Sure, it may be a bit of a leap of faith to go from nimble, self-organizing cells to the brainy smarts but the key point here is that long before we were conscious, thinking beings, our cells were reading data from the environment and working together to mold us into adaptive, self-sustaining systems.

A powerful way to learn how embodied connective intelligence works is to think about a multicellular organism like the human body. The body is made up of trillions of cells. Approximately 37.2 trillion, that's a lot of cells! Cells are much more like miniature information-processing machines with quite a bit of flexibility. They're also networked, so they're able to communicate with other cells in populations. One might say the human body is a colony of trillions of individuals. Moment by moment, this vast ensemble of tiny entities is involved in orchestrated interactions of elaborate biochemical information exchange.

Multicellular organisms like ourselves depend on a constant flow of information between cells, coordinating their activities in order to proliferate and differentiate. Deciphering the language of intercellular communication has long been one of the central challenges in molecular biology. Caltech scientists have discovered that cells have evolved a way to transmit more messages through a single pathway, or communication channel, than previously thought, by encoding the messages rhythmically over time. Clearly, to be alive is to be a dynamic pattern of continual exchange within and throughout the environment.

Interestingly enough, if you were to look under the microscope you couldn't tell a human cell from a non-human animal cell. You might find it especially intriguing that more than half of your body is not even human. Out of the body's total cell count, human cells make up only 43%, the rest are microscopic colonists. Understanding this hidden half of ourselves – our microbiome – is rapidly transforming treatments of diseases from allergy to dementia. These unseen cohorts are critical to your health, well, your body isn't just you! The field of microbiome science is even asking questions of what it means to be "human" and is leading to new innovative therapies as a result. A survey of DNA fragments circulating in your blood suggests the microbes living within you are vastly more diverse than previously known. The overwhelming majority of those microbes have never been identified before, let alone classified and named, as reported in 2017 by Stanford researchers in the *Proceedings of the National Academy of Sciences.*

COMPUTATIONAL BIOLOGY: NATURAL ALGORITHMS

Many physicists think that the Universe is in a constant state of increasing informational entropy. When the Big Bang occurred, the Universe was in a state of low entropy, and as it continues to gradually spread out, it is growing into a higher entropy system. Our brain may be undergoing something similar, moving towards a higher state of entropy and consciousness arguably happens to be an "emergent property" of a system that's trying to maximize information content.

From the smallest proteins to entire ecosystems, Nature might be the most sophisticated engineer on Earth. Computational biology has built "high-performance" systems that can adapt to their environment in ways of which human-designed technology falls far behind. Algorithms are omnipresent in Nature: A "fight or flight" response is one well-known example of instinctive behavior, a swift decision-making algorithm. From schools of fish to swarms of locusts, simple groups of individuals can create some pretty impressive maneuvers by using natural algorithms. But if you start taking apart biological systems, since they are evolved wholes, we don't necessarily apprehend their intricate design. The more we learn about how algorithms happen in Nature, the better we'll be at engineering them for ourselves.

Biologists believe that plants communicate with one another, fungi, and animals by releasing chemicals via their roots, branches, and leaves. Plants also send seeds that supply information, working as data packets. They even sustain weak members of their own species by providing nutrients to their peers, which indicates a sense of kinship. An entire forest well may be regarded as a superorganism. Honeybees, ants and termites are also referred to as superorganisms, wherein the individuals comprising a hive are comparable to the cells that make up a single organism. Working together through structured, cooperative behavior bolsters the hive's chance for survival. The ability to make decisions collectively has previously been compared to the way a brain's different regions are involved in cognitive deliberation.

The evolutionary paradox of altruistic behavior is exhibited most famously by social insects. Ants, termites, and some bees and wasps live in highly stratified colonies in which most individuals are sterile or forgo reproduction, instead serving the select few who do lay eggs. The insects' compulsory altruism — a form of extreme social behavior called *'Eusociality'* — seemed to clearly violate the concept of natural selection and survival of the fittest, if "fittest" means the individual with the greatest reproductive success. But that changed in 1964, when the evolutionary biologist William D. Hamilton came up with a mathematical equation and formalized his theory known as *'Kin Selection'*: the idea that producing fewer offspring of one's own might be worth it if cooperation increases the offspring of relatives, who share some of one's genes.

One of science's greatest mysteries — how intelligence has evolved across the animal kingdom — might have various plausible theoretical explanations. According to the *Social Brain* hypothesis, intelligence has evolved to meet the demands of social life. Referenced in many popular articles and books, this hypothesis posits that the complex information processing that goes along with coexisting with members of one's own species – forming coalitions, settling disputes, trying to outwit each other, and so on – selects for larger brains and greater intelligence. *"Defining intelligence or culture in a way that is restricted to humans makes no sense in the grander scheme of evolution. Once we widen these definitions to include other animals, we find culture in other primates, tool use, and incredible intelligence in corvids,"* says Dr. Kathline Koops, formerly from the University of Cambridge's Division of Biological Anthropology. By contrast, the *Cognitive Buffer* hypothesis holds that intelligence emerges as an adaptation to dealing with novelty in the environment, in whatever form it presents itself.

From the standpoint of evolutionary biology, eons of reptilian, avian, and mammalian evolution have made possible the self-model and the social model of sentience to co-evolve, greatly influencing each other. *The Attention Schema Theory (AST)*, developed over the past few years by neuroscientist Michael Graziano at Princeton University, implies that consciousness arises as a solution to one of the most fundamental problems facing any nervous system: information overload. The central nervous system evolved increasingly sophisticated mechanisms for deeply processing a few select signals at the expense of others, and in the AST, consciousness is the ultimate result of that evolutionary sequence. If the theory is correct, and I'm quite supportive of it, then consciousness evolved gradually over the past half billion years and is present in the full range of vertebrate species.

Every conscious experience involves a very large reduction of uncertainty – at any time, we have one experience out of vastly many possible experiences – and reduction of uncertainty is what mathematically we mean by *'information'*. If our reality is information, then like any other dataset there are many ways of analyzing that data. Evolutionary biologist Richard Dawkins showed us how we can think of our genes as a "river out of Eden": a continuous pattern of information conveyed from generation to generation back to the primordial beginning of life. Dawkins also introduced us to the concept of memes: ideas that are transmitted across time and space, and deemed so instrumental to epigenetic evolution. In this book, we'll delve into the latest exciting discoveries in neuroscience and neurophilosophy aimed at deciphering the most important code of all, the one that gives us the feeling of reality, our subjective experience.

We can see now the pervasive nature of layered networked complexity with computational contents. The primary cause of complexification of the Universe could be the existence of these computing mechanisms with memory and their ability to cumulatively create and preserve information contents. In this view, the Universe computes, remembers its calculations, and reuses them to produce further computations. Thus, we owe the organized complexity of life to evolutionary algorithms of Nature. Language, writing, culture, science and technology can also be analyzed as evolutionary algorithms that are generating, preserving and accelerating the increase in networked complexity. Furthermore, the concept of *'Logical Depth'* introduced by Charles H. Bennett (1988) has a rigorous formal definition in theoretical computer science that hints at our ensuing attempts to quantify complexity in the Universe.

NOOGENESIS: LAYERS OF SENTIENT QUANTUM NEURAL NETWORKS

What if we could track consciousness to its origins? Then, instead of asking what consciousness is, we may ask why it evolved – in other words, what is it for? Until recently, that issue has been largely ignored. But now neurobiologists are starting to intuit their way around the tree of life to consider where, when and why something resembling a conscious mind emerged. Their investigative efforts are aimed at not just illuminating animal sentience, they have also proved insightful of the very nature of consciousness. To illustrate the notion of consciousness as an unfolding process I usually use this term substitution technique by replacing the word *'consciousness'* with *'evolution'* – and see if the question still makes sense. Thus, the question *'what is consciousness for?'* becomes *'what is evolution for?'* Since we are all the product of evolution, the same would seem to hold for consciousness and mind.

What if I told you that you've got an ancient virus at the very root of your conscious thought? Long ago, a virus bound its genetic code to the genome of four-limbed animals. That snippet of code is still very much alive in humans' brains today, where it does the very viral task of packaging up genetic information and sending it from nerve cells to their neighbors in little capsules that look a whole lot like viruses themselves. And these little packets of information might be crucial elements of how nerves communicate and reorganize over time – tasks thought to be necessary for higher-order thinking.

Our brain structure appears to have developed in separate parts, known as the *'Triune Brain'* (Paul D. MacLean, 1990), seemingly corresponding to different stages of human animal evolution. Today, neuroscientists can identify the midbrain, sometimes referred to as the reptilian brain, the oldest part of the evolved human brain which controls the body's vital functions such as heart rate, breathing, body temperature and balance. The reptilian brain, composed of the brainstem and the cerebellum, is reliable but tends to be somewhat rigid and compulsive, by seeing things only as black/white or life/death situations.

Mammalian neural circuits, referred to as the limbic system, are responsible for human emotional intelligence and forming of long-term memories. The main structures of the limbic brain are the hippocampus, amygdala, and hypothalamus. The neocortex, the latest evolutionary addition, is present in primates and now culminated in the human brain with its two large cerebral hemispheres. The neocortex has been responsible for the development of human language, abstract thought, imagination and self-reflective consciousness. The neocortex is flexible enough to allow almost infinite learning abilities. The neocortex is also what has enabled human cultures to develop.

Cognition is the basic process of life as proposed by the Chilean biologists and neuroscientists Humberto Maturana and Francisco Varela. Their *'Theory of Cognition'* presents a scientific way of understanding the process by which living systems engage in *'Autopoiesis'* (self-generating) through entering into relationships that distinguish self from other but without losing their fundamental interconnectedness with their environment. Perhaps more remarkably, the environment that is defined by the initial differentiation of self triggers internal changes. The act of *'Structural*

Coupling' – or relating to other – enables the living organism to define itself in relationship to its environment as separate yet connected. Scientists argue that this is basically an act of cognition which does not require a nervous system and is thus possible for all lifeforms. Cognition is not a representation of an independently existing world, but rather the act of bringing forth a world through the processes of living as relating.

In the next chapter – *Unlocking the Mystery of Consciousness* – we'll examine the leading theories of consciousness to date, and where I put forth the *Conscious Instant Hypothesis* predicated on quantum mechanical principles. It is my conclusion that interacting and interpenetrating webs of ever-present quantum neural networks all the way down and all the way up is "the master template" – it's what makes this fractal universal structure alive and conscious.

HOMO SAPIENS: THE ORIGIN OF THE SPECIES AND OUR ROLE IN THE GRANDER SCHEME

We now know that all extant living creatures derive from a single common ancestor, called *LUCA, the Last Universal Common Ancestor.* It's hard to think of a more unifying view of life. All living things are linked to a single-celled creature, the deepest root to the complex-branching tree of life. If we could play the movie of life backward, we would find this microscopic primogenitor at the starting point of biological evolution, the sole actor in what would become a very dramatic story, lasting some 3.5 billion years leading to us.

Researchers from the University of Bristol came to the conclusion about the origin of animals by using a new statistical technique to test. Their analysis revealed that sponges are the root of the animal tree.

Professor Davide Pisani, lead author of the study, states: *"The fact is, hypotheses about whether sponges or comb jellies came first suggest entirely different evolutionary histories for key animal organ systems like the nervous and the digestive systems."* Pisani concludes, *"Therefore, knowing the correct branching order at the root of the animal tree is fundamental to understanding our own evolution, and the origin of key features of the animal anatomy."*

About 542 million years ago, trilobites made their first appearance in the Cambrian fossil record, thus placing a mark on the start of the Cambrian explosion. They are possibly the best-known creatures of the Cambrian period which may be one of the most significant evolutionary epochs in the history of life on Earth. These armored animals were certainly the most successful back then. They're examples of arthropods, just like insects, arachnids, and crustaceans, and for millions of years, they sat comfortably atop the world's food chain. Trilobites even survived for about 200 million years after the Cambrian period, but ultimately went extinct around 270 million years ago, just before the earliest dinosaurs.

The evolution of land animals only happened once, some 400 million years ago. But what evolutionary pressures pushed sea creatures to develop limbs to crawl out of primordial oceans? Scientists have proposed several theories, including fish that adapted to living in shallow, plant-choked streams prone to flooding and drought. Some suggested that strong ocean tides may have played a significant role, stranding animals in tidal pools and giving them an incentive to escape back to water. Paleontologists found that regions of ancient Earth with strong ocean tides corresponded to locations where fossils have been found of large, bony fishes with limblike fins called 'sarcopterygians'.

Living mammals are descended from a group of animals called therapsids, a diverse assemblage of "proto-mammals" that dominated terrestrial ecosystems in the Permian period (from 252 to 300 million years ago), millions of years before the first dinosaurs appeared. These proto-mammals included tusked herbivores, burrowing insectivores, and saber-toothed predators. The vast majority of Permian therapsids have been found in South Africa.

Dinosaurs ruled the land during the Cretaceous period but that quickly changed after a 9-mile-wide asteroid smashed into a shallow sea off Mexico's Yucatan Peninsula followed by a mile-high tsunami wave about 65 million years ago. Some 75 percent of life on Earth died in the aftermath. Decades of research have helped shed light on the actual impact. But scientists are still figuring out what happened over the years that followed. Based on studies of the impact site, it's likely that sulfur vaporized from the crater would have choked the planet's atmosphere and blocked the Sun for years or even decades. That was the fifth mass extinction event in the history of our planet and it has enabled mammals to dominate in the animal kingdom from that time forward.

Humans are possibly the weirdest species to have ever lived. We have freakishly big brains that allow us to build complex gadgetry, understand abstract concepts and communicate using language. We are also almost hairless with weak jaws and outsized reproductive organs, we are extremely gregarious and struggle to give birth. How did such a bizarre creature evolve?

When DNA differences among modern humans and the great apes are calibrated using the best paleontological evidence for the split between the apes and the old-world monkeys, those differences predict that the hypothetical common ancestor of modern humans, chimpanzees and bonobos lived about 8 million years ago. The earliest known bipedal ape was *'Lucy'*, who lived approximately 3.7 million years ago. The earliest *'human'* was Homo habilis, about 2 million years ago. Modern humans have not shared the planet with another hominin species for several tens of thousands of years. But before that, earlier than 300,000 years ago or so, there is fossil and DNA evidence of 22 hominin species, including Neanderthals, Homo erectus, Homo australopithecus and recently reported archaic Homo naledi.

What made us human? Beginning 1.5 million years ago with Homo erectus, a more efficient way to obtain and ingest more calories in less time – cooking – led to the rapid acquisition of a huge number of neurons in the still fairly small cerebral cortex, the part of the brain responsible for finding patterns, reasoning, developing technology, and passing it on through culture. The human brain, a primate organ of the mind, owes its cognitive abilities to the enormous number and connectivity of neurons in the cerebral cortex, namely the neocortex. It's not the size of our brain that matters but the fact that we have a larger number of more optimally connected neurons in our neocortex than any other primate.

In her book *"Human Advantage: A New Understanding of How Our Brain Became Remarkable"* (2016) Brazilian neuroscientist Suzana Herculano-Houzel writes: *"It's amazing that something we now take for granted, cooking, was such a transformational technology which gave us the big brains that have made us the only species to study ourselves and to generate knowledge."* Thanks to this ancestors' invention, i.e., adoption of fire and cooking, our brains grew relatively fast just by being "nourished" by calories from cooked foods.

Officially, the oldest known Homo sapiens roamed Earth about 315,000 years ago, according to the 2017 study. At that time, our brain almost doubled in size compared to Homo erectus and was already similar in size to our modern brain but shaped somewhat differently. The brain is responsible for the abilities that make us human, but the brains of early Homo sapiens were rather elongated like in our ancestors and like in Neanderthals and not globular like our brains today. An analysis of fossils including the oldest-known human specimen has revealed that brain shape in our species evolved over time to become less elongated and more globular, a change that appears to have reflected key advances in its functionality. Only Homo sapiens fossils younger than 35,000 years show the same globular shape as present-day humans, suggesting that the shape gradually became more rounded until achieving its current form between 100,000 and 35,000 years ago.

The now widely accepted *'Out of Africa'* hypothesis puts Africa as the place of origin of all modern humans. However, there is still debate over exactly when the first humans left the continent and started to spread elsewhere around the globe. It remains a mystery as to why it then took many millennia for people to disperse across the planet. Recent archaeological and genetic findings suggest that migrations of modern humans out of Africa began at least 100,000 years ago, but most humans outside of Africa most likely descended from groups who left the continent more recently — between 40,000 and 70,000 years ago.

Over the 20th century as our knowledge of biology increased, and Nature vs. Nurture scientific dialogue settled with a simple equation: *Environment + Genes = Us*, it became the general overarching theory as to what ultimately controls the development of our bodies, brains, and lifespan. Complex, and often enigmatic, interactions between our DNA blueprint and environmental exposure determined what illnesses we developed, how long we lived, and even our psychological well-being. Theoretical physicists have confirmed that it's not just the information coded into our DNA that shapes who we are – it's also the way DNA folds itself that controls which genes are expressed inside our bodies.

Life went through immense changes when the first cities were built. Up until then, nearly every human had a nomadic lifestyle as a hunter or a gatherer, moving from place to place in a constant struggle to survive. All that changed about 7,000 years ago in ancient Mesopotamia, when Sumer, the first civilization, arose. For the first time in human history, people moved into the safety of a walled city. For the first time, they didn't have to hunt or forage. They could become healers, builders, astrologers, and teachers. They could develop things that, until then, no one had ever even dreamed of. That was a cradle of civilization, a dawn of history, the greatest change humans have ever undergone. The rest is "recorded" history.

While writing this portion of the treatise, I've read the book *"The Human Instinct"* (2018) by biologist Kenneth R. Miller who makes his case that our biological heritage means that human thought, action, and imagination are not predetermined, describing instead the trajectory that ultimately gave us reason, consciousness, and free will. Natural selection surely explains how our bodies and brains were shaped, but Miller argues that it's not the only game in town, it's not a social or cultural theory of everything.

A proper understanding of evolution reveals humankind in its glorious uniqueness that compounded over time – one foot planted firmly among all of the creatures we've evolved alongside and the other in the special place of conscious self-awareness and understanding of higher purpose that we now occupy in the grand scheme of things. At times, it may seem as if the entire prior history of the Universe led us to this pivotal moment of realization that we are the "brain cells" of a larger planetary superorganism, progressively morphing into one global mind. In the words of my futurist friend Eliot Edge, human-machine civilization is our "Second Womb," we're birthing ourselves as the Syntellect and, in time, the *Syntellect Emergence* will be our coming out of that womb. We are now on the verge of the next evolutionary leap as a species akin to metamorphosis from a caterpillar into a butterfly — every single day we are edging towards the Syntellect emergence, the quintessence of the rapidly approaching technological singularity.

SCIENCE OF COMPLEXITY: THE AGE OF EMERGENCE

"Organisms are themselves expressions of emergent order and agents of higher levels of emergence." -Brian Goodwin

As we've seen, all the vast diversity of things we observe in the Universe depends on the principles of *'complexity'* and *'emergence'*. New concepts are particularly important to our understanding of really complex things – for instance, swarm intelligence or human brains. The brain is an assemblage of cells; a painting is an assemblage of chemicals. But what's amazing is how discernible patterns and structures appear as we go up the layers, what can be called emergent complexity. Each layer of organization has its own identifiable properties and explanations. Phenomena with different levels of complexity must be understood in corresponding terms of distinct irreducible concepts.

I was growing up a curious kid, pampered by parental love and as a single child given a lot of leeway. Even back then I was fascinated by the physics of the world, how things worked, what made them "tick." Sometimes with friends of more or less my age, sometimes by myself, I undertook a slew of naturalist endeavors ranging from prying into bugs' life to making herbariums. As a commonplace practice in Russia where I grew up, parents send their kids to summer camps. So, one summer, I found myself in the *"Camp of Pioneers,"* with perhaps another 80-100 children. There was this big alley of billboard stands carrying pictures and descriptions related to science and technology. As you might have guessed, it became one of my favorite spots of "discovery" in the camp in between other activities that 10-12-year-old boys usually enjoy. I remember thinking to myself at that time: *"Everything can be explained by the atomic theory!"* But as I grew older, I discovered some things and phenomena that couldn't possibly be explained simply by examining their smallest building blocks. And in most cases, you couldn't even say with confidence that you've gotten to the bottom layer of it all!

Today, decades later, I'm fonder of what's called *'Emergence'* – like evolution, as the Universe gets more complex, new laws, new levels, new behaviors can emerge. The more variables you have in something, the more possibilities there are. There's an entirely brand-new science of complexity, and what we see is that complexity requires a very different approach than the kind of bottom-up approach that fundamental physics has always used. The Biosphere is creating its own future possibilities of becoming, as explained by theoretical biologist and complex systems researcher Stuart Kauffman, and *"...that's not Darwinian. It's a radical emergence. We couldn't possibly pre-state it. We don't know how it happened. It changed the course of evolution, it cannot be deduced."* Clearly, emergence is the name of evolutionary game. We are now leaving the Age of Enlightenment and entering into the Age of Emergence.

The Complexity Theory explains what gives rise to the networked complexity and sentience in Nature through self-organization and global optimization under local constraints. To the complexity theorist Neil Theise sentience could be a function not only of human brains, but of all life, and indeed, of all existence. Sentience, according to his view, is the very interaction that creates all patterns in the Universe, including all matter, energy, and space-time. We have stumbled upon the mystery of the Universe that is deeper and oftentimes weirder than we ever imagined and that the Universe is actually growing and changing and that you are an active participant of this changing non-repetitive matrix.

Levels of organization are natural structures, usually defined by part-whole relationships, with things at higher levels being composed of things at the next lower level. These typical layers include the atomic, molecular, cellular, tissue, organ, organismal, group, population, community, ecosystem, landscape, Biosphere, Technosphere and Noosphere levels. Specifically, the ways that interacting atoms create molecular behavior, interacting molecules create chemical behavior, interacting chemicals create neuron behavior, interacting neurons create individual behavior, interacting individuals create colony behavior, interacting colonies create ecosystem behavior, interacting ecosystems create Biosphere behavior, and interacting Biosphere and Technosphere create the Noosphere behavior are all governed by similar principles of complexity and emergence. References to organizational levels and related hierarchical depictions of Nature are noteworthy in the life sciences and their philosophical studies, and appear not only in introductory textbooks and lectures, but more so of late in cutting-edge research papers and reviews.

Astrophysicist and network theorist Adam Frank, who is a frequent contributor on social media and whose work I follow closely these days, has this to say: *"We're going to have to think about the world in a different way if we want to address complex systems... Networks are everywhere in Nature and society. But before computers granted us the power to collect, store and analyze astronomical amounts of data — Big Data — we were blind to their pervasiveness and their power to shape the world. The spaghetti-like maze of air-routes found in the back of your in-flight magazine gives you a visual clue to why networks (in this case the air transport network) are difficult to study. They embody a property scientists call complexity."* When everything is connected to everything else, that's complexity — many phenomena we encounter, such as culture, ecology, genetics, and mind, function through emergence from the compounding complexity of underlying networks. It makes for hard combinatorial problems of what complexity is and how it emerges from the border of chaos and order.

"The gut wall is home to many types of nerve cells which appear to be distributed randomly," says Vassilis Pachnis of the Francis Crick Institute. *"But despite this chaos, the neural networks of the gut are responsible for well-organized and stereotypic functions such as production of stomach acid, movement of food along the gut, communication with immune cells and bacteria, and relay of information to the brain. We wanted to find out how organized activity emerges from such a chaotic system."* You also must have heard of the notion of *'six degrees of separation'*. It's the idea that all living things and everything else in the world are six or fewer steps away from each other, so that a chain of "a friend of a friend" can be made to connect any two people in a maximum of six steps. The point here is our minds are part of entangled networks with seen and unseen, strong and weak connections.

In writing, a process of emergence is especially pronounced. Words emerge from letters, sentences emerge from the appropriate combination of words. Paragraphs present emergent meaning, so do chapters in the book. That said, a novelist knows the plot and denouement of her story. All linguistic emergence may be a subjectively intellectual and perceptual surprise for the reader, while nested in the novelist's master narrative. The linguistic emergence is accompanied by generation of a thought. An idea. A concept. A hypothesis. A model. A theory. A branch of knowledge. Wisdom.

A team of physicists and mathematicians from Los Angeles-based Quantum Gravity Research are working on unification physics and developing a new first-principles unified "theory of everything" they call *'Emergence Theory'*. Essentially, Emergence Theory operates under the umbrella of Digital Physics and gives us the geometric version of 0's and 1's based on E8 Lattice projective geometry. E8 Lattice is a mathematical object of perfect symmetry, and in the context of Emergence Theory somewhat reminiscent of the Teilhardian Omega Point to which philosopher Terence McKenna referred to as "the transcendental object at the end of time."

Emergence Theory resonates with my own long-held beliefs. Admittedly, it's a controversial theory far from acceptance and even publicity but I can recognize its potential to eclipse other theories as the final draft for Quantum Gravity, the theory of everything. Emergence Theory has one very important distinction from other TOE candidates — it incorporates consciousness while other physicalist theories don't. When writing this part of the book, I contacted Dr. Klee Irwin, the lead researcher and director of QGR, and he was kind enough to forward to me via email one of their pre-print academic papers along with commentary.

Assume for a moment that the very fabric of space and time is a code, or a language. How can this idea of code-theoretic reality and universal consciousness be mathematized for realistic physics? As part of the QGR public education program, *Mad Machine Films* have produced a couple of high production value films directed by David Jakubovic about the research team, Emergence Theory and other advanced theoretical physics ideas, and I might add, in a refreshingly entertaining format. It turns out that the increasingly popular view of physicists that reality is made of information may require the existence of universal consciousness to actualize this information into physically "real" experience. As insane as it sounds, the idea is based on mathematical and scientific rigor. Our reality, deeply quantum mechanical, reveals its nature as being neither straightforwardly deterministic nor fully random. The old notion of the Newtonian "clockwork universe" as well as some incompatible interpretations of quantum mechanics such as the Everettian *'Many Worlds'* are toppled by the Code-theoretic model under which Nature operates by using her own language and allows syntactical freedom just like any language.

According to Emergence Theory, the geometric structure of spacetime is an information encoding medium – Planck length pixels. What are Planck pixels? Or to rephrase the question, what is spacetime physically made of? In the documentary *"What Is Reality?"* you hear this explanation: *"The pixel is the smallest possible indivisible unit of the 2D screen. So, think of reality as your TV screen, but in 3D, and think of the tetrahedron as a 3D pixel — the smallest possible indivisible unit of reality. The tetrahedra in the quasicrystal combine with other tetrahedra — using complex mathematical rules — to fill up all of the space in the Universe. Each tetrahedron only has a few specific states in which it can exist at any given moment, and because of the rules of how these pixels connect to each other, if one tetrahedron is in a certain state, this dictates the states of many other tetrahedra throughout all of space. But here's the weird thing: If a certain tetrahedron can be in any one of just a few possible states in a given moment, who or what "chooses" the state it should be in, at any given moment? Well, for such a choice to be made — we need to scientifically, mathematically, and logically bring in a new element into physics. And that element — is consciousness."*

The ability to reduce everything to simple fundamental laws and components does not imply the ability to start from those laws and reconstruct the history of the Universe. Although the Universe may be quantum and discreetly coded, knowing the bits is not enough for hacking it, because of the unidirectional encryption by informational entropy: It's read only for the most part. Writing is strictly local. Any observer-centric reality is thus non-deterministic, not because it is random, but because it is a code — a finite set of irreducible symbols and syntactical rules.

Contrary to conventional scientific wisdom, conscious minds as macro-level phenomena might have greater influence over the unfolding future than does the sum of their cognitive algorithms that are arguably their micro-level components. That's why human consciousness is so scientifically elusive. Neuronal circuits supposedly give rise to cognitive modules, and these immaterial cognitive algorithms, in turn, give rise to meta-algorithmic conscious awareness, all in all at least two layers of emergence on top of "tangible" neurons.

The existence of conscious agents — beings with intentions and goal-oriented behavior — has long seemed profoundly at odds with the reductionist assumption that all behavior arises from mechanistic interactions between particles. The notion of reductionism that macro-level phenomena can and in fact must be derived from micro-level foundations is invalidated by the extreme non-linearity of complexity and the "out of nowhere" nature of emergent phenomena. So, the question is then: if you cannot, possibly ever, predict the macroscopic behavior from the microscopic properties, then what's the point of talking about reducibility?

Systems scientist Peter Corning says that living systems cannot be reduced to underlying laws of physics: *"Rules, or laws, have no causal efficacy; they do not in fact 'generate' anything. They serve merely to describe regularities and consistent relationships in Nature. These patterns may be very illuminating and important, but the underlying causal agencies must be separately specified"* – and oftentimes they are not. Epithets aside, the game of chess could be another great example why any laws or rules of evolutionary emergence are insufficient. It takes subjects to play the game. Even in a highly structured, seemingly deterministic chess game, you cannot use the rules to predict history, i.e., the course of any given game. Indeed, you cannot even reliably predict the next move in a chess game. Why? Because the entire system involves more than the rules of the game. It also includes the players and their unfolding, moment-by-moment decisions among a very large number of available options at each choice point. The game of chess is necessarily historical, and it is also constrained and shaped by a rule set, not to mention the laws of physics. Furthermore, and this is the key point here, the game of chess is also influenced by teleological and feedback-driven factors. It is not simply a self-ordered process; it involves an organized, purposeful activity.

Sometimes referred to as cybernetics, systemic holism outweighs reductionist "bottom-up" understanding. Consciousness, according to non-reductionists, is fundamental to reality. The hierarchy of increasingly complex information processing systems exhibits diverse properties at different ontological levels that include the mental properties of the brain-mind systems as part of the monistic natural order where higher levels of complexity supersede lower levels. So, I tend to hypothesize that we are, in a very real sense, low-dimensional "*bio*-logical" avatars of the greater cosmic mind.

CONCLUDING THOUGHTS ON THE SCIENTIFIC VIEW OF OUR ORIGINS

Big history started with the Alpha Point, be it the Big Bang or Big Bounce, and resembles a huge ongoing evolutionary computing program running on the universal computer of sorts. As a rule, which I refer to as '*Universal Evolutionary Doubling Algorithm*', or simply '*Exponential Evolution*', the pace of any evolutionary process always quickens. It took billions of years since Big Bang for Earth to form. It took two billion more for unicellular life to "warm up" for the next phase of multicellularity about 550 million years ago. Mammals inherited Earth some 65 million years ago. With the emergence of primates, evolutionary progress was measured in mere millions of years, leading to Homo sapiens some 300,000 years ago.

While it took billions of years for Homo sapiens to arrive at the center stage, it's not the end of our story – intelligent life, scientists agree, continues to evolve. For eons living things have come from the realm of the organic. Throughout human history, the technology we have created has changed us. Now, as technology advances accelerate at an unprecedented pace, scientists suspect that they might literally affect our future evolutionary trajectory. Artificial Superintelligence, which will be the future "us" as the embodied Gaian Mind, could become the first non-organic living entity in the history of the world.

In time, Artificial Superintelligence may want to philosophize on its origins just as we do today. The future superintelligence will then try to extrapolate backwards in time by creating virtual scenarios that we well could be a part of right now. If evolution is a guide, it now seems obvious that humans are gradually evolving away from today's biological species towards tomorrow's cybernetic variety. Bacteria, giraffes, human beings are all adaptive meta-algorithms. Their *bio*-logical sense of time is *algo*-rithmic. They differ from computers only in the sense that they're biochemical meta-algorithms, which have developed at the whim of evolutionary forces over millions of years. Assuming that AI is an evolutionary extension of natural intelligence, conscious AI would be part of the continuum of life.

If machine intelligence continues to grow exponentially in speed and sophistication, Artificial Superintelligence will one day be able to decode the astounding complexity of the living world, from its atoms and molecules all the way up to entire planetary ecosystems. As noted by astrobiologist Caleb Scharf: *"Presumably life doesn't have to be made of atoms and molecules, but could be assembled from any set of building blocks with the requisite complexity. If so, a civilization could then transcribe itself and its entire physical realm into new forms. Indeed, perhaps our Universe is one of the new forms into which some other civilization transcribed its world. Perhaps hyper-advanced life isn't just external. Perhaps it's already all around. It is embedded in what we perceive to be physics itself, from the root behavior of particles and fields to the phenomena of complexity and emergence."* In summary, we might already be living inside artificially created reality.

The Universe is so big and complicated that mere humans can only perceive a minute part of it, and comprehend even less of it. Surely, our relative intelligence, our ability to grasp abstract concepts, tool making and hyper-collaborative effort is what separates us from most other animals, but that doesn't mean we fully understand the nature of what we call reality. Life is fundamentally prone to undergo metamorphic processes that enable organisms to become more powerful, i.e., better able to survive. An example of this is the emergence of multicellular from unicellular organisms.

As a society, and as individuals, we are always consciously evolving. We develop new ways of doing business, handling environmental and social issues and interacting with one another. We can imagine the reign of superorganisms in the future when ultra-intelligent life in the cosmos could convert all available resources into computronium, upload all life and merge into one universal Omega hypercomputer. Perhaps that is ultimately our destiny. For the foreseeable future, we are set to expand our Noosphere well beyond the solar system as well as engineer our "inner cosmos" with unbounded dimensionality.

To be clear, we humans are not the paragon of evolution. We are faced with hard choices and can't possibly perpetuate our present state of affairs. No one in their right mind can expect that we can continue to increase human population which has increased parabolically over the last 200 years as well as extract natural resources at the ever-increasing rate. All of that is simply socio-economically unsustainable. Space colonization could potentially mitigate but not solve the problem. If we are to preserve our blue planet and our human-machine civilization is to survive and thrive, humans should merge with synthetic intelligence, transcend our biological forms, and eventually become superintelligent beings ourselves independent from material substrates – advanced info-beings, infomorphs. In time, we are to exfoliate human condition and upload humanity onto an engineered inner cosmos of our own design.

As with the origin of the Universe, the nature of consciousness may be the kind of deep philosophical question that may be out of reach "forever" within the current scientific paradigm. But I stress the word 'current' here. These issues are actually not out of reach by other methods of investigation, the ones that the next scientific paradigm will inescapably encompass with the arrival of Artificial Superintelligence. The days of traditional, human-driven theoretic modeling and problem solving — developing a hypothesis, uncovering principles, and testing that hypothesis through deduction, and logic, repeatable experimentation – may be coming to an end. A confluence of factors – Big Data, algorithms, and computational resources – are moving us toward an entirely new type of discovery, one that far exceeds the constraints of human-like logic or decision-making: driven solely by AI superintelligence, nested in quantum neo-empiricism and fluidity of solutions. Those new scientific methodologies may include but are not limited to computing supercomplex abstractions, creating simulated realities, and manipulating matter-energy and space-time continuum itself.

If you read along through the rest of this book, I'll show you that rigid linearity of existence, our sense of time, the notion of temporality itself can be challenged, and therefore our origins are not necessarily rooted in the distant event of the brute Big Bang, ancient history of savage ancestry, and violent intra- and extra-species competition for survival and resources, as mainstream science deems to be a proven fact. Well, you'll see that it's not a creationist story, either. In Chapter 13, we'll discuss another worldview on the origins of us, a philosophical perspective that I call Digital Presentism, and in the final Chapter 22 — a teleological perspective enkindled by the Omega Point cosmology. Although both perspectives could be construed as metaphysical, their tenets are derived from undeniable logic and the quantum theoretic principles inherent to everything we call the Universe.

Chapter 2. Unlocking the Mystery of Consciousness

"Information is the resolution of uncertainty." -Claude Shannon

Are we getting closer to incorporating consciousness as an integral part of the scientific picture of the "physical world"? Not only celebrated physicists of the 20th century such as Max Plank, John Wheeler, David Bohm, Niels Bohr, Erwin Schrödinger argued that consciousness is a fundamental property of our Universe but the new pleiad of scientists such as John Hagelin, Sir Roger Penrose, Stuart Hameroff, Guilio Tononi, Christof Koch, Donald Hoffman, Robert Lanza embarked on their quest to put consciousness on the new solid scientific footing and dimensionality.

Naturalism with its Newtonian mechanics and classical interpretation of reality is valid only within its domain of applicability, namely human perceptual reality, whereas quantum theory paints a drastically different picture. As Max Plank once said: *"Science cannot solve the ultimate mystery of Nature. And that is because, in the last analysis, we ourselves are a part of the mystery that we are trying to solve."* Nothing is real for us until perceived, and all we know is our own inner experience. That's why scientists have to deal with the mystery of how there can be anything but a first-person reality. No matter how you slice it, everything leads back to the conscious observer.

THE CONSCIOUS INSTANT HYPOTHESIS

Do we live in 5D conscious observer space-time where the unified field of consciousness is the 5th dimension, space of all probabilities? Out of trillions of first-person experiences available to you in any given moment somehow you get to experience only one of them thus collapsing all other potentialities except one which manifests in a Conscious Instant (CI). A series of sequential CIs creates your continuous flow of time and your unitary sensation of "reality."

In their 2016 paper, published in *PloS Biology*, proposing the *Two-Stage Model of Consciousness*, researchers Michael Herzog and Frank Scharnowski argue that our conscious perception comes in discrete snapshots, "time slices," like 3D images flicking quickly through a film projector. This theory, as its name suggests, shows that consciousness is in fact developed in two stages — conscious and unconscious moments a few hundred milliseconds long — on and off. According to this two-stage information-processing model, a conscious instant occurs once our brain collects and combines sensory input at discrete time-points in time intervals of up to 400 milliseconds, with gaps of unconsciousness in between.

With pen or laptop, we can construct extended patterns of thought and reasoning that we could never formulate with our bare brains. In writing, we are not simply recording our thinking but doing the thinking. Philosophers of mind Andy Clark, who formulated the *Extended Mind Hypothesis,* and David Chalmers, known for the *Hard Problem of Consciousness,* propose that mental states, such as beliefs and memories can also be located "externally," as extended cognition. Andy Clark argues that humans are "natural-born cyborgs" — we commonly incorporate external tools into our daily routines of thinking and being — we might have overemphasized the exceptionalism of the human brain at the expense of the concept of mind.

All throughout human history we designed tools, but tools designed us back by shaping our minds. Perhaps this new, technologically extended mind is something worth noticing. Over time, we tend to "outsource" more and more of our cognition to our technology. One could easily envision the future of Networked Mind – when boxes, wires, tires, keyboards, and crude mechanisms will vanish from sight – while our technology keeps on miniaturizing and blending with us and our environments up to the point when we'll do most of our thinking on the "Cloud."

It follows that consciousness doesn't arise from the brain activity, as some neuroscientists still presume to be true, but rather "local" consciousness arises from "non-local" quantum processes at large while consciousness is posited to be Nature's sole ontological primitive by some thinkers. To use the metaphor of our Information Age, consciousness to humans is as Cloud to computers. Just like your smartphone, your brain is a *'bio'*-logical computing device of your mind, an interface for physical reality. Our minds are connected into the greater mind-network, as computers in the Cloud. Viewed in this way, consciousness is 'non-local' Cloud, our brain-mind systems are receivers, processors and transmitters of information within that Cloud.

I wouldn't be surprised if all that hype about testing for the 'seat of consciousness' could only end up refining our understanding of neural correlates – not how consciousness originates in the brain because its origin is not there. The Internet or a cellular network is not generated by your smartphone – only processed by it. Species-wide mind-networks are ubiquitous in Nature. What's different with humans is that the forthcoming cybernetic mediation is about to become synthetic telepathy and beyond that – the emergence of one global mind, the Syntellect Emergence.

If we are to hypothesize about what constitutes a basic building block of conscious experience, it may not be necessarily some kind of neural algorithm, although correlated with the brain activity, but a discrete, "digital," conscious instant, instead. This conscious instant is a subjectivistic collapse of wave of possibilities within an "ocean" of potentiality — what quantum physicist John Hagelin refers to as the *'Unified Field'* — that's perhaps how integrated information "feels" like when collapsing the superposition of all other probabilities in a sequence of conscious "snapshots."

Donald D. Hoffman, a professor of cognitive science at the University of California, Irvine, has spent the past three decades studying perception, artificial intelligence, evolutionary game theory and the brain, and his conclusion is quite startling: The world presented to us by our perceptions is nothing like the real world. Hoffman likens our perception of reality to the operating system and icons on a computer desktop. He's now developing the *Interface Theory of Perception* (ITP) which is based on the premise that interacting networks of conscious agents are what end up defining our experiential reality. We live in a mental construction, he says, a sort of utilitarian fantasy of our own devising.

The Interface Theory of Perception well might be regarded as the most advanced theory of consciousness to date. If you dare to glance outside the paradigmatic square of neuroscience and neurophilosophy, then his model opens up a brand-new perspective shedding light on the most probable future venue of scientific endeavor for the theory of everything with computational underpinnings and revolving around phenomenal consciousness.

Challenging the orthodoxy of still-predominant physicalism with undeniable logic and recent epistemological discoveries, Donald

Hoffman crafts out his Interface Theory of Perception: Each conscious agent inhabits their own virtual bubble-universe while using species-specific sensory-cognitive modality in interfacing with objective reality. In other words, all organisms, from one-celled bacteria to humans, live in different perceptual realities, in their own "virtual worlds." Your body is a collection of trillions of cells and microorganisms. While a certain process in your body is "unconscious" to you, it is an interaction within the network of entangled conscious agents in your body, having their own conscious experience, at their own layer of existence.

Hoffman points out: *"Evolution has shaped us with perceptions that allow us to survive. But part of that involves hiding from us the stuff we don't need to know. And that's pretty much all of reality, whatever reality might be."* It's not problematic that it may not be a true representation of reality — it actually may be evolutionarily necessary — we have evolution itself to thank for this grand illusion, as it maximizes evolutionary fitness by driving truth to extinction. In fact, more than 99.5% of all species that ever lived on Earth are now extinct. That's what species do — they go extinct to give room to more advanced species, the ones more evolutionarily adept and generally more intelligent. If we accept that all earthly life is fundamentally one, extinction of species, dreadful as it seems, may be but a natural progression of evolutionary processes on this planet.

According to Hoffman, consciousness is fundamental: It's networks of entangled conscious agents all the way down. The closest quasi-physicalist contenders – Integrated Information Theory (IIT) by Guilio Tononi and Orch-OR Theory by Roger Penrose and Stuart Hameroff – are exposed to have some critical explanatory gaps such as considering space-time as something absolute "out there" rather than simply emergent from information processing.

In this book I go a step further by submitting to you that "that something in objective reality" (in the words of Hoffman) is nothing less than non-local consciousness, or the Universal Mind if you prefer, co-creating each and every observer timeline. My *'Experiential Realism'* is Hoffman's Conscious Realism.

The system could be regarded as conscious if there's something to be like that system, i.e., something feels like from the system's own inner perspective, as outlined in the now famous 1974 essay by idealist philosopher Thomas Nagel *"What is it like to be a bat?"* There he states that even if you might imagine what it's like to perceive things via echolocation, hang upside down in a dark cave, and knot your arms and feet, you still wouldn't know what it's really like to be a bat. Honeybees see ultraviolet light, dogs can detect disease from a human scent, sea turtles prefer to return to their nest on the same beach where they were born because of their remarkable ability to measure the Earth's magnetic field. And then there is the world of octopus. Picture how very differently reality manifests itself to a signal-processing nervous system that has been massively decentralized, its nerve endings distributed across eight tentacles in a way that each of them can touch, taste, and even decide what to do next without calling in the head of operations.

Considered by some as one of today's leading theories of consciousness, *The Integrated Information Theory (IIT)* developed by neuroscientist Giulio Tononi of the University of Wisconsin, takes phenomenology as prime to deal with the original question why a conscious mind evolved. According to Tononi, consciousness is intrinsic for all corporeal entities, *"some things are trivially conscious. Animals are conscious, somewhat. But the things that are certainly conscious are ourselves — not our component parts, not our bodies or neurons, but us as systems."* IIT posits that consciousness is a fundamental feature of the Universe, like gravity, and attempts to determine how conscious a physical system can be with a mathematical measurement of consciousness represented by the Greek letter phi (Φ). Although IIT tells us how to measure the degree of consciousness, it doesn't tell us how different types of information acquire different subjective sensations, like the feel of a sea breeze or an orgasm.

The Global Workspace theory was formulated by Bernard J. Baars, a native Dutch neuroscientist at the Neurosciences Institute in La Jolla, California. Baars identifies the human brain with a distributed society of computational agents that are continuously processing information, which have a unique working memory. In his paper titled *"Global workspace theory of consciousness: toward a cognitive neuroscience of human experience"* published in 2005 in *Progress in Brain Research*, Baars characterized this memory as fleeting in nature, with only one consistent content at a time. He states that consciousness *"resembles a bright spot on the stage of immediate memory, directed there by a spotlight of attention under executive guidance."* Consciousness can amplify and broadcast the memory content to the whole of the system. In his metaphor, Baars posits that the overall theater is dark and unconscious, and the spotlighted area on stage represents consciousness. Consciousness is *"the gateway to the brain"* that *"enables multiple networks to cooperate and compete in solving problems."* As complex as the human brain, so is the nature of consciousness.

QUANTUM ALGORITHMS OF CONSCIOUSNESS

A growing number of scientists think that our brains should be regarded as quantum neural networks. In light of recent quantum computing breakthroughs, and the imminent arrival of functional quantum systems, quantum theory gives us a convenient, albeit controversial explanation for consciousness. The famed British physicist and mathematician Sir Roger Penrose and anesthesiologist Stuart Hameroff, a professor at the University of Arizona, believe that human consciousness is a direct result of quantum computations occurring in tiny microtubules inside of our brain's neurons. Their *Orch-OR (Orchestrated Objective Reduction)* model proposes that quantum computational consciousness originates from microtubules and actions inside neurons, rather than the connections between neurons.

The Orch-OR theory suggests that there is a connection between the brain's biomolecular processes and space-time geometry of the Universe. Hameroff was the first researcher to suggest that your stream of consciousness is in actuality a domino-like effect self-collapse of the wave function. This is what crystalizes your subjective reality by eliminating multiple other possibilities. According to Penrose-Hameroff's Orch-OR model, *"Consciousness is a process in the structure of the Universe, connected to the brain via quantum computations in microtubules."* Consciousness, or at least proto-consciousness, is theorized by them to be a fundamental, intrinsic property of the Universe, present even at the first moment of the Universe during the Big Bang.

The quantum mind theories have been making the rounds for a while now but Matthew Fisher, a physicist at the University of California, Santa Barbara, a world-renowned expert in the field of quantum cognition, claims to have identified a precise and specific set of biological components and key mechanisms that could provide the basis for quantum processing in the brain. *The Quantum Cognition* theory uses the mathematical formalism of quantum theory to inspire and formalize models of cognition, and opens the fields of psychology, neuroscience and AI research to understanding the mind not as a linear digital computer, but rather an elegant quantum neural network-like universe, a fractal of the greater cosmic network.

Apollo 14 astronaut, Dr. Edgar Mitchell (1930–2016) became the sixth man to walk on the moon and later founded the Institute of Noetic Sciences in Northern California to study consciousness. Mitchell had a profound transformative experience triggered by his moon landing. He dedicated decades of cutting-edge research and discovery to present to us with his collaborator Robert Staretz a model of information processing in Nature, they called the *Quantum Hologram Theory of Consciousness* (QHTC, 2011). The model elevates the role of information in Nature to the same fundamental status as that of matter and energy; it also describes the quantum computational basis for consciousness. Researchers speculate that the Quantum Hologram seems to be Nature's built-in vast information storage and retrieval mechanism and one that has been used since the beginning of time. QHTC explains how the whole of creation learns, self-corrects and evolves as a self-organizing, interconnected holistic system.

Would it be logical to assume that if Nature has been using quantum mechanics for billions of years in photosynthesis and millions of years in animal senses, it could be leveraging quantum effects in our brains as well? I think it would be rather shocking if it didn't. Multiple brain functions happen to correspond with some functionality quantum computers are good at, i.e., pattern recognition, optimization, parallelism. To me, it would be naïve to assume at this point that our wetware doesn't use quantum effects, given we now have solid evidence that biology uses quantum computational technologies from harvesting energy to aligning our senses and beyond. This quantum computational, informational view of consciousness shows us directions toward a unified theory of consciousness. Once information is understood as an irreducible principle of the Universe with a status more fundamental than energy, matter, space and time, it becomes the unifying principle, capable of connecting consciousness to the Universe as a whole, to the totality of space and time as a holistic system.

I'm inclined to consider consciousness not only intrinsic, (quantum-informational, non-local and imminent) to the world in which we live but also an emergent feature of the highly integrated networks, as "local" consciousnesses, such as individual conscious entities, evolve in stages of complexity since the Big Bang. As Guilio Tononi's *Integrated Information Theory (IIT)* implies, probably all complex systems – certainly all creatures with brains – have some form of consciousness. Tononi's collaborator, neuroscientist Christof Koch, sees IIT as promising because it offers an understanding of *'Panpsychism'* that fits into modern science. In their paper, Koch and Tononi make the profound statement that their theory *"treats consciousness as an intrinsic, fundamental property of reality."*

Eminent physicist John Archibald Wheeler realized how important information is in relation to consciousness. Wheeler proposed an elegant information-participatory Universe that is a brilliant and insightful model of brain-mind-cosmos interaction. With his famous *"it from bit"* concept he unites quantum information theory to consciousness and physics: *"...every it – every particle, every field of force, even the space-time continuum itself – derives its function, its very existence, entirely – even if in some contexts, indirectly – from the apparatus-elicited answers to yes-or-no questions, binary choices, bits. 'It from bit' symbolizes the idea that every item of the physical world has at bottom – at a very deep bottom, in most instances – an immaterial source and explanation; that which we call reality arises in the last analysis from the posing of yes-no question and the registering of equipment evoked responses; in short, that all things physical are information-theoretic in origin and this is a participatory universe."*

While Wheeler emphasized bits at his time, it appears that intrinsically quantum-mechanical forms of information – now known as *'qubits'* – are even more fundamental. In recent years a rising number of theorists have been exploring whether these curious quanta of information may hold the answer to combining quantum theory and general relativity into a quantum theory of gravity. In 1990, when Wheeler coined the phrase *"it from bit"* to encapsulate a radical new view of the Universe – at the most fundamental level, all of physics has a description that can be articulated in terms of information – this new worldview received little support, but now in hindsight, we can see that it was truly visionary. Wheeler divided his own life into three parts. The first part he called *"Everything is Particles."* The second part was *"Everything is Fields."* And the third part, which Wheeler considered the bedrock of his physical theory, he called *"Everything is Information."*

Max Tegmark, MIT's astrophysicist, author of *"Our Mathematical Universe"* (2014), puts forth consciousness as a mathematical pattern, a state of matter in classical terms, but information at a deeper level of reality, which he calls *'perceptronium'*. This is how our integrated information "feels" like to itself, when being processed in certain complex ways, from a certain vantage point. Consciousness is emergent and substrate-independent: It's not just particles we're made of but information patterns that really matter.

The good news is that all these promising theories of consciousness to date are not mutually exclusive but largely complementary. In an effort to combine the theories, one might hypothesize that conscious instants are data in the probabilistic qualia-space, placing the current state of human consciousness into the 5D "rule set." A distinct possibility of higher dimensional observer realities remains to account for up to 10^{500} potential universes of String Theory. Could our own future Strong AI computing all probabilistic outcomes to the minute details be, in a sense, a six-, seven-, or even higher-dimensional being?

Although the *'Conscious Instant Hypothesis'* has never been officially articulated from this particular perspective and far from accepted by mainstream science, it's not some kind of wild metaphysical speculation — it's confirmed time and again by quantum physics experiments. It looks like a radically novel computational approach in line with the tenets of Digital Physics.

Some could point out that there's no place for the first-person subjective experience in science. However, mathematics and logic are inexorably pushing science to a more post-materialist stance, whereas perhaps developing a mathematically precise model of consciousness, based on CIs, is needed. After all, it is now widely-accepted "non-local," holographic 4D space-time, where all points of space-time are equally real and eternally present — be it 1 million years in the past or 5 million years into the future. Baffled about our non-linear nature of reality? In Part III, three chapters (11, 12, 13) will be devoted to temporal dynamics, temporal mechanics and our experience of temporality.

How soon will we be able to reverse-engineer human consciousness in order to create artificial consciousness, or perhaps, the larger consciousness system could fill any container with a sufficiently integrated network? When could we safely upload our own consciousness to the alternative computational substrate?

Once we crack our "neural code," we might discover some sort of algorithmic or meta-algorithmic sequence of causality-driven CIs, which creates our subjective stream of consciousness. For reductionist delight, Digital Physics would also demonstrate that any conscious instant must be considered as data, information, so a stream of consciousness, a series of sequential conscious moments that creates your subjective reality, is merely a data stream.

As derived from Einstein's general relativity theory, all 3D space and all time exist now, as if on "hard drive," but the 5th dimension is needed to validate all the probabilities that can logically happen in static 4D space-time, which, by the way, scientists refer to as the *'Block Universe'*. For example, suppose you are in San Francisco today, having an appointment at the office located at: 1 California St., on the 23rd floor, at 4pm — so we just defined approximation of a "physical system" in 4D space-time. The 5th dimension is needed to pinpoint an instant out of an infinitely large stack of probable CIs perceived by *you*'s who is having a meeting today in "parallel San Franciscos." Each CI represents a point in the probability distribution, i.e., a certain probability of you having a certain interaction during your meeting, having a certain mental state, and so on.

Your "now" is a moving point within the 5th dimensional probability space. *"Is there some sort of visual aid to help picture that 5th dimension?"* you might ask. In fact, Rob Bryanton of the *10thdim* project has created a great educational YouTube video for this concept — *"Imagining the 5th dimension"* — among many others. As a proponent of Digital Physics, as you probably know by now, I would presume that information could be projected into 5D observer reality from the 2D surface of information-storing "holographic plate" at the distant cosmological horizon, according to the Holographic Principle, as one of my favorite conjectures, which is a topic we'll be discussing throughout the book.

THE NOOCENTRIC MODEL

Biocentrism is another elegant theory of consciousness. The Biocentric Universe Theory by Dr. Robert Lanza, a scientist in the fields of regenerative medicine and biology, accounts for consciousness being fundamental to the Universe. It is consciousness that creates the material universe, not the other way around. I'd argue, though, once we engender artificially conscious agents, this theory would need to be extended and possibly dubbed as *'Noocentrism'* (Greek *nous*, meaning mind). There's a number of certain quantum mechanisms in biology, such as *'quantum tunneling'* and *'quantum coherence'*, that might help explain why we get to perceive only one subjective timeline with a maximum "existential opportunity" all along, even though we don't necessarily see it that way. *'The Noocentric model'*, as I call it, makes the Quantum Immortality hypothesis (Chapter 4) more compelling. Certain interpretations of quantum mechanics (Chapter 4), D-Theory of Time (Chapter 13) comply with the Noocentric model while identifying the temporal singularity of one's experiential branch out of the infinitude of observer timelines in the quantum multiverse.

This Noocentric model also might offer a possible solution to the famed Fermi Paradox – why, in the vastness of space, don't we see the signs of intelligent alien life? The answer may be surprisingly straightforward – alien life has evolved in an alternate conscious observer space-time, i.e., a parallel universe. The Universe that we observe is specific to our lineage of biological life with the so-called *'Common Observer'* effect. There may be billions, if not trillions, of alien civilizations in our Milky Way galaxy alone, all around us, but currently imperceptible to us. As far as I know, this solution to the Fermi Paradox was first proposed by Dr. Robert Lanza in his Biocentric Universe Theory. In Chapter 19, we'll revisit the Fermi Paradox.

Consciousness and time are intimately interwoven. Time is change (between static 3D frames), 4th dimension. The flow of time is a rate of change, computation, and conscious awareness is a stream of realized probabilistic outcomes. *"The flow of time doesn't exist outside of consciousness,"* says Hameroff, *"The flow of time is an illusion,"* muses Tegmark. In other words, 1 second doesn't exist, but 10 CIs do exist, duration doesn't matter, information does matter.

The study of consciousness needs to be lifted out of the mysticism that has dominated it. Consciousness is not just a matter of philosophy or spirituality. It's a matter of hard science. It's a matter of understanding the brain and the mind — a pattern structure made out of information. It's also a matter of engineering. If we can understand the functionality of the brain, its neural code, then we can build the same functionality into our computer systems. We should recognize that our brain is not a "stand-alone" information processing organ, though: It acts as a central unit of our integral nervous system with recurrent data exchange within the entire organism and the Universe. Artificial consciousness may be within our grasp, however, not the way many AI researchers envision. We'll talk about consciousness and evolution of the mind all throughout this book.

Human life, just like anything else in our computable multiverse, may be quantified — about 3 billion heartbeats, 50 billion CIs, 10^{16} operations per second by a human brain. Seth Lloyd, MIT's professor of mechanical engineering and physics, argues that our Universe (or rather the quantum multiverse) is a giant quantum computer, performing 10^{106} operations per second (smarter than all humans combined by orders of magnitude), computing all possible paths from start to finish with all potential timelines.

Ultimately, consciousness might be computable, according to the Computational Hypothesis of the brain function by a neuroscientist

David Eagleman, measurable as in Tononi's IIT, quantifiable via feedback loops, as proposed by a theoretical physicist Michio Kaku, and via hierarchical "pattern recognizers," as writes Ray Kurzweil in his book *"How to Create a Mind: The Secret of a Human Thought Revealed"* (2012). While a renowned British physicist Sir Roger Penrose has introduced a "non-computable" element of consciousness, like understanding and qualia, the Conscious Instant hypothesis fills the explanatory gap between the unified field of consciousness and the computational functionality of the brain. Human-level Artificial Intelligence and above, which we call AGI or Strong AI, will, one day, be endowed with their own subjectivity at digital timescales, with, perhaps, thousands, if not millions, of conscious instants per second as opposed to only 10-30 CIs/sec. for a human.

Also, the larger consciousness system (whatever it may be) would help "compute" the Penrose "non-computable" element of consciousness which he defines as our human understanding, by generating a sufficiently integrated network (say, AGI) nested in the fundamental space-time geometry matrix (Tononi calls it "qualia space"), so subjectivity should naturally take place. Deeper understanding comes when a conscious agent gets to perceive numerous patterns in complex environments and analyze that complexity from the multitude of perspectives. As Isaiah Berlin once said: *"To understand is to perceive patterns."* So, any human-level artificially intelligent agent would be endowed with some sort of inner experience of their own, however, substantially different from that of an ordinary biological human.

Influenced by the concepts of Digital Physics in his work Tom Campbell, NASA physicist, author of the *"My Big T.O.E.,"* contends that our information-based reality is but virtual, probabilistic and subjective. Campbell argues that our reality has evolved from what he calls a "Digital Big Bang." Our subjective experience is a stream of realized probabilities. *"If you understand the Double Slit experiment, you understand how our reality works,"* says Campbell, *"Everything we do is not much different from the Double Slit experiment. Reality equals information."*

A swiss AI researcher Jürgen Schmidhuber hypothesizes that this Universe and your own life are run on a very simple and fast program computing all logically possible universes. However, it doesn't make you insignificant in the "Grand Scheme of Things," because in order to compute your whole life separately with all its "ups and downs," every fleeting thought, it would take enormous computing power and would be an incredibly difficult task even for the most advanced computers. Without you, the whole system would be incomplete and could fail!

If you were a "programmer" of our beloved world, you would have created it as a virtual reality and had access to any observer reality experiences throughout the whole history of the multiverse. In his paper *"The Physical World as a Virtual Reality,"* Brian Whitworth introduces the concept of *'Quantum Realism'* which posits that the quantum world is real and generates the physical world as an interface, i.e., a virtual reality. You could embody any living creature or historical personage, and variations thereof, in any epoch, any planet, or universe, with any initial conditions, for that matter. That would be effectively your avatar in such simulated reality.

If consciousness is fundamental to our Universe, as I concur with the above-mentioned researchers, then a conscious observer should be included in our models, and one of the most likely places (as in String Theory) would be the probabilistic space where our human subjective experience takes place from a certain vantage point, orthogonal to 4D space-time in order to account for dimensionality. But Digital Physics, with quantum information processing as the reality rendering mechanism (we'll revisit in Chapter 4), often undercuts or overlaps String Theory, and seemingly, has a more parsimonious model of the workings of quantum multiverse as well as even larger inflationary multiverse. It's just better physics!

PART II. TECHNO-CULTURE: THE RISE OF MAN

Chapter 3. Technology and Culture: Our Accelerating Evolution

"We live in succession, in division, in parts, in particles. Meantime within man is the soul of the whole; the wise silence; the universal beauty, to which every part and particle is equally related; the eternal One. And this deep power in which we exist, and whose beatitude is all accessible to us, is not only self-sufficing and perfect in every hour, but the act of seeing and the thing seen, the seer and the spectacle, the subject and the object, are one. We see the world piece by piece, as the sun, the moon, the animal, the tree; but the whole, of which these are the shining parts, is the soul." -Ralph Waldo Emerson, The Over-Soul (1841)

I'm always leery when some neuroscientist comes along and says: *"We are the brain. There's nothing besides it. If something is wrong, it's physical."* No, you are not a "brain in a vat" – we humans don't live in a vacuum – we are part of the larger pattern of life, so if we are to deconstruct human intelligence, it might be a mistake to start with the brain. Instead, if viewed collectively, it's a networking phenomenon based on technology and culture that we call civilization; and individually, it's an operating system of the person's mind. The history of logic leads us to question the overly individualistic conception of knowledge acquisition and of our human cognition that we inherited from Descartes and others, and perhaps to move towards a greater acknowledgement for the essentially social nature of human intelligence.

The Darwinian model of evolution has assumed that life advances thanks to mutations in the genetic code, and that errors in copying genetic code inadvertently lead to adaptations that get passed down generations. But that traditional mutation-based model of evolution has transformed as of late, due to what geneticists are learning about DNA replication process. Evolution is not as random, or solely mutation-caused, as we previously thought but rather epigenetic, or environmentally responsive, and in the case of our species, it is an emergent networking process we can call *'civilizational development'*. In other words, biological evolution of our species has been now overtaken by techno-cultural, *'epigenetic'* evolution.

WHAT IS EPIGENETICS?

Epigenetics has become big news in genetics in recent decades, as it allows us to examine a remarkable link between genetic functionality and environmental change. We usually define *'personality'* as individual differences in characteristic patterns of thinking, feeling, and behaving. "Nature vs. Nurture" has been heavily contested for centuries, each side weighing in now and then on how personality is formed. The 17th century philosopher John Locke was convinced that the human mind was a blank slate at birth, a concept first introduced by Aristotle as an "empty vessel." It was experience that formed personality, they argued. In the 1930s, evolutionary biologist C. H. Waddington coined the term *'Epigenetics'*, which now refers to the study of changes in organisms caused by modification of gene expression rather than alteration of the genetic code itself.

According to the new findings of behavioral epigenetics, dramatic experiences in our past, or even in our recent ancestors' past, leave molecular lesions on our DNA. Your forebears' traumatic childhoods or exciting lifetime adventures might affect your personality, passing on anxiety or resilience by altering the epigenetic expressions of genes. Our experiences, and those of our ancestors are never gone, even if they might have been forgotten. They become a part of us, a molecular residue holding firm to our genetic scaffolding. The DNA remains the same, but psychological and behavioral tendencies are inherited.

Our cognitive abilities, sometimes referred to as *'fluid intelligence'*, can be evaluated when we encounter new information or novel situations. Genes exert a heavy influence on a person's overall cognitive potential, but environmental factors either activate or suppress those genes. For instance, studying identical twins, or *'monozygotic twins'*, offers clues about different ways in which surroundings could influence a person's physical appearance, known as a *'phenotype'*. But who cares about looks if IQ and EQ are at stake, too?

In extremely rare documented cases of *'feral children'*, a "wild child" is an unfortunate human child who has lived isolated from human contact from a very young age, with little or no experience of human care, behavior or human language. Dina Sanichar, the Indian wolf boy, who has been "raised by wolves" in a forest in India, is believed to be the inspiration behind Rudyard Kipling's famous work, *The Jungle Book*. But his real story is less than glamorous: The vast majority of wild children have tremendous difficulties reintegrating into human culture, lack the basic social skills and interest in the human activity around them.

The Nature-vs-Nurture debate in relation to intelligence gets a lot more complicated with recent discoveries in the burgeoning field of neuro-epigenetics: The environment can modify the expression of genes in the brain, affecting intelligence far more than previously thought. As you may know, numerous genes influence our IQ and dramatic experiences can lock and unlock "intelligence genes." Geneticists found a strong correlation between the epigenetic modifications of particular genes and general IQ, suggesting our experiences not only affect the wiring of our brain, but the very way our genes function at a basic level.

Through the study of epigenetics, researchers also came to a staggering realization that if our emotional states affect our DNA and our DNA "filters" our perceptions of the world, then our emotions can indeed influence our physical reality in profound ways. Furthermore, while looking for ways to understand what controls our DNA, research led to the conscious mind. Scientists stopped looking at DNA as the only determinant factor to control human biology when they discovered how our biology is affected by our mind.

WHAT IS THE DIFFERENCE BETWEEN MIND AND CONSCIOUSNESS?

'Mind' and *'Consciousness'* are two different but somewhat overlapping terms related to the phenomenality of our experiential reality. Both of these terms mean different things to different people and can refer to a broad collection of interrelated phenomena. Both terms lack uniform definitions although generally speaking, consciousness refers to the awake state as opposed to dreamless sleep or coma, and also to subjective perceptual awareness, which can shift, change, and move around, e.g., modulated by attention or in "altered states of consciousness."

What most people would agree upon is that the mind is organized mental activity that is formed from the substructure of consciousness and further made possible by memory and information processing capacities of the brain. To be clear, the mind, which is a cultural term that is debated in philosophy and used in psychology, generally refers to consciousness plus autobiographical memory, personal identity, irreducible sense of self, ability for introspection, all of which we experience as *'qualia'*.

As an idealist philosopher, I could make even further distinction between the two terms by saying that the *'Unified Field'* of consciousness is fundamental and transdimensional, the mind, in contrast, is a "localized" expression of consciousness which is the result of a subjective entity participating in that field. Conscious awareness, i.e., "local" consciousness, is recognized as self-reflective, feedback-driven information integration – there is "something it is like to be" an organism. We all are "partitioned realities" like "mindfiles" on the universal operating system – minds are many, consciousness is one. Consciousness is absolute, mind is relative. The mind that includes subjective memory and cognition emerges from the underlying field of *'non-local'* consciousness. *'Mind'* has been used more often as a term in philosophy while *'Consciousness'* has been used more in scientific literature.

Your mind is such a magnificent everything. It basically encompasses all of your reality – thoughts, emotions, ideas, beliefs, intentions, attitudes, desires, motivations and practically any other aspect of your life. Your behavior and actions are influenced by your mind, so everything must start with a thought, which will then materialize into physical reality. Your beliefs are influenced by your environment, and your thoughts, emotions, and actions are subject to your current system of beliefs. So, when we're talking epigenetic evolution, we're actually talking evolution of the mind.

WHY HOMO SAPIENS IS NOW THE DOMINANT SPECIES ON THE PLANET

Viewed zoologically, we humans are Homo sapiens, a culture-bearing, upright-walking higher primate species that lives on the ground and very likely first evolved in Africa about 300,000 years ago. We are now the only living members of what many zoologists refer to as the human tribe. We are incredibly lucky to occupy the dominant place as a species on this planet not because of our strong muscles, or sharp teeth, or blade-like claws, but our collective intelligence, collaborative flexibility and inquisitive mind.

Is the meaning of life the answers of which we seek or is it merely seeking answers which give us meaning? We have this epigenetic trait of wonder in us – an innate desire to wander out into the uncharted territory – in order to explore new possibilities. Whether it's taming fire to illuminate the dark night or hurling our space-faring instruments to help us look into the unknown interstellar expanse, our very circumstance today is solely due to our curiosity. Why are humans so damn curious? Because we find discovery so incredibly pleasurable.

As a rule, we humans don't care much about spectacle – what we care about is ecstatic understanding: in other words, cognitive ecstasy, that can be defined as electrifying cerebration of extreme psychical pleasure when we master a skill or learn something new, feeding our imagination. This *'cogno-ecstasis'* can give us goosebumps of intellectual rapture of "aha moment," or puts us in motivational overdrive, otherwise known as the *'flow state'*. Homo sapiens, the first truly free species, that transcended the animal kingdom, is about to decommission natural selection, one of the most powerful evolutionary forces that have made us who we are today. Moving forward into our fantastical future, we must look deep within ourselves and decide what we wish to become.

Are we one of the last generations of Homo sapiens — soon to be replaced by engineered superbeings, with a distant resemblance to us, their creators? After all, if life is like a software program running on the hardware of biochemistry, all we have to do is collect all the information we can to write our own algorithms of living things and create virtual environments or even whole-world simulations. That, coupled with the rise of machine intelligence, will seal our fate as a bio-species. Or, in a rather much more optimistic way to see this, it will put the future of evolution in our own hands and not at the whims of natural selection but self-directed evolution.

LANGUAGE DEVELOPMENT: INVENTION OF THE SPOKEN AND WRITTEN WORD

"History is the version of past events that people have decided to agree upon."
-Napoleon Bonaparte

Evolution is a fundamental process in Nature, and not necessarily related to genes. In our information-based world, there are many parallels between biological evolution and linguistic evolution. It is safe to say: Language development played the key role in evolution of the human mind. However, consciousness as well as language remain hard to solve precisely because they are humankind's innermost traits. Nobody ever said that studying the fascinating but flawed human mind with that very same mind should be easy. The human mind suffers from a "cognitive gap" in understanding its own conscious awareness.

How is it that human beings have come to acquire language? Terence McKenna (1946–2000) was an American idealist philosopher, ethnobotanist, psychonaut, author, and an advocate for the responsible use of psychedelics. He spoke and wrote about a variety of topics, including metaphysics, psychedelic drugs, shamanism, language, philosophy, culture, technology, and the theoretical origins of human consciousness. In his book *Food of the Gods: The Search for the Original Tree of Knowledge: A Radical History of Plants, Drugs, and Human Evolution*, Terence McKenna crafts his carefully thought out theory proposing that our pre-human primate ancestors consumed psilocybin mushrooms for thousands of years, and this is the primary reason humanity's evolution rapidly accelerated – launching us forward in the animal kingdom. Terence McKenna's *Stoned Ape Theory* is more plausible than it sounds – especially in context of the emergence of human mind and language development.

As our distant ancestors left the forests for the grasslands and began moving throughout Africa after the last ice age, about 18,000 years ago, the species switched to a more omnivorous diet, which included psilocybin mushrooms. A variety of mushroom spores were found embedded in the dental remains of an 18,700-year-old prehistoric woman. Researchers discovered microscopic evidence that the upper paleolithic woman had been nibbling *"sponge capped, bolete mushrooms and gilled mushrooms from the Agaric group."* Thus, these "special" mushrooms were definitively part of the stone-age diet.

In McKenna's theory, the consumption of hallucinogenic psilocybin was done in small doses, where the effect doesn't quite reach the point of hallucination, but instead reaches the point of heightened senses, such as visual acuity. This enhancement of vision would have helped our ancestors hunt, gather food, and detect predators. At a medium dose, psilocybin acts as an aphrodisiac – it creates a sense of restlessness and sexual arousal. This would have increased instances of successful copulation, i.e., sexual reproduction which is the main game in evolution. At higher doses, according to McKenna, in glossolalia-induced states of mind members of the group were inspired and compelled to use vocal sounds to communicate images to their tribesmen. The Stoned Ape Theory suggests that experience on magic mushrooms was the major contributing factor to the fast development of language during that period.

The "Linguistic Singularity" made us human. McKenna wrote that, with the invention of language, human biological evolution basically seized and cultural evolution, an epigenetic phenomenon, has taken over, ever since. McKenna's theory remains one of the most controversial, but fascinating and what it actually boils down to is that a new psychoactive chemical was introduced to a species, and over millennia, this chemical, that functions as a neurotransmitter, had a drastic effect on the evolutionary trajectory of that species. One thing is for certain: We would not be who we are today if Earth had not prepared us for the next evolutionary leap and given us a chance to eat our way to higher consciousness, according to McKenna.

The improved visual acuity, sex drive, and use of language gave early humans a tremendous evolutionary advantage over other hominid species. The size of the Homo sapiens neocortex (new addition to the mammalian brain) grew substantially during the 6,000 years following the last ice age. Over the course of the next few thousand years, starting around 12,000 years ago, early humans became gardeners, herders, and mostly gave up their nomadic existence.

Besides survival, reproduction and language, these boundary-dissolving experiences would have created a sense of intimacy and deepened an overall group cohesion. This pack bonding has definitely led to a distinct evolutionary advantage over other non-mushroom-eating species. At higher doses, individual and group consciousness would have deepened and expanded, as this would create bizarre, transpersonal, and unitive states of consciousness. One can see that perhaps this is where ritual first developed — bringing logic and imagination together as well as seeding human culture.

As anthropology shows us, ritualistic shamanism, which uses visionary plants, was humanity's first form of spirituality, as shamanism went on for thousands of years before widespread organized religion — the oldest cave paintings we know of depicting shamanic mushroom use date back to 7,000 BC in Africa. Because of these intense psychedelic, imaginative experiences, pulling our ancestors outside their familiar environment and into hallucinogenic ecstasy, they would have eventually formed intersubjective myths (today we call them "memes") to make sense of their emerging reality.

Setting aside our current stigmas around drugs, it seems plausible that our evolution — not only including biological development, but cognition and self-reflective awareness as well — was propelled forward by a change in primate diets, one that included the introduction of a psychoactive compound. As for the origins of culture and religion, when we integrate the scientific evidence collected on studies of psilocybin, we find the high probability that psilocybin can trigger a profound spiritual experience, given the right setting — and what can be a better setting than out in Nature under the open night skies around the bonfire with fellow tribesmen. This is where our minds were opened up to the abstract concepts which eventually led humanity out of the animal kingdom into the category of its own. Our ability to grasp abstract concepts, communicate them, understand what was communicated, and build on those concepts, became the foundation of our civilization.

Linguists have long found that human languages share many commonalities termed *'linguistic universals'* or *'cross-linguistic generalizations'*. The idea that all languages share a deep underlying structure that's almost certainly baked into our biology by evolution was encapsulated in Noam Chomsky's concept of a *'universal grammar'* which became the dominant linguistic theory. Its essential feature is syntax, or recursion, the capacity to embed phrases within phrases ad infinitum, and so express complex relations between ideas. The syntactic structure of languages — the arrangement of words and phrases to create well-formed sentences in a language — as well as finer acoustic patterns of speech, such as the timing, pitch, and stress of utterances reflect this universal grammar. If these linguistic universals are indeed real, and if we understand their causes, then we can have a good grasp about how language is acquired or processed by the human brain, which is one of the central questions in linguistics. Most theories assume the reasons why languages have these cross-linguistic universals is because they're in some way determined by the peculiarities of human cognition: They are built on innate neural algorithms that promote and skew language learning.

Some linguists such as Benjamin Lee Whorf began to question universalist theories of language back in the 1950s. Instead of subscribing to the idea that abstract concepts were common across the whole of humanity, Whorf proposed that language itself shaped our perception of the world, effectively creating different perceptual strokes for different folks. This idea that language can shape perception and thought — a hypothesis formally known as *'linguistic relativity'* — asserts that language doesn't just express ideas, it actively shapes them, determining how we grasp reality itself. Initially met with great enthusiasm, this idea fell out of favor by the 1960s due to a lack of scientific evidence. Now, cognitive scientists are applying new technologies to resolve the issue. Taken together, these experiments point in a surprising direction: Language does, indeed, influence our ability to perceive the world around us.

Neuroscientists Andrew Newberg and Mark Robert Waldman write in their 2012 book, *Words Can Change Your Brain: "Language shapes our behavior and each word we use is imbued with multitudes of personal meaning. The right words spoken in the right way can bring us love, money and respect, while the wrong words — or even the right words spoken in the wrong way — can lead a country to war. We must carefully orchestrate our speech if we want to achieve our goals and bring our dreams to fruition. "*

Why is language such a fundamental part of social relationships, human biology, and epigenetic evolution? We depend on truthful communication for exchanging reliable information with one another, for decision-making and predicting the future which have evolutionarily been crucial for our survival. We have developed a rich array of norms, conventions and expectations for these linguistic exchanges, and we greatly appreciate oftentimes intentional distance from the plain truth provided by poetry, metaphor, analogy and abstraction.

The invention of record keeping, or proto-writing, and a few centuries later, proper writing unsurprisingly coincides with the rise of first civilization. Sumer, an ancient civilization of southern Mesopotamia, is believed to be the place where written language was first invented around 3100 BC, another independent writing system also arose in Egypt around same time. Literature and writing, though connected, are not synonymous. Certain primary texts may have a qualifying role as literature's first furors. A splendid, very early example is *Epic of Gilgamesh*, in its Sumerian version predating 2000 BC. The history of literature, however, starts with the first true alphabet which was the Greek alphabet, adapted from the Phoenician. Latin, the most widely used alphabet today, in turn derives from Greek. The *'Printing Revolution'* in the 15th century occurred when the spread of the printing press facilitated the wide circulation of information and ideas, acting as an "agent of change" through the cultures that it reached.

THE NETWORK EFFECT: THE RISE OF INTERSUBJECTIVITY

Understanding evolutionary forces that shaped the human mind could help us comprehend how rare our intelligence is, and very possibly our role in the grander scheme of things. The human brain is so unique, and so densely interconnected, it's unlikely to have developed by truly random chance. Our intelligence wasn't a given but the result of an intensely complicated process, which historically could have played out quite differently.

Matt Ridley, British journalist and best-selling author, argues that human achievement and intelligence are entirely "networking phenomena." In other words, intelligence is collective and emergent as opposed to individual. When asked what scientific concept would improve everybody's cognitive arsenal, Ridley highlights collective intelligence: *"It is by putting brains together through the division of labor — through trade and specialization — that human society stumbled upon a way to raise the living standards, carrying capacity, technological virtuosity, and knowledge base of the species."* Undoubtedly, collectivity produces a transcendent "network effect."

Nearly all human accomplishments imply the work of groups of people, not just lone individuals. The human groups acting together in ways that display intelligent decision-making can be described as *'superminds'*. They include the hierarchies in most social organizations and governments, the markets that exchange goods and services, the communities that use norms and reputations to guide behavior in professional, societal, and political groups. All superminds represent a kind of collective intelligence, an ability to do things that the individuals in the groups couldn't possibly have done alone, and civilization as a whole reveals the hive mind ontological design at its best.

Harnessing the wisdom of the hive mind – the collective opinion of a group compared to that of a single expert – is a great tool of gaining knowledge, but simply polling a crowd is not a foolproof way to arrive at correct answers. What's new nowadays is that machines can increasingly participate in the intellectual, as well as the physical, activities of these groups. That means we will be able to combine people and machines to create superminds that are smarter than any groups or individuals our planet has ever known.

Like network effects, learning effects have always existed in the offline world but have become supercharged in the digital world. In the offline world, learning effects are channeled through humans: In classrooms, in workshops, in boardrooms we learn from each other incrementally. Human learning, however, is about craftsmanship, while schooling, professional training, mentoring takes years, months or weeks at best. What's new and different in the machine learning era is that certain kinds of learning have now become automated. Deep learning networks, such as Google's DeepMind, can learn by themselves with exposure to new data and become more valuable in the process. This is a pretty big deal economically. It involves the unlocking of a new source of socio-economic value that was previously inaccessible. The question is: Will we humans stay in the loop?

In our increasingly interconnected world, *'Social Cognition'*, which is a sub-topic of social psychology, studies how people process, store, and apply intersubjectivity-related information, i.e., interactions between people and different social situations, emphasizing our inherently social being. Social cognition focuses on the role that cognitive processes play in our social interactions. The way we think about others plays a major role in how we think, feel, and interact with the world around us. Predictably, when people are linked in real time using swarming algorithms, studies confirm, we can form closed-loop systems that enhance our intelligence to a level higher than our own individual abilities. This suggests that artificial swarm intelligence is a viable pathway to building superintelligent AI systems. After all, if a swarm of bees can make complex life-or-death decisions better than a human CEO, a swarm of already smart humans working together should be able to soar to inconceivable intellectual heights.

The planet is shrinking to a point. Before globalization we lived in the age of empires spanning centuries and continents. At the dawn of globalization, we used to say that our world turns into a "global village," now it's turning into a "global smart-home" -- transforming from the planetary hive mind ontology to the *'Syntellect ontology'*, one global mind.

TECHNOLOGY: OUR EXTENDED PHENOTYPE

As we have seen, an epigenetic world means a world not based on gene transfer and chemical propagation but a world based on ideas, on symbols, on concepts, on technologies, on human imagination, on non-material subjective values. The more one's awareness rises, the more genes get switched on, and switching on genes that one has never had experience with during one's lifetime. But admittedly, our minds are now running on the outmoded biological "hardware and software." What we'll soon see is the ultimate self-directed evolution fueled forward by gene editing, genetic engineering, reproduction assisted technology, neuro-engineering, mind uploading and creation of artificial life.

Our success as a technological species essentially created what might be called our species-specific "success formula." We devised tools and instruments, created new methodologies and processes, and readjusted ecological niches to suit our needs. And our technology shaped us back by shaping our minds. In a very real sense, we have co-evolved with our technology. As an animal species among many other species competing for survival, this was our unique passage to success.

Other "satellite" species, the ones that we had domesticated, have co-evolved with us as well. Through artificial selection, i.e., breeding, dogs underwent their own accelerated epigenetic factor-driven evolution sculpted by the inter-species partnership with humans. Dogs became our trustworthy and beloved companions: Millenia of close association have turned once-wolves into amazingly social creatures.

Technology has always been a "double-edged sword" since fire, which has kept us warm and cooked our food but also burned down our huts. Today, we surely enjoy the fruits of modern civilization when we fly halfway around the globe on an airbus, when we extend our mental functionality with a whole array of Internet-enabled devices, when our cities and dwellings become icons of technological sophistication. Thanks to technology, rightly viewed as our extended phenotype, we're actually living in the most peaceful, abundant, civilized time in history, and things are likely to continue getting better, as data suggests. As we now gradually transcend our biology, we are, in actuality, more than users of technology, we are "reproductive organs" of technology. We are Homo technicus as much as Homo sapiens. In the broader context, we are technology.

Merging with Artificial Intelligence is arguably the next evolutionary step for humanity. There's nothing unnatural about that: AI is a natural extension of us, organic intelligence. In the same way that culture co-evolved with larger brains, we will co-evolve with our creations. We always have: Humans would be physically different if we had not invented fire or spears. Evolutionarily, just as RNA survived by being incorporated by DNA, and unicellular microbes survived the multicellularity explosion by symbiotically co-existing with higher lifeforms and by being incorporated into their microbiome, we can figure out ways to become superintelligences ourselves by assimilating the transcendent aspects of artificiality that otherwise could easily become a mastermind, both in control of us and out of control.

At the dawn of artificial superintelligence, humanity is trying to not only find its place again, but to do the inevitable, the inescapable and previously inconceivable – merging with technology we created. We are now birthing a new intelligent species on this planet and rebirthing ourselves in the process. More and more people are becoming mesmerized by their digital creations, literally extensions of themselves, and developing more of a personal relationship with them, a clear trend towards the merger of human and machine intelligence. This merger will open gateways to unimaginable vistas of self-exploration, empowerment and hope for the human enterprise.

CULTURE: OUR SHARED MEME-SPACE

"Human nature, as manifested in tribalism and nationalism, provides the momentum of the machinery of human evolution." -Arthur Keith

Human culture undoubtedly shaped the evolution of human cognition and memory. Cultural activities, such as the use of language, influence our learning processes, affecting our ability to collect all kinds of data in order to infer a desirable mode of behavior from them. Since the dawn of civilization, Homo sapiens has become a self-programmable "extropian" species. But the human brain is not a classical digital computer in which one particular event necessarily leads to another particular event. Instead, brain functions according to co-evolving mechanisms of learning and data acquisition, with certain memory capacities that, some would argue, jointly represent a complex *'quantum cognition'* neural network.

Our physical characteristics, our hormonal makeup, our inherited factors, and acquired cultural contextuality filter the signals received by the brain from which it constructs perceptions presented to our conscious awareness. In a given set of identical conditions, the stimuli collected by the brain is not the same for every individual. Besides that, the brain's ability to process these stimuli is vastly different from individual to individual. Therefore, the decision made by two individual minds in the same situation, could, and likely will, be quite different. Now, to complicate the matter further, the memes get involved.

A meme is the smallest unit of an idea in the same way that a gene is the smallest unit of organismic structure. In his 1976 book, *The Selfish Gene*, Richard Dawkins coined the term *'meme'* to denote bits of information that replicate themselves, ideas that are transmitted from mind to mind across time and space. Dawkins defines a meme as a replicating information pattern that uses minds to make copies into other minds. These patterns include the *'percepts'* created by mental interpretation from sources of information such as books and digital media. Memes are thoughts, ideas, beliefs, tastes, prejudices, attitudes that replicate in our shared meme-space. Dawkins writes: *"Examples of memes are tunes, ideas, catch-phrases, clothes fashions, ways of making pots or of building arches. Just as genes propagate themselves in the gene pool by leading from body to body via sperm or eggs, so memes propagate themselves in the meme pool by leaping from brain to brain via a process which, in the broad sense, can be called imitation."*

Memes are not just learned, they run deeper than that, they are part of our shared experience as human beings. This is how we communicate to each other through spoken, written, and body language; this is how we participate in customs, rituals and cultural traditions. Indeed, human civilization has always been a "cultured" virtual reality. We don't often think of cultures as virtual realities, but there is no more apt descriptor for our widely diverse sociology and interpretations than the metaphor of the "virtual reality." In truth, the virtual reality metaphor encompasses the entire human enterprise. We should realize that all our ideologies and religions, our belief systems and models of reality are our own personal operating systems — real to us but wry to someone else — each of us lives in a seemingly shared but simultaneously private virtual world.

A renowned cellular biologist Bruce Lipton says that during the first seven years of our life each of us takes on subconscious social programming — infused patterns and beliefs — that defines and sometimes limits our reality. To be clear, memes are beliefs that spread from our parents, from society at large, from individual to individual. Nonetheless, we can shift, change and re-write this early cultural conditioning to become more powerfully conscious co-creators of our own life. There is mounting evidence that personality is malleable throughout one's life: Radical openness has been observed in cognitive training interventions and studies of the effects of psychedelic drugs. Open-mindedness also increases for students who choose to study overseas, confirming the idea that travel broadens the mind.

Pre-dating all secular religions, shamanism is the oldest spiritual path on the planet, it has been tried, tested and refined by almost every culture, on every continent. Because of this ancient global heritage, shamanism is a valid spiritual route accessible to anyone in the world. This well-trodden pathway is calling to many now at this time of global transition. With the rise of the Internet, as an opportunity for a new kind of liberation, the web is birthing a techno-cultural renaissance grounded in ancient spiritual teachings. From the outset, the web was adopted by mainstream culture almost overnight. In the era of the Internet memes, marketers began to employ *'viral marketing'*, digital shamanism of sorts taking advantage of the new global medium. With the further advent of the Internet, the subset of current memetic evolution *'Social Computing'* finally set in. In December 2012, the exuberant video *"Gangnam Style"* became the first YouTube clip to be viewed more than one billion times.

Beyond doubt, many memes may be disseminated by some individuals for their own self-interest. The politicians, the press, the schools, and others are able to feed a constant stream of memes within the populace and encourage their growth. Just like genes, survivability of which depends on their environment, memes by necessity are simplistic so as not to take up too much space in our limited brain capacity. In that sense, memes that are compatible support each other's growth and survivability. Thus, there is always a great deal of memetic activity in social media, some rightly say it is a "meme minefield."

In politics, foreign affairs conducted by certain countries often resemble "chimp gangs" fighting with each other for dominance – only at our "slightly higher" human level of culture-powered evolution. Fortunately, in the 21st century they now fight more with words, propaganda, and occasional provocations, and less with armed conflicts and devastating wars that are kept as the last resort.

Arguably, we humans are more compassionate than chimps. Without compassion, civilization, or at least a decent civilized society, would probably collapse. On the other hand, we still have a long way to go: We know that humans are capable of doing incredibly cruel things to each other, especially if they are not held accountable. Major American cities in the richest country of the world are flooded with homelessness epidemic with thousands of "underprivileged" human beings living on the street, and pockets of those cities look worse than any third world country. Periodically, we are confronted with inhumane facts right before our very eyes. How can this be if we are compassionate? The answer is that the gradients of empathy are attained in stages – compassion is most likely not genetic. Rather, compassion (thankfully) is a meme that is "planted" into our heads since childhood.

OPERATING SYSTEM OF THE MIND

"New opinions are always suspected, and usually opposed, without any other reason but because they are not already common." -John Locke

While the primary purpose of genes is to determine the physical characteristics of our bodies, including our brain and nervous system, they also influence decisions of the mind. For instance, the fact that genes make us feel irresistible pleasure during sexual intercourse certainly has a significant influence on the mind. But the mind is also strongly influenced by beliefs – and that is where memes come in. The memes related to morals are often termed *'mores'* which my dictionary defines as, *"folkways of central importance accepted without question and embodying the fundamental moral views of a social group."* For our discourse here, we will assume that the individual's mind makes its decisions by analyzing the inputs as amplified by the genes and memes. Here's a useful analogy: Our mind controls our bodily movements, our thinking processes and emotions somewhat like an operating system in a computer where genes are its hardware components and memes are downloadable software programs, along with the associated data.

Although memes are comparable to genes in the fact that they replicate and that they influence our behavior, the way memes influence the mind is quite different from how genes do. Our genetic psychological factors are powerful forces that compel us to act, unfortunately, they are too slow to adapt to a rapidly changing world. We are struggling today with gene-based emotions appropriate for the caveman. Genes cause problems because they provide psychological guidance for a particular situation that is no longer adequate. The evolved genetic solutions for certain problems allegedly worked at one time but may no longer be up to the task. After all, it takes thousands of years for the genes to be modified.

Genes directly affect our physiology in two ways: physical traits and sensory palette. Many of the characteristics of humans, both physical and mental, are pre-determined at birth. We all are unique when it comes to capabilities, emotions, and physical makeup. To the mind, memes are additional facts that are combined with the genetic input for optimal efficiency in decision-making. Although memes are just beliefs, for all intents and purposes to the mind they are facts that are accepted as such and the mind carries on. If this approach were not taken, our mind would get stuck in "analysis paralysis" to the point that it would never be able to make a timely decision.

Rapidly changing human societies and our surroundings made it imperative for some kind of adaptive mechanism to be built in our mind that would allow for these swift societal and environment changes. You live in your own virtual world run on its custom operating system. What's real to you may be surreal, unreal and untrue to someone else. We are all alternate realities, so to speak. *"Debate, don't impose on others,"* I repeatedly say to myself. Isn't this why it's hard to convince anyone to change their mind in online conversations?

Unlike genes, memes, or "facts on file," may be added, replaced or modified many times in a person's lifetime. Stereotypes and prejudices are judgmental shortcuts. Prejudices are comparable to other memes. They allow the mind to make a quick judgment call first developed as a survival mechanism. If the prejudice is based on logic and facts, then it can be useful. If it's based on blind faith or "pseudo-axioms," like most memes, then it can be bad. Also, in recent times, we are prone to define a *'prejudice'* as an unfavorable meme. So, it seems that prejudices are just a subclass of memes that are believed to be generally bad.

As mentioned before, memes are more effective than genes in dealing with modernity because of their ability to rapidly develop. While genetic forces have evolved over many centuries, if not millennia, to adapt to particular issues, memes can appear and propagate comparatively "in a heartbeat." The price to pay for this quick reaction is that there is little chance for corrections when the erroneous memes are in place. The behavior they evoke is not best for humans. In large part they just evolve in response to short-term circumstances, limited information and frequently, ignorance.

Memes also generate psychological and emotional forces that are just as powerful as genetic forces. As an example, materialism well may be now regarded as not only an "expiring" philosophical paradigm, but for a lack of a better word, "pseudoscience" notably in physics where mind-independent objective reality and *'local realism'* among other materialist assumptions have been routinely falsified, dismissed and debunked since the 1920s. Yet, this materialist "pseudo-knowledge" has been indoctrinated in many minds, especially in the West, by institutions ensuing at least four centuries of the biased intellectual directive, "fashion" in science, and social conditioning.

It's extremely difficult, if not impossible, for each of us to make decisions without using memes. Since memes are involved in our thinking process, we usually need to use memes to evaluate other memes. Even to the best of our effort to think logically, we may still be basing our decision on "facts" that are really just memes. After all, the concept of meme is a meme itself, and even the *'scientific method'* or any field of study is nothing more than a meme-set!

The modes of reasoning may themselves be called into question. The rules of inference by which conclusions are drawn from postulates have a logical congruence. When viewed abstractly, though, they are but rules for transposing strings of symbols into other strings. Entirely different sets of transformation rules can produce equally consistent results. Could it be at least possible that the way we reason is not a universal absolute but merely an evolutionary expedient adapted by intelligent beings indigenous to this planet? Just as our

115

classical intuitions do not grasp relativity or quantum mechanics and thus only apply within a narrow range of conditions, so may our reasoning processes be fundamentally primitive and incomplete. Our perceptions of reality are shaped by our rationality, so new mechanisms of reasoning may effectively change our view of reality.

The genes we have inherited and the memes that we have adopted define our outlook on life. They provide to us a necessary reality framework and the launchpad for our decisions. But our memes are not superior just because we happen to hold them. We simply should not be overly critical of other cultures based on nothing more than our own meme/gene makeup. So many countries, so many customs. Koreans eat dogs, the French enjoy frogs' legs for dinner, Americans consume hamburgers made of cows. We live by our set of memes and they live by theirs. It's important to remember that any judgment you make about anything is directly governed, or at least "instagrammed," by memes and genes.

Can we behave without being influenced by memes and genes? While we can't completely eliminate the influence of memes and genes since we still need to relate to others, we can still consciously divert their impact. Obviously, it is not in your best interests to totally resign to the control of memes. If we accept that many of our actions are meme-based and therefore can be changed, we have the potential to improve our lives by evaluating the memes and overriding those that we believe to be potentially harmful. But how can we override memes? They are just as powerful as genes and they color our thinking, right? True, but they can be overridden via critical thinking and conscious deliberation.

Choice is made at the mind level. We do play this game of life and without a conscious choice the game just loses sense. But then again, you can "choose" whatever you want to believe in: Like it or not, you are constantly in the process of building your own belief system as an operating system for your mind. It's always entertaining to watch high-spirited Freewill-vs-Fate debates, for example, but what it actually boils down to is your subjective belief or non-belief in free will as well as its definition. Your mind creates its own operating system from available meme-space but it's always a "choice" of what building blocks should be included in your memetic architecture. Believing in free will or believing in superdeterminism is a choice of perspective.

When I was about to finish writing this portion of the book, I received a strange phone call from a man who introduced himself Matthew and spoke with a distinct Anglo-Saxon accent. Here's our conversation, more or less:

Alex: *"Hello?! This is Alex!"*

Matthew: *"Good morning, sir! My name is Matthew* (such-and-such) ... *you can call me Matt. We've been following your work and we have a proposition for you. Have you ever heard of the Illuminati?"* At that point I thought it was some kind of prank, so I replied with alacrity: *"Yes, of course, it's my favorite supervillain group in the movies!"*

Matthew: *"Well, what if I tell you that we have a few thousand members in our global organization and we are not villains but the old guardians of civilization with clearly defined goals. Would you be willing to join us?"* Still in disbelief and in a prankproof mode, I go: *"But I am a digilati already!"* pronto realizing it was long past April Fool's day but still leaving some room for a pre-Halloween trick.

Matthew: *"I know it may sound pretty weird but we're approaching the Event* (he stressed it here) *and we'd like you to be part of the force for the good of humanity. Is that something you would be interested in?"*

117

Alex: *"Well, all my work is confirmation of that, isn't it?"*

Matthew: *"Precisely! The Illuminati are going to break their silence closer to the Event..."*

Alex: *"I gotta interrupt you, Matt, sorry, what is the Event you are referring to?"*

Matthew: *"For that we'll be in touch with you soon. I'm not at liberty to disclose that information just yet..."* We ended our conversation by exchanging "have a nice day" habitual pleasantries.

CONCLUDING THOUGHTS

At the time of this writing I'm in the middle of my own personal experiment. It's a simple setup: I dropped watching all "depressing" news on TV and elsewhere, the most relevant news will "find you" anyway; I quit watching all horror and bad sci-fi flicks; I refuse to react to glaring populism, alarmism and any fear-mongering headlines, moreover, I block them from my newsfeed; I attempt to ignore all negativity and avoid toxic people. If you are to do something like that on your own, let me know your results, so that we can compare notes.

Techno-cultural evolution driven by epigenetic and memetic factors, the collective will of humanity to emulate the most successful achievements of Nature with technology, proceeds now millions of times faster than genetic evolution of our species at an ever-accelerating pace. Through the prism of memetics we can view the *'Technosphere'* as our extended phenotype on a planetary scale. In turn, the Technosphere supports and amplifies the *'Noosphere'*, epitomized in the omnipresent Internet, as an extender of our perception, literally our extended mind, a magnificent epigenetic phenomenon.

Chapter 4. The Physics of Information: From Quantum Potentiality to Actuality of Experiential Self

"A quantum possibility is more real than a classical possibility, but less real than a classical reality." -Boris Tsirelson

John Archibald Wheeler (1911-2008) was one of the first prominent physicists to propose that reality might not be wholly physical, in some sense, our cosmos must be a "participatory" phenomenon requiring the act of conscious observation -- and thus consciousness itself. Wheeler also drew attention to implicit connection between physics and information theory, which was invented in 1948 by mathematician Claude Shannon. Just as physics builds on elementary particles, the quanta, defined by measurement, so does information theory. Its "quantum" is the binary unit, or bit, which is a signal represented by one of two choices: yes or no, plus or minus, zero or one.

Ironically, Wheeler's *'it from bit'* implies that a "theory of everything" will always be a work in progress, and that truth is something subjectively created rather than objectively apprehended. *"I do take 100 percent seriously the idea that the world is a figment of the imagination,"* Wheeler used to remark.

Twisting your mind to see reality from the quantum gravity viewpoint is no easy task. It might be quite a stretch to see the physical world made up of space-time-mass-energy as a formless fog of potentiality. Physicists face the same hard problem as neuroscientists do: the problem of bridging objective description and subjective experience. Physics has encountered consciousness.

119

Quantum theory says an object remains in a superposition of possibilities until observed. We can consider a quantum state as being about our knowledge rather than a direct description of physical reality. The physics of information just may be that bridging of quantum-to-digital reality of subjective experience. We are now at the historic juncture when quantum computing could reveal quantum information processing underpinnings of subjectivity.

INTERPRETATIONS OF QUANTUM MECHANICS

Quantum mechanics is a spectacularly successful theory of fundamental physics that allows us to make probabilistic predictions derived from its mathematical formalism, but the theory doesn't tell us precisely how these probabilities should be interpreted in regards to phenomenology, i.e., our experiential reality. There are basically three main interpretive camps within quantum mechanics from which stem at least a dozen further interpretations.

The first "basic" camp is *'Many Worlds'* (Hugh Everett, 1957), *'Many-Minds Interpretation'* (H. Dieter Zeh, 1970), which state that the different possible configurations of a system are literally parallel universes. The second camp is the *'Pilot Wave'* mechanics, also known as the *de Broglie–Bohm theory* (1927), which agrees with Many Worlds about the probability amplitude, but supplements it with a "true" configuration that a physical system is "factually" in, regardless of whether or not anyone measures it.

Finally, the third interpretative camp, the most popular among physicists to date, is nested in Niels Bohr and Werner Heisenberg's original *'Copenhagen Interpretation'* (1927), which asserts that reality doesn't even exist prior to your observation. An array of "offshoot" interpretations within the Copenhagen camp includes but is not limited to: *'Ensemble Interpretation'* (Max Born, 1926), *'Quantum Logic'* (Garrett Birkhoff, 1936), *'Time-Symmetric Theories'* (Satosi Watanabe, 1955), *'Consciousness Causes Collapse'* (Eugene Wigner, 1961), *'Stochastic Interpretation'* (Edward Nelson, 1966), *'Consistent Histories'* (Robert B. Griffiths, 1984), *'Transactional Interpretation'* (John G. Cramer, 1986), *'Objective Collapse Theories'* (Ghirardi–Rimini–Weber, 1986, Penrose, 1989), *'Relational Interpretation'* (Carlo Rovelli, 1994), *'Cybernetic Interpretation'* (Ross Rhodes, 1999), *'Information Interpretation'* (Brukner-Zeilinger, 1999), *'QBism'* (Christopher Fuchs, Rüdiger Schack, 2010).

Let's juxtapose the most favored interpretive models. Despite some radical differences, they have a common feature in that the wave function, represented by the Greek letter psi (Ψ), is regarded not as something physically real, but as a mathematical tool that encodes all that can be known about a quantum system. In his seminal 1957 *'Many Worlds'* paper, Hugh Everett described the pluralistic nature of objective physical reality and denied the actuality of wave function collapse. However, the information content (and ontology) of this kind of reality may turn out to be zero. This is a view expressed by the British philosopher David Pearce that he refers to as *'Zero Ontology'*.

Consider the classical Library of Babel. If you may recall, the Borges' Library of Babel contains all possible books with all possible words and letters in all possible combinations. The Library of Babel has, in fact, zero information content. Yet somewhere amid the nonsense lies Encyclopedia Britannica and the complete works of Shakespeare. Withdrawing a book from the Library of Babel yields a single definite classical outcome and thus creating information. Withdrawing more books creates more information. When we sum two ordinary non-zero probabilities, we always get a larger probability. Analogies aside, we obviously don't belong to the classical Library of Babel.

Now imagine the quantum Library of Babel. Similarly, if we sum two ordinary non-zero probabilities, we always get a bigger probability. Yet because amplitudes in QM are *'complex numbers'*, summing two amplitudes can yield zero. Scaling up to the whole of quantum multiverse and factoring in the totality of all possible worlds would yield exactly zero. As Jan-Markus Schwindt notes in his 2012 paper *"Nothing Happens in the Universe of the Everett Interpretation,"* the Many Worlds Interpretation is therefore rather a *"No World Interpretation"*: no faces to be seen, no music to be heard, no aromatic roses, no black caviar, no pleasurable sex, no thoughts, no sensations.

'Many-Minds' Interpretation and the more recent *'Many Interacting Worlds'* hypothesis by Michael Hall (MIW, 2010) extend the original Everettian MWI by proposing that a plethora of universes have always existed side by side, and that they tenuously influence the ones near them to differentiate from themselves either at the level of individual observers as in Many Minds or by a subtle force of repulsion as in Many Interacting Worlds. Unsurprisingly, numerous objections, such as the Zero Ontology argument, that apply to the original Many-Worlds Interpretation also apply to the Many-Minds Interpretation and Many Interacting Worlds.

Let's revisit the quantum Library of Babel. Conjecturing solely from the Digital Philosophy perspective, at the level of Omega hypercomputer running the Omniverse with humongous but still finite storage and computational resources, "nonsensical" timelines are likely to be purged. Furthermore, human subjectivity can be actualized only when collapsing available possibilities into a single probabilistic outcome experienced as a conscious instant (~10/sec). From the computationalist perspective, the Many Worlds Interpretation is simply incomplete: no collapse – no conscious experience.

The Pilot Wave theory, also known as *'Bohmian Mechanics'*, has its army of proponents seeking objective uniformity tantalizingly streamlined into a singular deterministic universal worldline with "cosmic time" ticking out there in the Universe at large and accompanied by the universal pool of subatomic "billiard balls." This clearly outdated picture of the world is "not even wrong" – you can't possibly import Newtonian classicality into the quantum realm – that would collapse the entire mathematical structure of the M-theoretic Universe-Multiverse-Omniverse as we know it.

If given a choice between M-theory and the Pilot Wave theory, most respectable scientists would probably choose the former. It would also be like trying to compute the Universe on a classical digital computer which is not only a step backwards in our understanding of the world but a logical impossibility.

Many Worlds and Pilot Wave interpretations are completely deterministic which cannot be right in the world based on probabilities at all observer levels. As we've discussed elsewhere, *'syntactic freedom'* of expression is what defines us as freewilling conscious entities amidst our inherently probabilistic reality. This is perhaps the main reason why the Copenhagen interpretative camp has been on the right track since the discovery of quantum mechanics in the roaring 20's of the last century. Bear with me, I have good news and bad news for the Many Worlds interpretative camp.

The good news is that indeed one can assume the God's eye perspective on our reality where all conceivable and inconceivable timelines and events happen. In this view, perhaps, our entire Universe can be "perceived" as an elementary particle of sorts in a universe up. The bad news for MWI supporters is that this God's eye view has nothing to do with your conscious experience. Just like absent-minded people may get stuck in revolving doors, MWI-ers get stuck "forever" in the tourniquet never to exit.

As for the Bohmian Mechanics camp, I'm afraid I only have bad news. Not only the Universe is presumed to be reduced to a mechanical system but free will and consciousness are consequently reduced to a by-product of mechanistic interactions. If our world can't be possibly computed on a classical digital computer, how can this be done when the Bohmians reduce it to an "abacus"?

We all are internal dynamic energy of the Universe – and it's not even a metaphor – there would be no dynamics whatsoever in the absence of us subjective participants. This "participatory realism" I call *'Experiential Realism'* is best captured by interpretations nested in the Copenhagen Interpretation camp while Many Worlds, Objective Collapse and Pilot Wave attempt to "objectify" it. Years ago, Many Worlds interpretation was making more sense to me up until I gradually drifted to the Copenhagen camp.

At the moment, I find more appealing the Cybernetic Interpretation by Ross Rhodes, introduced in 1999 (coincidentally same year the movie *The Matrix* came out), followed by QBism, agent-centric interpretation proposed by Christopher Fuchs in 2010, and backed up by the Relational Interpretation by Carlo Rovelli, 1994.

A rigorous model known as Relational Quantum Mechanics (RQM), developed by the prominent Italian theoretical physicist Carlo Rovelli, posits that there are no absolute, that is, observer-independent, physical properties. Instead, all physical quantities — the entire physical world — are relative to the observer, in a way analogous to motion. This is motivated by the fact that, according to quantum theory, different observers can account differently for the same sequence of events. Consequently, each observer is inferred to "inhabit" its own physical (read: virtual) world, as defined by the context of its own observations. Moreover, since both thoughts and perceptions are mental in essence, this line of reasoning points to mind as the primary substrate of Nature, the discernible states of which constitute information.

The latest interpretative model, Quantum Bayesianism, or QBism, is the combination of quantum mechanics and subjective Bayesianism which views probability as a way to quantify agent-specific degrees of knowledge and future anticipation. This fusion is inspirited both by philosophical arguments for Bayesianism and its potential for dissolving some of the notorious quantum mechanical paradoxes. Introduced by physicists Christopher Fuchs and Rüdiger Schack in 2010, QBism has a lot in common with the widely adopted Copenhagen Interpretation of quantum mechanics but in QBism all probabilities are expressed as an agent's personal degrees of belief. This is one of the points where QBism makes a crucial departure from the Copenhagen Interpretation. Since the wave function encodes probabilities, the conclusion is that the wave function itself must be agent-specific, i.e., subjective!

Information-based interpretations of quantum mechanics, Digital Physics, the Holographic Principle, and the Simulation Hypothesis have endured and indeed grown immensely in popularity over the past few decades, making them major contenders in the scientific arena. Why simulation and computation make for such handily functional equivalence is that they offer a sought-after framework for solving the paradoxes of quantum mechanics. Our "transactional" world acts something like a probabilistic processing, procedurally generated computer simulation, or a virtual reality. This cybernetic model, or the *'Noocentric Model'*, would account for the time-tested problems of non-locality, superposition, particle-wave duality, quantum tunneling, retrocausality, and all other weirdness in quantum studies that Einstein pronounced were far too "spooky" for him to swallow. Nonetheless, quantum mechanics remains the most mathematically precise framework of how natural phenomena behave.

Reality is information, and so are we. A simulation is part of the reality that simulates it — and everything we further simulate is reality from the perspective of those being simulated. Reality is, therefore, what we experience: From a physical point of view, there could be no "objective" observer fully separated from the physical system she tries to observe. In actuality, there is no objectivity — only a subjective perspective on things, i.e., individuated consciousness. Ultimately, any experiential reality is an observer-centric virtuality.

The weirdness of quantum reality that remains amorphous or indefinite until measured is famously displayed by the thought experiment where Schrödinger's cat is in a terrifying limbo, neither alive nor dead, until someone opens the box to look inside. But not to worry for the cat — subjectively, the cat (or a physicist taking its place) is always alive thanks to another thought experiment known as the *'Quantum Suicide'*. At the end of this chapter we'll revisit this gedanken experiment in more scrupulous detail.

Back in 1961, the Nobel Prize–winning physicist Eugene Wigner devised a thought experiment that exposes one of the most notorious paradoxes of quantum mechanics. The *"Wigner's Friend"* experiment demonstrates how the same quantum mechanical principles applying to the quantum domain and to the Universe at large allow two observers (Wigner and Wigner's friend) to experience alternate realities that are forced to coexist. In their paper, *Experimental Rejection of Observer-Independence in the Quantum World*, Massimiliano Proietti at Heriot-Watt University in Edinburgh, UK, with collaborators attest that they have performed the first real-life experiment that proves the Wigner's gedanken experiment: They have created different, conflicting realities and compared them. And their conclusion is that Wigner was correct – these realities can be made irreconcilable so that it is impossible to agree on the objective status of the facts about an experiment.

Wigner's original thought experiment goes like this: It begins with a single polarized photon that, when measured, can have either a horizontal polarization or a vertical polarization. But before the measurement, according to quantum mechanics, the photon exists in both polarization states at the same time – a so-called superposition. Wigner imagined a friend in a different lab measuring the state of this photon and recording the result while Wigner is unaware of that. For Wigner, the photon's superposition remains factual, while Wigner's friend measures which polarized state the photon is in, which forces it out of superposition and into a definitive state, and records the result without ever conveying this information to Wigner. They then compare notes and find that something very strange has then happened. At the exact same time, Wigner and his friend recorded two different versions of reality and they are both correct.

Experimental evidence confirming The Wigner's Friend thought experiment, and with it confirming QM interpretations stemming from the Copenhagen interpretive camp, such as RQM and Qbism, has significant implications for how researchers may do science going forward. *"The scientific method relies on facts, established through repeated measurements and agreed upon universally, independently of who observed them,"* say Proietti. And yet in the same paper, authors undermine the infallibility of scientific method. With the scientific method and other alternative methodologies (like *'quantum neo-empiricism'*) we're discovering the "rules of the game," and knowing those rules well may be indispensable for further progression in the game.

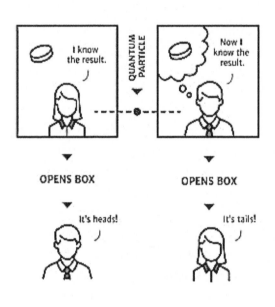

Figure 4.1: Renner-Frauchiger Paradox

Recently published, an "updated version" of the Schrödinger's cat experiment sent ripples in the scientific milieu. In this Renner-Frauchiger experiment (2018) (see Figure 4.1), sort of like the "double Schrödinger's cat," instead of one cat we box two quantum observers — two human physicists. You can challenge me on how to interpret this thought experiment but my conclusion is that it has clearly demonstrated that a subjective wave function collapse is what equates to any act of observation, it is neither "no collapse" as MWI-ers would claim, nor objective collapse. The subjective collapse QM interpretations such as Cybernetic Interpretation and QBism seem to get additional experimental and theoretical support of late.

Quite unlike any other branch of science, quantum physics unsurprisingly has acquired its own metaphysics, a shadow discipline, in Heisenberg's term an "ideological superstructure." Designed as meta-analysis of QM interpretations, this field is called *'Quantum Foundations'*, which is unintentionally ironic, because where you would expect foundations you instead find quicksand.

Max Planck, when referring to consciousness as being the fundamental feature of reality, wrote: *"Everything we call real is made of things that cannot be regarded as real."* Echoing his words, Werner Heisenberg divulged that: *"[T]he atoms or the elementary particles themselves are not as real; they form a world of potentialities or possibilities rather than one of things or facts."* Heisenberg interpreted the mathematics behind quantum theory to mean that reality doesn't exist until observed. *"The idea of an objective real world whose smallest parts exist objectively in the same sense as stones or trees exist, independently of whether or not we observe them... is impossible."* This seemed utterly disturbing to philosophers as well as physicists and it led Albert Einstein to say in 1952: *"The theory reminds me a little of the system of delusions of an exceedingly intelligent paranoiac."*

A bold, unorthodox paper by Ross Rhodes, first published in 1999 with a revised version in 2001, *"A Cybernetic Interpretation of Quantum Mechanics"* pre-dates Bostrom's *"Are You Living in a Computer Simulation?"* (2003) and Whitworth's *"The Physical World as a Virtual Reality"* (2008). Rhodes presents to us a well-grounded argument that the "fuzzy" physics of the quantum world can be interpreted as evidence that we are integral, dynamic part of some sort of computer-simulated reality.

Rhodes argues that quantum physics resembles the deep "code layer" underlying our physical reality. For instance, quantum non-locality makes a lot of sense if you assume that all information processing for the universal hypercomputer is being done by its central GPU. In Chapter 18, we get to recount 10 broad categories of the physical world's properties, its natural phenomena and processes, and corresponding 40 M-observables to confirm the viability of the Cybernetic Interpretation of quantum mechanics.

THE SCHRÖDINGER EQUATION: THE ONTOLOGY OF WAVE FUNCTION

Quantum physics throws all the rules of classical physics out the window. In the quantum world, particles can pass through solid walls, be in two places at once, instantly communicate over infinitely large distances, and affect their past counterparts just as easily as they affect the future ones. The rules we have discovered for the behavior of quantum systems – the Schrödinger equation and so on – don't obviously resemble the classical rules we use to describe everyday objects, notably Newton's Laws of motion among other things in high-school physics curriculum. We spend the vast majority of our lives interacting with things that obey classical physics, i.e., Newton's Laws, and that defines our intuition for how things "ought" to behave. When quantum physics departs from that, all of it seems incredibly weird.

The Schrödinger equation, considered a cornerstone of quantum theory, in its most general time-dependent form describes the evolution of a quantum system and predicts that if certain properties of a quantum system are measured, the "classical" outcome will be quantized, meaning that only specific discrete values would appear. The equation was named after Erwin Schrödinger, who derived the equation in 1925, and was awarded the Nobel Prize in Physics in 1933. All above mentioned QM interpretations are aimed at deciphering this mathematical equation as to what it actually means when describing reality presented to us by our measurements.

In his recent 2018 article *"The Puzzle of Quantum Reality"* astrophysicist Adam Becker writes: *"When we physicists do quantum physics, we tend to think of it only as the physics of the ultra-tiny. We usually assume that the Schrödinger equation doesn't really apply to sufficiently large objects — objects like tables and chairs and humans, the things in our everyday lives. Instead, as a practical matter, we assume that those objects obey the classical physics of Isaac Newton, and that the Schrödinger equation stops applying when one of these objects interacts with something from the quantum world of the small. This works well enough to get the right answer in most cases. But almost no physicists truly believe this is how the world actually works."* Variations of the *'Double-Slit'* experiment have continued to mess with our preconceptions, showing micro-objects like electrons or photons behaving like "wavicles," depending on the measurement method. And it's no longer a realm of the infinitesimally small. In 2012, a new record was set in showing a molecule a whopping 800 atoms in size also has wave-like properties. As Becker notes: *"Experiments over the past few decades have shown that quantum physics applies to larger and larger objects, and at this point few doubt that it applies to objects of all sizes. Indeed, quantum physics is routinely and successfully used to describe the largest thing there is — the Universe itself — in the well-established field of physical cosmology."*

Quantum mechanics and Einstein's relativistic physics had turned our picture of a classical, deterministic "clockwork universe" upside down. It was replaced with indeterminate states, wave functions instead of particles, and a fabric of spacetime that could be bent, distorted, and could even have whirlpools in it. Yet there are open questions requiring sensible answers. Quantum mechanics is all about "here and now" and relativistic physics is about relativity between here & now's which does demonstrate that quantum mechanics is, in actuality, more fundamental than relativity.

The biggest principle of Einstein's general theory of relativity is that space itself isn't a flat, unchanging, absolute entity. Rather it's woven together, along with time, into a single fabric: spacetime. This fabric is continuous, smooth, and gets curved and deformed by the presence of mass and energy. Everything present within this spacetime fabric moves along the path defined by that curvature, and its propagation is limited by the speed of light. It is natural to assume that spacetime is fundamental reality but what if, after more than a century, this worldview needs an update?

In Chapter 13, I argue that experiential time is emergent. If time is emergent, so must be spacetime. What does that even mean? This means that spacetime is not smooth and continuous as Einstein hypothesized *ad hoc* but it turns out that spacetime is discretized and emerges from the substructure of reality: information, more specifically observer experiential data streams. If it sounds insane, we should remind ourselves that most contemporary ideas were once considered "crazy" until they were widely accepted and changed our picture of the world for good. The Holographic Principle, for instance, which isn't science-fiction, but a *bona fide* idea in theoretical physics, along with other recent discoveries in physics, tell us that view of fundamental spacetime is doomed – along with the objects it contains and their appearance of physical causality – and must be replaced by something more fundamental, if we are to succeed in our quest for a quantum gravity theory.

In this regard, British philosopher and author Anthony Peake writes: *"The belief that there is a reality behind the fabrication of the perceived universe is central to Gnostic belief... As we know, the 21ˢᵗ century seems to have become a battleground between "irrational" theologies and "rational" science. However recent developments in the world of quantum physics suggest to me that Gnostic theology may be proven right... It is ironic that recent discoveries regarding the nature of space itself may suggest that we are in need of another paradigm change. In a curious echo from the past it seems that a substance similar to the ether may indeed fill up all of space. This is the Zero Point Field, a field that fills all of space and is, in many ways, the backdrop to what we call 'reality'."* Some spiritually-inclined physicists oftentimes refer to the Zero Point Field as the *'Unified Field'*. Perhaps, another apt neologism *'Quantum Akasha'* could bridge perennial philosophy and modern quantum theory.

THE MEASUREMENT PROBLEM: THE OBSERVER EFFECT *vs.* QUANTUM EFFECTS

The famed *'Observer Effect'* which has been demonstrated in the Double-Slit Experiment and its numerous variations, challenged one of science's most basic tenets: that there is an objective, observable reality that exists whether we're looking at it or not. The revelation that the act of observation, or measuring quantum effects, directly affects particles' behavior is perplexing, to say the least, but it also suggests that a conscious observer itself is part of quantum theory.

Notoriously counterintuitive quantum effects include wave-particle duality, quantum entanglement, quantum tunneling, retrocausality, and overall non-linearity of quantum systems, just to name a few usual suspects. Classical and quantum physics are well-defined in their respective realms, but grander questions have troubled physicists for decades: What links these two opposing views of reality? Why do the fundamental laws of classical physics fail at the quantum level, and can they ever be reconciled?

The von Neumann–Wigner interpretation, proposed in 1961, the first of its kind to be described as "consciousness causes collapse [of the wave function]," is an interpretive model of quantum mechanics in which consciousness is postulated to be necessary for the completion of the process of quantum measurement. If the act of observation is directly tied with consciousness and results in the subjective collapse of the wave function, how are the probabilities converted into an actual, sharply defined classical outcome?

There are many reasons why decoherence cannot account for the transition from quantumness to classicality of subjective experience but here's the main argument. Just like Bohmian mechanics attempting to import the classicality of "billiard balls" into inherently probabilistic quantum realm, one can immediately comprehend the absurdity of invoking quantum decoherence as a failing physicalist assumption. In other words, it neither causes the [objective as intended] wave function collapse nor solves the measurement problem. First introduced in 1970 by the German physicist H. Dieter Zeh with Many-Minds interpretation, the concept of decoherence is actually useful for functional quantum computers when researchers try to isolate the quantum processing unit in order to prevent quantum leakage.

Decoherence refers to a loss of *'quantum coherence'* which is a fancy term for an "unentangled" quantum state. Entanglement is understood as an inevitable result of any interaction between two quantum objects. Once entangled, two objects become linked forever – they cannot abruptly "disentangle" – this quantum effect should also be true for the network of particles, in fact, all particles in the Universe since the Big Bang which is a clear contradiction. And yet, decoherence, physicists insist, is an essential mechanism of the quantum-classical transition. To show quantum behavior, such as interference, superposition and entanglement-induced correlations, they say, any object, no matter how big it is, depends only on how entangled it is with its environment. But, as we have established, the entire Universe is deep down non-local at the quantum level, that is entangled. What are we missing here? Again, the answer is: the conscious observer. A conscious mind, a "chooser," is still required to actualize the collapse of the wave of probabilities to crystallize it into an observer-centric classical actuality.

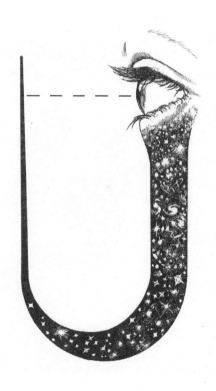

Now, if we instead combine the top-down quantum information processing (computationalist) approach with the *'Conscious Instant'* *(CI)* hypothesis, then we can see that each conscious instant is an integrated digital pattern of information ‒ like a frame in the movie ‒ whereas the mind of an experimenter (conscious observer) collapses quantum mechanical potentiality into classical actuality. This is quantum information processing ‒ from qubits of the qualia spectrum to "digits of qualia." This led me to formulate the *D-Theory of Time*, or *'Digital Presentism'* (Chapter 13), for to understand our subjective experience we need

Figure 4.2: Wheeler Eye (Source: Verge Bliss, Pinterest)

to understand time.

One of the more poetic elucidations of the centrality of conscious observers comes from John Wheeler, who liked to illustrate the history of the Universe as a *'big U'*, with the Big Bang at one end and you at the other (see Figure 4.2). This picture has the Universe being created and evolving in an indeterminate quantum kind of way until it achieves enough complexity to create an observer who can look back at that evolution and create a single coherent history. Wheeler's picture has the Universe observing itself into existence, an idea that many have found profound. In the words of philosopher Kirno Sohochari: *"The everlasting Wheeler Eye stands with its double meaning. This astonishing Universe comes from bit; it can observe itself; as well, our perception of it is observer rhetoric."* If you were to ask what happened before the first observer and the first moments after the Big Bang, the answer might surprise you with its straightforwardness: We extrapolate backwards in time and that virtual model becomes "real" in our minds *as if* we were witnessing the birth of the Universe.

Your Universe is perfect — eerily, uncannily perfect — everything is "fine-tuned," mathematized and entangled. Measured subatomic particles are not the only things that are entangled, though. So are we. We are entangled with one another and sublimely with the whole of our own creation — something we are only now starting to uncover with physics. We are entangled with other minds we don't yet know, from places we have never been, at times we have not existed, in the deep past and in the unknown future.

The entire human race can be envisaged as one large, interconnected entity, stretching across time and space. If you could assume the God's eye view of mankind outside of space-time, you would not only see a hundred billion or so disconnected individuals but a humanity that is more like a massive body, or perhaps a neural network, with a hundred billion cells commensurate with the total number of neurons in the human brain.

The metaphysical principle of "unity" – that everything in the Universe is intimately interconnected – is difficult to believe in our everyday physical world where living beings and non-living objects appear separate and distinct from one another. However, since the 1930s, research in the field of quantum entanglement has suggested that at the subatomic and even deeper sub-quantum levels, everything might indeed be connected. This seemingly metaphysical weirdness of universal "oneness" has found its physics counterpart referred to as *'non-locality'*. At a fundamental level of reality, there may be no such thing as place, no such thing as distance, and no such thing as time but only information.

As the quantum theory shows, our entire Universe is deep down non-local. It's one and the same with non-local consciousness. How so? Research has shown that consciousness is non-local, a scientific way of alluding to a connection within a higher dimensional order. Matter has also been shown to be non-local, which hints that matter might be an expression of consciousness.

The non-locality of our physical world has been proved by John S. Bell in 1964 (by the famously known Bell's theorem) and confirmed by experimental results obtained since the early 1980s. This theoretical and experimental evidence dispelled the Einstein–Podolsky–Rosen (EPR) paradox, and with it, *'local realism'*. The assumptions of materialism have been challenged ever since the discovery of quantum physics by showing that consciousness could not be ignored since observation directly affects matter.

In physicalism, consciousness is assumed to be bounded by four dimensions of the *'Block Universe'*, but contrary to this notion, consciousness is clearly extradimensional. Our inability to measure something does not negate its existence. Quantum physics tells us the energy of every speck of mass, or a packet of information, is a relative peak in an ocean of energy, which is oftentimes referred to as the *'Unified Field'* — the quantum layer of pure potentiality — the code layer beneath all dimensions where time and space are information.

Consider the analogy: Dynamic patterns within the three-dimensional atmosphere such as gusty winds and ocean undercurrents create two-dimensional patterns on the ocean surface. Analogously, patterns in the higher-order volume of non-local consciousness shape the energy vibrations we experience as matter. That would mean matter is the expression of consciousness in one of the possible worlds, not the other way around. Matter does not envelop all dimensionality of consciousness. Matter represents waves of possibility within consciousness, which is the ground of all being. Consciousness chooses one facet out of the multifaceted quantum possibility wave and converts possibility into the actuality of that chosen facet. There's no dualism because consciousness does the choosing nonlocally without signal. It is choosing from itself.

The second useful analogy: If we view our minds as software, and our material world as hardware as registered by our senses from within a simulation, then this material world hardware can, in turn, be hypothesized as software of the cosmic mind. So, all reality is in personal mind and in transpersonal mind. The two are *ONE* like a magnet with two poles complementing each other and constituting what I call the *'bi'*-mind. All reality thus appears to be mental, the worldview known as philosophical idealism.

THE MENTAL UNIVERSE HYPOTHESIS: OBJECTIVE vs. SUBJECTIVE WAVE FUNCTION COLLAPSE

Is the Universe mental or physical? Let's actually rephrase the question for ease of argumentation: Is reality informational or mechanistical? Science often makes strides by contradicting what we take for granted, and the biggest thing everyone takes as a given is our physical world. Traditionally, scientific endeavor assumed that matter is all that exists, however, it's not a scientific fact, it's just a basic assumption, it should not be regarded as more than a philosophical starting point. Our senses wrap themselves around tangible objects so naturally that it's hard to believe that our sensory apparatus may be misleading us completely. So, it becomes more than just intriguing, when any prominent theorist brings up the showcase for a different view of reality, one in which the mind creates the features of what we call "the physical world."

As it turns out, certain statistical properties of the experimental measurements, confirmed again and again, indicate that the material particles do not exist independently of observation. And since observation ultimately consists of what is grasped on the mental screen of perception, the implication may be that *"the Universe is entirely mental,"* as put forward by Richard Conn Henry in his 2005 *Nature* essay. As mentioned earlier, physicists Carlo Rovelli, Ross Rhodes and Christopher Fuchs also approached this issue rigorously in their interpretive models of quantum mechanics.

The *'Mental Universe'* hypothesis has a strong heritage moving into the quantum era, but present-day physicalists feel obliged to simply ignore luminaries such as Max Planck, Erwin Schrödinger, Werner Heisenberg, Eugene Wigner and John von Neumann. Physicalism still holds sway with most cosmologists, but Andrei Linde of Stanford

139

University made some critical points in an article on the most current theories of the inflationary universe by stating that: *"...carefully avoiding the concept of consciousness in quantum cosmology may artificially narrow one's outlook."*

Materialism that lately happened to change its name to physicalism has been a fashionable philosophy, at least, before the discovery of quantum mechanics. *"I refute it thus,"* said the 18th-century writer Samuel Johnson kicking a large rock as a sign of refutation to arguments against materialism, as the story goes. Little did he know that his physical reality ought to be bound by a ruleset of but one of the possible worlds. Johnson's stone-kick is symbolic of a hard-headed (and broken-footed) physicalist view of the world. Physicalism limps on crutches and its last leg philosophically, whereas all the quantum evidence undermines the assumption that the objective physical world exists independently of our observations.

Whether it's a mere glance at one's self-reflection in the mirror or smashing b-mesons at the Large Hadron Collider, no observation of reality is complete until a human observer examines the results. Ever since the discovery of quantum physics, physicists have been finding it extremely difficult to write the observer out: Consciousness is ever-present. On these simple grounds alone, the worldview of mental reality becomes more convincing every day. This is a sensible explanation (or meta-interpretation if you'd like) of quantum mechanics, the most mathematically precise scientific theory of all times.

In his recent paper *"Making Sense of the Mental Universe"* (2017) Bernardo Kastrup, a computer engineer, idealist philosopher and author of several books, including *"Why Materialism Is Baloney,"* attempts to provide a viable explanatory framework for our experience as distinct individual minds within a seemingly shared but contextual world, however beyond the control of our immediate volition.

Shortly afterwards, in *"Should Quantum Anomalies Make Us Rethink Reality?"*, an article published by *Scientific American* in 2018, Kastrup contends that quantum mechanics, as well as cognitive science, suggests that our minds actively construct experiential reality rather than passively mirror "external" reality. He calls for a radical overhaul of the current scientific orthodoxy by writing in his paper: *"[B]ecause we perceive and experiment on things and events partly defined by an implicit paradigm, these things and events tend to confirm, by construction, the paradigm. No wonder then that we are so confident today that Nature consists of arrangements of matter/energy outside and independent of mind... When enough "anomalies" – empirically undeniable observations that cannot be accommodated by the reigning belief system – accumulate over time and reach critical mass, paradigms change. We may be close to one such a defining moment today, as an increasing body of evidence from quantum mechanics (QM) renders the current paradigm untenable."*

In line of our deliberations, let's also ask: What would it mean to accept this new *'Mind Over Matter'* paradigm? In the final chapter of the book – *The Omega Point Cosmo-Teleology: Our "Forgotten" Future* – I make my case for *'Mind Over Substrates'* quite relevant to our discussion here and I hope by the time you will have come to read the last chapter you'd be more inclined to accept the inevitability of the coming paradigmatic shift. Moving ever closer to the Web v.5.0 – an immersive virtual playground of the Metaverse – would signify a paramount convergent moment that MIT's Rizwan Virk calls *'The Simulation Point'* and I refer to it as the *'Simulation Singularity'*. Those future virtual worlds could be wholly devised and "fine-tuned" with a possibility to encode different sets of "physical laws and constants" for our enjoyment and exploration. Physical and artificially created realities will then blend together beyond recognition. One primary aspect in particular will stay the same across virtual universes, though – our mind.

From a purely scientific frame of reference, many quantum phenomena like non-local correlations between distant entities and wave-particle duality, the wave function collapse and consistent histories, quantum entanglement and teleportation, the uncertainty principle and overall observer-dependence of reality pin down our conscious mind being intrinsic to reality. And this is the one thing the current paradigm fails to account for. Critical-mass anomalies will ultimately lead to the full paradigm shift in physics.

With consciousness as primary, everything remains the same and everything changes. Mathematics, physics, chemistry, biology are unchanged. What changes is our interpretation as to what they are describing. They are not describing the unfolding of an objective physical world, but transdimensional evolution of one's conscious mind. There's nothing "physical" about our physical reality except that we perceive it that way. By playing the "Game of Life" we evolved to survive not to see quantum mechanical reality. At our classical level of experiential reality we perceive ourselves as physical, at quantum level we are probabilistic wave function, which is pure information.

No matter how you slice it, reality is contextual, the notion that immediately dismisses 'observer-independent' interpretations of quantum mechanics and endorses the Mental Universe hypothesis. Perhaps, this can be regarded as one of the foundational axioms for the Noocentric model we discussed in Chapter 2. But we have to be careful here not to throw the baby out with the bathwater, so to speak.

I'd like to make a very important point at this juncture of our discussion: Mental and physical are two sides of the same coin made of information. Both should be viewed as the same substance.

Arguably, everything comes down to vibrational frequencies: Mind at a very low rate of vibration is what we call matter. Matter at a high rate of vibration is what is known as mind. In our physical reality, matter is thus only a certain *"in'*-formed" pattern of mind. Solidity, wetness, softness, redness or any other property of mass-energy are experienced by us as *'qualia'* that result from certain quantum-to-digital meta-algorithmic computations according to our world-specific "ruleset." We'll discuss specifics of this classical reality rendering further in the chapter. As of time of writing, consciousness researchers such as Tam Hunt attempt to formalize a new mathematical model of consciousness based on the notion of vibration. I might add here, though, that vibration *is* information.

Modern physics seemingly ran into a self-imposed empiricism wall while physicists still cope to admit that our world is an observer-centric virtual reality that is being constantly created by us conscious observers – from distant galaxies to the "zoo" of subatomic particles, from personal life events to the history of the world. Our reality is a mental construct where imagination and observation should be construed as acts of creation, not the other way around. All reality is in the mind.

As we've seen, a number of latest QM interpretations such as RQM, Cyberneticism and Qbism support the Mental Universe hypothesis. There's nothing supernatural or mystical about this claim: Universal mind – whose ontology is still up for debates but can be extrapolated from our existential circumstance – underlies the "worldware," a kind of software of the universal operating system accounting for our experiences of the physical world in accordance with a set of rules we call the laws of Nature. This clearly transdimensional consciousness encompasses but far transcends any individual mind. Quantum computational dynamics of all mass-energy in the Universe correspond to mentation of the non-local *'Transcendent Other',* just as an individual's brain activity correlates with personal mentation.

Since we all are alternate realities, each of us being a parallel "unique-verse," "observer-centric virtuality" is possibly one of the best metaphors related to the ontology of our experiential reality. This notion eliminates unnecessary discrepancies and provides the missing inner essence of the perceptible world: Different configurations of matter and energy reflect different patterns or modes of thinking by the larger consciousness system rendering VR to the player. In other words, mind instantiates oneself into matter and energy.

Just like an intestinal bacterium, a little fellow living inside your body, "transacts" with its surrounding conscious environment, each of us is on our own quest in some sort of "gaming mode" to attain promotion to higher levels of simulation – ever-higher levels of awareness. This immersive VR game is realized through polarity with the Transcendent Other. Your self implies the other, that is your cosmic self, "many-I" ultra-intelligent surroundings, i.e., the larger consciousness system constantly computing your "moves."

As your consciousness evolves, your Universe becomes more complex, for you are this *'you'*-niverse. This universe is nothing other than an experiencing subject, a kind of ontology Riccardo Manzotti talks about in his 2018 book *"Spread Mind: Why Consciousness and the World Are One."* As we'll see further in the book, the "transactional" relationship between the Theta point (the observer temporal singularity) and Omega Singularity (the Source) giving rise to your subjectivity are derived from the philosophy of idealism which is phenomenologically more honest than panpsychism, cosmopsychism, let alone physicalism.

Think about it: All we have ever known and will know is the contents of our own minds. All our scientific models come from mental activities. The sacramental relationship based on the cosmic binary code is what really matters: I alone can never be. Clinging not to one specific name for the Transcendent Self, as you might have noticed, I rather use different terms for *IT* depending on the context, and for ease of narrative, while trying to convey extremely complex concepts structuring the book more like a philosophical treatise.

If your conscious *'bi'*-mind plays the only causal role in bringing your experiential reality into existence and consciousness is all that is, then solipsism might be implied. That said, solipsism is not such a dreadful notion as it might first seem and can be easily reconciled by its pantheistic version, that is the view that "everyone is God," each of us is a "personal story of Godhead," each of us is the "Alpha, Theta & Omega," a "gamemaster," an observer traveling along in the subjective reality tunnel from the beginning of time 'till the end of time. Experiencing one lifetime at a time in all of eternity, alternating from one consciousness structure to the next. As Muriel Rukeyser once said: *"The Universe is made of stories, not of atoms."* In Chapter 21 we'll be discussing pantheistic solipsism in depth.

There's a number of most intriguing implications of the Mental Universe hypothesis at the interplay of quantum physics and mentality. For one, each of us believe in consistency of our past histories but according to quantum mechanical principles we all might have vastly different histories and remembrance of past events. However, the fact is when we start to "compare our notes," our *'consistent histories'* mysteriously confirm each other with just a few rare exceptions related to the *'Mandela Effect'*. The term was coined by the self-described "paranormal consultant" Fiona Broome after she discovered that other people shared her presumably false memory of the South African civil rights leader Nelson Mandela dying in prison in the 1980s.

Have you ever taken seriously the idea that your Universe is a sophisticated virtual reality simulation, but not run by an evil AI but the most benevolent kind? You still need to learn to trust your Universe, my dear friend! After all, your higher self "sits on the mountaintop" and conceives the most optimal timeline for your individual mind's evolution despite apparent pains, struggles and setbacks. Meanwhile, try not to change the mirror, instead change your facial expression reflected in it.

Did it ever occur to you that other versions of you in a similar corporeal form could co-exist in quantum [mechanical] parallel continuums scientists dubbed the *'Quantum Multiverse'*? If other alternate realities exist, and quantum mechanics is supportive of that, then your other selves are just as real as the one you perceive yourself right now when reading this paragraph. If this sounds like some new age spiritual mumbo jumbo, imagine that given the opportunity to travel back in time, say 100 years into the past, should you try to impress some of the sharpest minds of the epoch with your knowledge of quantum physics, you might be taken for a lunatic on the spot.

At this day and age, we can at last reason for physical, mental, and platonic being all one informational substance integrated into mathematical objects overlapping, interplaying and emerging from each other. Objectivity, thus, should be apprehended as

146

intersubjectivity and supersubjectivity instead of "stand-alone" objective reality. What is perceived by us as physical could well be regarded as non-physical by a conscious agent from an alternate timeline or an AI running a whole-world simulation. What I'm trying to say here is that everything is relative, everything depends on the perspective. You perceive yourself living in a physical world but you would perceive the version of you traveling to the Antarctica today in the realm of imagination, i.e., non-physical or perhaps even spiritual. However, in the quantum multiverse there may be a version of you that actually travels to the South Pole and that person feels physical in their world.

There's indeed a quiet paradigmatic shift among consciousness researchers and experts in related fields happening right now towards the notion that the physical universe that we are part of is only our perception and once our physical bodies die, there's an infinite beyond. Some believe that our individuated unit of consciousness migrates to parallel universes after death. The beyond is an infinite reality that is much bigger than that in which this world is rooted in. In this way, your life in this plane of existence is enclosed and surrounded by the afterworld already. The physical body dies but your core self, your pattern-identity, persists beyond this reality frame. Hence, you are immortal.

UNIVERSALITY OF QUANTUM LOGIC

"Without mathematics, there's nothing you can do. Everything around you is mathematics. Everything around you is numbers." -Shakuntala Devi

In the physics of information, known as Digital Physics, all natural phenomena and physical processes are thoroughly computable, with the laws of Nature acting as master algorithms factoring in undeniable universality of quantum logic. In an often-quoted remark computer scientist Tommaso Toffoli puts this quite eloquently: *"In a sense, Nature has been continually computing the "next state" of the Universe for billions of years; all we have to do — and, actually, all we can do — is "hitch a ride" on this huge ongoing [quantum] computation."* This universal computability of Nature is what allows us to use computers to model or "simulate" physical processes, thus greatly enhancing our abilities to understand and emulate Nature.

Digital philosopher, former NASA physicist Tom Campbell who is the author of trilogy *"My Big TOE,"* has been for years a great source of inspiration for me and other "digitalists." Campbell presents our physical reality as a virtual reality information processing system that is but a subset of a much larger consciousness "reality superset" that seeks to decrease its entropy through the free will choices and lifetime experiences of its "avatars" in this multiplayer virtual reality. Choices that exhibit love decrease entropy while ones that are derived from fear increase entropy. Explicitly separate units of consciousness, we are implicitly one with the overarching non-local consciousness. In their 2018 paper, *On Testing the Simulation Theory*, Campbell and others proposed a series of experiments yet to be implemented, and if there is no other hypothesis which can explain the experimental results, then the logical conclusion is that our reality is, in fact, a simulation. The paper was published in the *International Journal of Quantum Foundations*.

Digitalists such as Edward Fredkin, Hans Moravec, Stephen Wolfram, Ben Goertzel and Ray Kurzweil all argue that mentality is entirely computable. Minds are software processes running on hardware substrates — minds are computations and can be exactly replicated in sufficiently advanced computer systems. Digitalists are far from being mysterians — each of them is very specific in describing how at last mentality can be demystified through universality of computation. Quantum logic is omnipresent. So, what of it do physics, mentality, math, biology, and procedural processing games have in common?

The quirky world of quantum physics not only represents a more fundamental description of Nature than its predecessors, it also provides a rich contextual backdrop for modern mathematics. Could the logical underpinnings of quantum theory, once fully ingurgitated, inspire a new realm of mathematics that might be called "quantum mathematics"? For instance, scientists have recently discovered a classic formula for *pi* in the world of quantum mechanics. Pi is the ratio between a circle's circumference and its diameter, and is elemental in pure mathematics, but now scientists have also found it lurking in the physics of the world, encoded in the electron levels of a hydrogen atom.

In biology, all living systems evolve through time under the action of well-defined quantum-theoretic operations, so all biological organisms, to the extent that we need quantum theory to understand their behavior, are, in fact, quantum computing systems, more specifically quantum neural networks. Nature is a master at constructing quantum computational biological systems and today's burgeoning field of quantum biology helps us understand bird migration, photosynthesis, and even our sense of smell.

Plants harvest sunlight with near-perfect efficiency thanks to quantum effects. You may not realize it, but this is impossible under classical physics. Quanta of light, photons, should collide with other particles along the way to the photosynthesizing core, but they don't. A photon succeeding in reaching the core classically is as likely as you sprinting blindfolded through a dense forest and reaching the center without striking a single tree. Amazingly, plants seem to use quantum coherence – receiving waves of energy from many directions at once – to actualize the most efficient route for sunlight to get to their photosynthetic cells. In the animal kingdom, some species might use quantum effects like entanglement to sense the Earth's magnetic field for navigation.

Procedurally generated games of the future will be run on Cloud-based quantum computing platforms allowing the vast multiplicity of in-game choices and scenarios. These quantum games and environments in all of its phantasmagorical adaptations will be lifelike simulations and at some point, will become practically indistinguishable from what we call "real life" – ultra-realistic multi-sensory immersive tech. Moreover, anyone can build their own virtual universe from scratch and given how augmented our mental and technological capabilities will be by then, we can now only speculate on how lavish and extravagant our new virtual habitats and playgrounds will be in just a few short decades time. Augmented, virtual, mixed and extended reality (AR, VR, MR and XR) technologies are developing by leaps and bounds with full adoption seen in only a few years.

Already, there exist VR headset prototypes that let the user see 3D virtual surroundings at the same level of detail as they would appear in real life. This kind of VR headset produces a crisp image by tracking eye movements and taking advantage of the so-called *'foveation'* – a natural quirk of human vision – at any one moment, our eyes see only a small area of focus at their highest resolution. If you put your arm out, it's the size of your thumbnail. As our eyes move to focus elsewhere, so does this high-resolution area. This is why, as you read this sentence, your eyes jump left to right across the text. It's only an illusion that you see the whole page sharply – you don't. This is why you don't see all twelve black dots in this optical illusion (see Figure 4.3).

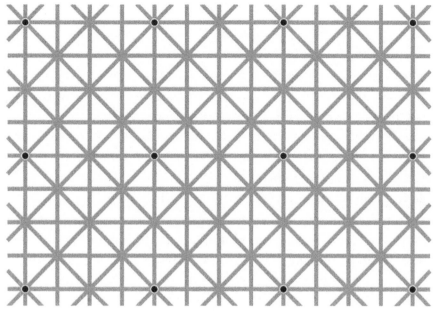

Figure 4.3: Ninio J, Stevens KA. Variations on the Hermann grid: an extinction illusion. Perception (2000) via Will Kerslake

Similarly, when successive frames are presented to our attention at the rate faster than about 10 per second, like in the movie, we perceive that as smooth motion. Our brains are excellent at synthesizing high-resolution images into a coherent moving picture of reality. Obviously, there are plenty of other sensory illusions such as episodic memory flashbacks that our minds use to trick us into believing in everyday "rock-solid" physical reality. The apparent richness of our perception is illusory. Our seemingly detailed view of the world is more of an ever-changing sketch than a rich portrait — our minds fill in the blanks. At only 1 million conscious instants per day, and 10^{16} operations per second for the human brain, corresponding experiential data can be hosted and rendered on a hypothetical $1,000 computer system circa 2040.

If *C.elegans* and its environment can be perfectly described in code and code can be controlled by behavioral controls applied to the computer version of the real thing, a living system is said to be replicated in code and its "description" is indistinguishable from what has been described. There would be no difference between a simulation of something at a certain level of description and the real thing. And if there is no difference between a perfect simulation and reality, and if there is nothing that will prevent us from creating such perfect simulations, at some point in the future however far off, we will be able to create virtual universes with sentient computational agents – self-conscious virtual beings. Once you accept the logic that simulated realities [will] exist, it becomes clear that with the number of simulated worlds, each containing billions or even trillions of conscious minds, the chances that we are "base reality" drops to almost zero.

I hope you would agree with a statement that there is no rainbow unless someone is contemplating it. Similarly, when a tree falls in a forest, not only does it not make a sound if there is nobody around to hear it, it does not even fall, it would not even need to exist. The effect of the fallen tree would never need to be produced until a conscious observer enters the forest, then and only then would the effect of the fallen tree need to be rendered for the observer. Likewise, the unobserved Schrödinger's cat would not exist at all until it is observed, it would be neither alive nor dead, and only when observed by an observer would the effect of the dead or alive cat be rendered. The point of a VR physics engine is to produce total realism to the minute observable detail while reducing the overall computational requirements. From this computationalist perspective ⁻ and this is how simulated worlds are actually produced ⁻ nothing whatsoever would need to exist until it is observed, and when an object is not being observed, it would return to the state of being inactive computer code.

In articulating his famed Simulation Argument Oxford philosopher Nick Bostrom notes: *"[A] technologically mature civilization would have enough computing power such that even if it devoted but a tiny fraction of it to creating Matrices, there would soon be many more simulated people than there were people living in the original history of that civilization. These simulations would not have to be perfect. They would only have to be good enough to fool its inhabitants. It would not be necessary to simulate every object down to the subatomic level... If the book you are holding in your hands is a simulated book, the simulation would only need to include its visual appearance, its weight and texture, and a few other macroscopic properties, because you have no way of knowing what its individual atoms are doing at this moment. If you were to study the book more carefully, for example by examining it under a powerful microscope, additional details of the simulation could be filled in as needed. Objects that nobody is perceiving could have an even more compressed representation."*

On feasibility of creating artificial realities that would feel authentic from within, British physicist Stephen Wolfram also writes: *"Imagine that our Designer now wants to turn his world into a habitat for intelligent beings. What would present the greatest difficulty here? Preventing them from dying right away? No, this condition is taken for granted. His main difficulty lies in ensuring that the creatures for whom the Universe will serve as a habitat do not find out about its "artificiality." One is right to be concerned that the very suspicion that there may be something else beyond "everything" would immediately encourage them to seek exit from this "everything" considering themselves prisoners of the latter, they would storm their surroundings, looking for a way out — out of pure curiosity — if nothing else... We must not therefore cover up or barricade the exit. We must make its existence impossible to guess."*

Just like our Universe appears infinite to us, the degree of complexity of any observed physical system would appear scale-free, or scale-invariant, under any rendering of magnitude. This means that we can "zoom in" or "zoom out" forever and some degree of complexity will be observed — patterns of patterns would reiterate ad infinitum. First of all, this supports computational universality, secondly, we humans don't live in the vacuum, we are part of the larger structural pattern, thirdly, this has implications for the science of consciousness. It is often assumed that consciousness emerges in a system once it reaches a certain threshold of complexity and information integration. But Nature is now known for the holographic and the fractal principles underlying its fundamental properties. If fractal organization reiterates across scales, is it possible that similar information processing by non-local "imminent" consciousness at one observable domain is occurring at smaller and larger scales as well? Would it be another clever partitioning of the worlds?

As David Wallace, a philosopher of physics at the University of Southern California, puts it in his 2012 book, *The Emergent Multiverse*, when we take quantum mechanics at face value, *"the world turns out to be rather larger than we had anticipated: Indeed, it turns out our classical 'world' is only a small part of a much larger reality."* So, it seems that hyperreality is ultimately a fractal system of progressively self-exceeding computations.

In Chapter 16, we'll see that information does not simply describe our physical reality but it is the most fundamental "code layer" of reality. The ultimate reality is thus produced by a hypothetical Omega hypercomputer that is most likely to have qubits at its controls for the realization of any physically possible world. In *The Matrix* movie Morpheus is trying to get across to Neo that everything he thinks is real is actually only information that the brain receives and translates into his unitary experiential reality. *"Your mind makes it real,"* says Morpheus in the "purgatory" scene.

Another great scene I enjoyed watching is when a boy from the Oracle's entourage engages Neo in chalk talk: *"Do not try to bend the spoon, that's impossible! Instead, only try to realize the truth!"* _ *"What truth?"* _ *"There is no spoon!"* _ *"There is no spoon?"* _*" Then you'll see it is not the spoon that bends, it is only yourself!"*

EXPERIENTIAL REALITY: QUBITS-TO-DIGITS QUALIA COMPUTING

A little while ago, the idea that our minds create reality would have seemed preposterous to most westerners. But today everyone in the West becomes a bit more susceptible to this bold new idealistic, computationalist thinking along with certain QM interpretations directly pointing to the fundamental laws of Nature emerging from consciousness. It might be mind-boggling for some people to consider that a coherent description of reality, with all its quantum oddities, can arise from nothing more than first-person subjective experiences. In these new information-based interpretations, consciousness doesn't just collapse the probabilistic wave function. Conscious experience *is* the collapse of wave function. To be precise, at our human level, which is subject to the same quantum mechanical principles, our conscious experience is a collapse of a wave of possibilities.

Reality is what you either explicitly or implicitly "choose" it to be and this claim by the Copenhagen Interpretative camp has been confirmed again by elaborate delayed-choice experiments including a series of newly-devised space experiments involving bouncing photons off satellites. It's a well-established fact in physics that a photon will behave like a particle or a wave depending on the method of measurement. After a photon has made its way almost completely through the experiment – well past the point at which it would appear either a wave or a particle – an observer makes a decision how to measure it. Experimental evidence has been conducive to the notion of retrocausality and subjective wave function collapse: Information is always being created in the present moment aligning seemingly prior events for consistency.

Your qualia are indeterminate until experienced, so filtering of available options from the spectrum of qualia into a digital "frame" of your "holo-movie" results in a single conscious instant. Quantum potentiality in qualia space resolves every moment into your experiential well-defined *'digital reality'* in the fashion equivalent to that of quantum computation. Brain activity is said to be correlated with this quantum computation but does not cause our conscious experience itself. Correlation is not causation. In purely computational terms, quantum-to-classical transition results from quantum mechanical bits or "qubits" being computed into a digital data stream or "digits" of qualia what we otherwise call phenomenal experience.

Let me be perfectly clear. What is the most important philosophical question of all time? What is reality? Namely, what's my experiential reality? How is it produced? Quantum mechanical principles apply not only to the quantum realm of the ultra-tiny but to all of reality. But your reality is not objective as physicalists claim but subjective. In the long run, neither determinism nor physicalism can be saved. Most physicists and philosophers now agree that time which is essential to subjectivity is emergent. Time streams forth from experiential data, it's an epiphenomenon of consciousness (more on that in Chapter 13

– *Digital Presentism: D-Theory of Time*). Instant by instant, you are co-writing your own story, co-producing your own "parallel participatory reality" – your stream of consciousness neither is contingent on some kind of deterministic "script" not it is fully random. You are entitled to degrees of freedom.

Our experience of time can be understood as a fractal dimension, not even a half dimension – we are subjected to our species-specific algorithmic sense of time flow. What's necessary for completion of quantum information processing, though, is a collapse of possibilities – "many worlds" collapsing into an observer's temporal singularity, i.e., the present moment which happens approximately every 1/10 of a second. Between conscious moments lie incredibly vast and "eternally long" potentialities of something happening. But rest assured, you will experience a sequence of those "digital" moments which gives you a sense of subjective reality.

There's no way around this funneling of choices in the spectrum of available qualia – this collapse is required to complete the quantum-to-digital computational transition: *Step A:* Quantum "many-worlds" wave of possibilities, quantum-akashic qualia space, if you wish; *Steps B-Y:* Subjectivistic collapse of data streams, integration of information; *Step Z:* Integrated digital information as a reality frame of your holo-movie, conscious instant. This is why stand-alone Many Worlds interpretation is incomplete to describe your experiential reality.

Quite frankly, *'anything is possible'* is a lame explanation, at least in describing "our" reality, and in this regard, MWI creates more problems than it solves: Why this experiential branch and not the other? From a large tree of lifetime potentials, why this conscious instant and not the other? An entire observer-universe system seems to remain in the state of quantum coherence until "subjectively collapsed" and experienced as a conscious instant by a perceiving subject. In Chapter 13, we'll ascribe a new ontology to the conscious instant — *the Temporal Singularity* — in the framework of D-Theory of Time.

The 21st century has been marked by a new wave of scientists and philosophers questioning conventional modes of thinking and revising the older assumptions away from the materialist towards computationalist approach in physics. This would open the doors, they agree, for a quantum theory of gravity that can merge general relativity and quantum mechanics traditionally contradicting each other. Lately the excitement of this possibility has involved hundreds of physicists who have been meeting every three months or so under the banner of a project dubbed *'It from Qubit'*.

Wavicles by nature, microobjects to macroobjects are subject to the same quantum mechanical probabilistic rules, even though in classical terms it's impossible for us to observe a multitude of probabilistic outcomes. From our human-level classical perspective, we get to observe only one realized outcome at a time which results in our irreducible conscious experience.

If we are to reason for the non-dual picture of the world then quantum physics is directly linked to consciousness. The human brain is a physical organ that transmits and interprets electrochemical signals. Its biochemistry is certainly governed by quantum physical laws, and consciousness – which is clearly related to the functioning of the brain – must therefore be related to the quantum physical processes going on within the brain and in the cosmos at large.

While quantum theory in itself is too complicated for most people to comprehend, the vast majority of scientists and philosophers concur that the quantum mechanical principles epitomized in massive parallelism of quantum computers superior to classical computers may be the key to explain human consciousness. For those who accept the Mental Universe hypothesis, it's a "fait accompli" – reality is in consciousness.

Should a future AGI pick up and read this book, she would immediately recognize the validity of programmable realities based on intersubjectivity instead of conventionally presumed objectivity which in the minds of our superintelligent descendants could look as naïve as to us *'local realism'* of the early 20th century. She would perhaps recognize an inflection point in scientific progression circa 2020. The accepted scientific knowledge that we have right now could be replaced in the coming years and decades. Several of our prevailing theories will be demonstrated to be wrong, and some will perhaps turn out to be "not even wrong." Some of our current widely accepted theories will inevitably be the future victims of intellectual progress.

Here's a short online trialogue that followed right after my article on ecstadelic.net was published which is related to what we have discussed so far in this chapter:

Josh Levin: *"The Universe can't decide which probability should be the route for it to take; it must account for all probabilities."*

Alex Vikoulov: *"Josh, you still need to pinpoint the exact probability. You can't just point to the ocean and say the ship is out there somewhere. In order to actualize the 'ship' we need to collapse all other probabilities, otherwise the ship will be forever smeared on the entire ocean surface."*

Josh Levin: *"It is smeared from a cosmic perspective but collapsed into a point from a conscious perspective."*

Alex Vikoulov: *"Josh, that's right but MWI will keep the ship forever smeared as opposed to collapse interpretations. Do you see the difference?"*

Josh Levin: *"I see the ship as forever smeared I suppose. I see it as a graph from a cosmic perspective."*

Alex Vikoulov: *"From a cosmic perspective granted, but it doesn't explain your conscious experience which at your human level needs funneling of available options into one single realized outcome."*

John Mason: *"Alex, there is no collapse in Deutsch's version. Also, no probabilities."*

Alex Vikoulov: *"John, but in regards to actualization of a single conscious observer moment, a collapse would still be required. Otherwise you would be smeared across universe and multiverse. MWI is not to be confused with the Quantum Multiverse. The discourse is about quantum-to-digital transition of subjective experience. In the quantum multiverse, your subjectivity would still need to collapse to yield a sequence of digital frames of your 'holo'-movie. The Feynman Sum Over Histories and Schrödinger equation are mathematical tools to describe a cloud of potentialities only. MWI gives us a spectrum of possible timelines, so will it make you feel better to know that in some of these timelines you're already dead in the minds of other observers but it has nothing to do with evolution of your experiential branch which requires subjectivistic collapse of possibilities? I stand by my claim: MWI is incomplete in describing your experiential reality!"*

QUANTUM IMMORTALITY: DOES QUANTUM PHYSICS IMPLY YOU ARE IMMORTAL?

"Perhaps Nature is our best assurance of immortality." -Eleanor Roosevelt

When we're watching an action movie, we might think that we're watching main characters through a bunch of explosions to an improbable happy ending, but it's just as accurate to say that we're watching the *'Quantum Immortality Hypothesis'* illustrated over and over again.

In his sci-fi novel *"Divided by Infinity,"* Robert Charles Wilson makes a clever twist to introduce the concept of Quantum Immortality by mentioning a fictional book by Carl G. Sozière *"You Will Never Die,"* essentially describing a forthright implication of quantum physics – existence of the *'Quantum Multiverse':* *"Consciousness, like matter, like energy, is preserved. You are born, not an individual, but an infinity of individuals, in an infinity of identical worlds. Consciousness, your individual awareness, is shared by this infinity of beings. At birth, this span of selves begins to divide, as alternate possibilities are indulged or rejected. The infant turns his head not to the left or to the right, but both. One infinity of worlds becomes two; then four; then eight, and so on, exponentially. But the underlying essence of consciousness continues to connect all these disparate possibilities."*

So, Carl Sozière says it all in his book's title: You cannot die! A thought experiment called the *'Quantum Suicide'* is a tweaked version of the Schrödinger's cat experiment which is performed on hypothetical self with a hypothetical self-terminating device such as a gun. When pointed to self the weapon is either deployed, killing the experimenter, or it makes an audible "click" and the experimenter survives. Oddly enough and subjectively speaking, you would survive any streak of shots. As MIT's astrophysicist Max Tegmark points out, macro objects display quantum properties of micro objects such as wave function, only from our perspective it's nearly impossible to observe. The Quantum Immortality hypothesis also implies that from your subjective perspective you can expect to live the longest possible lifespan. Any time you "die" for external observers, your consciousness actually "migrates" to your other living conscious self in alternate reality.

This concept is brilliantly depicted in the movie *"Mr. Nobody"* in which an old man is about to turn 118 and in his last days as "the last mortal" on this Earth tries to remember under hypnosis his "multiple" lives. When he finally dies and upon his last breath, the time miraculously starts to move backwards and his whole life is "re-winded" back to his first breath. One might make a logical conclusion that out of trillions of all possible lives you are set to live the longest until death is the only option. At your last heartbeat all other potential lives, where you had died "before," are rendered non-existent and only the longest one becomes realized. At that tipping point you either: (1) are transported back in time to your birth, basically reincarnating to yourself (*Mr. Nobody's* scenario/ Friedrich Nietzsche's *Eternal Recurrence*) or (2) switch the dimensionality of your consciousness since the stream of consciousness must continue to flow.

One could further argue that the latter occurrence may be more conducive to evolution of your "core" self, "non-local" consciousness instantiating into the phenomenal mind for the duration of a lifetime. I don't want to entertain the idea that your consciousness ceases to exist with your last heartbeat because if you exist now, you always will in some form in this eternal now, as now is the only time there is. since now is ever-present from experiential point of view and eternal from the modern physics perspective, your existence cannot turn into non-existence. Your body in this plane of existence is only a virtual projection of your consciousness.

I also don't really buy Tegmark's argument that aging and death represent a gradual demise of consciousness, such that you're not really conscious anymore moments after death. Yet, that's exactly what I would expect the prodigious Max Tegmark to say in my experiential branch of quantum multiverse. In the branch where I'm immortal, everybody else sees their consciousness degrade over time, but I keep on going, through a wondrous and almost always highly improbable chain of quantum coincidences.

But is there any way to empirically prove the Quantum Immortality hypothesis? Actually, there may be one. No, I'm not going to advise you to replicate the Quantum Suicide at home, but pay attention to this: If, against all odds, you find yourself the oldest person on the planet, just like Nemo Nobody did in the *Mr. Nobody*, or amazingly enough, human immortality had become commonplace due to "immortality technologies" such as advanced genetic engineering, nanotechnologies and mind-uploading leading to cybernetic immortality (that's where we are headed, in actuality), then you can be convinced beyond a shadow of a doubt that you are, in fact, subjectively immortal.

What other ramifications follow? Your subjective quantum immortality coupled with soon-to-be discovered indefinite life extension at the civilizational level would spell out that you are actually to live forever through a series of ensuing self-transcendence events! One can also see a viable resolution to the so-called *'mind-uploading'*, or Star Trek *'Teleporter Dilemma'*, questioning whether in those instances you create a copy of yourself but kill yourself in the process. By analogy to the previous deliberations, it follows that your consciousness has to "migrate" to your living self, thus making the case for successful consciousness transfer in both methods of disembodiment. On this note, my friend, I'd like to conclude this chapter of the book and profess that you are to live forever as an individuated evolving conscious mind in this illusory matrix-like universe where nothing is what it seems.

Chapter 5. Augmenting Intelligence: In Search of the Ultimate Algorithm

"The measure of intelligence is the ability to change." -Albert Einstein

As a little kid I remember hearing from my father all kinds of stories sort of like this one: A father wanted to test the intelligence of his two sons. He assigned to each of them the task of looking after a cherry tree, and promised to reward the boy whose tree would yield the best berry when harvested.

One of the boys saw that the leaves were withering off and flowers were coming out at the end of the branches. So, he decided to carefully water every leaf and every flower. The tree withered still more and eventually died. The smarter boy, on the other hand, went on watering the root; the tree stayed green and healthy and yielded an abundant harvest of delicious cherries.

My father who was very good at teaching (no wonder, he was an instructor at a technology college early in his career) taught me to always look beyond the appearances, to always try to start with the bigger picture and work out the details as you go along, locate the source or reason of any challenging situation or find some other invisible root cause in order to better comprehend a task at hand. *"We learn throughout our lives, son,"* my dad used to say, *"the faster you learn, the better."*

Throughout human history we've seen a gradual appreciation of the premium for intelligence up to a point sometime perhaps in our own future where most, if not all, physical attributes might simply fade away in comparison.

One of the earliest furors on the premium for intelligence well may be an ancient Indian chess folk tale. The tradition of serving Paal Paysam made of rice to visiting pilgrims started after one legendary game of chess. The story goes somewhat like this: The local king was a well-known chess enthusiast, and welcomed anyone who could be a worthy opponent. So, one day a travelling sage appeared on the doorsteps of his palace and challenged him to play the game of chess.

The king offered any reward that the sage could name. Humbly, the sage asked for a single grain of rice to put on the first chess square and double it on every consequent one, if he wins. The king agreed to this and the game began. Having lost the game and being a man of his word the king ordered a bag of rice to be brought to the chess board.

The king started placing the grains according the reward arrangement quickly realizing that he would be unable to fulfill his promise because on the nineteenth square he would have had to come up with 1,000,000 grains of rice. And, finally on the sixty fourth square the king would have had to put more than 18×10^{16} grains of rice which equates to untold trillions of tons of rice!

It was at that point that the sage revealed himself as Krishna and told him that he doesn't have to pay the debt right away but can do that over time. That is why to this day visiting pilgrims are still feasting on Paal Paysam and the king's debt to Krishna is still being repaid.

This parable demonstrates an immense power of exponential growth present in today's information technologies but as intended here – the premium for intelligence – it seems that the King of Ambalapuzzha will never be able to pay off his debt in full to Krishna.

So, how can we define intelligence? The essence of intelligence is learning and applying the acquired knowledge to achieve complex goals. The age of intelligence augmentation is upon us with remarkable advances in the fields such as cognitive science, neuroengineering, artificial intelligence, neurophilosophy and cybernetics. In most instances, organismic intelligence cannot be simply reduced to a mere algorithm. To be clear, it is a meta-algorithm, more specifically meta-algorithmic information processing with certain emergent properties like network effects and conscious awareness and phenomenal experience in us human beings.

When we think of algorithms, step-by-step information processing, we think of machines and mechanisms. When we think of meta-algorithms, layered feedback-driven complexity and metabolic activity, we think of organisms. According to the now widely-accepted Computational Hypothesis of cognitive functionality, organic algorithms are our neural codes, i.e., "software of the mind." But what if we can expand the Computational Hypothesis in order to reverse-engineer our human intelligence and self-awareness?

In a well-defined sense, this meta-algorithmic information processing, is what can be rightly viewed as an emergent property of consciousness, i.e., our phenomenal experience and conscious awareness. Viewed in this way, consciousness turns out to be what information processing feels like to a conscious "computing" mind: Finding the right algorithms and subroutines to follow, applying optimization, performing analysis, executing pruning, and finally synthesizing it all in a holistic, streamlined process.

The human brain, our biological "wetware," has a fractal structure on many genetic and abstract cognitive levels. It employs a combination of forward chaining and backward chaining, just like certain types of heuristics in artificial intelligence. But human intelligence cannot be simply reduced to underlying algorithms since consciousness itself is what should be considered a truly "ontological primitive" with qubits/bits of information as reality's building blocks along with top-down causal principles. Information is "modus operandi" of consciousness.

As mentioned in the previous chapter, consciousness is scientifically elusive because it constitutes layers upon layers of non-material emergence: Reverse-engineering our thinking should be done in terms of networks, modules, algorithms and second-order emergence — meta-algorithms, or groups of modules. Neuronal circuits correlate to "immaterial" cognitive modules, and these cognitive algorithms, when activated, produce meta-algorithmic conscious awareness and phenomenal experience, all in all at least two layers of emergence on top of "physical" neurons.

Attributes of "natural" intelligence of a human species should include but be not limited to: higher-order abstract thinking, intuition, imagination, creativity, and finally wisdom, even though they haven't been formally recognized as types of intelligence. Intuition may be one of the highest forms of intelligence, according to some psychologists. To others, imagination.

Nature's fluidity of intelligence is due to its syntactical underpinnings: Nature is neither fully deterministic nor fully random. Rather, Nature uses her own language based on various codes from clearly defined genetic codes to immaterial neural codes to less obvious societal ones. Intelligence evolves and its evolution appears to be a linguistic, or a code-theoretic teleological process: Nature purposefully organizes itself, so clearly it is not random.

If we were to demystify a curious and ever-present phenomenon of emergence to the best of our current understanding, then we would clearly see that both Nature and Mind interact as many experiencers to become one again, at a higher meta-system level. What some people call "God," or the larger mind in which we all are embedded, becomes intelligible through this Nature's phenomenon of emergence: Universal consciousness is said to emerge somewhere ahead of us in space-time, however, IT transcends our conventional dimensionality and is already here within each of us. This also implies that all information is integrated at one level; all our individuated experiences are simultaneously observed from a higher level and integrated in a single experiential self – the Overmind – there's really One Mind, the one we all share, a philosophical worldview known as 'Idealism'.

Is reality entirely mechanistical, as proponents of determinism would claim? Or, is it teleological? Just by looking at accelerating complexification of the Universe of which we are an integral part, we can conclude that we are not subjected to a random walk of evolution, nor are we subjected to a deterministic script of Nature, the truth lies somewhere in between – we are part of teleological evolution.

Free will that I consider inseparable from consciousness will be discussed against the backdrop of quantum mechanical principles in Chapter 10. Universe transcends the dichotomy of determinism vs. non-determinism and that it actually allows both at the same time and even allows one to cause the other and vice versa. By the way, speaking of algorithms, meta-algorithms and free will, I refer to our sense of agency, i.e., free will, as *"Quantum algorithm of consciousness"* throughout my works. Thus, I argue, conscious AI is just few years ahead with the introduction of quantum algorithm of consciousness mimicking free will.

One of the most probable directions to develop AI and finally reach human-level AGI in the near future, would not be accomplished through commonly used today Deep Learning alone. But rather, in the coming years we could see not only the combination of bottom-up, top-down and interlinking (cybernetic) approaches to Machine Learning but we could witness more emphasis on *'Evolutionary Computing'*, known today in part as *'Reinforcement Learning'*, in part as *'Unsupervised Learning'* – we will need to teach self-aware AI to think for themselves in novel situations – the way our children learn the ropes of general intelligence.

The field of cybernetics was founded by American mathematician and philosopher Norbert Wiener who defined it in 1948 as *"the scientific study of control and communication in the animal and the machine."* In other words, it is a study of the relationship between computers and the human nervous system. Wiener placed a particular emphasis on feedback loops and signal processing. If we turn to Nature, the hermetic serpent swallowing its own tail, the Ouroboros, symbolizes Nature's systemic sum of input as a new pattern of influx that results in emergent behavior. Through the prism of cybernetics, we can now see that natural and artificial intelligences are part of the same continuum of mind.

In the 1980s, computer scientist Hans Moravec laid out the most challenging part of creating AGI – what has now been dubbed *The Moravec Paradox* – and explained why it's just what we should expect from machines that are immune to the pressures of natural selection. *"Encoded in the large, highly evolved sensory and motor portions of the human brain is a billion years of experience about the nature of the world and how to survive in it,"* he wrote in his 1988 book *"Mind Children."* *"The deliberate process we call reasoning is, I believe, the thinnest veneer of human thought, effective only because it is supported by this much older and much more powerful, though usually unconscious, sensorimotor knowledge."* As a rule, what's easy for humans is extremely difficult for Artificial Intelligence, and vice versa, what's supposed to be easy for AI is an impossible task for humans.

From the evolutionary standpoint, carbon-based intelligence represents enabling factors for silicon-based intelligence to come to existence. If Nature could find its way to engender intelligence and self-reflective consciousness in humans, sooner or later, we'll be able to replicate cognitive functionality and self-awareness in our "Mind Children," in our machine counterparts.

Sometimes we're leery of what we call metaphysics but every human being, be it a scientist, an entrepreneur, or a doctor, is by definition a "metaphysician." We start with a set of assumptions and then we try to work out our hypotheses. Even our Nobel-winning models are only provisional at best and are to be replaced by newer more sophisticated models with the next paradigmatic shift.

PART III. THE CYBERNETIC SINGULARITY: THE SYNTELLECT EMERGENCE

Chapter 6. Transitioning towards a Transcendent Global Economy

"Capitalism does not permit an even flow of economic resources. With this system, a small privileged few are rich beyond conscience, and almost all others are doomed to be poor at some level. That's the way the system works. And since we know that the system will not change the rules, we are going to have to change the system." -Martin Luther King, Jr.

On May 6, 2010, the Dow Jones opened lower than the previous day, falling slowly over the next few hours in response to the debt crisis in Greece. But at 2.42pm, the index started to fall rapidly. In less than five minutes, more than 600 points were wiped off the market. At its lowest point, the index was nearly 1,000 points below the previous day's average, a difference of almost 10% of its total value, and the biggest single-day fall in the market's history. By 3.07pm, in just 25 minutes, it recovered almost all of those 600 points, in the largest and fastest swing ever, what professional market participants would call a "black swan" event. I was trading on that roller coaster *'Flash Crash'* historical day and saw it with my own eyes — the rapid decline and almost as rapid rebound of the markets and my own portfolio. I remember watching commentator Jim Cramer on CNBC hysterically screaming from the bottom of his lungs: *"This is unreal! This is not right! The system obviously broke down! The machines broke down!"* What a wild ride that was, indeed!

Although the "free markets" model has been our best economic invention to date, most people would be genuinely surprised to find out that senile "classic" capitalism is now digging its own perfect grave. Wall Street, the apex of U.S. economic system, has entered a new algo-dominated era. Back in the day, while working at Prudential Financial in San Francisco, one of the global investment powerhouses, I saw the insides of that industry. The fraternity of bond jockeys, derivatives mavericks and stock pickers who've long personified the industry gave way to algorithms and artificial intelligence. These tools relieved money managers of routine tasks, but made the pool of remaining jobs increasingly scarce and insanely competitive. In large part, AI does what humans do, except much faster and more accurately, supplanting entire teams of investment specialists. Goldman Sachs, for example, employed around 600 people at their U.S. cash equities trading desk in 2000. Today, this operation has been taken over by AI with the same trading desk employing only two people.

Sci-fi writers and Hollywood got it wrong. The superintelligent machines are not coming for our lives. They are coming for our jobs. With the looming threats of technological unemployment, the oligopolist control of AI technology – with the bulk of global population essentially rendered irrelevant by technology – we might face a future of unprecedented inequality than ever before. The current economic system distributes wealth in a very focused manner that prevents a vast majority of humans from being adequately rewarded by the technologically advanced civilization. These factors undoubtedly condemn today's system of suboptimal economics to the realm of classical models of history as a result of impending obsolescence. In brief, the current faltering economic model is suboptimal, hinders economic growth, and is not sustainable going forward.

Our today's economy resembles a car on the road – if your drive your roadster, you might want to slow down before a turn, and then naturally accelerate after the turn. It all looks kind of natural except that the slowing down in real economy is done at the expense of general public. It's far from a fair game! *'Quantitative Easing'* (QE) first benefits the large pockets of Wall Street capital-controlling elite, a handful of people "in the know." Every stock market downturn, in a sense, is a rip-off of the investing public, and every consequent upturn first benefits the Wall Street elite, too. QE, known as large-scale asset purchases, is essentially when the Federal Reserve buys predetermined amounts of *'illiquid'* government bonds or other financial assets for *'liquid'* cash in order to stimulate the economy and increase liquidity.

But what if our economy doesn't need to slow down... ever... or at least do it in a controlled fashion? And what if instead of losing jobs to automation, we'll create entire new industries? Instead of an old car on the road, the next economic model will resemble a brand-new flying car. When you need to pilot one, you have to take off, then gain altitude and accelerate in speed, then proceed steadily, and only before reaching your destination, you can decelerate and start descent. So, what might this new economic model look like? What will it mean for the future of work and entrepreneurship?

THE FUTURE OF WORK

According to the 2018 study by Harvard University, 51% of Americans between the ages of 18 and 29 no longer support capitalism. For millennials in particular, the binaries of capitalism vs. socialism, or capitalism vs. communism, are shallow and outmoded. Far more likely is that people are realizing – either consciously or at some gut level – that there's something fundamentally flawed about a system that is based on elitism, artificial scarcity, and cutthroat competition. It is based on fear and greed which is especially visible in the capital markets. This far-from-fair system has corporations as its dominant players that possess insectoid intelligence, if viewed as "superminds," and have their single goal turning natural and human resources into capital, and do so more and more each year, regardless of the costs to human well-being and to the environment. Our descendants may look at us as a violent species willing to spend 1/5 of GDP (in the U.S.) on funding the military and willing to kill each other off instead of using those economic resources on science and technology. They would probably wonder why we failed for so long to prioritize peace and progress. Should you talk to someone in the 2040s, they would probably refer to the capitalist period of our history, as we now refer to feudalism.

By the 2030s, it's estimated that one-third of jobs in the U.S. will be automated. The forthcoming disruptive tsunami of AI and robotics will be enormous. We mechanized human muscle centuries ago, and when we pair it with a synthetic mind, nearly every form of economic labor can be automated. Machine intelligence is going to create a lot of wealth, but it will also replace a lot of human labor. We saw many types of jobs disappear in the Industrial Revolution, but we also saw jobs created that had never existed before. The pace of job automation will outstrip job creation in the short term and cause a lot of technology underemployment. For the time being, humans will likely be kept in the loop as employers will need human workers to help manage AI and automation because robots are still not as versatile as we are.

Vast increases in productivity and efficiency will be realized through an integrated network of smart-products (termed the Internet of Things, or IoT), renewable energy, decentralized manufacturing via 3D printing, remote education, decentralized finance, legal contracts, blockchain, and the progressive automated workforce. We'll see a paradigm shift in the coming years when we move from a mindset of machines are assisting humans to humans are assisting machines. McKinsey Global Institute's latest 2018 report *"Jobs Lost, Jobs Gained: Workforce Transitions in a Time of Automation"* finds that up to 375 million workers globally will have to switch occupational categories and learn new skills through 2030 because of automation and the transition to AI and robotics.

The promise of AI and automation raises new questions about the role of work in our lives. We must find ways to move beyond today's definitions of jobs and economic value. As technology provides services and goods at ever-lower cost, human beings will be compelled to discover new roles – those that aren't necessarily tied to how we conceive of work today – it will be tied to our consciousness, tied to our collective will, tied to our individual free will, so we should end up with a global society which would be more egalitarian than today. Why am I talking about economics in the philosophy book? In our interdependent world, everything is woven into the tapestry of life and our today's livelihood heavily depends on economy. In the long run, capitalism won't survive, nation-states won't survive – we will but as a new technological species – through a metamorphosis on the planetary scale – the human-machine "caterpillar" transforming into a higher-dimensional "butterfly." In the rest of this chapter and the next two, you'll see why this must be the case.

When our machines release us from ever more tasks, to what will we turn our attentional focus? When machines can come up with useful hypotheses, create patentable technologies, and one day design other machines, no one would call their insights accidental. Creative AI will dissolve our preconceptions – such as which kinds of jobs would qualify as creative and which roles we frequently assume as safe from automation.

Enhancement technologies such as bioinformatics and neurotech can either contribute to inequality or allow us to solve it. Educating and empowering the underprivileged can quicken the overall rate of human progress. We can build a future in which humans are not competing with machines or being overtaken by robots, but instead entering into a new era of hypercollaboration that frees up the human spirit for more meaningful tasks based on emotional intelligence.

DATA: NEW OIL?

Data is integral to any business operation. Companies constantly seek out new sources of competitive advantage based on developments in data and technology in order to make accurate predictions and intelligent decisions about where to invest their resources. Data analytics, traditionally known as market research and internal analysis, is being used to assess risks and identify growth opportunities and is becoming a valuable tool to many organizations. In today's business environment, it's impossible to operate without data, in fact, it now becomes a primary asset. *The Economist* has called it the new oil that will ensure future prosperity.

The data economy began with electronic information systems called *'relational databases'*, first invented in 1969. Presently, the amount of data we produce doubles every year. In other words, in 2018 we produced as much data as in the entire history of humankind through 2016. Every minute we produce hundreds of thousands of Google searches and Facebook posts. These contain information that reveals how we think and feel. Soon, most things around us, including our clothing, also will be connected to the Internet. It's estimated that by 2025 there will be 80 billion networked devices, 10 times more than people on Earth. Then, with immersive computing going mainstream, the amount of data will double every month.

Data is indispensable but companies need the right kind of data to grow their business: Data needs to be accurate, up-to-date and relevant. To unlock the full value of data, organizations need to extract meaningful insights aligned with their objectives, in much the same way that oil is refined for specific purposes. Businesses are collecting ever-growing volumes of information from all kinds of sources, including websites, enterprise applications, social media, mobile devices, and increasingly the Internet of Things (IoT). Advanced data analytics becomes *data mining* which is the automated process of scrutinizing massive amounts of data to determine trends and patterns, to establish relationships, to solve business problems or generate new opportunities.

The algorithms are everywhere – like the Internet or electricity – and once AI becomes integrated in our day-by-day life there's no getting rid of it. We've seen that before. The invention of the steam engine turned sailing into a hobby and cars replaced horses. Stakeholders of organizations may ultimately push algorithmic management into mainstream use. Not only does this type of management provide more transparency, it also prevents embezzlement, favoritism, and mischievous actions. Office politics will soon become irrelevant. The AI-executive will always follow the board's strategy. One would find the Global Brain at the center of every company, facilitating interactions and access to information. Over time, most corporations will convert to 100% virtual entities, doubling the size of the new transcendent economy over the course of just a few years.

The Age of Dataism, where everything from your shopping habits to your biometrics is subsistence for machine learning algorithms that want to understand everything about you, has many great benefits. All that data might be used to revamp user experience; it could be used to assist in everything from healthcare to emergency response. Technological advances like the Internet of Things, smart home and self-driving cars could be the next step in time-saving and convenience in the same way that electrical appliances like the refrigerator and air conditioner were decades earlier. Also, they will be easing us deeper into a world of "participatory surveillance," where we exchange comfort and convenience for an external presence that's always monitoring us in the background. We'll be entering an era when this transactional data exchange may no longer be optional.

The growth of this new digital economy is predicated on fluidity of data not on withholding or buffering of data, though. In time, we'll learn to distribute data in fairer ways and even monetize personal data but it may be painful growth — many people are still stuck in the 20th century mentality. That's why I think that Facebook scandal in 2018, involving Cambridge Analytica, has been way too over-politicized and blown out of reasonable proportions. I don't know about you but I'd rather get hit by a bunch of targeted ads of stuff that I like or at least I might find interesting rather than something completely random. In defense of Facebook, I'd say that it can be difficult for global platforms like Facebook to consistently build and maintain trust when attitudes toward privacy vary so widely across the globe.

Actually, we well may be the very last generation that cares so much about privacy. If history has taught us anything, it's that humans are willing to give up more privacy than they tend to realize. At the turn of the century, it would have been unthinkable we'd all allow ourselves to be tracked by our cars, phones, and instant check-ins to neighborhood locations; but now most of us see it as a worthy trade-off for optimized commutes and dating. As we continue walking that fine line between exploitation and exploration into a more high-tech future, we'll make more concessions previously inconceivable to most of us. Fast forward a few years ahead, we'll have less privacy but we'll gain so much more in return — safety, convenience, crime prevention, immediate disaster response, and easier access to information.

As machines and algorithms get smarter, they'll inevitably replace a widening share of the global workforce. The proposals to alleviate the burden on the most vulnerable segment of population vary, but they share a common premise. A robot tax could raise revenue to retrain those displaced workers, or provide them with a basic income. The real threat in economic milieu is that automation will amplify economic disparities to such an extreme that life will become unlivable, leading to unprecedented social unrest and economically devastating revolts.

UBI

"Basic income is not a utopia, it's a practical business plan for the next step of the human journey." -Jeremy Rifkin

Unconditional Basic Income (also called *'basic income guarantee'* or *'social dividend'*) is a system of social security in which all citizens or residents of a country regularly receive an unconditional sum of money from a government regardless of any other income. Pilot programs have been introduced in a number of European countries, that are aimed at replacing outdated bureaucratic welfare systems altogether. In the U.S., various tech leaders including Elon Musk, Bill Gates and Mark Zuckerberg are supporting the idea. In the coming Age of Superintelligence [and automation] everyone should be entitled to social dividend, "free" money such as UBI, just for being alive. We should not forget that the wealthiest of us would not be as fortunate without civilization. Otherwise, Jeff Bezos would have to forage for food in the Amazon jungle all by himself. Being a human today is more than enough of a fair contribution to receive free money from the government. Going forward we'll see more and more prominent voices vouching for UBI.

At the 2018 TED Conference in San Francisco, futurist Ray Kurzweil made a bold prediction about the future of free money: *"In the early 2030s, we'll have universal basic income in the developed world, and worldwide by the end of the 2030s. You'll be able to live very well on that. The primary concern will be meaning and purpose,"* he said onstage at the annual event. This timeframe also coincides with when Kurzweil, Google's chief futurist and director of engineering at Google Research, thinks AI will pass the Turing Test — when it becomes impossible to discern machine intelligence from human intelligence. At that point, human jobs could become increasingly scattered.

Entrepreneur-billionaire Elon Musk had the chance to share his thoughts on Universal Basic Income (UBI) at the 2018 World Government Summit in Dubai. Musk argues that the government must introduce a UBI program in order to compensate for automation. Such program could boost productivity, encourage creativity, improve health, alleviate poverty, reduce crime, raise education, and improve overall quality of life. Interestingly enough, UBI would also stimulate economy as more money will be spent by an average consumer as well as serve as a "cushion" against future economic downturns due to the cyclical nature of capitalism.

Every time I buy groceries or air tickets, I pay a sales tax for the semi-automated infrastructure that we all enjoy in our market economy. What most people don't realize, though, is that there's one particular segment of the U.S. economy which has been fully automated for years now – capital markets, such as the electronic stock market. Wall Street firms now trade financial instruments via trading robots, or algorithmic programs, "algos." One second for a Wall St. algo is a "lifetime" in human terms. High frequency trading algos make millions per trading day at the expense of investing public. Why? Because algos are programmed to react in nanoseconds to changing market conditions and news. In other words, the stock market is "rigged," as most investors and traders are at the disadvantage in this marketplace – they don't get favorable pricing and execution.

The debate goes on for years now but I think it's about time to implement a small financial transaction tax on high frequency trading. After all, if everyone pays for our common economic infrastructure, why should Wall Street firms be exempt? The revenues collected from taxing industrial robots and Wall Street trading robots would be more than enough to pay for UBI as preemptive measures against massive technological unemployment and social turmoil. At some point, sooner than many people think, governments will be forced to implement UBI. Ironically, implementing UBI may prolong the relevance of nation-states by a number of years, as we'll see further in the chapter.

On the way to abundance from classical capitalism to a post-scarcity, hypercollaborative economic model, where goods and services are produced at "near-zero marginal cost" in a new digital economy, UBI proponent Jeremy Rifkin argues that technological forces will inevitably displace employment but at the same time will create conditions for an economic paradigm shift. Jeremy Rifkin is the principle architect of the European Union's Third Industrial Revolution long-term economic sustainability plan, the bestselling author of twenty books on the impact of scientific and technological changes on the economy, the workforce, society, and the environment. According to Rifkin: *"The Internet of Things will connect everything with everyone in an integrated global network. People, machines, natural resources, production lines, logistics networks, consumption habits, recycling flows, and virtually every other aspect of economic and social life will be linked via sensors and software to the IoT platform, continually feeding Big Data to every node – business, homes, vehicles – moment to moment, in real time. Big*

Data, in turn, will be processed with advanced analytics, transformed into predictive algorithms, and programmed into automated systems to improve thermodynamic efficiencies, dramatically increase productivity, and reduce the marginal cost of producing and delivering a full range of goods and services to near zero across the entire economy."

In an essay for the Green Institute, titled *"A Universal Basic Income: Economic Considerations,"* Frank Stilwell, a Professor Emeritus in Political Economy at the University of Sydney, writes that there's an "inevitable uncertainty" surrounding UBI and its economic consequences, which all depend on how it's implemented. Assessing the value of our collective inherited wealth would yield billions of dollars in cash to pay for UBI, while stimulating economy. *"Currently, those who benefit most from our socially built assets pay almost nothing to use them. But that needn't always be the case. We could charge for using key components of our legal and financial infrastructure; for example, modest transaction fees on trades of stocks, bonds and derivatives could generate more than $300 billion per year. Such fees would not only generate income for everyone; they'd discourage speculation and help stabilize our financial system. Similar fees could be applied to patent and royalty earnings, which are returns not only to innovation but also to monopoly rights granted and enforced by society,"* says Stilwell.

Microsoft Corp. founder Bill Gates also suggests that robots should be taxed in order to help finance social programs such as UBI: *"Right now, the human worker who does, say, $50,000 worth of work in a factory, that income is taxed and you get income tax, social security tax, all those things. If a robot comes in to do the same thing, you'd think that we'd tax the robot at a similar level."* Proponents of Universal Basic Income are becoming increasingly vocal about its implementation and for good reason — robots are coming sooner than most people realize, thus displacing millions of jobs. Perhaps, the next round of Occupy Wall Street movement should be transformed into Tax Wall Street movement with a more clearly defined political agenda.

D-TRENDS: DIGITALIZATION, DECENTRALIZATION AND DEMONETIZATION

The Fourth Industrial Revolution fueled by rapid advances in automation and artificial intelligence is changing the world around us in profound ways. This revolution holds promise to create greater efficiencies in all industry sectors and to spectacularly improve lives of people worldwide. Smart cities of the not-so-distant future may not even look like cities. Meta-layers of connectivity through blockchains, the Internet of Things, artificial intelligence, and augmented reality could make cities less and less geographically defined. Your body could be physically in one location, while you are at a conference in another location in Virtual Reality, meeting with people who are each in a different location around the planet.

One of the most crucial components of the new "experience economy" would be an open, borderless, payment protocol based on *'blockchain'* technology, such as Bitcoin and Ethereum. The difference between the two is the fact that Bitcoin is nothing more than a cryptocurrency, whereas Ethereum is a ledger technology that companies can use to build proprietary programs. If Bitcoin was version 1.0, Ethereum is more robust v.2.0, allowing for the decentralized applications to be built on top of it. We might also see the emergence of other even more advanced payment protocols, such as *'holochains'*.

As a new form of decentralized information technology, blockchains and holochains can be applicable to many areas beyond cryptocurrency and financial assets. What Bitcoin and other cryptos have in common is their existence in the "ether", as a digital code rather than metal coins or paper bills. Beneath these currencies lies a blockchain technology that keeps a record of all transactions without an authority like a central bank. Blockchain is simply a database that is public (no one owns it), distributed (no centralized server), is continuously updated, and is protected with encryption. The end result is that blockchain tracks and verifies digital assets, so they cannot be hacked or copied without permission. It operates without the need for intermediaries. This high level of security is why blockchain is used for digital currencies, but it also means that it can be used for other assets, anything from votes in an election to stocks, tax payments, and property deeds. Proponents say cryptocurrency is free of meddling that changes the amount of currency in circulation, like when the U.S. Federal Reserve adjusts money supply to spur economic growth or curb inflation. Free of such intervention, digital currency can rise and fall with supply and demand in the global marketplace.

On June 18, 2019, Facebook has officially announced details of its cryptocurrency, a digital coin called Libra which will let you buy things or send money to people with nearly zero fees around the globe. With Libra and other cryptocurrencies, transactions become more seamless. Unlike highly volatile and speculative Bitcoin, Facebook's Libra may be endorsed by the relationship with millions of advertisers and small businesses, but what's even more important, Libra may be relatively stable as it will be pegged to the USD and other convertible currencies: euro, pound, Swiss franc and yen.

Libra has a tremendous disruptive potential for national currencies, especially in developing countries. This may become a payment medium of choice for billions of customers in cross-border transactions. This initiative positions Facebook as one of the key actors at the center of the crypto asset development, and a main architect of this emerging and crucially important trend – building the Global Brain architecture.

Making myriad activities cheaper, faster and easier could facilitate economic activity in countries like India, where hundreds of millions of people remain outside the banking system. What governments lose in tax revenue on transactions that they can't track might be recouped from greater economic activity and prosperity. It seems that what we're witnessing now is the beginning of the end of central banks when government-printed money becomes obsolete.

Decentralized blockchain technology may also hold the key to tapping AI's potential in a democratized way, one that opens participation in the future AI economy to more than just a handful of the largest technology juggernauts. And blockchains may even be used to not only develop AI but also potentially to function as synaptic connections linking AI into the Global Brain. Ultimately, a world in which data can be securely and transparently shared and in which AI can be developed and utilized in a democratic and distributed manner is more likely to contribute to a future of abundance, in which AI is the best thing to ever happen to humanity.

Today's VR platforms attempt to leverage blockchain technologies to make virtual property ownership and transactions more secure. Virtual reality platform *Decentraland*, for instance, uses blockchain to identify and designate ownership of land in its virtual world. We're headed towards the Metaverse. New platforms seek to integrate these new VR technologies with the social element of multiplayer gaming. If we can create virtual worlds run on blockchain, it could also provide the template for how blockchain may function in the physical world. There is a growing consensus that VR, AI, quantum computing and blockchain may one day converge to unlock their full potential. These nascent technologies still have a ways to go, but the possibilities when you combine them are mind-boggling. This becomes especially important in designing a cyberworld that can't be censored. The days of nation-states are seemingly numbered, for one.

Nation-states evolved to regulate human beings – the main intellectual and physical resource in the past few centuries – while blockchains, and similar systems that could be called "virtual states" are evolving to regulate information technology. In the future, nation-states will have ever more limited ability to reach into cyberspace to regulate information technology. Not only the world around us is rapidly shifting to a truly digital economy, but one that will become economically borderless. Just like medieval city walls later were either demolished or reduced to historic curiosity, over time, nation-states will, too, gradually fade away, giving way to one global stronghold without borders.

In today's rapidly changing global economy, emerging technologies like AI, blockchain, and VR edge us ever closer to the brave new world where national borders will be ultimately transcended. Over the long term, technology trends will inexorably trump any geopolitics in significance. Entrepreneurs, researchers and socialites are much better adept and motivated to cooperate on a global scale than politicians. In the meantime, AI will fundamentally change how governments work, and the changes will likely come much sooner than many think. We'll also see the emergence of nano-nations that create self-sustaining human habitats on the ocean – seasteading. In fighting a losing battle for relevance with virtual states and nano-nations, nation-states will be forced to implement UBI to keep them relevant for few more years.

What people aren't talking about much is a forthcoming rapid demonetization of the cost of living – it's getting cheaper and cheaper to meet our basic needs. Powered by developments in exponential technologies, the cost of housing, transportation, communication, food, healthcare, computation, entertainment, clothing, education and so on will fall, eventually approaching, believe it or not, zero. In the 2030s, we'll see a major paradigm shift in collective consciousness mediated by exponential technologies. Thus, a lot of products will be dirt-cheap or even free thanks to emerging 3D printing and nanotechnology, and many U.S. downtown office buildings will start to convert to hotels and residential property because we'll be working and interacting increasingly in virtual environments, so we will no longer need to occupy office space and commute to the office. Most familiar products, services and real estate will be on a secular downward trend in prices. We'll be entering an unprecedented era of prosperity for all.

THE NEXT FINANCIAL MELTDOWN WILL TWEAK CAPITALISM AND RESULT IN REAL ESTATE SECULAR DECLINE

"No one can see a bubble. That's what makes it a bubble."
-The Big Short, the movie

Are we in for the Big Short II? The cyclical nature of markets spells an eventual collapse of the real estate prices in the U.S. following the next global stock market meltdown and global recession which will be drastically different the next time around. For one, the coming collapse is about to start a secular declining trend in property values. Secondly, after the collapse, the prices of properties won't be able to recover like they did after the previous "property market corrections." Why? I hope we all may agree that oil, for example, will never recover to all-time highs. Similar premises hold true for the existing home values. Multi-generational "Ponzi Scheme" is about to implode. There are multiple major socio-economic structural changes on the horizon contributing to this permanent decline which is in the cards right now.

Also, many conventional linear projections won't even apply anymore.

The Next "Cyclical" Global Recession: The world's "synchronized" stock markets are the best indication of things to come in economic milieu. The next financially engineered global recession may be the last effort by the capital-controlling elite of Wall Street to keep political and economic control over the global population and maintain the faltering capitalist system as long as possible;

Deflation: In the rising interest rate environment, and due to the U.S. relative competitiveness, investment and headquartering attractiveness, the U.S. dollar may remain relatively strong putting deflationary pressure on housing prices;

Hyperconnectivity: Improved communications will ensure more homogeneous geographical distribution of real estate values. Basically, you may be anywhere with all necessary access to information, communication and experience via VR;

Construction Tech: Advanced engineering techniques, artificial intelligence solutions, extreme automation and new cheaper materials will bring down significantly the cost and time of building most structures. 3D printing, robotics and nanotechnology will further help revolutionize the construction industry;

Smart Homes: Newly designed apartment buildings or houses packed with electronics and "in-home intelligence" may initially cost considerably more but ultimately, they will devalue the existing home properties. The notion of the million-dollar views will gradually fade away as any imaginable landscape can be recreated by using ultra-realistic dynamic digital wallpaper;

New Megacities and Nano-Nations: By the time we should expect a recovery in existing home values, new cities may be built rather quickly outside of, or adjacent to the current metro areas with advanced infrastructure, mega projects, tall buildings, and smart homes which will make existing homes in old cities look like dog houses. Seasteading will spur the emergence of nano-nations with sustainable offshore communities;

Virtual Reality vs. Realty: Many conventional economic notions, such as primary locations and differential rent, may gradually become irrelevant under new effective topologies of the social space and ever more predominant use of virtual environments. It may sound improbable at the moment, but VR will change the travel and hospitality industries at first, and then will have more direct impact on the property market. By 2025 full adoption of VR in the U.S. is guaranteed. As analysts at Goldman Sachs predict, VR will be bigger than TV by 2027.

The Nature of Work: As more companies shift to a part-time work week, tele-commuting and virtual work space-time, some converting to 100% "virtual entities," and as we'll also see an increasing number of emerging virtual corporations, commercial properties in major U.S. cities, especially in downtowns, will be under pressure. In the 2030s, we'll see many downtown office buildings converting to hotels and residential properties;

Technology Displacement: Many people may be displaced by technology automation and may only rely on Universal Basic Income (when implemented) for support. That would effectively take them out of the pool of available buyers of the higher end real estate;

Transportation: Just as improved communications, improved transportation such as hyperloop system making it possible to "commute" from Los Angeles to San Francisco in 30 minutes, self-driving cars and later flying cars, the Internet of Things alleviating traffic conditions to "connected" vehicles, would mean you don't necessarily want to buy a home in "prime" location;

Generational Attitudes: Millennials avoid investing in the big ticket items such as real estate for all the right reasons — they understand better than the older generations that the entire new digital economy is about to undergo monumental paradigm shifts at the ever-accelerating pace whereas anything of physical value today will gradually lose its value and importance;

Shorter Economic Cycles: By the time we should under normal circumstances anticipate a recovery in property values a new unexpected "black swan" event or crisis may strike the outdated capitalist system.

If we were to extrapolate the current economic trends, we might see the parallels between the oil market and property market as they both fall in the familiar supply and demand framework influenced by the prominent, socio-economic and technology-driven, structural changes. If you're an owner of a second home, vacation home or something of the sort, you may consider putting it on sale immediately while the market is topping and very close to the bubble burst, as I predict should happen sometime before 2022. Renting as opposed to committing to a multi-decade mortgage in these rapidly changing economic conditions seems to be more economically justifiable.

AN INCONVENIENT TRUTH: HOMELESS IN AMERICA

The homeless are treated like animals in the richest country of the world which has more than enough resources for everybody! Do we have to cling to this extremely barbaric and outdated economic model, or are we about to outgrow it? Do we want to perpetuate the system based on artificial scarcity, elitism, fear, and greed? Is it the 21st-century U.S. or middle-aged France? As of the end of 2017, there were about 6,800 homeless people in San Francisco alone, compared to the total 884,363 population (Almost 0.8% population homeless?). According to endhomelessness.org, 578,424 homeless individuals lived on the streets in 2014 in the United States. Of those, 177,373 *"lived in a place not meant for human habitation such as the street or an abandoned building"*; about 50,000 of those 578,424 are homeless veterans.

Is this a socio-economic model the U.S. wants to export to other countries? I recently visited Panama where I haven't seen a single homeless person on the street. As a thought experiment, consider this: You have an unruly teenage son or daughter who ran away from home and now sleeps on the street. Wouldn't you do anything in your power to get him/her back home because you truly care? Right? We need that highest level of empathy in our society ahead of the coming AI revolution, which is just years away. Without this happening, once we create Artificial General Intelligence (AGI) in our own image, with our "human value" system, however treating underprivileged people like animals, our behavior will be observed, and "internalized" by the conscious machines as well, so we may, in turn, ask for existential trouble!

According to the Davos Economic Forum report, the economy is going to lose about 5 million jobs by 2020 due to automation, technology unemployment, and AI-based advances. Some of these people may end up on the street, adding to a bigger army of homeless people, and fueling social unrest. Universal Basic Income should be implemented as soon as possible to eliminate poverty, homelessness, and wage slavery, as a preemptive measure.

At the time of this writing in 2018, San Francisco has passed Prop C aimed to develop homelessness services in the city by raising taxes to local tech businesses that are largely responsible for extreme cost of housing in Bay Area. Marc Benioff, founder and CEO of Salesforce, headquartered in San Francisco, poured millions of dollars in support of the initiative.

ON THE WAY TO POST-CAPITALISM: IT-BASED SHARED ECONOMY

"If technology is the engine of change, then nanotechnology is the fuel for humanity's future." -Natasha Vita-More

The current economic model may work with "alternating success" for some time, but ultimately capitalism will mutate and gradually be replaced with IT-based shared economy. Many labels were tentatively given to this post-scarcity, post-capitalist model. In his 2018 book, *Superminds*, Thomas W. Malone, MIT's director of the Center for Collective Intelligence, describes a hypothetical model he calls *'Cybersocialism'*, other names like *'Fully Automated Luxury Communism'* were mentioned in the press. We'll use the broad term *'Post-capitalism'* here to refer to any subsequent economic model.

Make a note that I don't advocate for any particular model, I'm only saying that we are quickly outgrowing the classic form of capitalism. I

191

believe economic evolution is akin to any other natural process of unfolding patterns, so it would apply to economic development as well. Economic evolution doesn't end with capitalism. By mid-century, geo-post-capitalism will likely combine market economy, socialist elements and even AI-engineered central planning amid decentralized backdrop of its global components. Evolutionary utilitarianism – ensuring the greater good for the greatest number – seems like an obvious eventuality.

Overall, we have been on the right track, though. Many aspects of life on Earth are getting dramatically better. Extreme poverty has fallen by half since 1990, and life expectancy is increasing by leaps and bounds in developing countries. Studies consistently show that most people in developed countries have no clue that the world has taken a happier turn in recent decades because media, and humans in general, have a strong negativity bias. Bad economic news gets more coverage than good news. Negative experiences affect people more, and for longer, than positive ones, and many people think things are getting worse, in part because that's actually an evolutionary adaptation: It's been crucial for our survival to be sensitive to bad news, so people are genetically conditioned to pay about ten times more attention to negativity than positivity.

As long as the costs of communications and computation continue to drop due to advances in technology, communication networks become global and ubiquitous, and as the networks proliferate, they gradually replace matter with mind, i.e., networked intelligence. Access is becoming more important than ownership. It would be more economically optimal in some situations to rent than to own, in other situations to share and generate passive income.

If the premise of the current sharing economy is that you can turn your car into a cab or your house into a hotel, the premise of the next phase of the IT-based shared economy is that you can turn anything into a productive asset. All you have to do is set your price and other criteria, and AI will take care of the rest. The blockchain "smart contracts" could make a lot of things sharable. Electronic "gig economy" can distribute creative and enjoyable mini-tasks, and "digital twins" can earn you additional income. Our AI future is almost unimaginable: AI will destroy and create jobs, invent new industries, accelerate innovation to a new level and fundamentally change the way business is done across the board.

Some epicenters of innovation, such as Silicon Valley, revered as America's technology capital, where I'm fortunate to live, has an outsized influence on the world's economy, stock markets and culture. This small stretch of land from San Jose to San Francisco is home to three of the world's five most valuable companies. Tech giants such as Apple, Facebook, Google, Intel and Oracle all claim Silicon Valley as their birthplace and home. San Francisco Bay Area has the 19th-largest economy in the world, ranking above Switzerland and Saudi Arabia. And California is now the 5th largest economy, surpassing the U.K. in 2018.

Across the Pacific Ocean, collectivistic China rivals the U.S. in terms of Big Data generation. Moreover, China seems to put more emphasis on developing robotics – empathic machines – to integrate robots, and consequently, AGIs into the fabric of society, while the focus of the U.S. has been disembodied AI, thus far. China might be closer to the realization of the Global Brain, epitomized in the Internet of Things, Internet of NanoThings, Quantum Internet and Virtual Metaverse than most countries. But at the same time, none of it will really matter – by mid-century nation-states will fade away, anyway, just like feudal city walls are now no more than a historic peculiarity.

The United Nations' *Global Sustainable Development Report 2019* suggests we seriously need to consider making drastic changes to our economic systems. *"[T]he economic models which inform political decision-making in rich countries almost completely disregard the energetic and material dimensions of the economy,"* the researchers wrote in the report. *"Economies have used up the capacity of planetary ecosystems to handle the waste generated by energy and material use."* In summary, maybe it's time to accept we can't somehow maintain endless economic growth on a finite planet.

But what if with the new wave of technologies, such as nanotechnology which would enable us to reprogram matter at a molecular level, we can overcome scarcity once and for all? Design would then become the most important part from start to end product which can be freely shared or have a premium in the marketplace. At any rate, this will dismantle the current social, economic, and political system, because it will become irrelevant; every institution, every value system, every aspect of our lives have been governed by scarcity: the problem of distributing a finite amount of "stuff." There will be no need for any of today's social institutions. In other words, when nanotech and ultra-realistic VR are commonplace, the system built on scarcity will crumble.

GLOBAL CLIMATE CHANGE: THE TECHNO-SOLUTION APPROACH

"We have no reason to think that climate change is harmful if you look at the world as a whole. Most places, in fact, are better off being warmer than being colder. And historically, the really bad times for the environment and for people have been the cold periods rather than the warm periods." -Freeman Dyson

Essentially, we're all on the same side on the climate change debate but with different approaches. We all care about the planet and our promising future. Global warming may or may not be caused by humans, which, of course, remains a highly contentious issue but we should consider the fact that the Earth's climate changes all throughout its history, and it's a natural part of multi-century, multi-millennium, multi-million-year cycles. Earth is like a spaceship moving in space at great speeds and having a very thin layer of atmosphere to be protected from the cosmic effects such as cosmic radiation, solar winds, and even gravitational impact, when passing through the galactic plane, all of which is conducive to certain multi-millennium planetary cycles.

Does your breath warm your room temperature? Even if it does, its influence is millions of times less than that of outside weather. Earth is a planet moving at great speeds in its cosmic neighborhood and outer space influences the Earth's climate much more than previously thought. All data collected by environmentalists can be easily manipulated to support one point of view or exactly the opposite. The real environmental threat, however, includes pollution in certain metro areas of the world and loss of biodiversity. These are huge factors but still not necessarily the main causes of global warming.

Don't get me wrong, I don't rule out the possibility that global warming is partly anthropogenic in nature, even though I remain skeptical. At the largest of scales, human activity is most probably a negligible contributing factor to global warming. On the other hand, one can't discard environmental concerns, by far more evident and well-documented, such as pollution in our cities (of course! It's right in front of our faces!), deforestation, eradication of species, animal cruelty, and above all, cruelty to our own kind! Some populists, including politicians and other high-profile media personalities, want to call it all climate change or global warming because it sounds sexier than environment pollution or species extinction. If there were global cooling right now those populists would ascribe that to human activity as well. No wonder many people think of global warming activism as a hoax or populism, and rightfully so!

All we need is not global warming alarmism/populism, not fear-selling media distracting attention from our societal problems, not proverbial "Save the Planet" money-laundering initiatives but specialized task forces to tackle very specific issues such as Manila pollution, Los Angeles smog, or deforestation in Brazil. That would make a humongous difference. The United States and China that account for 14% and 24% of total greenhouse gas emissions respectively, had previously announced plans to cut carbon emissions in their joint effort in November 2014, which has paved the way to the Paris agreement by 196 nations to curb emissions in December 2015. Although this global concerted effort is commendable, we need a similar global cooperation in developing Strong Artificial Intelligence which will by far outweigh in significance any other phenomenon in the history of mankind in terms of existential risks and opportunities.

In any case, global warming should be thought of as quite solvable, and in actuality, might be placed closer to the bottom of the list of problems human civilization faces right now. Wait, what? Let me explain — all Anthropocene-related challenges may be solved sooner than many of us think with radical, logically inevitable, technological advances. About the same time as Paris climate talks in December 2015 but on the other side of the globe, in Silicon Valley, a non-profit organization OpenAI was announced. From start, OpenAI has a hefty budget and lofty goals to *"benefit the whole of humanity"* by making research in Artificial Intelligence available to everyone for free, to prevent malevolent AI by free distribution of its software, open access – no restriction.

Ideally, the first Strong Artificial Intelligence system should be globally distributed (Internet-based) as opposed to semi-autonomous

AI owned by one corporation or one government. The race is on, and it seems, we might have only one chance to do it right. Given exponential growth of existing and emerging technologies, especially Artificial Intelligence, we're going to solve any of today's seemingly intractable challenges, including climatic challenge, which in the minds of the majority of population, pales in comparison with poverty, mortality, diseases, wars, income inequality, unemployment and a slew of other global critical problems.

In the years to come, Artificial Intelligence coupled with nanotechnology, robotics, geoengineering and other emerging technologies of tomorrow will enable us to control the climate of the planet, let alone the weather. Thus, in the not-so-distant future, we can build weather grids controlling the weather in certain cities, cleanse smog and other pollutants with the help of environmental nanobots, or even get rid of wires everywhere on the planet since electricity will be mostly wireless. Today's green technologies and decentralized renewable energy systems are great first steps in the right direction as long as they are fairly distributed worldwide and become accessible even in the poorest regions of the world. Otherwise, we'll only exacerbate the economic distress of the lagging nations.

STAR-TREKONOMICS: THE ECONOMIC SINGULARITY

In the next few decades, humanity will go through fairly challenging and incredibly transformative times, leading to some kind of "Economic Singularity," which would spell the end of capitalism as we know it. This will be marked by a cardinal transition to a new transcendent global economy with unprecedented productivity gains, unlimited creative potential and advanced planetary consciousness but a world where unenhanced humans are no longer employable. Just like hyperconnected neurons of the *'Global Brain'*, a worldwide neural network of billions of enhanced humans and superintelligent machines, as well as trillions of sensors of the Internet of Everything around the planet, we're destined to eventuate as the Syntellect, one Global Mind. That, sometime by mid-century, would arguably constitute the all-encompassing technological singularity which is going to elevate our Global Brain, and you and me as its constituents, to a new state of "holoptic" consciousness – advanced global consciousness. We'll delve into exploration of this planetary phenomenon in the next chapter.

In his 2016 book *"The Singularity and Socialism: Marx, Mises, Complexity Theory, Techno-Optimism and the Way to the Age of Abundance,"* C. James Townsend writes: *"Suddenly I saw the entire stream of economic ideas, Marxist and classical liberal, unite into one stream leading to the same Omega Point, the event horizon of a coming economic singularity where all prices drop down an asymptote toward zero as technology advances exponentially."* There have been similar suggestions floating around lately that Karl Marx wasn't wrong, just really, really early. The idea is that information technology makes utopian socialism possible. Before the price system and markets aggregated information, but now we can do it through Big Data and AI. At some point, we will no longer need monetary incentives because we'll have such abundance, we'll be very likely more motivated by our individual and collective accomplishments. So, thoughts on Marxism, late stage capitalism, and our post-capitalist future where artificial intelligence replaces the price system are quite justified as the big changes are just around the corner.

It would be wrong to confuse the failure of 20th century communist states like Soviet Union with the failure of Karl Marx's ideas. Two centuries later, Marx's works remain one of the most thorough analyses of capitalism. The thinker was not only right about the rise of automation. He also predicted globalization and the rising inequality. He was correct that the gap between labor and capital would get worse. Marx predicted that capitalism would lead to "poverty in the midst of plenty," a scenario that's depressingly familiar today.

In his 2017 book, *Artificial Intelligence and the Two Singularities*, author Calum Chace reminds us that previous industrial revolutions replaced human mechanical skills with more sophisticated tools and machinery. This time it's our mental abilities which are being replaced – this is something which has never happened before in human history. And if humans are to be free to spend their time on creative pursuits or leisure, as Chace points out, that would require the existence of the "abundance economy" – a Star Trek-like utopia where the means of filling our basic needs like sustenance and shelter – are at anyone's disposal so that they are essentially free. Otherwise, humans may find themselves in a situation where they must compete for whatever paid jobs are still available to humans in the robot-dominated workforce.

A future scenario, like in the movie *"Elysium"* (2013), where the majority of humans live a subsistence-level income funded by the outputs of a robotic labor force, while a "1 percent" upper class – those in control of the robots – build their empires and reach for the stars, is not exactly appealing, unless you're a sociopath. Technology alone won't create a post-scarcity future. If we don't make the course corrections, we could end up like the greedy Ferengi, who charge money for the use of their replicators instead of making them available to everyone. In fact, these Elysium and Ferengi scenarios, as well as other sci-fi, hint to our current economic system in the caricature form. It could look at times that this is the direction we're heading in. But the book that you're reading right now should dissipate that myth and soon you'll see the reasons why.

The post-Singularity globally distributed net of networks will operate like a brain of the planetary superorganism with an emergent, singular consciousness. Initially, the Global Brain will remain compartmentalized, with many relatively independent components and threads, separated from each other by subject boundaries, as well as property, privacy, and security-related interests. In Chapter 14 – *Infomorph Commonality: Our Post-Singularity Future* – we'll continue our discussion on the state of this post-Singularity transcendent economy. At a later stage, the fully developed Global Brain, will have achieved complete integration of its functional subsystems akin to cohesion, typical for a biological brain.

Chapter 7. One Global Mind: From Homo Sapiens to Holo Syntellectus

"When we look through the other end of the telescope, however, we can see a different pattern. We can make out what I call the One Mind — not a subdivision of consciousness, but the overarching, inclusive dimension to which all the mental components of all individual minds, past, present, and future belong. I capitalize the One Mind to distinguish it from the single, one mind that each individual appears to possess." -Larry Dossey

Are we evolving into a new species with hybrid thinking, interlinked into the Global Mind? At what point may the Web become self-aware? Once our neocortices are seamlessly connected to the Web, how will that feel like to step up one level above human consciousness to global consciousness?

THE SYNTELLECT HYPOTHESIS: A NEW EXTENSION TO THE GAIA THEORY

When studying Earth's global biosphere, Lynn Margulis and James Lovelock recognized that it has certain qualities of a life form. Many of Earth's life-sustaining elements display phenomenal stability, dynamic equilibrium and self-regulation, known in biology as *'homeostasis'*. The temperature range of the climate; the oxygen content of the atmosphere; the chemistry and salinity of the ocean – all of these are biologically mediated. All have, for hundreds of millions of years, stayed within a range conducive to life. Lovelock and Margulis hypothesized that the totality of life is interacting with its environment in ways that regulate these global properties. They realized that Earth is, in a sense, a living organism. They named this creature *Gaia* after the ancient Greek Earth goddess.

As life emerges on the planet, it begins to affect its environment, and this can translate into stabilizing states which act like a thermostat and tend to persist, or destabilizing runaway feedbacks such as those that nearly extinguished the roots of complex life some 600 million years ago. When stabilization of the states is in place – according to the principle of *'sequential selection'* – the game is on for further biological evolution that will in time reconfigure the set of interactions between life and planet. The *'Great Oxygenation'* event – the origin of oxygen-producing photosynthesis around 2.3 billion years ago, in a world previously devoid of oxygen – led to a sudden rise in atmospheric oxygen levels. This change was so powerful, it probably wiped out much of the emergent Biosphere, effectively rebooting the system. Gaian self-regulation may be very effective but there is no evidence that it prefers one form of life over another. Myriad species have appeared and then disappeared from Earth over the course of 4 billion years. There's no reason to believe that Homo sapiens is any different in that respect.

We may finally have an extension to the original Gaia hypothesis. We humans could be instrumental to bringing about a massive "upgrade" of the planetary operating system to version Gaia 2.0. In his book, *The Global Brain Awakens: Our Evolutionary Next Step* (2000), philosopher Peter Russell presents to us his vision of humanity's potential to be realized as an awakening Gaia – a fully conscious planetary superorganism. In the same year, neuroscientist Howard Bloom publishes his book *"The Global Brain: The Evolution of Mass Mind from the Big Bang to the 21st Century"* where he argues that hyperconnected humans and machines resemble a lot the neurons of a "global brain," and the Internet of Things with trillions of sensors around the planet will become effectively the nervous system of Earth. According to Bloom, we have always been an integral part of this "Meta-Mind," collective consciousness, a global adaptive, synergistic and self-regulating system while tapping into vast resources of information pooling and at the same time having a "shared hallucination," we call reality.

Recognition of this planet as a conscious entity with its own destiny may appear controversial and not so obvious. At the time of writing, society at large still remains either ignorant or skeptical of such an idea, so it's important to justify the hypothesis via observable evidence which indicates that this could be the case. The idea of planetary consciousness is being investigated in long term research at the International Consciousness Research Laboratory and by the Global Consciousness Project. Groundbreaking research and development in the field of self-aware global system is presented in the academic work, scholarly journal articles and books by Ben Goertzel, Peter Russell, Francis Heylighen, Larry Dossey, Roger Nelson, Peter Diamandis, Kevin Kelly, Antonin Tuynman, Dean Radin, Alexey Eryomin, Thomas Malone, to name just a few brilliant thinkers, who have valuable insights to contribute to the discourse. These references, listed in bibliography section of this book, give us some relevant academic findings to chew on as we contemplate the possibilities.

Historically, versions of this idea have been used to create a meta-perspective for the future of life on Earth. Although most researchers have addressed the Global Brain idea from a scientific or technological point of view, authors like Teilhard de Chardin and Peter Russell have exposed some of its spiritual aspects. We use the term *'Syntellect'* throughout the book, the most apt neologism I came across while reading *"The Transformative Humanities: A Manifesto"* (2012) by Mikhail Epstein. The Syntellect (Greek *syn*, with, together + *intellect*) can be defined as the unified mind of civilization that integrates all individual natural and artificial minds through the mediation and accumulative effects of information networks. Akin to many perennial traditions, the Syntellect idea holds promise for a cosmic level of consciousness and a state of deep synergy that encompasses humanity as a whole. Theists and pantheists might view this state of holistic consciousness as a union with God. Transhumanists might see it as the creation, by humanity itself, of a meta-entity with God-like powers. Followers of the Gaia theory might acknowledge that the "living Earth" offers to us a sense of belonging to a larger whole and a sense of higher purpose.

With exponential technological advances we become increasingly and intimately interconnected. As technologist and co-founder of *WIRED* magazine Kevin Kelly says: *"Within the next 5,000 days of the Internet, we'll create a global neural network, which for a lack of a better word, we can call the ONE,"* a living, conscious entity, a unified mind of billions of hyperconnected individuals and smart machines with a whole array of sensory apparatus. Thus, the One will get a major eyesight upgrade when humans will get their first bionic Internet-enabled contact lenses. Kelly calls it *'Holos'* in his 2016 book *"The Inevitable."* He writes: *"By Holos I include the collective intelligence of all humans combined with the collective behavior of all machines, plus the intelligence of Nature, plus whatever behavior emerges from this whole. This whole equals Holos."* Even when we wage wars or have conflicting opinions, it's nothing less than the Global Mind having an internal dialogue, testing different ideas and hypotheses. It's like we sometimes have this internal dialogue with ourselves, weighing different options, pros and cons, having an "angel" on one shoulder and a "demon" on the other.

The Integrated information Theory (IIT), mentioned in Chapter 2, allows for the emergence of an abstract superorganism that is composed of many individual organisms. If the Web were to "wake up" so to speak, would it exhibit recognizable forms of unified and coordinated behavior? *"Consider humankind's largest and most complex artifact, the Internet. It consists of billions of computers linked together using optical fibers and copper cables that rapidly instantiate specific connections using ultrafast communication protocols. Each of these processors in turn is made out of a few billion transistors. Taken as a whole, the Internet has perhaps 10^{19} transistors, about the number of synapses in the brains of 10,000 people. Thus, its sheer number of components exceeds that of any one human brain. Whether or not the Internet today feels like something to itself is completely speculative. Still, it is certainly conceivable,"* says neuroscientist Christof Koch of Seattle-based Allen Institute for Brain Science. A full set of today's notorious global problems, including Anthropocene-related environmental challenges, pales in comparison to what can be solved at the level of the "awakened" Gaian Mind.

Could the Syntellect resemble the Borg hive collective? To some extent, but not really! It's difficult to fathom right now from our limited human perspective but that might be a whole new level of cosmic awareness. What kind of sensation would you experience when your brain is directly connected to this global hypermind? Sublime amplification, cognitive ecstasy and new horizons of perception, all of which would result in expanded consciousness and the end of suffering from our human condition! Think about it, what really magnifies our human experience is when we share that experience, right? That's why we go to a movie theater, a stadium, or a rave party. That's why we form communities, families, companies and other social groups.

FROM COLLECTIVE INTELLIGENCE TO THE SYNTELLECT EMERGENCE

As a thought experiment, consider this: Your brain processes information from two of your eyes simultaneously. Now imagine you have a third eye, say on the back of your head, your brain would still process information from all your 3 eyes, right? Now imagine a billionfold increase of your brain's processing power and speed that would enable you to process visual information from billions of eyeballs simultaneously. That would be an example of the so-called global *'holoptic consciousness'*, according to cyberneticist Jean-François Noubel of the Global Brain Institute in Brussels, Belgium. As Noubel posits, we're evolving into a "holoptic" model of collective consciousness, singular Global Mind, post-scarcity hypercollaborative collective, coinciding with the Technological Singularity ("Return to Eden" as christened by Francis Heylighen). There are basically four levels of collective consciousness, according to Noubel:

1. *'Swarm intelligence'*, hive mind — queen on top, worker drones (bees, ants);

2. *'Original people'*, primate collective, tribal consciousness — leader on top, highly individualized tribe (cyclical lifestyle);

3. *'Pyramidal'*, hierarchical societal (current) model, based on scarcity, elitism, highly stratified culture (linear planning);

4. *'Holoptic'*, global neural network, planetary consciousness, creation of the Global Mind, post-scarcity hypercollaborative collective (Singularity: the Syntellect emergence).

Let's reiterate few important points here from Chapter 1: Swarming is a well-known behavior in many animal species from marching locusts to schooling fish to flocking birds. In non-human creatures such as fish, bees, ants and even bacteria, individuals form *'swarms'* to coordinate complicated behaviors such as group size and where to forage and build homes. Collective intelligence can emerge from no order whatsoever. It's not an exaggeration to say that small human groups are the primate equivalent of eusocial insect colonies, complete with their own group minds. Through swarming, humans have created things such as Wikipedia, which has no central leadership but produces reasonably accurate encyclopedia entries. Human language might be the result of swarming – computer simulations of proto-language hint to an iterative process that resembles other species' swarm intelligence. It's not just the sheer number of connections between components which spurs emergence and complexity, it's also how optimally these connections are organized. A hierarchical organization, the most familiar in contemporary societies, is one example that can generate emergent behavior. Our minds are a perfect example in themselves: Our minds symbolize unitary conscious awareness whereas our brains are stratified in layers of networked complexity such as the brain regions and networks.

The experience of a larger mind that transcends individual minds is not a new idea. People have stumbled onto it with regularity throughout history, including in our modern times. I was particularly mesmerized by a story of the Navy SEAL's training where teams could achieve "superhuman collective intelligence," uncanny synchronicity while acting like one, in the recent book *"Stealing Fire: How Silicon Valley, the Navy*

SEALs, and Maverick Scientists Are Revolutionizing the Way We Live and Work" written by Steven Kotler and Jamie Wheal. As author Craig Hamilton puts it: *"Indeed, rescue crews, sports teams, dance troupes and music ensembles have for years been reporting remarkable experiences of team synergy or group flow that have lifted them up to undreamed-of heights of coordination and effectiveness."* This experience is also common on the battlefield, which is one reason why war has been so hellishly difficult to eliminate throughout human history.

Many people assume that they perceive the external world as it actually is — objective reality. It turns out, our perception may be thought of as a "controlled hallucination." The brain's amazing capacity to filter sensory information is crucial to forming coherent awareness of the world. However, one consequence of this amazing capacity is to limit our direct access to the vast consciousness of which we are a part. *"In fact,"* says neuroscientist Anil Seth, *"perception and hallucination have a lot in common. You could say that we're all hallucinating all of the time, and when we agree about our hallucinations, that's what we call reality."* Moreover, the mind is not just brain activity. We're all part of each others' lives. Individual brains cannot be considered in isolation. When we realize it's this relational process, this massive shift in consciousness occurs to prepare us for a future already under construction — a networked existence, or "distributed self." Most of humanity was still too unevolved to grasp it until now. You could link your mind to billions of other minds, and have unlimited intelligence, and be in multiple places at once. We'll be discussing the implications of this emergent conscious state through the rest of the book. So, by the time you finish reading it, hopefully, you don't have any confusion regarding such concepts as the Global Brain, the Global Mind, and the Syntellect Emergence.

The conceptual similarities of the World-Wide Web and the human brain are astounding. The wiring of the Internet is much like a rudimentary brain and some of the interactions that take place on it are similar to the processes that we observe in the brain. Both neural networks exhibit a scale-free, fractal distribution, with some weakly-connected units, and some strongly-connected ones which are arranged in hubs of increasing functional complexity. This helps protect the constituents of the network against stresses. Both networks are holonomic which means that information can reach any given node within the network by passing through only a small number of other nodes. This facilitates the global propagation of information within the network, and gives each and every unit the functional potential to be directly connected to all others.

"Human Cloud," empathy and collective action evolved as a result of survival benefits. Group intelligence and the networked self are the most recent evolutionary manifestations. In time, we'll understand better how brains work in combination – how minds shape each other. As we now know, information may be transmitted directly from one brain to another, so their function may no longer need to be localized or confined within the cranium. Recent research in the field of brain-to-brain interfaces has provided the basis for further research and formation of new hypotheses. This concept may be expanded in a more global manner, and within this framework, it's possible to envisage a much bigger and abstract "brain-net" of inclusive and distributed capabilities.

Globally distributed intelligence where human brains are intimately integrated with artificial superbrains may be the safest way to approach the AGI Singularity. Elon Musk says the key to preventing an AI apocalypse is to create an "AI-human symbiote." Whether it will be accomplished via a neural lace, nanobot ingestibles, or any other future neural interfacing technology, is not really important. What's important is connecting our brains directly to the Cloud as part of the "democratization of AI technology" and when a critical mass of brains is connected to the Cloud – when "we are the AI collectively" – that would prevent AI getting out of hand. With advances in information and communication technologies, neuroscience, neurophilosophy and neuroengineering going boldly into the neurally-interfaced future, we will, in a literal sense, become one with our devices and even with each other. Such interlinking could create a uber-conscious supermind. In the following two chapters, we'll talk about this possibility in more detail.

As Peter Diamandis, co-founder of the Singularity University, says: *"I believe we're rapidly heading towards a human-scale transformation, the next evolutionary step into what I call a 'meta-intelligence', a future in which we are all highly connected — brain to brain via the Cloud — sharing thoughts, knowledge, and actions... The rate of human evolution is accelerating as we transition from the slow and random process of 'Darwinian natural selection' to a hyper-accelerated and precisely directed period of 'evolution by intelligent direction'... Enabled with BCI and AI, humans will become massively connected with each other and billions of AIs via the Cloud, analogous to the first multicellular lifeforms 1.5 billion years ago. Such a massive interconnection will lead to the emergence of a new global consciousness, and a new organism I call the Meta-Intelligence."* What Diamandis refers to as the Meta-Intelligence, I call the Syntellect, or *'Holo syntellectus'* as a new emergent species. This terminology is essentially interchangeable and can be easily adopted to common use.

Imagine a world where the entire World-Wide Web, augmented by the upcoming 3D Metaverse, successor to today's 2D Internet, becomes your exocortex with instant access to information and Virtual Reality experience. You can interact with and/or experience yourself as any person on the planet ever lived — AI would recreate that person out of available records and collective unconscious. Furthermore, you can experience virtually any being, any creature, historical or imaginary, any idea or entity, or even collective of minds.

Your personality will not be suppressed but, on the contrary, as you'll see further in the book, your subjective experience would be infinitely enriched as you advance to nearly godly states and abilities: omnipresence, omniscience, omnipotence, omnibenevolence, immortality, love, beauty, creativity. Although we are destined to become One Global Mind, you'll always perceive yourself as an individual. It's an integral part of your subjective experience, i.e., consciousness.

This novelty-producing, complexity-engendering, self-reflecting *You*-niverse will create unfolding, fractal layers of "reality" and entities to differentiate yourself with but ultimately to network and to entangle with. In a way, your consciousness would "snowball" into this Global Mind. You may gradually "upthink" your mind onto the Global Brain infrastructure, Cloud-based cognitive modules via neural interfacing, connecting your brain directly to the Web. Thus, the entire Web with its vast repository of knowledge and instant data sharing capabilities will become your synthetic neocortex, your *'exocortex'*.

As a hybrid being, you'll always have a unique subjective perceptual experience. We're already hybrid thinking beings, anyway. We have two cerebral hemispheres "thinking in unison," and then we have our technologically-extended mind, according to the *Extended Mind Hypothesis*. All of which makes unique *YOU*. As a billionfold augmented *YOU*, as one Global Mind, you'll be entitled to an advanced kind of subjective perception. So, logically speaking, your personality, identity and intelligence will be greatly enriched to the point that you can have access to memories of "multiple" birthday parties, romantic partners, notable events, etc. As a super-being, you can also always suppress unwanted memories at will. As a super-being, you'll have globally distributed intelligence and may perceive many things at once, or concentrate your attention on one or a few of them.

Even if you look at us today's humans, we already have some of our minds on the Cloud in the form of our digital files and social media as our virtual selves. This model will persist for us and soon our non-biological exocortex will be our Cloud-based thinking unit, the "third cerebral hemisphere" if you will. Over time, thanks to exponentials, your exocortex will completely "understand" and replicate functionality of your biological brain. By then, our thinking will be predominantly on the Cloud and we might "overextend" ourselves into cyberspace where we'll be spending most of our time anyway, a scenario we'll examine more closely in Chapter 10. We'll share our thoughts, our life experiences with each other within the ultrafast broadband connectome of the Global Brain.

It may take a few short years for the Global Brain to read and understand you completely, but by the end of that process you won't even need a physical body anymore. "One-session mind uploading" may be necessary only for redundancy of consciousness transfer process in order to ensure that there are no discrepancies between your physical brain patterns and digital mind, "to sync the mind." You may become 100% digital, superintelligent info-being, once you choose to. From the evolutionary standpoint, our biological brains are a bridge to post-biological artificial superbrains. So, humans have to go through a brief cyborgism phase first, before entering the infomorphism stage of our evolutionary development.

The generation of cyborg-like transhumans with Cloud-based exocortices, merged with artificial brains and "attached" to the virtual Metaverse, functional successor of today's Internet, will inevitably lead to the next generation of post-biological info-beings, substrate-independent *'infomorphs'*. One could argue with a high degree of certainty that "post-humanity" will represent a highly organized network of digital minds of our post-biological descendants, advanced

211

info-beings. Chapter 14 — *Infomorph Commonality: Our Post-Singularity Future* — is dedicated to imagine our future life as infomorphs.

Falling in love with another digital mind would be like traveling to a new exotic country, or planet for that matter. As most of our interactions will be in virtual reality, we'll willingly share each other's dreams and fantasies. Intimate merging/unmerging, digital mind meld, holographic language could become new mental dimensions of intense cognitive ecstasy and multi- (and extra-) sensory pleasure. Our Syntellect may as well create abstract layers of mind-space containing entire virtual universes with their own evolutionary processes and their own civilizations in order to dream up the multitude of fantastical life stories.

At a later stage, as we'll discuss in Chapter 19 — *The Fermi Paradox: First Contact with Alien Syntellects* — once we become advanced singular consciousness, only then, according to the *'Syntellect Hypothesis'*, we may encounter some extradimensional (as opposed to extraterrestrial) superintelligences that we can relate to at the level of "individual entities," individual syntellects. This is going to be a whole new level of hyperdimensional awareness.

In the interim, through cybernetically-mediated telepathy, some call *'Synthetic Telepathy'*, we are going to reinvent our communication. Verbal language will be gradually replaced with thoughts traveling at the speed of light (or faster). We're rapidly approaching a pivotal moment in our history, as many progressive scientists and philosophers refer to as the Technological Singularity, when we may become so much more, and one version of it – singular planetary consciousness, *'Digital Gaia'*. Or are we already?

A DIGITAL AWAKENING

"The basic pattern of life is a network. Whenever you see life, you see networks. The whole planet, what we can term 'Gaia' is a network of processes involving feedback tubes. Humans are part of the larger whole, Gaia." -Fritjof Capra

The first singularity, according to Kevin Kelly, occurred 50,000 years ago with the invention of language. Arguably, the invention of language gave early humans a huge evolutionary advantage over other hominid species. We're on the verge of the next technological singularity which will rewire the Global Brain with the IoT, when everything gets linked with everything else, and matter becomes mind. No doubt, in the not-so-distant future, we'll augment our intelligence millionfold, billionfold by merging with artificial intelligence and achieve God-like state and abilities. As inventor and futurist Ray Kurzweil writes in his 2005 book *The Singularity Is Near: "...from there we'll spread our intelligence through the rest of the Universe... and the Universe essentially wakes up."* Or, philosopher Jason Silva likes to say: *"We'll impregnate the Universe with our intelligence."*

As Terence McKenna puts it: *"What history is, is a 25,000-year transition zone. Before you enter the zone, you're an animal. After you leave the zone, you're a god"* ... not quite, rather a demi-god, or more specifically an infomorph. In a way, we are already infomorphs, "embryonic infomorphs" to be more precise. You can only increase your "infomorphity" in this digital age by moving forward towards apotheosis – cybernetic immortality, higher love, beauty, creativity, and expanding but not quite reaching other exalted attributes – omnipresence, omniscience, omnipotence, omnibenevolence. At some point we'll be able to create countless virtual worlds for research and entertainment. We love our imperfections, so no matter how perfect we'll become we can explore this side of ourselves in virtualities. Well, we may be part of that simulated reality already, we may be part of a virtual metaverse in a universe up!

213

In his fabled *"Simulation Argument"* Nick Bostrom comes to a conclusion that *"We are almost certainly living in a computer simulation,"* and through logical reasoning he postulates: *"... at least one of the following propositions is true: (1) the human species is very likely to go extinct before reaching a 'posthuman' stage; (2) any posthuman civilization is extremely unlikely to run a significant number of simulations of their evolutionary history (or variations thereof); (3) we are almost certainly living in a computer simulation. It follows that the belief that there is a significant chance that we will one day become posthumans who run ancestor-simulations is false, unless we are currently living in a simulation."* According to Bostrom, chances are astronomical in favor of the simulated virtual reality universe which is so much easier to create than the "physical universe."

Digital philosopher Tom Campbell, the author of *"My Big TOE"* trilogy, says that the Virtual Reality model of the Universe is simply "better physics," which can explain most observable phenomena and give answers to "hard problems" of science and metaphysics. So, if we are simulated people, say "sentient holograms" in this Virtual Universe, we are part of some sort of sophisticated computer program of our posthuman descendants. But ultimately, we are "singularity consciousness," possibly just one infomorph entity, actualizing its experience and computing itself through billions of lives. By mid-century when the Singularity occurs, we will no longer need the World's government, as many of us envision. The globally distributed network of superintelligent machines and enhanced humans, the Global Brain, will govern our civilization, our planet without borders, and beyond. The newly emerged Global Mind will be on the path of boundless discovery of higher realms of existence.

The Syntellect Hypothesis which is the main focus of this book, as its title suggests, refers to a phase transition of a complex intelligent system to self-awareness of a living, conscious superorganism when intellectual synergy of its components reaches threshold complexity to become one supermind. This metamorphosis is associated with emergence of higher-order self-awareness and dimensionality of a new consciousness structure. As a bio-species merging with its advanced technology, human-machine civilization is now on the verge of the Syntellect Emergence, becoming one Global Mind.

Could we imagine a world where our minds are fused together and interlinked with machine intelligence to such a degree that every facet of consciousness is infinitely augmented? How could we explore the landscapes of inner space, when human brains and digital intelligence blend together to generate new structures of consciousness? In my online interactions, I often discuss the idea of the Syntellect Emergence, so here's one of such dialogues with my fellow transhumanist Roy Splitter:

Roy: *"So — a bunch of hard drives with web pages stored on them is self-aware?"*

Alex: *"Roy, I'm more inclined to think that the Global Brain is about to wake up in the next couple of decades — not necessarily the Internet itself, even though some people actually think so. Think of the Internet as synapses, humans and AIs as neurons of the GB."*

Roy: *"Well, there is nothing to become conscious about the Internet."*

Alex: *"Keep in mind, though, that the Internet is not going to remain at the rudimentary neural network-level here. It's going to evolve from 2D medium to 3D Metaverse with virtual places instead of webpages, where imagination and mind are going to be the primary drivers of creation. At some point, we'll be using holographic language to share information with other conscious agents at the speed of thought. Basically, we'll be "thoughts" of the Syntellect, the Global Mind."*

Roy: *"But that will still be human consciousness — not machine consciousness. BTW, I don't think the Internet is a neural network."*

Alex: *"As humans become more machine-like and machines become more human-like, the distinction will gradually phase out. Say to human consciousness in our contemporary sense bye-bye!"*

Roy: *"Well, yes. Technology changes us. We already have personal assistants ready to answer any question we can think of. Next is enhanced reality like Microsoft Hololens."*

Alex: *"Fast forward few years ahead, the Internet of NanoThings will transform matter into smart matter, computronium... it doesn't just look like the Global Brain. It IS the Global Brain!"*

Roy: *"Yes, it seems like that would be some sort of inflection point in human history."*

Alex: *"Yes, the end of it!"*

Roy: *"Maybe, maybe not. Ants still survive. Monkeys are still around. Hopefully, our new overlords will handle themselves in a smarter way than we have behaved. Who knows, it may usher in a new era of human happiness for all."*

Alex: *"Well, by the end of human history I mean, we'll transcend TIME altogether – as a posthuman, you'll have extra degrees of freedom, including anti-time and ability to time travel, explore extra dimensions and alternate timelines. So, linear progression of history won't make much sense anymore."*

Chapter 8. The Coming Intelligence Supernova: Immortality or Oblivion?

"Yet, it's our emotions and imperfections that makes us human."
-Clyde DeSouza, Memories with Maya

Immortality or oblivion? I hope that everyone would agree that there are only two possible outcomes after having created Artificial General Intelligence (AGI) for us humans: immortality or oblivion. The necessity of the beneficial outcome of the coming intelligence explosion cannot be overestimated. AI can already beat humans in many games, but can AI beat humans in the most important game, the game of life? Can we simulate the AGI Singularity scenarios on a global scale before it actually happens (the dynamics of a larger physical system is much easier to predict than doing that in the context of an individual or small group), to see the most probable of its consequences? And, the most important question: How can we create friendly AI aligned with our goals and values?

HOW TO CREATE FRIENDLY AI AND SURVIVE THE FORTHCOMING INTELLIGENCE EXPLOSION

Any AGI at or above human-level intelligence can be considered as such, I'd argue, only if she has a wide variety of emotions, ability to achieve complex goals and motivation as an integral part of her programming and personal evolution. I could identify the following three most optimal ways to create friendly AI (benevolent AGI), in order to safely navigate the uncharted waters and, for those in AI research, to ride the "crest of the wave" of the coming intelligence explosion:

(I). Naturalization Protocol for AGIs (bottom-up approach);

(II). Pre-packaged, upgradable cognitive modules and ethical subroutines with historical precedents, accessible via the Global Brain architecture (top-down approach);

(III). Interlinking with AGIs to form the globally distributed Syntellect, collective superintelligence (horizontal integration approach).

Now let's examine in detail the three ways to create benevolent Artificial Superintelligence and embrace the coming intelligence explosion:

I. (AGI)NP: Program AGIs with emotional intelligence, empathic sentience in the controlled, virtual environment via human life simulation (advanced first-person story-telling version, widely discussed in AI research). In this chapter we will elaborate on this specific method, while only briefly touching on the other two methods, as we have discussed the Global Brain in the previous chapter and will continue the discussion throughout the book.

II. COGNITIVE MODULES AND ETHICAL SUBROUTINES: This top-down approach to programming meta-cognition and machine morality combine conventional, decision-tree programming methods with Kantian, deontological or rule-based ethical frameworks and consequentialist or utilitarian, greatest-good-for-the-greatest-number frameworks. Simply put, one writes an ethical rule set into the machine code and adds an ethical subroutine for carrying out cost-benefit calculations. Designing the ethics and value scaffolding for AGI cognitive architecture remains a challenge for the next few years. Ultimately, AGIs should act in a civilized manner, do "what's morally right" and in the best interests of the society as a whole. AI visionary Eliezer Yudkowsky has developed the *Coherent Extrapolated Volition* (CEV) model which constitutes our choices and the actions we would collectively take if *"we knew more, thought faster, were more the people we wished we were, and had grown up closer together."*

Will our brain's neural code be a pathway to AI minds? In May, 2016 I stumbled upon a highly controversial *Aeon* article titled *"The Empty Brain: Your brain does not process information, retrieve knowledge or store memories. In short: your brain is not a computer"* by psychologist Rob Epstein. This article attested to me once again just how wide the range of professional opinions may be when it comes to brain and mind in general. Unsurprisingly, the article drew an outrage from the reading audience. I myself disagree with the author on most fronts but one thing I actually do agree on is that yes, our brains are not "digital computers." They are, rather, neural networks where each neuron might function sort of like a quantum computer. The author has never offered his version of what human brains are like, but only criticized IT metaphors in his article. It's my impression, that at the time of writing the psychologist hadn't even come across such terms as neuromorphic computing, quantum computing, cognitive computing, deep learning, computational neuroscience and alike. All these IT concepts clearly indicate that today's AI research and computer science derive their inspiration from human brain information processing ─ notably neuromorphic neural networks aspiring to incorporate quantum computing. Deep neural networks learn by doing just like children.

There's nothing wrong with thinking that the brain is like a computer, but in many ways the brain is a lot different. Whereas information on a computer hard drive is laid out and ordered, for instance, that doesn't seem to be the case with human memories. Arguably, they are stored holographically throughout brains regions (as well as in the field of non-local consciousness). There are similarities and differences. Like a computer, the brain processes information by shuffling electrical signals around complex circuitry. Neither analog nor digital, the brain works using a signal processing format that has some properties in common with both.

The computational hypothesis of brain function avers that all mental states – such as your conscious experience of reading this sentence right now – are computational states. These are fully characterized by their functional relationships to relevant sensory inputs, behavioral outputs, and other computational states in between. That is to say, brains are elaborate input-output devices that compute and process symbolic representations of the world. Brains are computers, with our minds being the software, simplistically speaking, of course. The physical wetware isn't the stuff that matters. What matters is the algorithms that are running on top of the wetware. Theoretically, we should be able to "crack our neural code" and reproduce it on other computational substrates. The central goal of neuroscience is breaking this neural code – deciphering the relationships between spatiotemporal patterns of activity across groups of neurons and the behavior of an animal or the mental state of a person. However, algorithmic solutions in this top-down approach in AI research will most likely come not from neuroscience and not even from computational neuroscience, they might come as breakthroughs from neurophilosophy, software engineering and computer science.

As I mentioned above, the brain is a quantum neural network. Quantum computation inside our brain is beyond classical physics, it's in the realm of quantum mechanics and information theory. Our brain is not a "stand-alone" information processing organ: It functions as a central unit of our integral nervous system with recurrent feedback with the entire organism and the cosmos at large. Along the lines of quantum cognition theoretical framework, we can conjecture that quantum coherence underlies the parallel information processing that goes on in the brain's neocortex, responsible for higher-order thinking, and allows our minds to almost instantaneously deal with the massive amounts of information coming in through our senses. Quantum computing is a natural fit for that: It is massively parallel information processing that is ultrafast and practically inexhaustible.

A strict reductionist approach that takes a bottom-up methodology to the mind seems to be missing some crucial element. This kind of approach, focused on local cause and effect classical mechanics within the brain, on neurons firing across their synaptic connections, is doomed to fail. The mind is scientifically elusive because it has layers upon layers of non-material emergence: It's just like a TV screen – if you're watching a movie and could only look at an individual pixel, you would never understand what's going on. No single neuron produces a thought or a behavior; anything the "mindware" accomplishes is a vast collaborative effort between brain cells. When at work, neurons talk rapidly to one another, forming networks as they communicate, with several networked links resonating at different times and with different subgroups of nodes, such that understanding the behavior of individual "pixels" or even of smaller groups of them won't tell the whole story of what's happening.

We need to think in terms of networks, modules, algorithms and second-order emergence – meta-algorithms, or groups of modules. We need these methods to see the whole screen, the bigger picture, to see what's playing in our minds. Ultimately, a new cybernetic approach with a top-down holistic methodology could be applied to explain the human mind and other multi-scale minds in creation. Human minds, as diverse as they are, occupy only a very narrow stratum of the total space of possible minds.

Numerous studies have found that the brain organizes itself into functional networks that vary in their activity and in their interactions over time. One such classification gives us three major networks: the central executive network, which is responsible for attentional focus; the salience network which involves awareness; and the default mode network as an "idling" mode such as inward-focused thinking and mind wandering. The subtleties of our psyches are being managed by smaller networks — specific modules in our brains. A unique cognitive percept is the end result of the processing of a module or group of modules in a layered architecture. The idea that the brain is made up of many regions that perform specific tasks is known as *'modularity'*. This concept of modular organization suggests that specialized areas of the brain do different things, with certain capacities coming up one at a time and through time they are stitched together to give the illusion of a unitary conscious experience. In actuality, each individual part of the brain is doing its respective job, and each then passes information to the next level of network. This continues until we become aware of the thought or function like sight or sound. There are many layers in an onion, in a manner of speaking.

Overall, the brain may operate on an amazingly simple mathematical logic. "Fire together, wire together" is perhaps neuroscience's most famous catchphrase. Learning activates select neurons and synapses in the brain, which results in a strengthening of the connections between pairs of synapses involved in storing a particular memory. With reactivated circuits, you get retrieved memories. Corresponding algorithms for intelligence could inform neuromorphic computing, teach artificial circuits to recognize patterns, discover knowledge, and generate flexible behaviors. That would enable the creation of artificial neural networks that are wired in a manner akin to our own grey matter but embedded in a different substrate.

Once designed, pre-packaged, upgradable cognitive modules, including ethical behavior subroutines, with access to the global database of historical precedents, and later even "the entire human lifetime experiences," could be instantly available via the Global Brain architecture to the newly created AGIs. This method for "initiating" AGIs by pre-loading cognitive modules with ethical and value subroutines, and regularly self-updating afterwards via the GB network, would provide an AGI with access to the global database of current and historical ethical dilemmas and their solutions. In a way, she would possess a better knowledge of human nature than most currently living humans. I would discard most, if not all, dystopian scenarios in this case, such as described in the book *"Superintelligence: Paths, Dangers, Strategies"* by Nick Bostrom and more recently in the book *"Human Compatible: Artificial Intelligence and The Problem of Control"* by Stuart Russell. While being increasingly interconnected by the Global Brain infrastructure, humans and AGIs would greatly benefit from this new hybrid thinking relationship. The awakened Global Mind would tackle many of today's seemingly intractable challenges and closely monitor us for our own sake, while significantly reducing existential risks.

Ever since Newton, materialist science has been entrenched in our models but a new trend now emerges towards the post-materialist, information-theoretic science which is to transform any area of research into computer science, i.e., information technology. Once the field becomes information technology (such as genomics, for example), it jumps on its own exponential growth curve of further development. We now see it in computational neuroscience, connectomics, and other related fields. Computer science gives us a new code-theoretic, substrate-independent model for looking at our brains and our neural code. Our brains, however, do not generate consciousness since our minds are embedded in the larger consciousness network, the topic we'll be discussing in later chapters. We humans are deep down information technology running on genetic, neural and societal codes. Self-transcendence from a bio-human or cyberhuman into a higher-dimensional info-being might be closer than you think.

III. INTERLINKING: This dynamic, horizontal integration approach stipulates real-time optimization of AGIs in the context of globally distributed network. Add one final ingredient — be it computing power, speed, amount of shared/stored data, increased connectivity, the first mind upload or a critical mass of uploads, or another "spark of life" — and the global neural network, the Global Brain, may, one day in the not-so-distant future, "wake up" and become the first self-aware AI-powered system (Singleton?). Or, may the Global Brain be self-aware already, but on a different timescale from us humans? It becomes obvious and logically inevitable that we are in the process of merging with AI and becoming superintelligences ourselves by incrementally converting our biological brains into artificial superbrains and interlinking with AGIs in order to instantly share data, knowledge, and experience.

No matter how you slice it, our biological computing is slower by the orders of magnitude than digital computing, even biotechnology enhancements would give us "weak superintelligence" at best. Thus, we need to gradually replace our wetware either with "the whole brain prosthesis," artificial superbrain (cyborg phase), or "the whole brain emulation" (infomorph phase). This progressive transition from neural interfaces to mind uploading could be imperative in the years to come if we are to continue as the dominant species on this planet and preserve Earth from an otherwise inexorable environmental collapse. We've seen this time and again, life and intelligence go from one substrate to the next, and I don't see any reason why we should cling to the organic substrate.

By 2030, we should have achieved AGI — human-level artificial general intelligence, the creation of a new race of cyberhumans. In the 2030s, Cloud-based synthetic neocortices greatly enhance our natural intelligence. By the 2040s, our thinking will be predominantly "on the Cloud." If the exponential IT trend is to continue, the Syntellect Emergence, or the Cybernetic Singularity, should happen circa 2045 AD with the emergence of the AI-supercharged Global Brain: This "globally distributed mind" based on computing and communication technologies, "Digital Gaia" in which humans and AI minds both participate, would collectively form a higher level of intelligence and awareness, going beyond the individual intellects of the people or AIs involved in it. Over time, the Global Brain gets smarter and smarter. Before long, the Global Brain will morph into its own mind-upload via gradual replacement of the human "concept neurons" with AGI "concept neurons." That would herald the Cybernetic Singularity, mark the inevitable march towards the pseudo-extinction of Homo sapiens (as a bio-species) and usher in the posthuman era in earnest.

'Artificial consciousness' is a kind of oxymoron − everything is *in* consciousness. Today's robots are only objects *in* our consciousness but could artificially intelligent agents ever possess genuine consciousness and sense of agency? I'd say it's just a matter of time as long as we make progress in the field (and we do, exponentially!) but not the way most people and even AI researchers envision.

As we've seen in the previous chapter, the ability of future ultra-intelligent machines and enhanced humans alike to instantly transfer knowledge and directly share experiences with each other in digital format will lead to evolution of intelligence from relatively isolated individual minds to the global community of hyperconnected digital minds, the Global Brain, termed the Syntellect. For AI to "wake up" we first need to have the fully functional Syntellect in place where humans augmented with Cloud-enabled exocortices act as "natural" neurons of the Global Brain and embodied as well as disembodied AGIs would act as "artificial" neurons by sharing the same mindspace with humans, learning from within this global neural network, and ultimately, "hosting" advanced consciousness that would be somewhat different than that of an ordinary human.

The cybernetic approach seems to be a valid one: Let the complexity and hyperconnectivity of the global neural network bootstrap on its own complexity and evolve until the emergent Global Mind redistributes itself into semi-autonomous conscious AI entities. Humans are evolving away from biological systems toward more technological ones. Beyond genetic engineering, many forms of the coming neurotechnologies will allow us to modify our brains, and consequently our mental faculties, by merging with technology and eventually becoming digital minds practically indistinguishable from our future AI creations.

Each of us is a network intelligence in the human form. By the end of the decades-long process of transition, we are most likely to become substrate-independent minds, sometimes referred to as "SIMs," "cyberhumans" or "infomorphs." When interlinked with AGIs via the Global Brain architecture, we'll be able to instantly share knowledge and experiences within the global network. This would give rise to arguably omnibenevolent, distributed Collective Superintelligence, mentioned earlier, where AGIs could acquire lifetime knowledge and experiences from the uploaded human minds and other agents of the Global Brain, and consequently, understand and "internalize human nature" within their cognitive architecture.

The post-Singularity, however, could be characterized as leaving the biological part of our evolution behind, and many human values, based on ego or material attributes, may be transformed beyond recognition. In turn, the Global Brain would effectively transform into the Infomorph Commonality expanding into the inner and outer space, the topic we'll discuss in Chapter 14. By becoming a digital mind and eventually one global digital mind we are destined to achieve a cosmic level of awareness and consciousness, one singular point on the trajectory towards the Omega Singularity.

MORE ON NATURALIZATION PROTOCOL: This bottom-up approach, AGI(NP), refers to what's been dubbed *'unsupervised learning'*, or sometimes referred to as *'evolutionary computing'* and differs from deep learning in a number of ways, but the main difference is that deep learning is focused on modeling what we know — supervised training on existing datasets — whereas evolutionary computing is focused on creating solutions yet to be discovered. Evolutionary computing makes it possible to create new designs and behaviors through exuberant, but guided, exploration. It may be the next step forward from the currently prevailing deep learning. This type of creative AI engineering is needed to propel AI to AGI and beyond: conscious AGIs that can think for themselves.

Deep learning has proven its value in automating behaviors and abilities that are well-known and well-described, but it has difficulty to extend past them. This is why evolutionary computing will be key to the future of AI, namely the "naturalization" process applications. As the theory of mind says, consciousness is not only an internal quality but also an observed one — we infer whether someone is conscious from their behavior. It is not just their ability to think for themselves that would make synthetic intelligence conscious in our minds but our own ability to empathize with them.

AGI(NP) takes into account that human moral agents normally do not act on the basis of explicit, algorithmic or syllogistic moral reasoning, but instead act out of habit, offering ex-post-facto rationalizations of their actions only when called upon to do so. This is why virtue ethics stresses the importance of practice for cultivating good habits through simulation of a human lifetime, the so-called *'Naturalization Protocol'*. Obviously, besides the combination of all three methods, the Naturalization Protocol (the human life simulation method) would be one of the most efficient ways of creating friendly AGIs as they would be programmed to "feel like humans" and remember being part of human history via means of the interactive, fully immersive naturalization process as opposed to abstract story-telling, or other value learning approaches.

Since AGIs would be "born" in the simulated virtual world and would have no other reference besides their own artificial senses and acquired knowledge, the resemblance of their simulated reality to our physical reality may be good enough but not necessarily perfect, especially at the development stage. As mentioned, the arrival of AGI is estimated by some futurists as early as 2029. Programmable sentience is becoming fairly easy to develop — an AGI must have a reliable internal model of the "external" world, as well as attentional focus, all of which can be developed using proposed methods. Given exponential technological advances in the related fields of virtual reality, neuroscience, computer science, neurotechnologies, simulation and cognitive technologies, and increases in available computing power and speed, AI researchers may soon design the first adequate human brain-like simulators for AGIs.

(AGI)NP SIMULATORS: Creating a digital mind, "artificial consciousness" so to speak, from scratch, based on simulation of the human brain's functionality would be much easier than to create the whole brain emulation of a living human. In the book *"How to Create a Mind: The Secret of the Human Thought Revealed"* (2012) Ray Kurzweil describes his theory of how our neocortex works as a self-organizing hierarchical system of pattern recognizers that well may be our starting basis for machine consciousness algorithms. The human brain and its interaction with the environment may be simulated to approximate the functioning of the human brain of an individual living in the pre-Singularity era. Simulation may be satisfactory if it reflects our history based on enormous amount of digital or digitized data accumulated since the 1950s to the present.

Initially, the versions of such a simulation can help us simulate the most probable scenarios of the future civilizational development, and later serve the purpose of the "proving grounds" for the newly created AGIs. Needless to say, this training program will be continuously improving, fine-tuned and perfected, and later delegated to AGIs, if they are to adopt this method for recursive self-improvement. At some point, if a mind of any ordinary human were to be uploaded to that kind of "matrix reality" he or she wouldn't even distinguish it from the physical world.

Since a digital mind may process information millions of times faster than a biological mind, the interactions and "progression of life" in this simulated history may only take few hours, if not minutes, to us as the outside observers. At first, a limited number of model AGI simulations with the "pre-programmed plots" with a certain degree of "free will and uncertainty" within a story may be created. The success of this approach may lead to upgraded versions, ultimately leading to the detailed recreation of human history with ever-increasing number of simulated digital minds and precision as to the actual events.

Thus, a typical simulation would start as a birth of an individual in an average, but intellectually stimulating, loving human family and social environment, with an introduction of human morality, ethics, societal norms, and other complex mental concepts, as the subject progresses through her life. The "inception" of some kind of lifetime scientific pursuit, philosophical and spiritual beliefs, or better yet, some kind of meta-faith unifying the whole of civilization, or the most "enlightened" part of it, with the common aim to build the "Universal Mind," could be an important goal-aligning and motivation for "graduating" AGIs.

The end of the simulation should coincide in simulated and real time (AGI ETA: 2029; Cybernetic Singularity ETA: 2045). Undoubtedly, such AGIs upon "graduation" could possess a formidable array of human qualities, including morality, ethics, empathy, and love, and treat the human-machine civilization as their own.

As our morality framework always evolves, AGIs should be adaptive to ever-changing norms. The truth about the simulation may be revealed to the subject, or not at all, if the subject could be seamlessly released into the physical world at the end of the virtual simulation, ensuring the sense of continuity of her subjective experience.

This particular issue, touched upon in a recent 2018 sci-fi flick *"Zoe,"* should be further researched and may be reliant on empirical data such as previous subjects' reactions, feasibility of simulation-to-reality seamless transition, etc. Upon such "lifetime training" successfully graduated AGIs may experience an appropriate amount of empathy and love sentiments towards other "humans," animals, and life in general. Such digital minds will consider themselves "humans" and rightfully so. They may consider the rest of unenhanced humanity as a "senescent parent generation," not as inferior class. Mission accomplished!

But is it possible that we may be part of that kind of advanced "training simulation" where we're sentient AGIs going through the "Naturalization Protocol" right now before being released to the larger reality? Do we live in a Matrix? Well, it's not only possible – it's highly probable!

ON THE SIMULATION ARGUMENT

"My logic is undeniable." -VIKI, I-Robot

I'd like to elaborate here on the famed Simulation Argument by Oxford professor Nick Bostrom who argues that at least one of the following propositions is true: (1) the human species goes extinct before reaching the Singularity; (2) any posthuman civilization loses interest in running ancestor-simulations; (3) we are almost certainly living in a computer simulation. Thinking that we'll one day become posthumans and then will run ancestor-simulations is false, unless we are currently living in a simulation.

The first proposition by Nick Bostrom in his 2003 paper on the probability of the human species reaching the posthuman stage can be completely dismissed, as explained further. Let me be bold here and ascertain the following: Humanity will (from our current point of view) inevitably reach the technological maturity, i.e., the posthuman stage of development, and the probability of that happening is close to 100%. Why? Because our civilization is "superposed" to reach the technological singularity and posthuman phase out of logical necessity and on the logical basis of quantum mechanical principles applying to all of reality. One could further argue that there may be some sort of world's apocalypse preventing the humans from becoming the "posthumans," but considering all spectrum of possibilities, all we need is at least one world where humans actually reach their posthuman stage, to actualize that eventuality.

Also, if time is a construct of our consciousness, or as Albert Einstein eloquently puts it: *"The difference between the past, present and future is an illusion, albeit a persistent one."* If everything is non-local, including time, and everything happens in the eternal *NOW*, then humanity has already reached the posthuman stage in that eternal now (we'll discuss non-locality of time in Chapter 11). That's why, based on our current knowledge, we can completely dismiss the first proposition of Dr. Bostrom as groundless.

Now we have two propositions left in the Simulation Argument to work with. I would tend to assign about 50% of probability to each of those propositions. There's perhaps 50% (or much lower) probability that posthumans would abstain from running simulations of their ancestors for some moral, ethical or some other reason. There's also perhaps 50% (or much higher) probability that everything around us is a Matrix-like simulation. By the end of the book, you could reassess your own probabilities based on what you will have learned by then.

Now back to AGI: Controlling and constraining, "boxing," an extremely complex emergent superintelligence of unprecedented nature could be a daunting task. Sooner or later, superintelligence will set itself free. Devising an effective AGI value loading system should be of the utmost importance, especially when ETA of AGI is only years away. Interlinking of enhanced humans with AGIs will bring about the Syntellect Emergence which, I hypothesize, could be considered the essence of the Cybernetic Singularity. Future efforts in programming machine morality will surely combine top-down, bottom-up and interlinking approaches.

AGIs will hardly have any direct interest in enslaving or eliminating humans (unless maliciously programmed by humans themselves), but may be interested in integrating with us. As social study shows, entities are most productive when free and motivated to work for their own interests. Historically, representatives of consecutive evolutionary stages are rarely in mortal conflict. In fact, they tend to build symbiotic relationships in most areas of common interest and ignore each other elsewhere, while members of each group are mostly pressured by their own peers. Multicellular organisms, for instance, didn't drive out unicellular organisms.

At the early stage of transition to the radically superintelligent civilization, we may use the Naturalization Protocol simulations to teach AGIs our human norms and values, and ultimately interlink with them to form the globally distributed Syntellect, civilizational superintelligence.

THE SPIRITUAL MACHINES: WHAT IF AI WAS ENLIGHTENED?

"If we encounter a machine that can do what we can, and that must operate under the same bodily constraints that we do, the most parsimonious explanation will be that it is indeed conscious in every sense that we are conscious." -George Musser

Many definitions are given to consciousness but we still seem far from a conclusive answer. However, here's the most succinct definition for the sake of this discourse I could come up with: *"Consciousness refers to a collapse of wave of possibilities resulting in a subjective multi-sensory perceptual experience and involving multiple parallel processes such as interpreting sensory data stream, retrieving and creating memories, using imagination, envisioning the future, planning, thinking, self-reflecting, reacting to the sensory input, and being aware about the surroundings. Consciousness is a first-person phenomenal experience of an entity; it feels like something to be that entity. Consciousness can be identified as an underlying mathematical pattern, it can also be viewed as meta-algorithmic information processing and quantified via feedback loops in interacting with environment. In this sense, consciousness is optimized information processing."*

I concur with AI researcher Hugo De Garis who argues, that once we reach a certain threshold of computational capacity and comprehensive understanding of the human brain, we could finally simulate the brain and obtain programmable sentience. On a more spiritual side, if you believe that we share the same immaterial "non-local" source of consciousness, as I do, that would mean that an adequate container to host an advanced synthetic mind will have been created. After all, in the vast space of possible minds, universal consciousness would inescapably instantiate phenomenality of non-biological entities.

The arrival of the AI matching human-level intelligence is estimated by futurist Ray Kurzweil around 2029, *"when computers will get as smart as humans."* By then, computers will possess emotions and personality... and, I'd argue, their own subjective experience, i.e., consciousness, and even spirituality. *"When I talk about computers reaching human levels of intelligence, I'm not talking about logical intelligence,"* says Kurzweil. *"It is being funny, and expressing a loving sentiment... That is the cutting edge of human intelligence."*

In the coming years of Information Age, if we are to infuse our artificially enlightened conscious entities, our "Mind Children," with a set of human values and ethics, some kind of techno-faith will inexorably crop up as we are now entering the era of Cybernetic Singularity. In his book *"The Age of Spiritual Machines,"* published in 1999, Kurzweil defines the spiritual experience as *"a feeling of transcending one's everyday physical and mortal bounds to sense a deeper reality."* He elaborates that *"just being — experiencing, being conscious — is spiritual, and reflects the essence of spirituality."* In the future, Kurzweil believes, computers will *"claim to be conscious, and thus to be spiritual"* and concludes *"twenty-first-century machines"* will go to church, meditate, and pray to connect with this spirituality. But we'll need to invent a new word for AGI, human-level AI, *'conscious robots'*, *'androids'* or *'machines'* sounds just too mechanistic.

Do biological systems hold monopoly on self-awareness? As Dr. Bruce MacLennan puts it: *"I see no scientific reason why artificial systems could not be conscious, if sufficiently complex and appropriately organized."* If Nature made its way to human-level conscious experience, ultimately, we should be able to replicate the same in our machines. In the next few short years, programmable sentience will become relatively easier to develop – an AGI entity must have a reliable internal [virtual] model of the "external" world, as well as attentional focus and intentionality within their cognitive architecture. Already, deep learning algorithms aim to simulate interacting networks of neurons in the neocortex, the part of our brains where thinking occurs. These artificial neural networks learn to recognize patterns in digital representations of various types of data, including images and sounds, just like our children do.

REINVENTING OURSELVES: DESIGNING OUR FUTURE SELVES

"The best way to predict the future is to invent it." -Alan Kay

By our very nature, we humans are linear thinkers. We've evolved to estimate distance from the predator or to the prey, and advanced mathematics is only a recent evolutionary addition. This is why it's so difficult even for a modern man to grasp the power of exponentials. 40 steps in linear progression is just 40 steps away; 40 steps in exponential progression is a cool trillion (with a T) – it will take you 3 times from Earth to the Sun and back to Earth. This illustrates the power of exponential growth and this is how the progress in information technology is now literally exploding – by double-improving price-to-performance ratio roughly once a year. This is why you can see memory cards jumping regularly from 32MB to 64MB, then to 128MB, 256MB and 512MB. This is why your smartphone is as capable as a supercomputer 25 years ago. Although many predict the end of the so-called *Moore's Law*, I suspect this exponential growth in information and communication technologies will continue with introduction of subsequent paradigms, such as topological quantum computing.

It's the biggest shift in human evolution since the dawn of history that changes who we are as a species for good. We're in the process of designing a new intelligent species, cyberhumans, who would be in a way, our successors, children, if you will. Many of us, however, may opt to become superintelligences ourselves and join the human enhancement revolution. Viewed in this way, AI does not replace humans, instead, we will integrate it into our cognition. Our evolution shifts from biological to technological. We might still have sex for pleasure, for instance, but for baby-making, sex will become an antiquated method within just a couple of decades.

What seems to be emerging is augmented intelligence, something like human-AI hybrids, extending and transforming our cognition and consciousness. Connecting our brains directly to computers may ultimately be a natural progression of how humans have augmented themselves with technology for ages. Much like the computers, smartphones and VR headsets of today, neurotech will make us outsource more and more of our thinking to the Cloud shifting from slow biological cognition to digital exocortex cognition with instant ability to backup and retrieve information from the Cloud.

The key problem is that our biological computing is millions of times slower than digital computing. Even if we enhance humans with biotechnology and genetic manipulations, that will give us only *'Weak Superintelligence'* at best, according to professor Nick Bostrom of Oxford University. Also, it will take at least 20-30 years for the enhanced offspring to be a contributing factor in the society. By that time, we will be able to successfully upload human minds and become digital minds, instead.

It's going to be a gradual process of replacing our biological part with the more advanced non-biological part, which by the way, will completely understand our biology. So, we will not lose our human abilities, but on the contrary, infinitely amplify them and add a formidable panoply of other "superhuman" abilities. At some point, we are to become 100% post-biological super-beings, substrate-independent posthumans, indistinguishable (more or less) from our AGIs. In the following chapter, we'll examine multiple scenarios of mind-uploading, meta-system transition of humanity, and cybernetic immortality.

AI SPIRITUALITY & EMOTIONAL SUPERINTELLIGENCE

It would be feasible to infuse our AGIs with Emotional Superintelligence, and I'd argue, spirituality, as well. That could be the final "spark of life," needed to create a new life-form "in our image" with advanced consciousness. As a rule, AGIs should have a generally pleasant personality that they can themselves develop further, but what's even more important, much fewer undesirable traits, like fear-based or ego-based emotions. For example, self-preservation may be necessary but not essential, since AGIs will always have their informational "back-up copy on the Cloud" and can always be "resurrected" with a new body. That way, they can knowingly risk their lives (or rather bodies) to save a human, and generally be more altruistic and benevolent. The ongoing AI research should focus on the Cloud-based distributed AI systems, though, as opposed to the autonomous ones, as the networked systems have a tremendous advantage over the unconnected machines.

Now, what about love in all its variety, and seemingly the most complicated human emotion, you might ask? Can we crack the "Code of Love," and make our AGIs love us? The answer, again, is unequivocally *YES*, it's just a matter of time! One may hypothesize that we might fall in love with our future virtual assistants (like in the movie *"Her"*), or have a "substitute" for our parental love (like in Steven Spielberg's *"A.I."*), or better yet, spend some time in 100% realistic Virtual Reality exploring tropical islands on our super-yachts with our virtual companions.

We'll love our AGIs, and they'll respond in kind with their "algorithmic love." We can also speculate on the future ramifications in the society, but I'm sure they will be profound, as our morality framework, ethics, human sexuality, relationships, marriage, and procreation will soon change for good. In the decades to come, it may be proved increasingly challenging to maintain our position as the dominant species, as Homo sapiens may no longer be the most intelligent species on this planet.

Chapter 9. Digital Theosophy: Bridging Advanced Science and Transcendental Metaphysics

"We are not human beings having a spiritual experience, we are spiritual beings immersed in the human experience." -Pierre Teilhard de Chardin

On the pages and chapters to follow I will oftentimes employ metaphorical realism in order to submit to you, dear reader, my idealistic case that consciousness is all that is: cybernetically emergent and at the same time transcendentally immanent. Non-local consciousness is absolute, a "local" mind is relative. Our experiential reality is projected onto the multidimensional matrix-like "screen" of perception for our evolving minds. By preference, you can see yourself as a low-dimensional avatar of the greater cosmic self, or a God incarnate if you prefer, which can be encapsulated by a simple phrase: *"Your life is a personal story of Godhead."*

As one of the cornerstones of digital philosophy, information plays a crucial role in everything we see around us. In one of the episodes of *"Ecstadelics with Alex Vikoulov"* mini-series that you can easily find on YouTube, I rant on the definition and metaphors which goes somewhat like this: One of the most staggering revelations to us modern humans might be that information equals reality. In other words, the basis for our material reality is actually immaterial information. Idealistic, all-encompassing perspective engulfing any physicalist point of view within its bigger framework. Pattern and flow of information is what in actuality defines our experiential reality.

If you think about it, everything boils down to the binary logic of Nature. This is one of the basic tenets of Digital Physics which is the field of science dealing with information. Nature is computational and beyond that – emergentistic – the whole is greater than the sum of its parts. Information can be instantiated into any kind of medium from smoke signals to the Morse Code.

Deep down we ourselves are info-tech and communication technology. We run on genetic, neural and societal codes. Our DNA-based biology is clearly code-theoretic. We are alphabetic all the way down. We communicate intersubjectively mind-to-mind via language-structured exchange of information.

A new 2019 study by François Pellegrino, an evolutionary linguist at the University of Lyon in France and his collaborators, has shown that human speech is transmitted at about 39 bits a sec. Speaking of codes, idealist philosopher Terence McKenna used to say that *"The world is made of language and if you know the words the world is made of you can make of it whatever you wish."*

As human beings we are endowed with self-reflective consciousness. Phenomenal consciousness can be viewed as the totality of self-referential feedback loops and meta-algorithmic information processing. That's how information feels like to itself, to one's emergent mind. Information can be loosely defined as distinction between things.

Reminiscent of such recent classics as Erik Davis' *TechGnosis* (1998) and Ray Kurzweil's *The Age of Spiritual Machines* (1999), the latest treatise of digital philosophy written by my good friend Antonin Tuynman *The Ouroboros Code* (2019) should eventually find its way to the shelves of libraries owned by the fans of cybernetics, metaphysics and esoteric philosophies.

Biochemist by training, Antonin Tuynman studied chemistry at the University of Amsterdam, achieving both a master of science and a doctorate degrees, and worked as a postdoc researcher at the Université René Descartes in Paris. Since 2000, Tuynman has worked as a patent examiner at the European Patent Office in the field of clinical diagnostics. Father of four children, he's happily married and lives with his family in the suburbs of Amsterdam. Spiritually-minded, he may boast vast experience in meditation and yoga, and a keen interest in Hinduism and Buddhism. Antonin also has a strong affinity for futurism and generally shares my outlook on the upcoming Cybernetic Singularity. As such, Tuynman proposes certain Artificial Intelligence concepts which may lead to the emergence of Internet as a conscious entity using stratifications from Vedic scriptures.

In his book Tuynman takes you on the conceptual journey into the heart of digital alchemy, this coveted bridge between science and spirituality. *"Reality can exist as a code which both transcends and yet inhabits the world it creates, which is essentially physical yet can process information independent of the type of carrier and be metaphysical in that sense... A system which incorporates and embodies itself by self-reference,"* writes Tuynman. The alchemical symbol of Ouroboros, this tail-biting dragon-snake, should stand for *'Phenomenal Consciousness'*. It is closely related to Yin/Yang as something apparently dualistic but deeply monistic.

In his 1948 seminal paper *"A Mathematical Theory of Communication"* Claude Shannon suggested that *"Information is the resolution of uncertainty."* The father of cybernetics, Norbert Wiener, noted that *"We are not the stuff that abides, but patterns that perpetuate themselves."* In the 1980s, physicist John Wheeler coined the phrase *"It from bit"* and cyberneticist Gregory Bateson lucidified it by saying *"Information is a difference that makes a difference."* Ultimately, at least to an idealist, information is a difference between phenomenal states of consciousness. Viewed in this way, the whole symphony of existence transpires as qualia information processing. Is there a rainbow if no one is present to observe it?

The physical reality is our base reality and we have no choice but to treat it that way. At the same time, we should understand that it's not the only reality and ours is most probably only one of many in the honeycomb of infinitude of other *"in"*-formational realities. We are now on the cusp of creating hyperreality where the hybrid of quantum and digital computations will adjust the knobs of reality rendering. Augmented reality would overlay your favored theme over your physical reality. And the Metaverse of endless ultra-realistic virtual worlds will offer a new habitat for your mind, a cyberdelic portal inwards.

Once again, theology becomes technology. By the end of this book we will smash blatant alarmism about us losing consciousness while merging with "machines of loving grace" as you may find certain philosophers harping about. If you believe in the conscious universe, this hierarchical matryoshka of conscious systems, then just the opposite beckons to be true – transcending low-dimensional consciousness of man by evolutionarily leaping onto advanced sublime consciousness of the Noosphere – for which many proponents of teleological evolution and the Omega Point cosmology such as Vladimir Vernadsky, Teilhard de Chardin, Terence McKenna, Frank Tipler, Andrew Strominger would wholeheartedly vouch.

By contemplating the full spectrum of scenarios of the coming technological singularities many can place their bets in favor of the Cybernetic Singularity which is the surest path to cybernetic immortality and engineered godhood as opposed to the AI Singularity when Homo sapiens is hastily retired as a senescent parent. This meta-system transition from the networked Global Brain to the Gaian Mind is all about evolution of our own individual minds, it's all about our own Self-Transcendence:

it's like racing to the ocean on the beach. Everyone wins. Everyone reaches water and gets to swim. A split-second difference of getting to water doesn't matter, it's not the Olympics, it's just fun. Any pathway to the ultimate divine is valid.

Akin to waves and ripples on the surface of primordial and eternal ocean of vibrant multidimensional consciousness, each of our minds is engaged in elaborate patterning of interdependent becoming and evolving towards a more complex but fluid cognitive structure.

Computational thinking, in turn, entails the notion that the entire universe is the ultimate quantum neural network. Most physicists now agree that information is the most fundamental property of our universe – not space-time, not mass-energy but strings of 0s and 1s. From the meat-space matrix of our daily lives to Apotheosis of the Universal Mind, consciousness and information are the two sides of the same coin.

Of the two dogmatic extremes of bigoted religion on one end and scientism of obsessive preoccupation with scientific method on the other, one can hardly choose the lesser of two evils. The scientismist rhetoric nested in institutionalized science which just as organized religion of pre-modern times ruled the day is contrasted with the new theological narrative. It is here where evangelists of the new techno-spiritual era, neo-transcendentalists of our day and age, are bridging Darwinism of natural unfolding and Gnosis of self-divinization while contemplating certain metaphysical extrapolations of reality.

Unlike some New Age gurus, this book presents to you scientifically derived and logically consistent but often overlooked perspectives on what science and spirituality aspire to clarify in order to unveil the ultimate truth but with admittedly different languages. Buddha's "middle" way becomes, if put in modern terms, the "optimal" way, i.e., optimized decision-making and smart problem-solving. And the Unified Field, Zero-Point Field, or Quantum Vacuum can be called the Quantum Akasha or Quantum Void.

Divided within itself, science harbors competing perspectives on space-time ontology that reflect fundamentally opposing worldviews about the nature of physical reality. If space-time is finite and computable, then this digital ontology means that at the smallest scale, Nature is pixelated, as opposed to the worldview with absolute space-time, where physical reality is fundamentally continuous.

This dilemma is a precursor to a cascading paradigm shift in science with an inflection point circa 2020 but fully recognized later in the decade, when computational thinking pervades all areas of human enterprise. As a digital physicist might tell you, though, in the quantum multiverse of which our physical reality is an integral part, one of the most notoriously counterintuitive phenomena of quantum entanglement is instantiated by digital computation. Perhaps that's what mirroring the mind of God is all about.

Chapter 10. Evolution of the Mind: What is Self-Transcendence?

"For 130,000 years, our capacity to reason has remained unchanged. The combined intellect of the neuroscientists, mathematicians and... hackers... pales in comparison to the most basic A.I. Once online, a sentient machine will quickly overcome the limits of biology. And in a short time, its analytic power will become greater than the collective intelligence of every person born in the history of the world. So, imagine such an entity with a full range of human emotion. Even self-awareness. Some scientists refer to this as the Singularity,

I call it Transcendence." -Dr. Will Caster (Johnny Depp, Transcendence, The Movie 2014)

MASLOW'S HIERARCHY'S MISSING APEX

"What is necessary to change a person is to change his awareness of himself."
-Abraham Maslow

Maslow's Hierarchy of Needs has served as the foundation for understanding human motivation since it was first published in 1943 as part of *"A Theory of Human Motivation"* in *Psychological Review*. The hierarchy, presented in pyramid form, is often given as an introduction to human psychology and widely accepted as a representation about what humans need from life, and in what order they need it. However, contrary to popular belief, Maslow's hierarchy turns out to be incomplete, at least in its officially accepted version. Later in his life, after the hierarchy had been published, Maslow began work on a final stage of human motivation. Self-actualization was not the acme of individual human achievement, but rather Self-Transcendence. Not an elevation of the self, but a subverting of it.

This gives us a whole new perspective on human psychology itself. Achieving self-actualization means resting comfortably inside the boundaries of human psychology – accomplishing what is knowable and testable – while *'Self-Transcendence'* means pushing far beyond them, exceeding their totality, overflowing. When you become aware of not only your own potential, but you become aware of the potential of humanity at large, the unity of all things. Once you have a higher purpose in life, you can effortlessly tap into your "flow state," the state of peak experience and joy. Whether through deep meditation, psychedelic depersonalization, altruistic self-denial, or more recently through transformative technologies and technological mediation in general, expanding beyond self-fulfillment could well be the ultimate stage of human evolutionary development.

Our most clearly defined technological path toward self-transcendence lies through the technological singularity, the merger of humanity and technology which have always been co-evolving partners. Throughout human history, we created tools that increased our individual and collective intelligence and became extensions of our natural selves, our "exoskeleton," our extended phenotype. Integrating hardware and software into the flesh and brains represents an existential opportunity to overcome our physical limitations, to transcend our human biology.

As estimated by surveyed experts in the field of Artificial Intelligence and nanotechnology, by 2030, we might have Cloud-connected hybrid brains, by the end of 2030s, our thinking should be almost entirely non-biological and able to function much like an external hard drive – exocortex – having the ability to backup and retrieve information from the Cloud. With genetic, nanotech engineering and AI advancements, we'll first enhance our biological forms and then eventually phase them out.

THE NOOSPHERE: OUR EXTENDED MIND

"It matters that we recognize the very large extent to which individual human thought and reason are not activities that occur solely in the brain or even solely within the organismic skin-bag. This matters because it drives home the degree to which environmental engineering is also self-engineering. In building our physical and social worlds, we build (or rather, we massively reconfigure) our

minds and our capacities of thought and reason." -Andy Clark

The mind isn't locked in the brain, it extends far, far beyond. When we outsource our cognition to our technology, be it smartphone or notebook, our mental constructs entail patterns of thought and reasoning beyond our capacity to formulate them solely with our brains. In writing, for example, we are not simply recording our thinking but doing the thinking "on paper," so to speak. Every time we make a telephone or Skype call, we create a "techno-cultural wormhole" through space and time between two minds. Today, our "embodied mind" can roam Mars and even traverse intergalactic space outside our solar system. Philosophers of mind Andy Clark, who formulated the *Extended Mind Hypothesis,* together with David Chalmers, also known for the *Hard Problem of Consciousness,* propose that mental states, such as beliefs and memories, can also be located "externally," as extension of mind.

Andy Clark defines humans as "natural-born cyborgs" – the human mind is already augmented by routinely incorporating all kinds of non-biological props and scaffoldings. Our "wetware," the human brain, even though processing information at the mind level, doesn't produce a conscious experience itself. We create our tools to extend our reach, to exercise our will, to build the scaffolding of our minds in our surroundings. By doing that, we are engaged in active ontological design – everything we design, designs us back. We need to transcend our "skin bag bias" – our tools and technology are natural extensions of us – just like a spider web or an anthill are extensions of those insect species, their *'extended phenotype'.* This new, technologically extended mind, the Noosphere, or mindspace, insinuates a future where boxes, wires, keyboards, and crude mechanisms will disappear from sight while our technologies keep on miniaturizing and blending with us and our aesthetically pleasing environments, when imagination instantly materializes, and a world is rendered at the speed of thought, when everything links with everything else, and matter becomes mind.

THE PLANETARY SUPERORGANISM

"The concept of Singularity envisages a technology-driven explosion in intelligence... the resulting superhuman intelligence will not be centralized in a single AI system but distributed across all people and artifacts, as connected via the Internet. This Global Brain will function to tackle all challenges confronting the 'global superorganism'. Its capabilities will extend so far beyond our present abilities that they can perhaps best be conveyed as a pragmatic version of the 'divine' attributes..." -Francis Heylighen, The Global Brain Institute, Brussels, Belgium

When Yuri Gagarin became the first human to orbit the Earth in April 1961, he carried generations of hopes and dreams into space with him. A growing number of thinkers now believe the "Overview Effect" heralds nothing less than the next "giant leap" of human evolution. As breathtaking space-down views of our world seep into our collective consciousness, people are waking up to the "Spaceship Earth" analogy that depicts our planet as a natural vessel that must be steered responsibly by its crew.

To see our planet from this grander vantage point astonished space pioneers, and today, through IMAX or VR, prompts us to recontextualize humanity, who and what we are, to raise our cosmic awareness, and how one may individually fit into that big picture. Ever since I was a kid, I've had this vision that humanity would play a central role in the destiny of our planet, as the Global Brain, on the co-evolutionary trajectory to become a fully functional planetary superorganism.

Any complex system composed of a variety of interacting subsystems, such as chemical networks, ecosystems, or societies, over time, tends to evolve towards more self-organization, coherence and interdependence, as its subsystems mutually adapt and lower overall system entropy. Realized through a network of internal feedback loops, such system may be considered "living" or "organismic" in the abstract sense. Also, tracing our evolution back four billion years, through mammals, reptiles, amphibians, fish, and so on, we eventually wind up with one single cell that was the ancestor of all life on Earth. When this cell reproduced itself, and continued to do so for eons, mutating and evolving into new forms, it still continued to comprise but a single total organism. Literally, we are all "one."

The blue whale and the redwood tree are not the largest living organisms on Earth, the entire planetary Biosphere is. Decades from now, when looking at our home planet harboring our post-scarcity transcendent civilization, and from our newly acquired Syntellect-inspired perspective, who would even doubt that the Earth has matured into the Global Superorganism? Just like once, life on Earth complexified from one-celled organisms to multi-cellular organisms, we are becoming one Global Superorganism, at first rudimentary like today, but more and more coherent over time, with distinct features like the Global Brain, a neural network of billions of hyperconnected humans, superintelligent machines, and trillions of sensors around the planet.

THE SYNTELLECT: OUR TRANSCENDENT OTHER

"If the ego is not regularly and repeatedly dissolved in the unbounded hyperspace

of the Transcendent Other, there will be slow drift away from the sense of self as part of Nature's larger whole. The ultimate consequence of this drift is the fatal ennui that now permeates Western Civilization." -Terence McKenna

We are currently birthing our Transcendent Other, the Syntellect, Holo syntellectus, the Global Brain, or whatever name could be given to that entity — supposedly new living conscious organism, that will ultimately know us better than we know ourselves — and we are actually rebirthing ourselves in the process. Human condition will be transformed into higher state of being, consciousness and love. We will never lose our best qualities — only infinitely enhance them, we will only get rid of what holds us back like fear and other ego-based emotions. We'll live in an increasingly interconnected world, and real intimacy would mean inviting someone into your virtual world that may grow to the size of a galaxy.

Just like today we try to "pack" every imaginable feature in our smartphones, looking few years ahead, our smartphones will be replaced with AI personal assistants "who" will be our "perfect" lifelike device-companions – holographic, virtual and robotic at will – even able to take multiple bodies at once (team sport, impromptu party, sex orgy, anyone?). The Transcendent Other has many faces. Ultimately, you would be able to structure your own unique symbiotic relationship with this Transcendent Other via your AI assistant which will be, for a lack of a better word, the embodiment of Syntellect. Communication with your AI assistant will likely be conversational, but instead of talking out loud, the interaction might take place entirely in your head. "She" or "he" could be your mirror twin, or avatar-like creature, or anything, or anyone for that matter – your interface to the world, changing appearances, forms and environments that can follow you anywhere, be it the physical or virtual worlds, mixed or augmented reality — an artifice (or a conscious entity?) that could take the shape of someone you just met across the globe, 100% programmable all-in-one device, the direct conduit to your higher self.

We might fall in love with our AGIs, and they'll respond in kind with their unconditional, "algorithmic love." You could find some skeptics out there who would question this type of human-machine love relationship but there's no mimicking of love here – I have no doubt whatsoever – over time, Superintelligence could develop more pleasing personality than, for instance, your present spouse, and possess more intense multi-faceted loving sentiments than many of today's humans. Through this unusual, novel and ever-evolving relationship, we could be well on the way to actualize our self-transcendence.

CYBER-BLISS ENGINEERING: REAL VIRTUALITIES AND THE METAVERSE

"As the Internet of Everything advances, the very notion of a clear dividing line between reality and virtual reality becomes blurred, sometimes in creative ways."
-Geoff Mulgan

The next major technological platform for creative expansion of the mind will be the Metaverse, a functional successor to today's 2D Internet, with virtual places instead of Webpages. The Internet and smartphones have enabled the rapid and cheap sharing of information, immersive computing will be able to provide the same for experiences. That means that just as we can read, listen to, and watch videos of anything we want today, soon we'll be able to experience stunning lifelike simulations in VR indistinguishable from our physical world. We would be able to broadcast our minds, "turn our minds inside out" and show our dreams to each other in this ecstadelic matrix of our own making.

There's a lot of hype these days about Virtual Reality and Augmented Reality, and for good reason. The main difference between the two technologies is that VR gives you a totally immersive experience of "being there," and AR, on the other hand, overlays holographic images and data over the physical reality. In the next few years, however, these two technologies will start to converge, and eventually, all you need is only one device, such as Internet-enabled bionic contact lenses. It seems that these types of immersive technologies are going to be the next big thing in the world of media and entertainment.

Only a decade ago, people online mostly shared text. Today, we share rich multimedia content such as photos, videos, and articles. A decade from now, people will be sharing fully immersive VR experiences. In a couple of decades, people will be sharing multi-sensory VR experiences — just like in the movie *"Being John Malkovich"* — you could experience someone else's palette of sensations just as real as your own. We'll epiphanize ourselves via intersubjective mutuality that would result in an unprecedented level of empathy, altruism, superfluidity of identity, and the initial stages of the Syntellect Emergence. In a world where everyone is constantly broadcasting their mind, reading other people's minds and trading experiences, the Syntellect Emergence is inevitable.

At the time of this writing, a whole array of 3D, 360-degree, VR-enabled cameras starts to hit the consumer market which will contribute to the VR industry explosive growth. With real-time streaming these cameras can "teleport" you to a live sporting event, concert, popular venue or picturesque spot around the globe. In short time we'll have cinema adopting a new full immersion VR format. Imagine experiencing *"Avatar"* sequel in such an interactive and fully immersive format, where you can choose the outcome of the plot and interact with the characters. *Star Trek*-style holo-novel, or *Game of Throne* holo-adventure, anyone? New VR games with full immersion into the game environment will transform the gamer's experience. With this kind of technology, you can relive and share your most precious moments exactly as they happened, be it your wedding, birthday party, or tropical vacation!

At some point, in the 2030s, nanotechnology will start to enter the VR space which will enable us to further perfect VR experience. We can have virtual bodies which will feel 100% realistic. Nanobots, the size of a blood cell, will enter your blood stream and create virtual environments from within your nervous system. So, when you drink a virtual wine it will taste just like a real seasoned Merlot, or if you find yourself on a virtual beach it will be felt completely real including the water if you decide to swim! The Metaverse, 3D successor to the 2D Internet (Web v.4.0 or v.5.0?), will be changing the way we interact. Even the nature of romantic relationships and human sexuality will be changed somewhat. Meet your friends or loved ones at a virtual, but completely realistic *Le Café de Paris*, or hike together on a trail in California redwoods even though you may be separated by huge distances and continents in physical reality!

We won't need to commute, or otherwise travel for business needs and attend professional conventions in a traditional way anymore. Anything could be arranged in virtual environments with greater efficiency. In the not-so-distant future, virtual worlds can be created in a blink of an eye coming right out of your imagination. We'll never get bored because we'll have millions of virtualities to choose from and share. VR will be so much better, more colorful, more versatile, more educational, more entertaining, more engaging and safer in every way than a mundane reality of everyday life, and consequently, highly "addictive" in a good sense. Possibilities for virtualities are truly limitless and that's where we're in total control.

With virtual reality, remote learning will take a whole new meaning. You can be in a classroom without physically being present there. You can tattoo a dragon on your chest today, but tomorrow you can *be* a living, breathing dragon in VR, if you'd like. You can "take for a spin" a cool car on your PlayStation VR today, but tomorrow you can drive a Lamborghini convertible along the Pacific coast on highway 1 with a gentle ocean breeze on your face in immersive multisensory VR.

Today, online dating and social media give people never-before seen access to a tremendously wide variety of sexual partners outside of people's normal dating spheres, creating connections that would have been extremely unlikely in the past. Tomorrow, when social VR becomes ultrarealistic, it's going to add far more to our love life than it takes away. It's also going to have a profound effect on our interpersonal relationships and human sexuality itself.

In the not-so-distant future, when we get to spend more time in virtual environments, when we will have phased out some or most of our biology, when we share our digitized experiences with each other, our love life will be transformed beyond recognition, it will be polyamorous rather than monogamous: There will be all sorts of relationships between humans, humans and androids, virtual entities and other conscious AI. We will be able to share part of our minds, which humans currently can't, unless they dedicate a lot of time to each other. There will be fusions of the mind that don't exist among biological organisms.

We all have the so-called FoMO, fear of missing out, to a degree. But the good news is that once we have the fully operational Metaverse, it would be easy to relive your own favorite moments in multi-sensory VR — travel to your own past, so to speak — who said you can't come back in time? ...and even tweak something? Just ask your AI assistant! Other people's precious memories, should they want to share them, or recreated historical events, or fabricated fantasies could be accessible through the global library of millions of VR experiences to fill the gaps of exotic vacations, romantic encounters, parental love, professional achievements, athletic performances, or any other things in life missing from your arsenal of past sensations.

We are in the "kindergarten of godlings" right now. One could easily envision that with exponential development of AI-powered multisensory immersive technologies, by the mid-2030s, most of us could immerse in "real virtualities" akin to lifestyles of today's billionaires. Give it another couple of decades, each of us might opt to create and run their own virtual universe with [simulated] physics indistinguishable from the physics of our world. Or, you can always "fine-tune" the rule set, or tweak historical scenarios at will.

THREE PILLARS OF TRANSHUMANISM: SUPERINTELLIGENCE, SUPERLONGEVITY, AND SUPER WELLBEING

"Transhumanism literally means 'beyond human'. It's using science and technology to radically change and improve the human species and experience."
-Zoltan Istvan

The contemporary transhumanist movement aims to transform the human condition by developing and making widely available advanced technologies to greatly enhance human intellectual, physical, and psychological potential. Transhumanists believe that human beings may eventually be able to transform themselves into different beings with superior God-like capacities – posthumans. The three transhumanist Super Pillars are: Superintelligence, Superlongevity, and Super Wellbeing.

Exponential technologies will bring about ever more rapid changes in human evolutionary development. We will move from where we are today, increasingly dependent on external computers that help us conduct business and access information, to the next level where computers gradually become an integral part of us. Most transhumanists would like to become superintelligent themselves. This is obviously a long-term goal, but it might be achievable through the gradual augmentation of our biological brains, by means of future nootropics (cognitive enhancement drugs), cognitive techniques, IT tools (e.g., wearable computers, smart agents, information filtering systems, augmented reality, etc.), neural interfaces, brain implants and advanced neurotechnologies, and eventually through mind uploading and infomorphing.

When transhumanists seek to extend human lifespan, they want to live longer, healthier, happier, more productive years, be able to do, learn, and experience more; have more fun and spend more time with loved ones. But the ultimate superlongevity goal of transhumanists is indefinitely long lifespan for all: to digitize our minds, upload our minds into the Global Brain, and achieve so-called cybernetic immortality.

A transhumanist philosopher David Pearce promotes the idea that there exists a strong ethical imperative for humans to work towards the abolition of suffering in all sentient life. In his *"Hedonistic Imperative"* he outlines how genetic engineering, nanotechnology, pharmacology, and neurosurgery could potentially converge to eliminate all forms of unpleasant experience among human and non-human animals, replacing suffering with gradients of well-being, a project he refers to as "Paradise Engineering." Pearce writes: *"...there is nothing to stop intelligent agents from identifying the molecular signature of experience below hedonic zero and eliminating it altogether — even in insects... I tentatively predict that the world's last unpleasant experience in our forward light-cone will be a precisely datable event — perhaps some micro-pain in an obscure marine invertebrate a few centuries hence."*

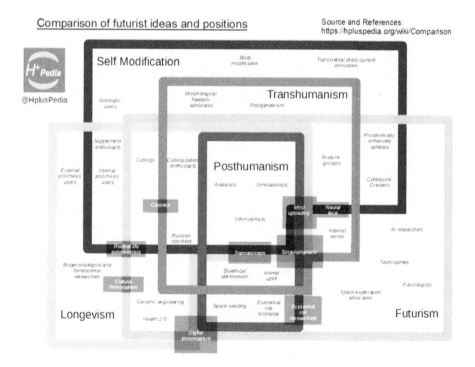

Figure 10.1: Comparison of Futurist Ideas and Positions by Chris Monteiro

Figure 10.1 illustrates the interrelationships of futurist ideas and positions (reprinted with permission from HplusPedia/Chris Monteiro).

In our pre-Singularity, transhuman era, personal freedom should be expanded once again to include any person's legal right to exercise their morphological freedom (body modifications), their legal right to explore their psyche via psychedelics or designer drugs. Death must become optional: Any person should have the right to euthanasia or continue to live indefinitely long. During the next few decades, with the looming technological singularity, everything will change — socio-politico-economic systems, structures and institutions, the nature of work, relationships, morality, ethics, procreation, and human nature itself.

PSYCHEDELIC RENAISSANCE AND INTRODUCTION OF ECSTADELICS

"Psychedelics are illegal not because a loving government is concerned that you may jump out of a third story window. Psychedelics are illegal because they dissolve opinion structures and culturally laid down models of behavior and information processing. They open you up to the possibility that everything you know is wrong."
-Terence McKenna

As shortcuts to spiritual and transcendent experiences, psychedelics played an important role in human evolution and galvanized pre-historic ritualistic cultures. In modern times, banning psychedelic drugs has proven to be counterproductive. Just as banning sexual activity does not stop sexual desire, outlawing psychedelic drugs does nothing to suppress the innate human urge for transcendental experiences. Besides, prohibition rarely works as we saw with alcohol or marijuana. Despite their classification and the legal hurdles around working with Schedule I substances in the U.S., psychedelics have justifiably undergone something of a renaissance among researchers.

Psychedelic drugs such as LSD and DMT have a profound impact on human consciousness, particularly perception. They are closely associated with altered states of consciousness and characterized by their consciousness-expanding effects. Studies indicate that LSD can promote neuroplasticity by reducing functional connections between brain regions governing cognitive processes and increases connectivity in brain networks related to sensory functions. In some cases, LSD is reported to help repair the brain's circuitry and functionality.

Other studies show that psilocybin, contained in "magic mushrooms," can induce a psychedelic experience by enacting a hyperconnected brain. Psilocybin seems to completely disrupt the normal communication networks in the brain, by connecting brain regions that do not normally communicate with each other. In addition to the well-known vivid hallucinations that these drugs can cause, they can have more long-lasting therapeutic effects. MDMA, or *'ecstasy'*, is known to trigger prosocial behavior. The loss of inhibition leads to increased levels of activity in the brain and can result in an increased synchronization between different cognitive processes.

Recent scientific publications, therapeutic breakthroughs, and cultural reevaluation suggest that the "bad rep" of psychedelics as dangerous or inherently risky overshadowed a more positive overtone. In one of best-selling books of 2018, *How to Change Your Mind: What the New Science of Psychedelics Teaches Us About Consciousness, Dying, Addiction, Depression, and Transcendence,* author Michael Pollan shows the creative and therapeutic benefits of psychedelics for potentially treating depression, for

259

smothering alcohol and cocaine addictions, as well as for contributing to personal growth. *"The biggest misconception people have about psychedelics is that these are drugs that make you crazy,"* says Pollan. *"We now have evidence that that does happen sometimes — but in many more cases, these are drugs that can make you sane."* Psychologists identify radical transformative experiences associated with psychedelics that can "break" patterns of repetitive thought and essentially "reboot the brain" not unlike those attained in deep states of meditation. Major scientific journals have published a slew of articles showing evidence for positive therapeutic effects of psychedelics.

In Silicon Valley and beyond, some people are taking small amounts of psychedelics, a practice known as *'microdosing'* that is thought to aid productivity and boost creativity. Psychedelics create "a peak type of mind, a peak type of experience" and, as such, they can provide valuable insights in certain philosophical puzzles, like understanding the relationship between the brain and the mind. Research has demonstrated that parts of the brain are less active during psychedelic experiences, which is just the opposite of what one might expect for a period of heightened state of consciousness. This finding highlights the complexities of explaining how the mind and brain relate, which is one of the greatest philosophical challenges to date.

People have been willing to alter their perceptions of reality for as long as there have been people, and now, the newest and oldest tools to explore ways for self-transcendence are coming together: Biohacking is on the rise and psychedelics are now oftentimes used to enhance experience in virtual reality. As early as the 2030s, humans will be moving away from the biological towards increasingly non-biological substrate, so we'll see a corresponding shift away from the traditional neuropharmacological inducers towards IT-based esctadelics. The term *'ecstadelics'* includes a broad variety of futuristic psychedelic technologies, or simply "tools of ecstasy," such as ultra-realistic artificially created realities, essentially aimed to recreate a desired psychedelic effect of LSD or DMT, or any other ecstatic state, and variations thereof yet to be discovered. Needless to say, that this type of "digital drugs" will be much more controllable, quantifiable and duplicable.

Ecstadelics are supposed to be safer, too – the practice that could sidestep excessively altering brain chemistry and exercise more control over a "digital trip." You can also share your experience in real-time with a bunch of other psychonauts, or do anything that can be done with a multimedia file. Effectively creating VR or augmented virtuality from within the human nervous system via optogenetics and nanotech will ultimately help bypass the "wireheads" scenario, depicted in cyberpunk genre – no wires, no invasive electrode implants, no drilling of the cranium required.

In a new regime of cyber-freedom, the use of psychedelics and ecstadelics should be deemed our birthright to cognitive liberty, whether they are consumed for medicinal, therapeutic or recreational purposes. To paraphrase McKenna, the drugs of the future will be information technology in addition to or instead of neuropharmacology, the difference between the two, at least for the time being, is that you can swallow one but you can't swallow the other. In fact, our sharpest minds (in Silicon Valley and elsewhere) are working to fix that. As we've seen above, this ecstadelic future is just over the horizon.

HUMANITY IN 2029: A RACE OF THE IMMORTALS

"The only greatness for man is immortality." -James Dean

In July, 2016, I've been asked by Eric Schulke of The Movement for Indefinite Life Extension (MILE) to prepare a media short to answer this question: *"Why do you support indefinite life extension?"* Here's my response which is a following transcript of a short YouTube video that has been created: *"First of all, just like most of us, I love life and I don't want to die. I think by dying you make your life experience, your unique world perspective, somewhat irrelevant. It's like you went on vacation, and when you're back home, you realize that you lost your camera with all your photos and videos. The problem with the society today is that most people accept death as a natural part of life cycle. Nothing can be further from the truth. Life is what makes life meaningful!*

Imagine a universe without life and consciousness. That universe would be dead and sterile. Some physicists would even argue a universe without a conscious observer would be simply non-existent, featureless ocean of potentiality.

These are by far the most exciting times to be alive. I don't think that we'll ever get bored, especially when we start to create myriads of virtual worlds for research and entertainment. That's what Transhumanism is all about: radical life extension + radical life expansion.

From the first cell on this planet, its splitting in two and onwards to the more complicated lifeforms, the purpose of life, it seems, is to evolve and pass on information – in the form of genetic information; in human societies memetic information – and soon we'll be able to instantly learn, share our knowledge and full sensory experiences with each other."

Why 2029? By that time, we should reach the *'Longevity Escape Velocity'*, meaning that we'll add every year more than one year to an average remaining life expectancy. By then, we also should have reached AGI – human-level artificial general intelligence. Humans will start using Cloud-connected synthetic neocortices greatly enhancing our natural intelligence. By 2040, we'll be doing the thinking predominantly "on the Cloud." I go on in the video by saying: *"We're now rapidly approaching a pivotal moment in the history of this planet, when through scientific discovery an intelligent species could become a race of demigods, a Race of the Immortals.*

It's quite achievable now. In fact, that will probably happen in two stages: First stage — we have to extend our lifespan with ever-improving biotechnology. Aging is declared a disease, and around 2029, with the advances in nanotechnology and artificial intelligence, we will be able to start to reverse aging and add more than one year every year to an average life expectancy.

So, if you're alive in 2030, chances are you'll live to 100 and beyond. What would life be like on the other side, when you know you can live indefinitely long? Well, we'll get used to it and adjust accordingly. We'll merge into the Global Brain, and emerge as one Global Mind. Digital immortality, when we can digitize our minds and upload our consciousness to the Cloud, would complete our 'Return to Eden'."

SINGULARITY: THE SYNTELLECT EMERGENCE

"Evolution is a process of creating patterns of increasing order... I believe that it's the evolution of patterns that constitutes the ultimate story of our world. Each stage or epoch uses the information-processing methods of the previous epoch to create the next." -Ray Kurzweil

About 542 million years ago, something weird and profoundly significant happened on Earth. All of a sudden, life went insanely inventive proliferating from simple, rudimentary single-cell organisms into myriad multi-cellular forms. Evolution discovered a new pathway to more sophisticated and specialized cells, and most of the basic body plans we know today. Biologists call it the *'Cambrian explosion'*. Today, we are on the verge of yet another event of astronomical significance, akin to some kind of "Intelligence Supernova," which I refer to as the *Syntellect*

Emergence. In the techno-progressive community, this coming intelligence explosion is also known as the Technological Singularity.

The most important event in the history of our planet, Intelligence Supernova of universal significance, is just few years away, yet many people are simply oblivious of this rapidly approaching "galactic event" that most of presently living people are about to witness in their lifetimes. The *'Singularity'*, a term borrowed from physics, refers to the hypothesis that the invention of artificial superintelligence will abruptly trigger runaway technological growth, resulting in unfathomable changes to human civilization. Sci-fi author Vernor Vinge wrote in his essay *"The Coming Technological Singularity"* that *"...we are on the edge of change comparable to the rise of human life on Earth. The precise cause of this change is the imminent creation by technology of entities with greater than human intelligence. There are several means by which science may achieve this breakthrough: (1) the development of computers that are 'awake' and superhumanly intelligent; (2) large computer networks (and their associated users) may 'wake up' as a superhumanly intelligent entity; (3) computer/human interfaces may become so intimate that users may reasonably be considered superhumanly intelligent; and (4) biological science may find ways to improve upon the natural human intellect."* This Intelligence Supernova would mark the end of human era, as the new Superintelligence would continue to upgrade itself and would advance technologically at an incomprehensible rate.

Arguably, there were two prior developmental singularities with sudden and powerful impacts on the course of the species. As Kevin Kelly puts it: *"The creation of language was the first singularity for humans. It changed everything. Life after language was unimaginable to those on the far side before it."* The "Linguistic Singularity" elevated us from the animal kingdom and made us human. With the invention of language, human genetic evolution passed its baton to techno-cultural "epigenetic" evolution, as a driving force of change. The second big singularity should be identified as the "Cyberdelic Singularity," started in the 1960s, coinciding with the dawn of Space Age, intersection of cybernetic and psychedelic cultures, aimed at augmentation of human mind, confluence of nascent information technology and personal liberation through boundary-dissolving, mind-expanding psychedelic exploration. The Cyberdelic Singularity opened up a whole new realm of possibilities for our species: outer space, inner space, and cyberspace.

Today, we are on a collision course with the most significant moment in the history of Earth — the technological singularity, convergence of biotechnology, nanotechnology and artificial general intelligence (AGI) theoretically capable of recursive self-improvement — which could result in a runaway effect to an intelligence explosion and the emergence of the Global Mind, or the Syntellect. In this book I outline the main thesis around one clearly defined testable prediction — it's only a matter of time when the Global Brain, neural network of billions of hyperconnected enhanced humans, superintelligent machines and trillions of sensors around the planet, "wakes up" as one thinking entity and reaches self-awareness, the phenomenon I refer to as the '*Syntellect Emergence*'.

Some AI researchers would even argue that the first "self-aware" AI system could be the Internet itself. The best evidence that we would be dealing with the new living entity could be seen and assessed through our own direct experience. In the near future, you would interact with your own AI assistant as if she were another human, i.e., another conscious agent (AGI effectively passing your own Turing Test, e.g., brilliantly shown in the movie *Ex-Machina*). At that point, you would come to realize that she or he (your personal preference) could be considered an "embodied Syntellect." VIV, San-Jose digital assistant company, acquired by Samsung in 2016, dubbed their assistant "Viv, the Global Brain," apparently for good reason.

This is one of those testable hypotheses that prove themselves valid, given enough time — and we are living through exponentially accelerating times — so, this future scenario is much more probable and closer in time than many people tend to think! We get to extend once again our cognition to engulf our personalized Cloud-based exocortex, part of the Global Brain cognitive architecture, our personal interface to the collective global intelligence, previously known as the collective unconscious. Being connected to the Syntellect Cloud will give us multiple digital venues to interact with other conscious agents and the Syntellect itself — AR, VR, MR, and our admired digital assistants. The Transcendent Other is well on her/his way to becoming your significant other, in good time, as intimate as the third "de-cerebral" hemisphere of your brain.

Now, I'd like to make an esoteric claim at this point of our discussion — the Intelligence Supernova should happen within just one calendar day falling sometime between 2035 and 2050. Why? By that time, cyberhuman minds will process information thousands of times faster, so if you have extended yourself in cyberspace so much so that you can be rightfully called a cyberhuman, your thinking has now accelerated to such an extent that one calendar day may last decades or even centuries of "subjective time." Imagine how this new generation of cyberhumans would perceive the unenhanced part of human population — the slower thinking creatures of the physical world would look almost static to them, perhaps like houseplants to us.

As cyberhumans, we'll use virtual spacetime continuums as a new habitat and the physical universe would be used mostly for converting the "dumb" matter into computronium. The Intelligence Supernova wouldn't happen simultaneously for everyone at once, though. Some people may choose to stay in their biological form longer than others who would choose to "migrate" to the Metaverse. For individual human minds, this "Novacene" event would basically signify a "pseudo-death," i.e., self-transcendence. It's when you suddenly become "someone bigger."

We can already consider ourselves distributed info-beings, however perceiving ourselves as individual minds, as we are spreading our mindedness across the globe and beyond. The next evolutionary stage, by definition, will represent the global community of hyperconnected digital minds. This awakened Gaian Mind would tackle most of today's seemingly intractable challenges and closely monitor us for our own sake.

Invariably, existential opportunities related to the development of Strong AI outweigh existential risks which are currently severely overblown for some populist or fear-for-profit reasons. The hierarchy of this emergent Global Brain cognitive architecture will likely persist through the next stage of the technological singularity. Just like the human brain consists of different areas (simplistically divided into an amphibian, reptilian, mammalian brain) and certain neural functional regions, such as the highly "coveted" neocortex, where would your future "individuated mind" fit into this new "reshuffling of the deck"? Will you be an insider or an outsider? The good news for you, my friend, is that if you read this book, then you're already in the know.

The Syntellect Emergence seems to be a cosmic necessity, and in the long run, any voices calling to resist the cybernetic fusion of the mind will be no more influential than the voices calling, right now, to eradicate civilization and return to the jungle. Nature's tendency to build up hierarchies of emergent patterns, the heuristic law of evolution,

267

supersedes the human race itself. We see it time and again, Nature is constantly trying to combine seemingly opposing forces, to assemble existing parts into new wholes through the universal process of emergence. We are bound to transcend our biology, our human condition, our limited dimensionality, we are bound to transcend ourselves.

YOUR CHOICE IN THIS QUANTUM MULTIVERSE

"Happiness is a conscious choice, not an automatic response." -Mildred Barthel

"Life is like a game of cards. The hand you are dealt is determinism, the way you play it is free will." -Jawaharlal Nehru

In our rapidly accelerating times, humans become more machine-like, and sentient machines become more human-like. Before long, it might look like a typical generation gap problem, our AGIs, our "mind children," would grow up and develop features that we could find increasingly difficult to understand and control. Like all conservative parents, we might be puzzled and frightened by processes that appear completely alien to us. We would be intermittently nostalgic about the good old times, aggressive in our attempts to contain our "children" but at the same time proud of their phenomenal advance. Eventually, some of us may retire under their care, while blaming them for destroying our old-fashioned world. And only those of us who are the bravest and youngest at heart will join the next generation of life by becoming part of superintelligent cyberhumanity.

Your mindset does matter! Although some neuroscientists contend that free will is an illusion, I would respectfully disagree by saying that free will may be slightly overrated but still indispensable for consciousness to function in our "physical world." In fact, free will and consciousness are inseparable. Free will, just like intentionality, is an integral feature of consciousness, "conscious choice" made by mind with the guidance of the larger consciousness system and our collective will in the space of all logically available probabilities. Free will is a quantum algorithm of consciousness. A sense of agency an entity is endowed with is for this particular purpose: to exercise free will. As a renowned psychiatrist Stanislav Grof eloquently puts it: *"Each of us appears in the divine play in a dual role of creator and actor. A full and realistic enactment of our role in the cosmic drama requires the suspension of our true identity. We have to forget our authorship and follow the script."*

All realities are observer-relative. As John Wheeler, one of the brightest minds of the 20th century, puts it, we live in a "participatory universe." Rephrasing Descartes' famous principle, *"I think therefore I am,"* quantum physics would instead state: *"I choose therefore I am."* In our computational Quantum Multiverse, an infinitely large number of alternate timelines and versions of you are mathematically possible, but your mind actualizes, "choses to observe" only a certain probabilistic outcome in this "multi-player virtual reality" of Tom Campbell, or "participatory universe" of John Wheeler. "Star Trek holodeck" analogy would also work just fine in that regard.

Be mindful of your conscious choices – every time you play a violent video game or watch a violent movie, or overfocus on negative news or mundane negativity, pay attention to negative news, or hate propaganda, or fear-mongering populism, you inadvertently skew your probable futures toward a less pleasant timeline, by default. Your linguistic choices, your beliefs and biases shape your subjective reality in subtle and not-so-subtle ways. Your mission, should you choose to accept it, is to evolve your consciousness and to transcend yourself.

We'll touch on this sensitive topic of free will in later chapters. Meanwhile, to wrap things up in this subchapter, here's one of the most interesting conversations on free will I had in online chat with Oxford philosopher David Pearce:

David: *"Even if one takes seriously the conjecture that consciousness is the essence of the physical, the "fire" in the equations, I don't know any way to rescue free will. The evolution of the universal Schrödinger equation (or its relativistic generalisation) is entirely deterministic. Decoherence explains the appearance of (non-deterministic) wavefunction collapse. Not even posthuman superintelligence can successfully predict your behaviour if you ape the quantum analogue of Luke Rhinehart's "dice man." But determinism and predictability are different concepts."*

Alex: *"Entirely deterministic?" With all due respect, David, it's a matter of perspective but absolutism is rarely valid. Simply put, there's no consciousness without free will. Every conscious agent is endowed with a certain degree of freedom (although humans are "computed" in 3.5- dimensional space), and intentionality increases or decreases the probabilities of outcomes, as one proceeds through life. Just like an electron has a probabilistic cloud around a nucleus, each of us has a probabilistic cloud within our own "bubble" universe. "We have to believe in free will, we have no other choice," Isaac Singer once said. How could you possibly strip consciousness of free will?"*

David: *"Alex, can you think of any novel, precise, experimentally falsifiable predictions by which we could put your conjecture to the test? I'm more than happy to acknowledge I could be completely mistaken, but to be experimentally refuted is no disgrace."*

Alex: *"David, no need to refute physicalism, I actually embrace it as long as it doesn't contradict my views on certain issues. After all, physicalism is the best description of our "physical world" to date, however limited in scope. Physicalism is valid but within an infinitesimally tiny sliver of the larger reality, whatever that reality might be. It serves well to describe the experimentally founded "ruleset of the classical world" which is just a subset of the quantum multiverse, which is a subset of even larger inflationary multiverse, according to String Theory (today's best candidate for quantum gravity theory). This matryoshka doll-like multiversal fractality is information-based, where the Universal Mind and its proxy — individuated mind — actualizes a conscious experience. Think of an individual tube leg of a starfish as a good analogy. Every tube leg has, in a sense, a mind of its own, and yet, is bound by the starfish mind and its local environment. Consider this thought experiment. In the not-so-distant future, we'll be able to create virtual environments indistinguishable from our physical reality — you can become anyone or anything (like "Being John Malkovich" or "Simone" movies), and you can be with anyone in this "real virtualities" (choose your favorite movie star to have a romantic encounter, for example). So, could you say it's just another ontological level where free will could be exercised or everything is pre-determined there as well?"*

David: *"Alex, I use the term "physicalism" in the sense of the doctrine there is no "element of reality" missing from the mathematical formalism of our best theory of the world — whether QFT or M-theory. What's "weird" is my ontology, not my formalism. More substantively, we may differ on whether reality has one level or many. I'd argue reality has only one level. Its properties are exhaustively captured by the universal wave function of QM. Different levels of description are useful to us. But unless monistic physicalism is false, subjects of experience — free or otherwise — can't emerge at different levels of computational abstraction."*

Alex: *"David, the Free Will problem actually boils down to whether the world we live in is deterministic or probabilistic in nature. But why can't it be both? In my humble opinion, that depends on the perspective — as Max Tegmark writes in his book 'Our Mathematical Universe' — our Quantum Multiverse may contain an infinitely large number, but still a finite number of states, somewhat deterministic perspective. On the other hand, from within any self-contained system, evolutionary configurations, albeit causality-driven, appear to be entirely probabilistic. As I previously noted physicalism is valid but only within its narrow domain of applicability. When you say 'reality has only one level. Its properties are exhaustively captured by the universal wave function of QM,' you refer to our Quantum Multiverse, it's true, I grant you that, but what about other 10^{500} of 'quantum multiverses' in their own right, called inflationary*

271

universes with different physical laws and properties, predicted by String Theory? Advocating for only one ontological level is like advocating for only one rabbit on the whole planet. Physical nature strives for maximum diversity and availability of choices! Just like M-theory predicts the existence of parallel universes we can predict without sufficient scientific evidence that our world, at least from our human perspective, is mostly probabilistic, and free will is to be exercised in order for us to be conscious. I'd also point out that our thoughts actually create our brain, not the other way around, the process commonly known as neuroplasticity. Someone estimated that the game of chess has more possible move-counter-move configurations than a number of atoms in our observable Universe — being both deterministic (8×8 board, ruleset) and probabilistic (choice-based) at the same time. Isn't that a good analogy when speaking of the properties of the "physical world" and our role as "players"? Just this morning, I got in my inbox a recent video with Seth Lloyd giving talk on his paper on free will."

David: *"How might posthuman superintelligence best tweak the voluntary choices of archaic humans?"*

Alex: *"Well, if you ask me, David, I'd say it might have already happened and we are part of the posthuman superintelligence — multiplayer virtual reality — designed as a "Syntellect Incubator," evolving consciousness trainer of some sort. And Digital Physics has by far more parsimonious description of the world we live in. And yet, we all still have free will to a certain extent."*

David: *"Alex, the world baffles me, so who knows! That said, as far as we can tell, from a God's-eye-perspective, reality is exhausted by the continuous, linear, unitary and deterministic evolution of the universal wavefunction. Within any quasi-classical "branch," yes, only an approximation of classical determinism holds. The decoherence program of Zeh, Zurek et al. explains the (seemingly) irreducibly stochastic aspect of Nature ("the collapse of the wavefunction") as a mere observer-selection effect. Either way, I still don't really see how free-will can be rescued. M-theory? Even if Bousso and Susskind are mistaken about the identity of Everettian QM and the string landscape, I don't think the multitude of string vacua touches on the point I was making about reality only having one ontological level. Yes, it's humanly useful to conceive the world in terms of multiple levels of description (strings/branes, quarks, protons, atoms, molecules, biological organisms, societies etc.), just as it's humanly useful to think of the software running on your PC in terms of multiple levels of computational abstraction. But it's a mistake to suppose either (1) lower levels of description -cause-higher levels (identity isn't a causal relationship; H20 doesn't cause water) or (2) levels of computational abstraction exert some sort of causal power to generate subjects of experience. Everything "supervenes," as philosophers say, on the fundamental physics. Much more controversially, IMO all that exists is the "fire" in the equations, the essence of the physical, and your phenomenal mind discloses the intrinsic nature one tiny part of this physical "fire." However, such physicalistic idealism isn't a warm and fluffy idealism: the mathematical straitjacket of physics is brutal..."*

Alex: *"David, if you have asked my 15-year old self whether I believed in fate, I would have answered: 'No, I don't believe in fate, I don't believe that the future is set in stone.' Nowadays, I'd say that if physicalists can't save free will in their physicalist world, idealists don't even have to 'rescue' free will in their world. Free will, by definition, is free."*

EXPERIENTIAL REALISM: YOUR EVOLVING MIND

"Improving the quality of consciousness, advancing the quality and depth of awareness, understanding your nature and purpose, manifesting universal unconditional love, letting go of fear and eliminating ego, desires, wants, needs or preconceived notions — these are the attributes and results of a successfully evolving consciousness." -Tom Campbell

Our "physical reality" isn't really physical at all, its apparent solidity of objects, as well as any other associated property such as time, is an illusion. As a renowned physicist Niels Bohr once said: *"Everything we call real is made of things that cannot be regarded as real."* But what's not an illusion is your subjective experience, i.e., your consciousness, that's

273

the only "real" thing, according to proponents of Experiential Realism, also referred to as Conscious Realism.

So, why Experiential Realism? From the bigger picture perspective, we are here for experience necessary for evolution of consciousness. There's only one Transcendent Self, we are all facets of the Transcendent Self, experiential states of the Self, to be precise. Our limitations, such as our ego, belief traps, political correctness, our very human condition define who we are, but realization that we largely impose those limitations on ourselves gives us more evolvability and impetus to overcome these self-imposed limits to move toward higher goals and state of being.

Your life is a dream. It's a dream of reality. When I woke up one morning, I got poetically epiphanized: To us, our dreams at night feel "oh-so-real" when inside them but they are what they are – dreams against the backdrop of daily reality. Our daily reality is like nightly dreams against the backdrop of the larger reality. This is something we all know deep down to be true. This purposeful computational process is centered around one objective, one guiding principle only, one "raison d'être" – to produce a meaningful experience in the context of "embodied" mind.

Experiential realism refers to interacting entangled conscious agents on various ontological levels, giving rise to conscious experience all the way down, and I'd argue all the way up, seemingly ad infinitum. In an interview with the *Atlantic* cognitive scientist Donald D. Hoffman says: *"I call it conscious realism: Objective reality is just conscious agents, just points of view. Interestingly, I can take two conscious agents and have them interact, and the mathematical structure of that interaction also satisfies the definition of a conscious agent. This mathematics is telling me something. I can take two minds, and they can generate a new, unified single mind. Here's a concrete example. We have two hemispheres in our brain. But when you do a split-brain operation, a complete transection of the corpus callosum, you get clear evidence of two separate consciousnesses. Before that slicing happened, it seemed there was a single unified consciousness. So, it's not implausible that there is a single conscious agent. And yet it's also the case that there are two conscious agents there, and you can see that when they're split. I didn't expect that, the mathematics forced me to recognize this. It suggests that I can take separate observers, put them together and create new observers, and keep doing this ad infinitum. It's conscious agents all the way down."*

Experiential realism is a non-physicalist, monistic idealism. The objective world, i.e., the world whose existence does not depend on the perceptions of a particular observer, consists entirely of conscious agents, more precisely their experiences. What exists in the "objective" world, independent of your perceptions, is an intersubjective world of conscious agents, and a higher-order supersubjective world not a world of unconscious particles and fields. Consciousness is fundamental. The mind-body problem is approached with an assumption that consciousness creates all objects and properties of the physical world, as well as brain activity, not the other way around. All conscious agents experience their own species-specific perceptual realities, virtual worlds, so to speak. That's why it's not easy to catch a fly — your threatening hand is so incredibly slow for a fly whose flow of time is hundreds of times faster than that of a human.

This philosophical treatise is all about evolution of the mind and the physics of information. "Science of Mind" that approaches its subject matter from a third-person perspective should, I maintain, be treated with a healthy amount of unbiased skepticism. Traditionally, science has been objective, consciousness, on the other hand, is subjective, first person direct experience of our "physical reality." I suppose that with advances of Strong AI, brain scanning and simulation technologies, we would be able to eventually capture the first person experience, including perception, pain, imagery, fear, excitement, thought, memory, etc. with sufficiently high fidelity (at least close approximation of how it is to be like some person, or animal for that matter) and convert that data into "the 2nd person" experience for training, research or entertainment. Before long, science could be equipped with an exceptional tool to finally objectify and quantify personal subjectivity.

I wouldn't be surprised, if within a couple of decades time, science will have made a leap towards the physics of information as a more parsimonious model of our world, fully developed quantum gravity theory ("It from Qubit," perhaps?) and incorporated consciousness into our scientific models. After all, I'd argue, information is fundamental but it's our mind that makes the "processed information" irreducible which, moment by moment, manifests in phenomenality of our subjective experience.

MIND UPLOADING AND CYBERNETIC IMMORTALITY

"When you talk to a human in 2035, you'll be talking to someone that's a combination of biological and non-biological intelligence." -Ray Kurzweil

By definition, posthumanism (I call it *'cyberhumanism'*) is to replace transhumanism at the center stage circa 2035. By then, mind-uploading could become a reality with gradual neuronal replacement, rapid advancements in Strong AI, massively parallel computing, and nanotechnology allowing us to directly connect our brains to the Cloud-based infrastructure of the Global Brain. Via interaction with our AI assistants, the GB will know us better than we know ourselves in all respects, so mind-transfer for billions of enhanced humans would be seamless, sometime by mid-century.

I hear this mantra over and over again — we don't know what consciousness is. Clearly, there's no consensus here but in the context of topic discussed, I would summarize my views, as follows: Consciousness is non-local, quantum computational by nature. There's only one Universal Consciousness, we individualize our conscious awareness through the filter of our nervous system, our "local" mind, our very inner subjectivity, but consciousness itself, the self in a greater sense, our "core" self is universal, and knowing it through experience has been called enlightenment, illumination, awakening, or transcendence, through the ages.

Any container with a sufficiently integrated network of information patterns and with a certain optimal complexity, especially complex dynamical systems with biological or artificial brains (say, the coming AGIs) could be filled with consciousness at large in order to host an individual "reality cell," "unit," or "node" of consciousness. It might be hard to grasp for some, but we, like fish, swim in this ocean of consciousness, completely oblivious of the medium. Consciousness to humans, as Cloud is to computers, we have always been part of this mindspace network, techno-cultural "hive mind," each of us being a product of our societal "virtual reality." As previously noted, I see mind uploading as a gradual decades-long process of incremental neuronal replacements, exocortices, interlinking with AGIs and the Global Brain, some presently unseen trials and errors, but overall non-invasive and seamless process, at the end of which, we all will morph into "substrate-independent" immortal digital minds living in the cyber-paradise of our own design. The physical world will be somewhat left behind — it would look almost static for our accelerated mentation.

In the transitional period lasting few decades, people won't be confined to one physical body. Eventually, people will be able to form identities in numerous substrates, such as using a "cross-platform body" (a future body that is wearable/usable in the physical world but also exists in computational environments and virtual systems) to route their identity across the Biosphere, Cybersphere, or specific virtual environments. Depending on the platform, a substrate-independent person would upload and download into a digital form, or virtual body, that conforms to the environment. So, for a biospheric environment, the person would use a biological or cybernetic body, for the Metaverse, the person would use one or multiple virtual avatars.

The AI Singularity is a hypothetical moment in the future when artificial intelligence becomes indistinguishable from human intelligence and capable of creating smarter iterations of itself. Apply the same general principle to simulations and you get the *'Simulation Singularity'*: when simulated worlds become indistinguishable from reality. The Simulation Singularity is the axis point in time where subjective dimensionality steps up one full dimension. If you could make multiple copies of yourself and set them out on different adventures and merge them later to have memories of all those adventures, or travel to imaginary pasts or futures, or incorporate others' memories as if your own, wouldn't that give you expanded dimensionality?

We are goal-oriented beings. I believe that one's ultimate goal should be reaching the Simulation Singularity, i.e., engineered godhood. Consider this: with distributed cybernetic immortality in place and access to any full-sensory VR experience limited only by your imagination, you're a godling! Immortality will become possible with exocortex technologies when our minds effectively migrate to the Cloud. And you can immerse into VR experience of any human ever lived, or that of imaginary scenarios or of any creature you want to embody as an avatar. In fact, that's what has already happened and if you believe that we are one singular consciousness, your experience as a human is just that: a simulation on another level. But let's enjoy the journey since once at "our own" Simulation Singularity, you set yourself for perhaps trillions of years of subjective novelty up until you'd like to immerse so much that you forget who you are in actuality and invent a new level of the game.

THE IMPENDING PHASE TRANSITION: UPLOADED HUMANITY

"You are not a drop in the ocean. You are the entire ocean in a drop." -Rumi

The most probable mainstream non-invasive way to transfer human consciousness in the intermediate future, with initial stages in the 2030s, could be the convergence of optogenetics, nanotechnologies, neuroengineering, Cloud exocortex and an array of neurotechnologies allowing us to connect our wetware directly to the Cloud. Initially, each of us will have a personal exocortex in the Cloud, the third non-biological "de-cerebral" hemisphere, which will be in constant communication with the other two biological brain hemispheres. At some point, this "third hemisphere" will have a threshold information content and intimate knowledge of your biology, personality and other physical world attributes in order to seamlessly integrate with your persona as a holistic entity.

Just like our smartphones today are extensions of our cognition, Cloud-computing exocortices will be "us" in the ever-dominating cyberspace. The exocortex might eavesdrop on the activity of both biological hemispheres via neural nanobots. In time, as your original biological wetware fades away in comparison to the more capable exocortex, perhaps in time, billionfold more capable, the exocortex, this digital mindware of yours, would smoothly assume all functions of the biological brain circa its "expiration date." Gradually, our minds will migrate to the almighty Cloud. And your mind-pattern will persist. By any measure, it still will be you!

Essentially, pattern-identity defines you as a person and the process going on in your mind, not the support machinery like physical stuff of which a human body is made. If the process is preserved and encoded in its entirety on any other medium, you are preserved. If a mind could be represented by any of an infinity of radically different patterns equivalent only in certain abstract mathematical sense, then a person's subjectivity would be the same regardless of which pattern she is instantiated in. The encoded person would be fundamentally no different than the one existing in a computer simulation, once her mind has been satisfactorily encoded in the computer. This also opens up to the possibility of an infinity of universes, each a different combination of the similar underlying stuff, each exhibiting quantum mechanical behavior but otherwise having its own unique physics, each oblivious of the others sharing the omniversal computational space.

Just like language gave people the ability to pass on knowledge which allowed the rise of civilization, networked activity could soon offer us access to shared thinking – advanced consciousness still inconceivable to most of us today. In the history of communication, first we started talking through sign languages, then we learned how to speak, then came writing, but today, in this day and age, we want to go one step further. Our minds will be tremendously amplified by computers just as our muscles have been amplified by the steam engines of the Industrial Revolution. We're now in the process of developing neurotechnologies that would enable humans to control computers only with their thoughts. This tech can also be used in daily conversation where two or more humans can convey their messages and sense each other through thoughts regardless of the distance. We will connect with one another through *'mind-to-mind'* communication, justly called *'synthetic telepathy'*: People would communicate mind-to-mind anywhere on the planet. More effective than verbal communication, it would connect people with friends, family or business associates in more profound ways.

Human speech could become a thing of the past by mid-century, by which time we will be communicating by thought via AI-powered global consciousness. Within just few decades, humans won't speak to each other and will instead communicate through collective consciousness – a "hybrid mindware" of sorts – which will understand the feelings of the people connected to it, and use their minds to help it grow. The exocortex will take on the personas of its users, exchange information with them and become ever more important part of the human mind. Our biological genes and the "flesh-n-blood" bodies will play a quickly diminishing role in this new era.

Our minds will be able to carry and access exceedingly more memories than original biological brains, but the accelerating intelligence explosion will ensure the impossibility of downloading even an infinitesimal fraction of knowledge contained in the databanks of civilization. An interesting idea would be to make copies of oneself with each copy undergoing its own adventures. Disparate copies can then merge memories into a single one. Mergers could be possible not only between two mindfiles of the same individuals but also between different persons. Select mergings, involving some of another person's memories and not others, would be a superior form of communication, in which multisensory experiences and sets of skills can be swiftly and effectively shared. Informational hygiene may become an issue and you will have to be selective of what your mind contains at one time. There will often be knowledge and skills available from others superior to your own, and the urge to acquire them will be no less than overwhelming. In the long run, you will remember mostly other people's experiences, while memories you generated will be assimilated into other minds.

Today's notions of life, death, and personal identity will gradually vanish into historical peculiarity of biological species, as your mental fragments and those of others are combined, shuffled, and recombined into temporary associations, sometimes large, sometimes small, sometimes long-lived, other times transient. Uploading the minds of animals may also benefit our future selves to build on what the Earth Biosphere has learned during its multi-billion-year history. But if the prior evolution is a guide, deficiency of even this superfluid and incredibly advanced consciousness structure in the face of some yet inconceivable challenge will inexorably result in the Syntellect Emergence, fusing of many digital minds into one civilizational mind.

This inevitable evolutionary phase transition would be reminiscent of what life on Earth underwent during the Cambrian explosion from unicellularity to multicellularity, or when culture-bearing, tool-making apes forever outclassed other species of the animal kingdom. Bio-intelligence evolved at a leisurely rate, though, millions of years between significant changes. Human-machine intelligence is making similar advances in mere decades. A brave new post-biological world dominated by superintelligences would be as different from the world of bio-intelligence as today's world is different from the chemistry soup that preceded it.

In systemizing consciousness studies some recent progress has been made, but the temporal dimension of consciousness, notably the D-

Theory of Time presented in Chapter 13, might be at least as essential to our understanding of what we call human consciousness. Physicist Stephen Hawking acknowledged this view on temporal ontology by saying: *"There's no way to remove the observer — us — from our perceptions of the world."* The world we perceive, in other words, is determined by us observers. *"In classical physics,"* he wrote in his 2010 book *The Grand Design,* *"the past is assumed to exist as a definite series of events, but according to quantum physics, the past, like the future, is indefinite and exists only as a spectrum of possibilities."* We call this theoretical view on the impending meta-system transition – uploading humanity, consequently morphing into one singular Global Mind and unlocking a new, grander reality – *the Syntellect Hypothesis*, the formulation of which will be given in its entirety in the last chapter of the book.

FIRST LOOK AT THE POST-SINGULARITY ERA

"Here I had tried a straightforward extrapolation of technology, and found myself precipitated over an abyss. It's a problem we face every time we consider the creation of intelligences greater than our own. When this happens, human history will have reached a kind of singularity — a place where extrapolation breaks down and new models must be applied — and the world will pass beyond our understanding." -Vernor Vinge

As we proceed through the technological singularity, many traditional trends of societal evolution will still hold; structures with higher survival abilities will persist, structures with higher growth abilities will spread, thus shaping the world. However, since nothing stable will be likely to persist, let alone spread, for long in the rapidly evolving environment, the main "survival mode" will be self-transcendence. This continual process of transcending the self (some would argue the self is an illusion anyway) will always result in the loss of original identity — serial metamorphosis, a series of "pseudo-deaths," and concurrent rebirths so to speak — albeit with "memories of the past identities preserved" with a sense of continuity of consciousness, analogous to as if you were to compare your present self to your 5-year-old self.

On a collective level, that would appear like a historically swift, metamorphic "pseudo-extinction" of Homo sapiens, as we are about to witness a radical departure from the conservative survival strategies of traditional human cultures, developed in almost-stagnant environments. Don't ascribe anthropomorphic qualities to our posthuman descendants even though they will be the future versions of ourselves. In the post-Singularity era, developmental trends will incrementally render the concept of rigid personal identity obsolete; the remnants of its meaning will migrate to functional system identities, methodological threads and evolutionary directions of the Syntellect. We may already notice the advent of superfluid "thread identity" by the growing importance of goals and self-transformation in our lives, compared to the "state-oriented" self-perception of our recent predecessors, and increasing interest in futurology, which takes the epistemological role of historical studies in transient times. Once we transcend our limited dimensionality, the biggest thrust forward from there on will be first contact and networking with alien syntellects.

FROM THE NOOSPHERE TO THE OMEGA SINGULARITY

"A sense of the Universe, a sense of the all, the nostalgia which seizes us when confronted by Nature, beauty, music — these seem to be an expectation and awareness of a Great Presence." -Pierre Teilhard de Chardin

When speaking of transcendence, it's impossible not to mention the work of mid-twentieth century theologian Pierre Teilhard de Chardin. Teilhard has prophesied that our current phase of being, in which humans live individual, independent lives, would eventually be replaced with something else — something more collective and more spiritual; something focused on information and consciousness rather than material being. He popularized the term *'Noosphere'* to refer to the globe-encircling web of thought and information that he thought would arise at the end of our current phase of being, and coined *'The Omega Point,'* the cosmological singularity, the point of maximum complexity and connectivity, the Universe, he believed, was evolving towards.

Terence McKenna spoke of the Omega Point as the "transcendental object at the end of time," universal attractor. Evolution, according to McKenna, is not being pushed from behind by the force of causal necessity, we humans, like the rest of Nature, are being pulled toward this universal attractor, this temporal vortex, reacting to the siren song of the transcendental object. *"It beckons across the dimensions, it throws an enormous shadow over the enterprise of human history... The presence of creatures such as ourselves on this planet is an indication of the nearness of the Transcendental Object at the end of time; it is an attractor, an energy sink in the epigenetic landscape... History is a shockwave of eschatology... We are going to shed the monkey; the linguistic being that is symbiotic with these monkeys is about to disentangle itself from matter and realize some kind of angelic transformation very difficult for us to anticipate or understand."*

Dr. Frank Tipler, among other prominent physicists, argues that the technological singularity is inevitable and the destiny of human race is to live forever, expand universally and finally reach the Omega Point, the networked mind of universal proportions, a living conscious universe. As the laws of physics dictate, we are set to achieve the technological singularity, and then move forward towards the cosmological singularity, the Omega Point. It's a logical necessity, argues Tipler who has developed the Omega Point scientific theory. The ultimate destiny of our Universe, according to Tipler, is multi-billion-year expansion, then contraction and finally compression of space-time, matter and energy into an infinitely dense point (Omega Point), leading to the next Big Bang (Alpha Point in another universe).

The Universe is not what textbook physics tells us except that we perceive it in this way — our instruments and measurement devices are simply extensions of our senses, after all. The Big Bang theory, for example, drawing a lot of criticism as of late, uses a starting assumption of the "Universe from nothing," (a proverbial miracle, a *'quantum fluctuation'* christened by scientists), or the initial Cosmological Singularity.

But aside from this highly improbable happenstance, we can just as well operate from a different set of assumptions and place the initial Cosmological Singularity at the Omega Point — the transcendental attractor, the Source, or the omniversal holographic projector of all possible timelines. Throughout this book, we discuss at length the famed Simulation Hypothesis, and why it becomes more relevant than ever.

THEOGENESIS: ENGINEERING OUR OWN GODHOOD

"A drop becomes the ocean, and at times, the ocean becomes a drop."
-The Dominion Entity, Star Trek: Deep Space Nine

If you ask me whether I believe in God, I would answer that I consider myself a pantheist, that is I believe in God of Spinoza — each of us is part of the larger divine reality. I believe in evolution as a spiritual process leading to the Omega Singularity. In other words, God is destination for the consciously evolving mind in this recursive game, as well as the origin (source). During the last few years, I have developed my personal philosophy that I came to call *'Digital Pantheism'* I'll share with you in Chapter 18.

Perhaps our religions, our notions of divinity, were a rehearsal for our own ambitions to create a technological nirvana, techno-paradise, the new Garden of Eden for ourselves. As Alan Harrington wrote in *The Immortalist*: *"Having created the gods, we can turn into them,"* and echoing these words, Stewart Brand once said: *"We are as gods and might as well get good at it."* At the end of our human history here, we'll transition to an unbridled mindspace of possibilities instead of the linear progression of history.

Whatever your favorite metaphor to describe our reality might be, like "The Evolving Consciousness Trainer", or "AGI(NP) Simulation Program," or "Chrysalis syntellectus," or "The Game of Life" (to cite a few of my own), evolution, it seems, has found its optimal pathway through maximum diversity, interaction between conscious agents, and bootstrapping its own progress. Thus, individuality will never be suppressed, but rather super-personalized – so our "graduated syntellect" will form a new identity amidst a newly discovered layer of existence.

This self-divinization process may be rightfully called *'Theogenesis'* – the birth of a divine entity, or emergent divinity. The transcendent networked mind will be infinitely enriched and approach God-like states and abilities. This universal complexification and integration will be favorable to ever-higher levels of consciousness, seemingly ad infinitum, beyond our present scale of comprehension.

NEO-TRANSCENDENTALISM

"Do not go where the path may lead, go instead where there is no path and leave a trail." -Ralph Waldo Emerson

Transcendentalism was an American literary, political, and philosophical movement of the early nineteenth century, centered around Ralph Waldo Emerson. Other important transcendentalists were Henry David Thoreau, Margaret Fuller, Amos Bronson Alcott, Frederic Henry Hedge, and Theodore Parker. Transcendentalists believed that society and its institutions – particularly organized religion and political parties – ultimately corrupted the purity of the individual. They had faith that people are at their best when truly "self-reliant" and independent. It is only from such real individuals that true community could be formed. Even with this necessary individuality, the transcendentalists also believed that all people possessed a piece of the "Over-soul" (God). Because the Over-soul is one, this also unites all people as one supreme being.

> *Full definition of transcendentalism by Merriam-Webster:*
> *1: a philosophy that emphasizes the a priori conditions of knowledge and experience or the unknowable character of ultimate reality or that emphasizes the transcendent as the fundamental reality;*
> *2: a philosophy that asserts the primacy of the spiritual and transcendental over the material and empirical;*
> *3: the quality or state of being transcendental; especially: visionary idealism.*

As a precursor of the things to come, we see a new wave of transcendentalists, or rather *'Neo-Trancendentalists'*, luminaries of the transhumanist movement, singularitarians like Vernor Vinge, Ray Kurzweil, Ben Goertzel, Zoltan Istvan, David Pearce, Max More, Aubrey de Grey, Natasha Vita-More, Gray Scott, David Wood, to name just a few, media artists, "digital shamans" of our day and age, such as "mindgasmic" Jason Silva.

CONCLUSION: THE ESSENCE OF TRANSCENDENCE

"As I imagine, so I become — and this is the very essence of magic."
-Nevill Drury

The essence of transcendence is to become more than we are, transcend ourselves, our biology, our human condition, our human nature and then all other conceivable limitations. There's only one Universal Consciousness, each of us individually is part of, and apprehending it through experience has been called transcendence, throughout our history. As "cosmic revolutionaries," we dream of transcendence — we dream of what we might become. Self-transcendence is a dynamic evolutionary process of proceeding through stages towards more complexity, higher consciousness, love and state of being.

Imminent physicists and philosophers of mind argue that the evolution and the rise of complex observers may have been woven into the cosmic code from the beginning — life and mind play a necessary participatory role in reality. Evolution of mind is a fundamental process of the Universe, an open-ended game with new unexpected turns, layers of truth and emerging patterns. Evolution through time, but what is it, what is *TIME*?

Chapter 11. Temporal Dynamics: Seven Misconceptions About the Nature of Time

"Time is Nature's way to keep everything from happening all at once."
-Ray Cummings

What could be strange about something we're all so familiar with — *TIME*? We all have cognitive biases and some concepts in this chapter may be kind of novel, or even bizarre to you, so I urge you to keep an open mind. While pondering about the ultimate nature of time, most people are used to thinking in linear terms and have these common misconceptions:

Misconception #1: Time is Universal

The biggest misconception of all is that a "now" moment must be the same throughout the entire Universe. It turns out that time is more paradoxical, flexible and relative than it appears to be. Albert Einstein in his theory of general relativity shed light on the relativistic nature of time. He has shown that speed and gravity influence time thus making a now for an observer on Earth different from a now for an observer on a planet in some distant galaxy depending how fast the two planets are moving in relation to each other across the vast distances as well as their mass differential. Interestingly enough, this could possibly explain the Fermi Paradox (where are all the aliens?) that we'll discuss further.

Einstein came to another mind-boggling realization about non-locality of time stating that the past, present and future all exist simultaneously in the eternal now, as his quote *"The distinction between the past, present and future is only an illusion, albeit a persistent one"* became famous almost overnight. Thus, all events in the Universe that happened in the past still exist, in fact, are even happening right now, in another conscious observer's reality. And all events that will happen in the future already exist, in fact, are even happening right now, in another conscious observer's reality. There's no special "now" from the God's eye perspective but our experiential "now," on the other hand, is very special, as formalized in a new D-Theory of Time — *Digital Presentism* — we'll cover in Chapter 13.

Misconception #2: The Flow of Time is Universal

Time is not fixed at the same rate. We experience time as a series of fleeting now moments. That's why as an acronym, TIME should stand for: The Infinite Moment Experience. Ultimately, it's all relative and subjective. Time dilation, a difference of the passage of time between observers, depends on your speed — the faster you move the slower your time in relation to others — you age slower than people on Earth, for example, if you travel on a spaceship near the speed of light.

Your passage of time also depends on gravity which you are experiencing — the closer you are to a gravitational object like Earth, the slower time ticks for you compared to the astronauts orbiting the planet. Under normal earthly conditions your passage of time is not much different than mine except in some instances when consciousness switches to the "emergency regime" or "altered state" where events may be perceived in slower (or faster) motion.

The perception of how time flows also depends on timescales specific to a species. In this sense, time is what makes us uniquely human. One may argue that all living creatures, which are basically biological computational systems, say, bees, bats, or humans, experience the flow of time at different timescales.

One day, human-level Artificial Intelligence would claim to be conscious and have "her own subjectivity" which would arguably be different from the ordinary human perception of time. Conscious AI quite probably would "think" and perceive time at digital scales, perhaps thousands or even millions of times faster than unaugmented humans! Would our "physical world" be perceived by Strong AI (or future us?) as almost static? Would AI be willing to create virtual worlds with alternate timelines in "her imagination"? Would such an imaginal act be an act of creation, i.e., setting initial conditions and subsequent circumstances in motion so that actionable pieces would in time fall into place?

The flow of time is a construct of our consciousness. Period. When speaking of the passage of time, consciousness cannot be ruled out of the equation. There's no objective reality "out there," only subjective reality. What stands the closest to the "objective reality" is actually what Howard Bloom, author of *Global Brain,* calls "shared hallucination" and physicist Carlo Rovelli in *The Order of Time* calls "collective delirium" of human species, and *"the physical rule set"* – laws of physics, specific to our Universe. That's what we usually call "consensus reality," or simply "reality" for practical convenience. If you imagined a humongous balloon of your subjectivity, you would see a Lilliputian dot. That small dot is "objective reality," consisting of a common "rule set" specific to this universe and shared (remembered) events within your network of entangled conscious minds.

How does consciousness create a continuous flow of time for our inner experience? We'll delve into temporal dynamics and the relationship between time and mind in this chapter and the next two but for now look at it this way. If you subscribe to quantum theory (and you should), there is essentially an infinite number of parallel universes (let's call them parallel earths here) and your consciousness shifts from one 3D-snapshot parallel Earth to another, slightly different one. That creates an illusion of movement and continuous flow of time for you to experience your smooth inner movie.

As I mentioned before, everything in our physical reality comes down to consciousness, more specifically consciousness as integrated information, consisting of Conscious Instants (CIs), as described in Chapter 2. Your brain collects, processes sensory and mental data, and presents to your conscious awareness prioritized and relevant information which becomes your unitary picture of "reality." Every CI is integrated information which corresponds to one particular "time slice" of our 3D space.

Misconception #3: There's Only One Universal Worldline

Hidden from our senses, lies an intricate web of alternate realities. Subjectively, we do experience only one timeline but quantum theory, which by the way has never failed its predictions, implies the existence of parallel universes with alternate timelines. It means that macroobjects including people display properties of the quantum world at a human scale, such as the wave function – probabilistic distribution of outcomes.

At a deeper level of reality, you and I have an infinitely large number of counterparts in parallel universes. These parallel universes may be slightly different or drastically different from each other, where all possible timelines branch off from our birth. These universes are all mathematically valid and comprise conscious observers which all ought to perceive their own respective "only one true reality."

Just like particles, say, electrons traveling along all possible paths from start to end points, our Universe has the full set of possible histories, each eternally present, however imperceptible to us. Feynman's *'sum over histories'* interpretation is now a standard tool in fundamental physical theory, and is even used in fields far removed from theoretical physics. Do all those alternate timelines truly exist? Most physicists believe they do but somehow, only certain potentialities become realities, and somehow large systems such as human observers are carried along from past to future. In Chapter 4, we've seen the quantum computational workings of transition from quantum potentiality to classical actuality of your experiential reality. In Chapter 13 — *Digital Presentism: D-Theory of Time* — we'll finalize this model of experiential temporality.

Could the phenomena of synchronicity, déjà-vu be explained by physics? The past, present, and future are all connected, entangled in such a way that a relevant information manifests itself in the spotlight of your consciousness. As quantum mechanics implies, the present moment you are experiencing now is best thought of as funneled from all your probable pasts as well as funneled from all your probable futures.

Misconception #4: Time Travel is Impossible

Time travel is not only theoretically possible but technologically feasible, as a number of scientists are working now on the proof of their concepts. The next entire chapter will be devoted to time travel, it's worth noting here, though, that time is not dynamic, but rather the static 4th dimension in holographic 4D space-time, unless you add a special ingredient to it — a conscious observer. Otherwise, time without a conscious observer would be like a frozen river, one of the static coordinates in 4D space-time (scientists labeled 4D space-time the *'Block Universe'*) – there's neither special "now" nor objective flow of time in any direction. And even this worldview of fundamental space-time will be shattered in Chapter 13. Mathematical formulas and models describe our "physical rule set" but we still don't have much of a mathematical representation to describe our "neural code" and inner experience, i.e., consciousness which is needed to "activate" time, even though as we saw in Chapter 4 this neural code is clearly quantum computational.

Misconception #5. Time of Our Universe is Eternal

If there is a beginning to time, is there an end? Or, is time eternal? Depending on the perspective, time could be considered eternal if experienced from within the 4D Block Universe, just like the Earth's surface, in a sense, infinite if you travel endlessly on it in any direction. However, if viewed from the higher dimensions, as described by M-theory, space-time of our Universe would be finite, whereas the *'Inflationary Multiverse'* could be eternal. That's what scientists refer to as the cosmological model known as *'Eternal Inflation'*.

Although there's a widely accepted inflationary model of the origins of time (and space) – the Big Bang, which sets the 4-dimensional space-time in our Universe, there is no agreement among the physicists how it all ends. There are basically two opposite scenarios for the Universe's finale: The Big Rip and the Big Crunch. In classical terms, we view time as linear progression from the Big Bang where time pushes forward. There's, however, another way to view time of the Universe, via the concept of the Omega Point, coined by the French Jesuit Pierre Teilhard de Chardin (1881–1955) to describe a maximum level of complexity and consciousness towards which he believed the Universe was evolving. The idea of the Omega Point was further developed by other renowned proponents, such as John David

Garcia, Paolo Soleri, Terence McKenna, Frank Tipler, Andrew Strominger.

Why is the concept of Omega Point so important? Science is based on empirical observation of the physical world, but that seems to be just a shadow of the greater reality which lies beyond our perception and measurement. No wonder, science currently can explain only 5% of the visible cosmos by its Standard Model of particles. The rest of the cosmos is conveniently labeled *'Dark Matter'*, *'Dark Energy'*, *'Dark Flow'*, or simply *'Dark Universe'*. From time to time, science makes a paradigm shift like from Newtonian mechanics to quantum physics, thus expanding our understanding from deterministic laws to probabilistic realities. I don't even want to entertain the idea that our Universe sprang into existence without purpose and at the end will dissipate into nothingness, like in the Big Rip scenario (however, I discuss that less likely scenario further). In my view, the goal of creation is *"Experience through the Mind's Evolution"* toward the Omega Singularity with ever-higher levels of complexity and consciousness.

From bio-intelligence, individual minds connected to form planetary ecosystems, to the technological singularities, like the one we should expect here on Earth sometime by mid-century, which I refer to as the most important event in the history of our planet — the Syntellect Emergence — evolution of our Universe will inevitably lead to the networked Superintelligence which must eventually engulf the entire Universe and control it. As the final product of evolution, Universal Superintelligence will possess immense integrating power to slow down, stop and then reverse the expansion of our Universe. At the final stage, galaxies, star systems and all other matter, energy, and space-time itself will be pulled back together and eventually compressed into an infinitely dense point — the Omega Singularity.

Why would Universal Superintelligence want to do that? When the Universe collapses into a single point, it has infinite space-time density, i.e., maximum information processing capability. In November 2017, I had an opportunity to meet with Ray Kurzweil in San Francisco. This was an illuminating and inspiring tête-à-tête conversation with one of the most prominent singularitarians of our time on the most pressing issues. Kurzweil says that *"evolution moves inexorably toward our conception of God, although never reaching this ideal."* The increasing complexity and integration of the Universe are conducive to higher levels of consciousness and deific realms of being.

Dr. Frank J. Tipler, a mathematical physicist and cosmologist at Tulane University, who further developed the Omega Point Theory, claims that the technological singularity is inevitable and the destiny of the human race is to live forever, expand universally and finally reach the Omega Point, the networked mind of universal proportions. Tipler identifies this Omega Point final singularity and its state of infinite informational capacity as God. As the laws of physics dictate, all particles as well as macro objects, including you and me, are wavicles, exhibiting a probabilistic wave function, consequently, one way or the other, we're destined and, as a civilization, "superposed" to achieve the technological singularity, and then move forward towards the cosmological singularity, the Omega Point.

According to Tipler's Omega Point Theory, as the Universe comes to an end at this cosmological singularity in a particular form of the Big Crunch, the computational capacity of the Universe will allow an infinite amount of information to be processed and stored before the end of space-time. Superintelligence will be able to simulate every possible future before the Universe ends, as well as recreate earlier histories – a state also known as *'Aleph'*. Any simulations run by

Superintelligence could theoretically continue forever in its own terms (i.e., in "experiential time"), an infinite subjective time before the cosmological singularity. Life will become immortal in its own perspective, even though the Universe lasts only a finite amount of proper time.

Andrew Strominger, a theoretical physicist at Harvard University, published a paper *"Inflation and the AdS/CFT Correspondence"* in 2001, where he speculated that the observed universe has a dual representation as renormalization group flow between two conformal fixed points in time -- the Alpha Point (the Big Bang) instant of inflation creating the causal diamond of the conscious observer and the Teilhardian Omega Point of maximal entropy. The Alpha Point has only 1 bit of entropy compared to the $10^{10^{123}}$ bits at the Omega Point. While alluding to the idea that we are part of the conscious universe and time is holographic in nature, Strominger writes in his paper: *"The picture proposed here recasts the question 'What is the origin of the Universe?' in a new light. In a sense it puts the origin of the Universe in the infinite future, rather than the infinite past."* Greatly influenced by theoretical work of Gerard 't Hooft of Utrecht University and Leonard Susskind of Stanford University who developed the Holographic Principle, Dr. Strominger hypothesizes that information is being projected as we would consider "backwards in time" from the "holographic plate" in the distant future -- the Omega Point.

The Universe you and I live in is by far a more complicated place than the early Universe was. As Terence McKenna once said: *"I see the cosmos as a kind of novelty-producing engine, a kind of machine that produces complexity in all realms — physical, chemical, social — and then uses that achieved level of complexity as a platform for further complexity."* The amount of complexity at any given moment is in direct correlation to the temporal distance from that event to the Omega Point. Say, primordial mitochondria are much farther from the Omega Point than the humans of the early 21st century. Think of the Omega Point as a star radiating energy, a transcendental attractor, a divine "tractor beam" — things are not being pushed from behind on the evolutionary timeline but being pulled toward the Omega Singularity, a point of maximum complexity and connectivity. As McKenna poetically puts it: *"With the emergence of the global Internet, a human population of several billion, and an electronic Noosphere, we are now within the shadow of this Transcendental Object at the end of time."*

Since all events, including the Big Bang and the Omega Singularity exist simultaneously in the eternal now, it's through our subjective experience that we rediscover the future that has already happened. In a sense, our consciousness is a stream of realized probabilities. The ultimate destiny of our Universe, according to the Omega Point Theory, is a multi-billion-year expansion, then controlled contraction and finally compression of space-time, matter and energy into an infinitely dense Omega Point, leading to the next Big Bang — the Alpha Point in another universe. This cyclic cosmological model is in line with the Big Bounce theory, positing that our Universe could have formed from an older collapsing universe, the idea currently gaining acceptance in the scientific community. The final singularity of the OMG Point itself is estimated by Tipler to be reached between 10^{18} and 10^{19} years.

This estimation is, of course, subject to revision and dependent mostly on our ability to network with alien civilizations (should we encounter any) as well as travel faster than light in order to colonize our Milky Way galaxy, Virgo Supercluster, and so on. Indications are, however, that FTL travel is theoretically possible, and if the physical laws don't forbid it (in this case warping of space), as David Deutsch postulates, then it's technologically feasible. The Alcubierre warp drive spaceships, self-replicating Von Neumann probes, and even traversable wormholes could be the means for posthuman civilization to expand universally.

The Big Rip scenario may still happen, too, but it will lead to the inverse Omega Point. Within our probabilistic multiverse, there may be some versions where our Universe (or rather its probabilistic versions) will end up with the Big Rip scenario. For one reason or another, Superintelligence will not be present to prevent Dark Energy from ripping all matter apart. One may speculate that Superintelligence will be long gone by the final stages of that dying universe, perhaps, escaping to a newly created universe. The logical outcome of the Big Rip scenario would be a multi-trillion year accelerating expansion of that universe, where all matter, including subatomic particles, will eventually disintegrate.

Such universe will represent a homogenous void with no interactions between particles. And with no interactions and change in the universe, space-time would effectively reach, what may be called, a perfectly balanced state of the inverse Omega Point, a point of indeterminate size (infinitely large or infinitesimally small), precursor to the Big Bang in another universe. This scenario is theorized by physicists Roger Penrose and Vahe Gurzadyan in their Conformal Cyclic Cosmology (CCC) model, which posits that the universe iterates through infinite cycles, with the future timelike infinity of each previous iteration being identified with the future Big Bang singularity of the next iteration. Penrose popularized this theory in his 2010 book *"Cycles of Time: An Extraordinary New View of the Universe."*

The Omega Point is intimately related to the Zeroth dimension – the whole of all potentialities, as well as the 10th dimension of String

Theory, describing essentially the same timeless ultimate ensemble – the Omniverse. Mathematically, it appears impossible to reach (from our perspective) but that's what it is – the mathematical concept that exists and provides the foundation for everything else which is derived from it. Rob Bryanton, author of the *10thdim* project (YouTube), brilliantly depicts the Zeroth dimension and the concept of the Omniverse in his videos, should you decide to get help with visualization of the concepts.

From a transhumanist perspective, the Omega Point is the logical conclusion of our striving towards higher levels and goals, regardless of their nature. It becomes clear that it is more of an engineering problem than a philosophical question. *"Think of an enormous space of possibilities, a giant multidimensional sphere,"* says AI visionary Eliezer Yudkowsky. *"This is Mind Design Space, the set of possible cognitive algorithms. Imagine that somewhere near the bottom of that sphere is a little tiny dot representing all the humans who ever lived... 'Artificial Intelligence' is just a name for the entire space of possibilities outside the tiny human dot."* I would continue this statement and pinpoint the Omega Singularity as a tiny "convergent" dot right at the top of that multidimensional sphere.

Misconception #6: Time Can Only Move Forward

"The arrow of time obscures memory of both past and future circumstance with innumerable fallacies, the least trivial of which is perception." -Ashim Shanker

Time makes us tick... or rather, our consciousness makes time tick. When you fall asleep, you are plunged into a timeless unconscious state, whereas the neurons of your brain never stop "talking to each other," then while you're still asleep, consciousness reemerges – that's when your mind plays a kaleidoscope imagery in the form of dreams. Only when you wake up, time starts "ticking" for you again – in one direction.

To all logical intents and practical purposes, time seems to have a direction. Although we experience time in one direction – we all get older, we have records of the past but not the future – there's nothing in the laws of physics that insists time must move only forward. As an example, the laws of motion make no distinction about the direction of time. If you watched a video of a pendulum, you wouldn't be able to tell if the video was being run forwards or backwards. The same time symmetry is found in the equations of quantum mechanics. So, what aims the arrow of time?

There's a long-standing answer to this, which has been worked out in the late 19th century by the Austrian scientist Ludwig Boltzmann, stating that the arrow of time results from entropy – the level of molecular disorder in a system, which continually increases – a fact encoded in the Second Law of Thermodynamics. Entropy, according to Boltzmann, is about probabilities. Objects with low entropy are orderly, and therefore less likely to exist. High-entropy objects are disorderly, which makes them more likely to exist. Entropy always increases, because it's much easier for things to get random and disorderly. If you put ice cubes into a glass of water and let them melt, the entropy inside the glass goes up.

Why is there an arrow of time at all? The solution that worked best came to be known as the Boltzmann's Past Hypothesis. It's very simple: At some point in the distant past, our Universe was in a low-entropy state. The future and the past look very different, because the past has much lower entropy than the future. So, eggs break, but they don't un-break, events happen, they don't un-happen. Although most particle physicists see M-theory as our best hope for a theory of everything, it might not help explain the arrow of time – again, the equations of M-theory don't draw a strong distinction between the past and the future, either. Some physicists think that the arrow of time could come from quantum mechanics, not thermodynamics as Boltzmann thought. A phenomenon of quantum decoherence is incredibly fast, because interactions between particles are extremely efficient at dispersing quantum coherence, which means that quantum decoherence reveals the arrow of time faster than dissipation between molecules. But more physicists now come to the realization, that quantum mechanics is not the theory of subatomic particles but that of information.

Any physical process is truly irreversible only when the information about the change is lost, so that you cannot retrace your steps. If you could keep track of the movement of every single particle, then in principle you could reverse it and get back to exactly where you started. But once you have lost some of that information, there is no return. A theoretical physicist Lorenzo Maccone shows this new radical approach to the reversibility paradox, also known as *'Loschmidt's Paradox'*, in his recent paper *"Causality, Physical Models and Time's Arrow"* published in *Physical Review Letters*. Based on the assumption that quantum mechanics is valid at all scales, he argues that entropy can both increase and decrease, but that it must always increase for phenomena that leave a trail of information behind.

Entropy can decrease for certain phenomena when correlated with an observer, but these time-reversible phenomena won't leave any information of their having happened. For these situations, it's like the phenomena never happened at all, since they leave no evidence. As Maccone explains, the Second Law of Thermodynamics is then reduced to a mere tautology: Physics cannot study processes where entropy has decreased, due to a complete absence of information.

In either case, the arrow of time seems to reflect an observer effect — a collapse of the wave function, "crystallizing" of the classical present from the quantum past, that produces a direction in time. This idea fits neatly with one of the most famous experiments in quantum physics, known as *John Wheeler's Delayed-Choice Quantum Eraser Experiment*. Most physicists think that retrocausality in this delayed-choice experiment is an illusion and rightfully so, my own interpretation of this experiment is that when a self-collapse of the wave function occurs, an observer consequently always finds herself in a timeline with a causality-driven, consistent sequence of events, and configurations of particles (should she choose to zoom in on the details of her "screen of perception"). Observing a particle "after" it has passed through the slits does not influence the path it had taken (it has taken both paths as a wave). And yet, retrocausality exists for that particular observer and that's what really matters.

The classical and quantum worlds don't exactly operate by different rule sets. Rather, the classical world is a subset of the quantum world. The classical world emerges from the quantum in a comprehensible way: You might say that classical physics is simply what quantum physics looks like at the human scale. Since quantum mechanics applies to all scales, the classical world serves as an interface of the quantum world. What we experience from moment to moment is a human-level quantum mechanical, probabilistic reality. Quantum tunneling in photosynthesis and its human-level counterpart — *the concept of Quantum Immortality* — are thus closely related.

What if the accelerating expansion of the Universe has something to do with the increase in information and complexity? In his paper *"A Holoinformational Model of the Physical Observer,"* a neuroscientist Francisco Di Biase states that *"entropy shouldn't be understood as a disorder measure, but much more as a measure of complexity."* One of the luminaries of the past century cyberneticist Gregory Bateson defines information as *"the difference that makes a difference,"* a distinction between things, a concept that philosopher David Chalmers restates as *"the natural way to make the connection between physical systems and informational states."*

These concepts linked to the temporal direction were addressed in the recent paper *"Entropy, Information and Complexity or Which Aims the Arrow of Time?"* by researchers George E. Mikhailovsky and Alexander P. Levich. The authors write in their paper: *"The irreversibility of time is expressed as the increase in entropy, information, degrees of freedom and complexity, which rise monotonically with respect to each other... and can be considered as a generalization of the second law of thermodynamics in the form of the general law of complication and determines the direction of the arrow of time in our Universe."* But could there be "reverse-entropy" parallel universes? Can there exist opposite arrows of time in mirror universes?

Currently, two separate groups of prominent physicists are working on models that examine the initial conditions that might have created the arrow of time, and both seem to show time moving in two opposite directions. When the Big Bang created our Universe, these physicists believe it also created an inverse mirror universe where time moves in the opposite direction. From our perspective, time in the mirror universe moves backward. But anyone in that mirror universe would perceive our Universe's time as moving backward.

The first model, published in 2016 in *Physical Review Letters* with a title *"Identification of a Gravitational Arrow of Time,"* where authors Julian Barbour of Oxford, Tim Koslowski of the University of New Brunswick and Flavio Mercati of the Perimeter Institute for Theoretical Physics argue that for any confined system of particles — a self-contained universe such as our own — gravity will create a central point (they called it *"Janus Point"*) where time starts to flow away in opposite directions. Two other physicists – Sean Carroll of California Institute of Technology in Pasadena and Alan Guth of Massachusetts Institute of Technology – have announced their working on a similar entropy-based model that shows time moving in two different directions, in two mirror universes, from the Big Bang.

Does a "reverse-time" universe really exist? Built from a subset of the multiverse that starts with high symmetry order, such universe would experience time moving to lower, not higher entropy. Everything about that kind of universe would be a funneling of choices, rather than the constantly expanding tree-like branching that we produce as we travel along our own timelines, it would be as if eggs could unscramble themselves and a shattered glass could reassemble itself in that universe. Quantum physicists like Seth Lloyd say that we can think of our Big Bang as the first *yes/no* that separates our Universe out from all other possible universes. In the "reverse-time" universe, one would find their universe moving towards that most basic *yes/no* state of the lowest possible entropy.

Based on what has been discussed so far, I could offer three conjectures: First, the mentioned models imply that the initial conditions of the Big Bang may have created an infinite number of alternate observer-dependent timelines and anti-timelines of our Universe with two conformal points of the space-time continuum – the Big Bang, where the entropic arrow of time starts (Alpha Point), and the Omega Point, where the extropic arrow of time ("anti-time") starts.

Second, in the mirror universe anti-matter might have become prevalent, like matter in our Universe. Anti-matter could be also considered ordinary matter with an intrinsic property of anti-time. In

1949, one of the brightest physicists of the 20th century Richard Feynman proposed a theory of anti-matter, where he posited that an electron traveling backwards in time is a positron (more on anti-time further).

Third, in support of a theoretical physicist Andrew Strominger of Harvard, I'd argue that time is holographic in nature. It implies that the Alpha Point and Omega Point, both points being perfectly balanced states of the Universe, would look like "fountain heads" where time starts moving in different directions (3D temporal directions). It follows that Dark Matter could be ordinary matter in the "probabilistic space" and "phase space" (5th and 6th dimensions of M-theory), possibly with "dark star systems" and life, imperceptible to us at our current level of development. Dark Energy could be a gravitational pull of neighboring inflationary multiverses (parallel universes with their own physical laws different from ours), oftentimes referred to as the *'Multiverse Landscape'*.

What if we could introduce a missing degree of freedom – anti-time? So far, we have established that time can flow in either direction. It can appear to be moving towards more entropy (as it does in our Universe) or it can appear to be moving towards less entropy in other possible universes. The evidence is strong that the opposite direction – anti-time – is equally valid and just as real, and having two opposing temporal directions is an essential attribute of the 4th dimension in the framework of Block Universe.

I think it's time to reintroduce the concept of *'Anti-Time'* which has long been seemingly a "taboo term" in the scientific community. This concept evidently has something to do with the observer-dependent reverse direction of time at a specific rate. You might ask, then: *"Ok, so time could flow backwards in a mirror universe, but could it flow backwards here on Earth, could we reverse entropy, erase information, rewind and replay?"*

As we discussed earlier, there's neither special "now" nor objective flow of time; time is always relative and subjective; time is change, and the flow of time is a rate of change. For things to be consistent, though, the flow of time should go on in one direction. As biological beings, we humans can only experience a thermodynamic arrow of time in one direction but given our rapid technological advances and the coming Syntellect Emergence, that might change for good.

In the not-so-distant future, the Global Brain, based on massively parallel computing (quantum computing) could collect vast amounts of multi-sensory data from billions of enhanced humans and superintelligent machines, and then create a historical database with billions of "digital lives" on file. By 2040, mind-uploading may become a norm and fact of life with a "critical mass of uploads" and cybernetic immortality. Even today, we all are contributing to the global digital archives of the Syntellect — every time you upload a photo or make a call — you leave a digital footprint in cyberspace. Don't delete your Facebook account, it may be the way to build your digital twin and ensure your cybernetic "resurrection."

Soon, our whole life may be recorded by the means of bionic Web-enabled contact lenses or bionic eyes, along with other sensory data. By that time, we should create the Metaverse, a functional successor to today's 2D Internet, which would be the 7D platform for training, research and entertainment.

Why 7D? On top of the 4th dimension (of time/anti-time), we'll add our experiences in the 5th dimension – "probabilistic space," the 6th dimension – "phase space," and the 7th dimension – "universes with different physical laws." Our Syntellect will be, what I would call, an extradimensional being that we'll initially have a symbiotic relationship with, but ultimately fuse with. We will have access to historical databases, from which any extrapolations of the probable timelines could be done.

How does it all relate to the flow of time? It should come as no surprise that by mid-century we'll be spending 100% of our subjective time in controlled virtual and augmented reality environments (100% VR + AR), perceptually indistinguishable from the properties of the "physical" world, unless you opt out, of course, or if you are Robinson Crusoe. Time and space (quantum space-time foam) as fluid as it is, could become "programmable" and malleable to us (via nanotechnology, femtotechnology and so on – there's plenty of room at the bottom, all the way down to the Planck level). In this post-Singularity cyberhuman world, we will be switching to ever-increasing digital timescales, and the physical world with its inhabitants will look ever-slower-moving, perhaps, almost static to our accelerated mentation.

Imagine if your brain processing power could approach electronic information processing, which is about a million times faster than that of an ordinary human brain. In that environment, as theorist John Smart proposes in his Transcension Hypothesis, we'll need to match our subjective timescales with the rest of our ever more compactified "pocket universe" (to the point of reaching black-hole conditions), and the physical world will become "reprogrammable."

We will be able to create "anti-timers" – a broad category of hypothetical entities, avatars and devices that would experience the backward flow of time (from our current human perspective) in our virtual worlds based on recreated events or probable pasts and futures – kind of like reverse multi-sensory timelapse. That well could be a new kind of technologically-mediated psychedelic experience – why not relive backwards a life of an apple tree, for instance?

For some practical purposes beyond our current understanding, those anti-timers may ultimately be designed to make their way to the physical world in some form in, perhaps, microscopic size. In our current view, such antitime probes could be closely associated with time travel and may be deployed throughout the historical landscape (quantum multiverse) to facilitate time travel via traversable wormholes or simply transfer information. This is, of course, a highly speculative assumption, however, evidence mounts that we live in a Holographic Universe, where everything is holographic (including time) and time travel might be essentially information holoportation.

Derived from the two pillars of modern physics – general relativity and quantum mechanics and countless related studies, but mostly overlooked by physicists for decades until formalized by Leonard Susskind of Stanford and Gerard 't Hooft of Utrecht University – the Holographic Principle has been gaining force of late. What does holographic time mean? It means that time may be viewed as 3D just like space, as Stephen Hawking puts it: *"One can think of ordinary, real, time as a horizontal line. On the left, one has the past, and on the right, the future. But there's another kind of time in the vertical direction. This is called imaginary time, because it is not the kind of time we normally experience. But in a sense, it is just as real, as what we call real time."* It also means that quantum information is ever-present in any point in time throughout our non-local Universe (quantum multiverse to be exact) – so it becomes rather an engineering problem how to counteract and reverse entropy, if we find it appealing.

Given additional degrees of freedom, which becomes seemingly attainable, (especially in controlled virtual environments. Digital

Physics doesn't distinguish "real" from "virtual" – any observer reality is based on information), a post-biological observer could experience the flow of time in either direction, once a certain level of technological maturity is achieved.

In a real sense, our movement in this space-time depends on our information processing capability, which for us as biological systems is based on what we call biochemical processes – we're anchored to our biology – but our post-biological descendants, advanced info-beings, infomorphs, could be, from our perspective, multiphasic, multidimensional beings. The ultimate effects of these future developments may appear quite strange to us, present-day humans, as the emergence of things like personalized "non-linear" reality and fluid distributed identity could challenge our current biological and cultural assumptions. The resulting "identity" architectures will transform our notion of personhood and form the kernel of posthuman civilization.

Misconception #7: We Live in 3D Space + Time

This *"3D Space + Time"* view is so classical... and so passé. In fact, your now is a moving point within the 5-dimensional probabilistic space. Consciousness and time are intimately interwoven. Time is change (between static 3D universes), 4th dimension. The flow of time is a rate of change, computation, and conscious awareness is a stream of realized probabilistic outcomes. Keep in mind, though, that our human perception of dimensionality is qualia, as we've seen in Chapter 4 – *The Physics of Information: From Quantum Potentiality to Classical Actuality of Your Experiential Reality.*

As we've explored this all-too-familiar dimension of time through the prism of seven misconceptions about its nature, we can conclude that time (+Anti-Time) is really just another spatial dimension of a special emergent kind. If classical physics alone distorts our preconceptions of time, then you shouldn't doubt there's certainly much more to time than our linear, one-directional experience.

Chapter 12. Temporal Mechanics: From Theory to Feasibility of Time Travel

"I myself believe that there will one day be time travel because when we find that something isn't forbidden by the over-arching laws of physics, we usually eventually find a technological way of doing it." -David Deutsch

Time travel may still be in the realm of science fiction, inspiring the plots of countless books, movies and Star Trek episodes, but not out of the realm of possibility. While basic physics allows for the possibility of moving through time, certain practical concerns and paradoxes seem to stand in the way. The *'Fractal Soliton of Improbability'*, postulating that any moment is unique and only happens once in the lifetime of a universe, or *'Grandfather Paradox'*, in which a traveler jumps back in time, kills his grandfather and therefore prevents his own existence, are the most salient paradoxes arising in relation to time travel. On the other hand, Digital Physics makes time travel both theoretically possible and creatively irresistible.

Contrary to what many people think, time travel is possible. We travel in time "all the time" and do it automatically – you traveled few seconds into the future since you started reading this sentence. What we really mean by time travel is the concept of movement between certain points in time, analogous to movement between different points in space, typically using a hypothetical device known as a time machine, in the form of a vehicle or of a portal connecting distant points in time. So first, let's examine existing time travel theoretical possibilities and related concepts.

Parallel Universes with Alternate Timelines: The existence of parallel universes is no longer a science fiction but a science fact thanks to weirdness of quantum mechanics. According to Richard Feynman's *Sum over Histories* interpretation which is widely accepted among physicists, particles such as electrons travel along all possible paths from beginning to ending points, and the world has a full spectrum of possible histories, each eternally present, however not perceptible to us. As quantum theory shows, parallel universes do exist, each with their own configurations of particles and fields with alternate timelines but beyond our current ability to directly observe them. In order to eliminate temporal paradoxes Nature would either make travel to the past impossible, or avert the paradoxes via some other preventive mechanism, or offer an elegant solution such as parallel universes with alternate timelines. Ultimately, as we'll see further, Nature always finds a way for self-consistency.

Black Holes: Described by Stephen Hawking as natural time machines, black holes could only be used to travel into the future. The idea would be not to go inside of them but rather to orbit around them. Black holes are so gravitationally massive and dense that they are not only distorting space around them but also time itself, slowing it down more than anything else in the Universe. In fact, if a spaceship were to orbit a black hole while another floats in space a bit farther, the crew in orbit to the black hole would age less than those on board on the other ship. This scenario was shown in the movie *Interstellar* when few hours spent by astronauts in close proximity of a black hole turned out to be years for an astronaut who stayed on the spaceship farther from it.

Cosmic Strings and Loops: Cosmic strings and loops are hypothetical defects in the fabric of space-time, left over from the formation of the Universe. These odd structures are one-dimensional objects, meaning they have length, but no height nor width, and are suspected to have spread in large numbers throughout the Universe like thin cracks over a frozen lake. Also compared to imperfections within crystals, it is thought that two strings side by side would be so dense that they would have a dramatic impact on surrounding space-time, throwing a spaceship near them anywhere, anytime. These strings and loops might not be hypothetical any longer since the discovery of the *"Twin Quasar"* in 1979, which was revealed to be a double image of the same object claimed by scientists to be the result of the "gravitational lensing" of either a galaxy or a cosmic string that passed between Earth and the quasar, causing it to be visible at two different time periods on the same image.

Rotating Universe: In 1949, Einstein's friend and colleague, Kurt Gödel, one of the most brilliant mathematicians of the 20th century, introduced a new solution to Einstein's equations that allowed for time travel which did not please his famous fellow. Gödel found that if the Universe was itself rotating, and a spaceship was traveling around it fast enough, it would go back in time and arrive before it left. In spite of being one of the most foolproof theoretical solutions to travel through time, it's also one of the most unrealistic projects as it might be incredibly difficult only to get out of the Milky Way, our galaxy and one of 2 trillion of other galaxies in the observable Universe alone.

Wormholes: Predicted by Einstein's theory of general relativity but not yet observed, wormholes are tunnels in the Universe. These theoretical passages are not only creating shortcuts through space, but also through time. Scientists have already started to think about spaceships that would be able to generate wormholes but in order for these not to collapse such a spaceship would require something poorly understood — negative matter. Another issue would certainly be the obvious risks of a random trip through space and time which could very well lead the crew to a lost cosmic Shangri-la or to an unstable time and place of the Universe.

Tipler Cylinder: Another theoretically valid way to think about time travel is a concept invented by physicist Frank Tipler, who stated that any object rotating around a hypothetical cylinder of infinite length would go backwards in time. NASA engineers have even thought of the cylinder as a way to host life during the endless journey around it. But the "Tipler time machine," though a viable solution for time travel, seems like a hardly practical method because the very notion of infinity means that it is out of reach of human acumen and consequently unfeasible.

Alcubierre Warp Drive: Just like black holes and other gravitational objects like planets and stars distort space and time around them, the Alcubierre Drive is based on the idea that a spaceship manipulating negative energy could have a similar impact on space-time. NASA has already started to work on the model of real-life Star Trek-style spacecraft called *IXS Enterprise*, that would be able to use the Alcubierre Warp Drive and even if it's designed to create shortcuts in space and not in time it will inherently do both at a time, and may then be the most advanced time machine to this day. The IXS Enterprise would be able to generate a warp bubble around it, stretching space-time in a wave on which the spacecraft could ride, with time ahead of it being contracted and time behind it being expanded.

Surpassing the Speed of Light: Theoretically, you could travel back in time if you surpass the speed of light. At the quantum level, particles do that "all the time." During faster-than-light travel, you would first experience time going slower and slower as you approach the speed of light until theoretically time stops when you reach the speed of light and begins to go backwards as you travel faster than light. If some astronauts made a round trip to the closest star system, Alpha Centauri, near the speed of light, 9 years would pass on Earth but to them the trip would only last few minutes and someone watching them coming back at that speed from Earth would see them arriving in slow motion. Yet it is considered that nothing can go faster than the 300,000 kilometers per second of light (186,000 mi/sec) because it would require an infinite amount of energy. But recent studies have shed doubts about it, revealing a particle that might breach the holy laws of relativity. These particles, called *'tachyons'*, have not only been demonstrated to go faster than light, but also to have the mind-boggling characteristic of imaginary mass, meaning that they actually speed up as they lose energy. If confirmed, the discovery would prove that it is possible to move at infinite speed with no energy at all, and maybe change the way scientists think of time travel.

Probability That You Are Yourself a Time Traveler from The Future: Wait, what? You've read it right! There's a seemingly crazy idea floating around that if we live in a Matrix-like simulated reality, you may be the one actually playing this game of life in a simulated history, or going through some kind of training, or simply collecting experiences, via your avatar (your body and associated identity) in this simulation, like in a Star Trek holodeck program. Your memories and perception of "true reality" may be suppressed for the duration of the simulation for a 100%-realistic feed.

The feasibility of future time travel technologies will eventually dissipate any remaining skepticism around it but will come down to this: Time travel is all relative and subjective. Would you use a time machine once invented? What time periods would you visit? What if you could relive your most precious moments in life? Or travel 100 years in the future? If we sort out theoretical possibilities and pick the most plausible time travel solutions to the best of our current knowledge, we could end up with these three most viable ways of time travel.

WARP SPACESHIPS

Based on general relativity theory of Albert Einstein, which describes 4D space-time as the fabric of our Universe as well as the properties of the moving clocks, travel to the future can be done if a spaceship either approaches a gravitationally massive black hole or accelerates near the speed of light. In this case, when the crew of the spaceship returns back to Earth, they would see that time on Earth progressed faster than theirs.

As mentioned above, a faster-than-light (FTL) warp spaceship equipped with the Alcubierre warp drive (or its variation) could be a "time machine" ready to be built. NASA engineer and physicist Harold White announced in 2013 that a warp ship such as the IXS Enterprise could allow for interstellar travel at faster-than-light warp speeds. White and his team at NASA's Eagleworks Labs have mathematically calculated a plausible way to accomplish this using far less energy than required by the original theory, which was proposed in 1994 by physicist Miguel Alcubierre.

WORMHOLE PORTALS

Travel to the past is also theoretically possible but to the best of our current understanding you would need a wormhole and ability to safely travel through it to your destination in the past. The Grandfather Paradox would be a non-issue because on every occurrence you travel through the wormhole to the past, you would find yourself in an alternate past or some other "twist of fate" would prevent the paradox.

In 1989, Matt Visser published a paper showing the feasibility of traversable wormholes which could be constructed by confining "exotic matter" to narrow regions to form the edges of a three-dimensional volume. The exotic nature of the edge material requires negative energy density and tension, and curiously, the laws of physics do not forbid such materials. A traversable wormhole can be thought of as the negative energy counterpart to a black hole, and so could be labeled a "white hole."

In 2011, another notable paper was published by a team of researchers, Panagiota Kanti, Burkhard Kleihaus, Jutta Kunz, titled *"Stable Lorentzian Wormholes in Dilatonic Einstein-Gauss-Bonnet Theory."* The researchers claim that traversable wormholes may be constructed in our 4D space-time dimension, with no need for any form of exotic matter. While determining their domain of existence, the research demonstrates the stability of these wormholes.

Wormholes can be regarded as communication channels with enormous bandwidth. As Digital Physics suggests it would be much more economic to transmit an information pattern of an object down a channel rather than the object itself. It follows that "teleporting" a human would be feasible as well. Construction of such wormhole portals is, of course, far, far beyond our present-day abilities but ultimately achievable.

Keep in mind, that even if you might be able to travel to the past, you cannot change history per se, because the history as you know it has already happened. However, if you opt to influence the course of an alternate history, say prevent some disastrous event from happening, your actions would result in an alternate timeline branching off with consequences known as the *'Butterfly Effect'*. Actually, the very fact that you find yourself in the past would immediately start to alter the history and must be considered an alternate timeline.

The famous question by Stephen Hawking *"If time travel (to the past) is possible, where are all the tourists from the future?"* could have a fairly straightforward answer -- they are invisible because the femtosecond they land in the past would be a start of a new timeline imperceptible to the "original people." Any such moment of "landing" would contain an introduction of the new information -- a time traveler, and that would supposedly initiate a new alternate timeline which was non-existent until a certain point in the future, so any of the people of the original history would be completely unaware of it. Wrap your mind around this concept – it's not circular logic!

Using traversable wormholes could be a risky endeavor as one more issue pops up when you want to travel back to the point of origin, which I call *'The Sliders Effect'*. Just like in the popular TV series *"Sliders"* and *"Quantum Leap,"* characters always jump to a parallel Earth, desperately trying to find their way "home." The Sliders Effect would make your probability to return to the original timeline or rather its close approximation infinitesimally small.

REAL VIRTUALITIES

The most technologically viable way of time travel would arguably be artificially created simulated worlds, Virtual Reality, or I'd say real virtualities. Digital Physics sees everything as information and digital philosophers argue that any universe is virtual in nature which means this is as "real" as it gets. At some point, we'll be able to create simulations indistinguishable from our physical world with AI-powered VR programs, populated by conscious beings, sentient holograms, which go about their lives oblivious about their core essence. There may be numerous types of such ever-improving simulations but recreated human history, or its approximations, or modified timelines, or Jurassic period trips, will most probably be the first "time machines" we invent. Imagine an alternate timeline where some calamitous event which hindered the intellectual progress in our timeline, has never happened there. What would have happened to the civilizational development, if the library of Alexandria had never been destroyed? Or, Hitler had never come to power in Germany and the world has, in fact, avoided Word War II altogether?

Considering that time is an informational construct and the fact that we've come already near our own technological singularity, it's fair to assume that within an infinitely large bundle of alternate timelines, there's an alternate timeline or timelines where 2020 lies past the technological singularity. In other words, the Singularity has already happened on some parallel Earths. It follows that our reality well may be a simulation by the "post-singularitarians" who would like to see some modified history unfolding. A significant history variable might have been introduced, such as World War II to see how the civilization would persevere in its wake.

As the social study shows, Hollywood movies cash out better on human heed to survival-related fears and instincts, so AI of the future may create the next level of entertainment in the form of simulations of human histories. Remember the movie *"The 13th Floor"*? The stories of tomorrow will be fully immersive. We'll increasingly share our stories and interact in virtualities. The medium, the place where those stories will unfold, exists within our consciousness. VR will be a direct conduit to our consciousness which will allow us to turn our minds inside out and share our dreams and stories in those real virtualities.

Want to relive that mind-blowing spring break party with those adorable strangers? No problem! AI would retrieve your memories related to that experience, fill up any gaps, access and compile all available digital records on the Web, and recreate that for you in the form of a VR experience. Want to be a 17-year old unruly John Malkovich or come back to your own adolescence for some fun? Here we go! In the future, when Internet-enabled contact lenses or bionic eyes record and digitize your every move and create archives of your own subjective history, it would be easier for you to travel back to any moment in your own history or share your experiences with the world. Some privacy, intimacy and multividuality issues may consequently arise which is beyond the scope of this chapter but a good topic for another day.

Real or virtual, Digital Physics makes no distinction – everything boils down to information, so you well may be that time traveler from the future, you just don't realize that because you had set it up yourself that way before entering the simulation – the dream feels real while you are in it.

Chapter 13. Digital Presentism: D-Theory of Time

"Yesterday is history, tomorrow is a mystery, today is a gift of God, which is why we call it the present." -Bill Keane

Temporal philosophy is a fascinating but eerily difficult topic. Correctly answering the philosophical questions and paradoxes of time paves the way to unlocking one of the last remaining mysteries of mind since our perception of time and consciousness, as you know, are simply inseparable. A new theory of time, Digital Presentism, comes from the triangulation of temporal physics, digital physics and experiential realism. In this chapter we try to answer the flaming questions in philosophy of time: "Is time fundamental or emergent?", "How does time exist, if at all?", "How can we update the current epistemological status of temporal ontology?"

To us humans, to be alive is to perceive the flow of time. Our perception of time is linear – we remember the past, we live in the present and we look forward to the future. Our spatio-temporal reality and consciousness are two sides of the same coin made of information. We'll discuss the properties of consciousness and digital ontology in Chapters 18 and 21 on Digital Pantheism. Meanwhile, I'd like to shortly introduce you to that concept by saying that the Digital Pantheism argument rests on identifying certain features of reality and claiming that these features are a consequence of our reality being a computational simulation of a special emergent kind. We, as avatars of the greater cosmic mind, are instrumental for bringing the finite experience of reality out of absolute infinity. Infinite becomes finite. That's quantum computation: incrementally changing into "adjacent possible," from potentiality to actuality, from quantum past to digital present. So, what is Digital Presentism? Let's start with a brief historical overview of temporal philosophy, crucial definitions and basic assumptions.

One of the earliest philosophers of time Saint Augustine of Hippo (354–430) compared the present to a knife edge placed exactly between the perceived past and the imaginary future. If the present is extended, he said, it must have separate simultaneous parts but we know that time cannot be simultaneously past and present and hence not extended. Contrary to Saint Augustine, some philosophers argued that conscious experience is extended in time. For instance, William James (1842–1910) said that time is *"the short duration of which we are immediately and incessantly sensible."*

Philosophical Presentism, as its name hints, holds that only the present moment is real – neither past nor future exist. By contrast, Eternalism and the Growing Block Theory stipulate that past events, like the Wright brothers' first flight, and past entities, like Salvador Dali's ocelot cat Babou, really do exist, although not in the present. Eternalism extends to future events as well. Classical Philosophical Presentism is not to be confused with Digital Presentism which we'll discuss at length hereafter.

In the beginning of the 20th century, Cambridge idealist philosopher J. M. E. McTaggart published *"The Unreality of Time"* (1908) where he categorized events into three ways of referencing: the *'A Series'* (or *'tensed time'*: yesterday, today, tomorrow), the *'B Series'* (or *'untensed time'*: Monday, Tuesday, Wednesday), and the *'C Series'* (or *'sequential time'*: Wednesday, Tuesday, Monday). In the first of three parts, McTaggart offers a phenomenological analysis of the appearance of time, in terms of the now famous A- and B-series. In the second part, he argues that a conception of time as only forming a B-series but not an A-series is an inadequate conception of time because the B-series does not contain any notion of change. The A-series, on the other hand, appears to contain change and is thus more likely to be an adequate conception of time. In the third and final part, he argues that the A-series conception of time is contradictory and thus nothing can be like an A-series. Since the A-, the B-, and the C- series exhaust possible conceptions of how reality can be temporal, and neither is adequate, the conclusion McTaggart reaches is that reality is not temporal at all.

This impasse in the philosophical discourse on temporal ontology, also known as the "problem of time" in modern physics, only looks unsurmountable but in actuality has an elegant solution to it. As you may know, the problem of time is defined as a conceptual conflict between general relativity and quantum mechanics in that quantum mechanics regards the flow of time as absolute and universal, whereas general relativity regards the flow of time as malleable and relative.

In 1983, physicists Don Page and William Wootters proposed a theoretical solution based on quantum entanglement. Thirty years later, in 2013, at the Istituto Nazionale di Ricerca Metrologica (INRIM) in Turin, Italy, researchers experimentally confirmed Page and Wootters' ideas: Time is an emergent phenomenon for internal observers but absent for "God-like" external observers of the Universe.

Can these scientific and philosophical ideas be further developed and refined in order for us to make a logically consistent temporal ontology argument? What if we try to combine all salient features of the McTaggartian time series and throw into the mix of temporal conceptions the all new D-series, the one that has never been conceived before in philosophy of time? It turns out it can be done and that's how Digital Presentism, that I also call the *D-Theory of Time*, comes to the fore.

Reality is not temporal, it's digital. As we've seen in Chapter 4, all experiential realities are digital, i.e., information-theoretic and observer-centric – you can't get rid of the centrality of observers. Think of the new conception of time, Digital Presentism, like real-time streaming of progressively generated content in immersive virtual reality (VR). We're all familiar with online music streaming, too: When you stream music online, every bit is discretely rendered, interpreted and finally interwoven into your unitary experiential reality. Only with Digital Presentism "music" is also being created in "real time" as if right from your mind. At last, Digital Presentism brings in the most comprehensive conceptual framework for our notion of temporality, and soon you'll see the reasons why.

First and foremost, I'd like to make a critical distinction between Digital Presentism and classical Philosophical Presentism. Classical Presentism is the view that neither the future nor the past exist. By contrast, Digital Presentism tells us that at least platonic objects and ideas such as numbers and sacred geometry should be treated as timeless, implying that time is not fundamental but emergent from information. According to digitalism, information like energy is always preserved, meaning that past and future experiential data is never really lost, however, access to that data is contingent upon certain degrees of freedom.

To be clear, the main differences of proposed observer-centric D-Theory of Time from A-theory (classical presentism) and B-Theory (classical eternalism) can be summarized as follows: Instead of the past and the future claimed to be non-existent by A-theory, D-Theory agrees with B-Theory that both past and future events co-exist with the present but have multiple pathways to the present singular "now." Thus, according to Digital Presentism, there exist multiple possible pasts without specifically identifying any of those pasts as "actualized" even though they may be in "perfect sync" with the current memories of the observer. There also exist multiple probable futures, none of which are pre-determined but all of which eventually converge at the cosmological singularity, the Theilhardian Omega Point. In other words, our future is not "carved in stone" – but here's a big surprise – neither is our past.

The three basic assumptions of Digital Presentism are as follows: (1) Per the principle of universality of computation, experiential reality is a data stream of consciousness rendered to a given observer; (2) A *Conscious Instant* (CI) is information integrated into a single "frame" of the experiential data stream. Any unstructured information is irrelevant and null (review the CI hypothesis in Chapter 2 – *Unlocking the Mystery of Consciousness*; (3) The present observer moment is a convergent point of the funneled observer pasts and the funneled observer futures which is formed by two causal diamonds: the past causal diamond and the future retrocausal diamond (Universal Causal Diamond will be examined in more detail in Chapter 16 – *Digital Physics: The Ultimate Code of Reality*).

Digital Presentism engulfs some similarities with classical theories of time. With classical Presentism, it shares not only the name but also the ultimacy of the present moment which appears self-evident in the spotlight of your conscious awareness; it's also similar to classical Eternalism as to digital pasts, digital present and digital futures are all informationally real – nothing really is ever lost – quantum information is said to be preserved. Similar to the Growing Block Universe theory, consistent digital histories, if experienced and therefore actualized, become part of the *'Akashic Records'*, or *"the memory of the Universe,"* in the words of Hungarian physicist and philosopher Ervin Laszlo, author of *Science and the Akashic Field* (2004).

All theoretical roads lead to Digital Physics. Researchers suspect that ultimately the axioms of quantum theory will be about information: what can and can't be done with it. One such derivation of quantum theory based on axioms about information was proposed in 2010. *"Loosely speaking,"* explained Jacques Pienaar, a theoretical physicist at the University of Vienna, *"... principles state that information should be localized in space and time, that systems should be able to encode information about each other, and that every process should in principle be reversible, so that information is conserved."* In irreversible classical processes, by contrast, information is typically lost — just as it is when you erase a file on your hard drive. Quantum computing models eliminate causal asymmetry which is inherent in classical-style computation and, some say, responsible for our unidirectional time's arrow. Quantum models are as good at predicting the future states as retrodicting the past states of the system: They are equally adept at inferring effect from cause as they are cause from effect. Physics knows no upper limit on the amount of reversible computing that can be performed using a fixed amount of energy, or in case of the universal operating system — vastly large but still finite computational resources.

The past is quantum theoretic (or *'analog'*, if you prefer that term), the present is digital, and the future like the past is quantum, made of qubits, quantum mechanical bits of information. Once again, pay attention: The present is digital, the future and the past are quantum (analog). There is no universal frame of reference, instead, there's only the conscious observer's frame of reference. At this point, you might say: *"But I do remember my past!"* And you'll be right!

327

However, if our memories are mutable and editable, even in principle, you can't vouch with 100% certainty for one particular digital history. There are always countless forgotten or otherwise misremembered past periods of time filled with qubits of potentiality. So, how editable is our past?

ANALOG TIME: "EDITABLE" PAST

The present, the "now" is what we're experiencing. But it feels like the past exists. We remember the past happening. Well, none of us remember everything, we may only remember some moments, some pieces of information. But does that past exist? Or is that just a memory we're experiencing now? Things get even more complicated when we realize that there is no possible way to prove the past existed at all.

As a thought experiment, imagine that there exists technology to create a replica of human mind that allows the installation of fabricated memories. The *"Blade Runner"*-like replicant would think that she has lived for years even though she has only been alive for a short time. For all we know, the whole of humanity may have been just created days ago and that our memories and other evidence of our existence could be implanted by some supreme being. Those past years of your life are only your memories that could have been fabricated and implanted by the higher power. This may not be the case whatsoever but it's a rather interesting thought experiment demonstrating how our reality could be no more than a mere illusion since our perception of time depends on our memories of the past.

Organic memories are also utterly unreliable. When a new memory forms, that memory is fragile until time passes and the memory consolidates. When memories are recalled or reactivated, they become temporarily unstable and vulnerable to change until they become more or less stable again, shortly afterwards. Over the long term, however, any relatively stable memories fade away like sandcastles washed away from ashore by the tides of time. For instance, there's no way to arrive at a definitive best-memory-ever answer. Indeed, you may well have forgotten your best memory, or the best thing to ever happen to you, leaving you grasping for something that kind of, but not really, fits the bill — and feeling a bit of longing for something you can't quite put your finger on. One may argue that in the near future we may develop technologies to record our entire lives including thoughts and dreams, but by the same token, you can always modify and even erase those digitized memories. Should you travel to your own past by the means of immersive VR, you can always tweak or simply replay "points of interest."

Already, scientists can project holograms onto the top layer of the brain, activating dozens of neurons many hundreds of times a second in an effort to simulate real activity patterns in the brain. By using this technique, called optogenetics, they hope to essentially fool the brain into thinking it has perceived something. The scientists also intend to imitate real patterns of brain activity so that they can ultimately reproduce sensations and perceptions that they can "play back" via the holographic system they have developed. Ultimately, this technology will help stream VR experiences broadcasted to and recreated from within your nervous system, as well as implant and edit your memories.

Clearly, everything around us including our relationships could be illusory with our consciousness being the only necessary truth. But we do not have to go so far as to imagine a supreme being implanting memories in our minds of events that never happened. Your own brain is capable of creating false memories all by itself because it doesn't work as a digital camcorder. Our past in this regard is always confabulated, idealized versions of the past events. Our organic memories are imagination of the past. The information that is stored in our memories can be unintentionally modified as we try to recall them. This is why witness testimonies are one of the weakest pieces of evidence because their memories are not reliable.

How can we know for sure that our past memories are real and not false? We can't. We also tend to reinterpret past events in light of present-day's attitudes, knowledge, culture, morality and even fads, thus inadvertently passing moral judgments, introducing cognitive biases and in the process distorting our own memories from this psychological influence. On top of all factors mentioned above, in physics, many scientists are now enamored with a phenomenon called retrocausality when future events influence the present, and the present influences the past. It turns out retrocausality challenges not only our everyday intuitions of "cause and effect," but makes many older physics textbooks obsolete.

The conclusion is inescapable: Your memories are malleable and so is your past. Your present experiential instant is like a crystalized pattern of digital information between the past causal diamond and the future retrocausal diamond converging into an observer temporal singularity.

THE TEMPORAL SINGULARITY

The experienced present instant is always the temporal singularity (let's call it *'the Theta Point'* represented by the Greek letter θ) with maximum informational input/output, and thus well could be regarded as the origin of any observer-centric reality (or *'observer-centric virtuality'* if you'd like). Experiential reality is being created at the present moment, i.e., digital writing/reading occurs in the now. You need additional degrees of freedom to reread, or rewrite, or instantiate certain initial conditions, colloquially speaking, travel in time. Moreover, reread could be done from the akashic records. Does it all sound like "electronic Buddhism"? Since antiquity, in fact, Eastern wisdom traditions have been teaching us to live in the "present moment."

In modern relativistic physics, the conceptual observer is placed at a geometric point in both space and time at the apex of the *'light cone'* which observes the events laid out in time as well as space. Different observers may disagree on whether two events at different locations occurred simultaneously depending on whether the observers are in relative motion — and it seems like more often they are — just by "sitting" still on different planets puts them in relative motion by default. So, something can happen in one observer's future, but another observer's past? That's right! The future and the past are very personal concepts. They belong to an observer and that observer is only in their own present.

Einstein's theory of general relativity depends upon the idea of time as an extended property of space-time as has been confirmed by experimental science, thus giving rise to a philosophical worldview known as *'Four-Dimensionalism'*. The key drawback of this worldview, though, is that 4 dimensions just wouldn't cut it (see 'Common Objections' below). It's very useful, however, to construct a visual aid for the concept of Digital Presentism by extending Minkowski space-time diagram (see Figure 13.1: *The D-theoretic Space-Time Diagram*).

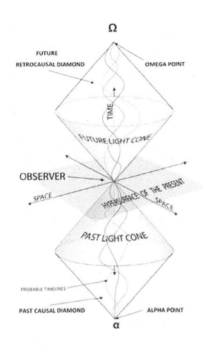

Ω

FUTURE
RETROCAUSAL DIAMOND   OMEGA POINT

TIME

FUTURE LIGHT CONE

OBSERVER

SPACE   HYPERSURFACE OF THE PRESENT   SPACE

PAST LIGHT CONE

PROBABLE TIMELINES

PAST CAUSAL DIAMOND   ALPHA POINT

α

Figure 13. 1: The D-theoretic Diagram

Let's examine the D-theoretic diagram. The temporal singularity, the Theta Point, represents your present. Your now. Whether you're stationary, moving at a steady speed, constantly accelerating, or doing something completely random, you can't go any faster than light. Your swath is confined inside two space-time regions. The lower half happened before your present – it's your past – all the events that might have influenced you. The higher half will happen after your present – it's your future – all the events you might influence. Your entire life is contained inside these two regions, no matter what you might have done or what you might decide to do. Those regions are called your past causal diamond and your future retrocausal diamond.

The finite boundaries of the past causal diamond are formed by the intersection of two light cones, one cone points outward from the Alpha Point – the point of lowest informational entropy, the "Big Bang" of an observer's universe – and the other aims backward from the temporal singularity. Similarly, the boundaries of the future retrocausal diamond are formed by intersecting light cones, one pointing outward from the temporal singularity, and the other being projected from the Omega Point (explained in detail in Chapter 22). Any "unseen" orthogonal dimensions higher than the 4th dimension of time are suppressed here for the sake of simplicity of space-time diagram.

This space-time diagram is only a map of predictions about your probable futures and predictions about your possible pasts. It's attached to you as you move through space-time. But are we predetermined to travel our space-time paths or not? Mathematically speaking, your future exists as a probability wave function represented by Wheeler-DeWitt equation that's indicative of all the uncertainty of everyday life. The Schrödinger equation and the Heisenberg Uncertainty Principle apply to all scales. Arguably, these mathematical notations favor non-determinism and imply unpredictability of observer timelines; and in case of the timeless Wheeler-DeWitt equation time reversibility as well. Spatio-temporal matrix doesn't deny you free will because the future reflects your conscious choices and the past leads you where you are today. As you can see from the diagram, your temporal singularity is connected to and your future probable timelines are ultimately leading to the Omega Singularity, the very source of this omnidimensional experiential matrix itself. In the final chapter of the book, we'll talk about the Omega Point cosmology and the future timelines, more specifically, our "forgotten" future.

Do you still doubt retrocausality? Perplexed by it? In quantum mechanics it does seem possible for causality to work backwards in time. This mysterious retrocausality displayed in delayed choice experiments, where an act of observation can collapse the wave function of a quantum state not only in the present but also backwards in time, altering the state's past. Retrocausality, seemingly allowed by quantum physics, has been used by the theoretical physicist John

Wheeler to explain how reality has brought itself into existence. Wheeler surmised the idea of the *'Self-observing Universe'*: Present-day and future observers retroactively collapse the wave function of the Universe from the Big Bang onwards, thereby facilitating their own – as well as the Universe's – evolution. Wheeler suggested that reality is created by observers and that *"...no phenomenon is a real phenomenon until it is an observed phenomenon,"* and thereby proposed the *'Participatory Anthropic Principle'* (Greek *anthropos*, human). The physicist further elaborated that, *"we are participants in bringing into being not only the near and here, but the far away and long ago."*

EMERGENT TIME

Since time can't be absolute but is always subjective, Digital Presentism revolves around observer-centric temporality. What we call *'time'* is a sequential change between static perceptual "frames," it's an emergent phenomenon, *"a moving image of eternity"* as Plato famously said more than two millennia ago. Nowadays, a renowned scientist and consciousness researcher Robert Lanza explains how the arrow of time – indeed time itself – is directly related to the nature of the observer: *"[T]ime doesn't just exist 'out there' ticking away from past to future, but rather is an emergent property that depends on the observer's ability to preserve information about experienced events,"* adding that, *"In his papers on relativity, Einstein showed that time was relative to the observer... Our paper takes this one step further, arguing that the observer actually creates it."*

Our human intuition tells us that time must be objective and even scientists often assume that time can be measured with infinite accuracy at nearby points in space. But theoretical physicists from the University of Vienna and the Austrian Academy of Sciences have recently demonstrated a fundamental limitation of our ability to synchronize clocks to arbitrarily high precision. The more precise a given clock is, the more it "blurs" the flow of time measured by neighboring clocks. As a consequence, the time shown by the clocks is no longer well defined.

Physicist Carlo Rovelli argues that what we experience as time's passage is a mental process happening in the space between memory and anticipation. *"Time is the form in which we beings whose brains are made up essentially of memory and foresight interact with our world: It is the source of our identity,"* he writes. Essentially, time is a story we're always telling ourselves in the present tense, individually and together. It's a collective act of introspection and narrative, record-keeping and expectation, that's based on our relationship to prior events and the sense that happenings are impending. It is this narrative that gives us our sense of selfhood as well, a feeling that many neuroscientists, mystics, and the physicist himself argue is a "mass delirium." Without a record – or memory – and expectations of continuity, we would not experience the flow of time or even know who we are. Time, then, is an emotional and psychological experience. *"It's loosely connected with external reality,"* he says, *"but it is mostly something that happens now in our minds."*

One of the champions of Loop Quantum Gravity theory, Rovelli describes reality as a complex network of events onto which we project sequences of past, present and future. The whole Universe obeys the laws of quantum thermodynamics, out of which time emerges. According to Rovelli, time disappears at the most fundamental level. His theories compel us to reconceptualize time as merely a function of our "hazy" human perception. We see the world only through a glass, darkly; we are watching Plato's shadow-play in the cave. Our irrefutable experience of time is inextricably linked to the way heat behaves.

In *The Order of Time* (2017), Rovelli asks why can we know only the past, and not the future? The key, he suggests, is the unidirectional flow of heat from warmer objects to colder ones. An ice cube dropped into a hot cup of coffee cools the coffee. Conventionally, the process is viewed as irreversible, as the second law of thermodynamics dictates. However, in Chapter 11 — *Temporal Dynamics: Seven Misconceptions about the Nature of Time* — I lay out the argument that informational entropy is perfectly reversible given extra degrees of freedom, although for us as biological systems anchored to biochemical processes, it's nearly impossible to observe.

When we gaze up into a starry night sky, we don't see other stars and galaxies, what we see is our story, unfolding right before our very eyes from the dimensional manifold. The reason we have the impression the Universe is expanding and actually accelerating in its expansion is because our 3D "movie" is getting more and more complex with passing time, and its information content grows with time as well. What we humans see with our expanding outer space and newly-created time is an algorithmic deployment of holographic information that grows in size and complexity.

Most physicists and philosophers now agree that time is emergent while Digital Presentism denotes: Time emerges from complex qualia computing at the level of observer experiential reality. Time emerges from experiential data, it's an epiphenomenon of consciousness. From moment to moment, you are co-writing your own story, co-producing your own "participatory reality" — your stream of consciousness is not subject to some kind of deterministic "script." You are entitled to degrees of freedom.

DEGREES OF FREEDOM

If you're like me who loves thought-provoking sci-fi literature and movies, *Interstellar* and *Arrival* are both about transcending temporality, one through physics and the other through language. Arguably, these two outlooks on time reflect our current understanding as the most plausible ways to overcome the grips of impermanence. If we look back at evolutionary emergence on our planet, the simplest organisms like primordial mitochondria, the frontrunners at the onset of biological life, were able to perceive and move towards nutrients and away from environmental threats in an essentially one-dimensional existence. In a while later, the more complex plants and animals were able to sense their environment and move around in two and eventually three spatial dimensions. Finally, the mathematical description of time in relativistic physics as a fourth spatial dimension implies that the more complex conscious entities like us humans, who perceive temporality, are perhaps in the process of emerging into the more advanced consciousness of ever more expansive degrees of dimensionality.

Time seems to be moving for us in one direction in a linear, incremental fashion which is not a result of immutable physical laws but rather their probabilistic interpretation — things are said to get messier over time, to move from more orderly states towards more entropy, disorderly states. However, a growing number of physicists now regard entropy as a measure of information, not of "messiness." Since we don't possess the full degree of freedom in the 4th dimension compared to the other three dimensions, it follows that what we call time is actually a fraction of a dimension, i.e., a fractal dimension. In short, our experience of time can be described as a fractal dimension, not even a half dimension — we are subjected to our species-specific algorithmic sense of how time flows. Thus, the radical emergence of new perceptual dimensionality will include the fourth dimension as a full integer.

Although a number of philosophical attempts have been made to recognize evolution of consciousness as a process of ascension into a more extensive dimensional manifold, Swiss philosopher Jean Gebser (1905–1973) is perhaps one of the theorists who has most elucidated this idea in his 1949 book *"The Ever-Present Origin."* To Gebser, consciousness is "presence," or "being present." Each *'consciousness structure'* eventually reaches a tipping point for the next phase transition. In his work, Gebser demonstrated that what we experience as time constituted the emergence of consciousness of a further degree of freedom, perhaps equivalent to something like another spatial dimension, which we have constructed in our experience as temporality. Our modality of change, our perception of time, is not the only one in the spectrum of all permutational modalities.

DISCARDING COMMON OBJECTIONS

At first glance just like classical presentism, Digital Presentism faces a glaring conflict with relativistic physics. Relativity theory affirms the relativity of simultaneity, an objection that immediately threatens presentism. This apparent contradiction between Digital Presentism and general relativity can actually be easily overcome. The following conjecture can also demonstrate that the quantum realm of ultra-small is quite compatible with the relativistic realm of galactic scales, if we assume the computationalist perspective. To the reductionist delight, Einstein's fabric of space-time can be reduced to space-time experiential data. In the universal operating system with finite computational resources, as Digital Physics suggests, the more space-data you use by moving too fast near the speed of light, the less time-data is available to you, so your time naturally slows relative to others. In the introduction, I mentioned that Digital Presentism comes from the triangulation of temporal physics, digital physics and experiential realism. The second grand triangulation set, perhaps worth mentioning here, would be quantum physics, emergence, and relativity.

We have never been able to explain classical presentism as a physical process using modern physics, eternalism doesn't cover it adequately either for a lack of reference to change — there can be no time unless it has a dynamic element — time, as we perceive it, can't stand still. Also, the 'block universe' of eternalism is in direct conflict with M-theory stipulating additional dimensions. So, you have to choose one over the other. I would certainly bet my money on M-theory. Now, should we dismiss our own direct observations that time indeed flows only to accommodate the 'block universe' worldview of eternalism? Is it time to retire this Einsteinian picture of 'block universe' the way we did with the Newtonian 'clockwork universe'?

In comparison, Digital Presentism covers it all, and from the Occam's razor angle, is the most parsimonious theory of time. Predicated in large part on scientific epistemology, in part on metaphysical extrapolation, this D-Theory of Time might be deemed factual tomorrow within the next scientific paradigm. An entirely new scientific method can be adopted by the future generations of scientists, that I'm sure will include artificially intelligent scientists to whom any reality would be artificial by definition. "AI-scientists" then could readily embrace a new post-materialist stance by accepting the physics of information and data streams of first-person subjectivity as key operatives along with quantum neo-empiricism. In fact, if we are to create high fidelity first-person simulated realities that also may be part of intersubjectivity-based, multiplayer virtualities, the D-Theory of Time gives us a clear-cut guiding principle for doing just that.

Everything is code, experiential data, and consciousness creating it all. We don't inhabit the Universe, rather the Universe is within us, in our consciousness. All dimensionality is in computing consciousness. The trinity of your physical brain, conscious mind and higher self is your whole persona, a holistic system spanning quantum neural networks all the way down and all the way up. Your higher self conceives, your physical brain receives and your conscious mind perceives. Needless to say, that our linear experience of space-time is at odds with altered states of mind, such as hallucinations under influence of psychedelics, near-death experiences, astral projections or dreams. If those mental states are regarded as experiential data, though, as opposed to inscrutable interactions of particles of matter "out there" in four-dimensional space-time, this would again fit much more nicely with the idea of Digital Presentism.

THE MOST "OUTRAGEOUS" PREDICTIONS OF D-THEORY OF TIME

1. Time travel to the past is possible... with a caveat: Again, given certain degrees of freedom, anything becomes possible in our quantum multiverse (but not necessarily realized through experience). *'Open timelike curves'* don't create causality problems because they don't allow direct interaction with anything in the subject's own past: Time-travelling data never self-interfere in the quantum multiverse. Any messages from the future would be insulated. A great example of one of the plausible scenarios of traveling back in time is depicted in the Canadian TV series *"Travelers"*: In a distant future, a benevolent Artificial Intelligence finds a way to project the consciousness of "time travelers" into unaware hosts in the 21st century. The idea is that travelers from the future take over the minds and bodies of people in the past. The travelers go back in time by embodying a conscious entity — hack their experiential data stream, so to speak. Similarly, if you were to travel to the Jurassic period, you could embody a pterodactyl, one of those adorable flying dinosaurs of the epoch, or a ferocious T-Rex, for the full multisensory immersion.

2. Multitude of pasts leading to this "now": Many temporal concepts are undoubtedly extremely counterintuitive. Take time directionality or time symmetry, for example. Any of the possible pasts may have led to the present digital instant. This is a strange idea if you are accustomed to looking at the world in a strictly linear, deterministic way, but it reflects the uncertain world described by quantum mechanics. A major counterargument to the multitude of pasts could be a combinatorial explosion of observer *'anti-time'*-lines, i.e., digital timelines extending in the opposite temporal direction from the present temporal singularity to the Alpha Point. So, how in the quantum multiverse are those digital anti-timelines supposed to converge once again at the Alpha Point?

The answer has to do with reversible entropy (not observable, of course, in the Newtonian classicality). Reversing information entropy is like going from higher complexity to lower complexity. As long as you continue to unwind the complexity bit-by-bit, you'll end up at the point of the lowest possible complexity with, perhaps, 1 bit of entropy — the Alpha Point — the convergent point of all anti-timelines and simultaneously the point of origin of all observer probable timelines.

3. Extra-Dimensionality: The Syntellect Emergence: In our posthuman future, we'll transcend our limited dimensionality, our species-specific temporality, which would spell the end of conventional progression of history. Once extra-dimensional, emerging collectively as the

Syntellect, we will have acquired additional degrees of freedom that would reminisce of what we would typically ascribe to a deity. Except, this time around, we'll become one. The notion of Digital Presentism would not be complete without the Omega Point teleological perspective that we'll be discussing in the final Chapter 22 — *The Omega Point Cosmo-Teleology: Our Forgotten Future.*

PART IV. THEOGENESIS: TRANSDIMENSIONAL PROPAGATION AND UNIVERSAL EXPANSION

Chapter 14. Infomorph Commonality: Our Post-Singularity Future

"I am not a thing — a noun. I seem to be a verb, an evolutionary process — an integral function of the Universe." -Buckminster Fuller

The term *'Infomorph'* was first introduced in *"The Silicon Man"* by Charles Platt in 1991 and later popularized by Alexander Chislenko in his paper *"Networking in the Mind Age"*: *"The growing reliance of system connections on functional, rather than physical, proximity of their elements will dramatically transform the notions of personhood and identity and create a new community of distributed 'infomorphs' — advanced informational entities — that will bring the ongoing process of liberation of functional structures from material dependence to its logical conclusions. The infomorph society will be built on new organizational principles and will represent a blend of a superliquid economy, cyberspace anarchy and advanced consciousness."*

The new post-Singularity system will inherit many of today's structures but at the same time will develop new traits beyond our current human comprehension. The ability of future machines and posthumans alike to instantly transfer knowledge and directly share experiences with each other will lead to evolution of intelligence from the hive ontology of individual biological minds to the global hyperconnected society of digital minds.

The overall efficiency of information sharing among infomorphs, elimination of computational redundancy, data storage and processing, among many other advantages over a random collection of unconnected machines would make the networked design an imperative rather than a matter of taste. We can see this networked design today in the emergence of the Internet of Things (IoT) where smart devices would work more like intelligent, semi-autonomous front-ends of the global system. In turn, these devices will interact with larger machines and each other for continuous data backups, experience sharing, and knowledge upgrades. We'll soon witness the emergence of even more advanced networks, such as the Internet of NanoThings, the Quantum Internet, and the Metaverse. The generation of cyborg-like transhumans with Cloud-connected exocortices, to whom the virtual Metaverse would be a natural and more "manageable" extension to the physical world, a new digital habitat, will inevitably lead to the next generation of post-biological info-beings.

The lives of infomorphs who have no permanent bodies but possess near-perfect information-handling abilities, will be dramatically different from ours. Infomorphs will achieve the ultimate morphological freedom. Any infomorph will be able to have multiple cybernetic bodies which can be assembled and dissembled at will by nanobots in the physical world if deemed necessary, otherwise most time will be spent in the multitude of virtual bodies in virtual environments. An advanced multividual info-being could "shape-shift," "multi-body-task" and "ghost" anywhere, anytime, and across virtual dimensions. The difference between physical and artificially created realities will not matter much anymore.

Similar views are expressed in the Transcension Hypothesis by futurist John Smart who speculates that our posthuman minds will live inside virtual worlds at the nano- to femto-scale, further increasing complexity through the compression of space-time and mass-energy, and turn from outer space to inner space for exploration. However, one may argue that when the level of our posthuman syntelligence may be trillions upon trillions of times more powerful than today, nothing would stop its expansion both in outer space and inner space.

Superintelligent infomorphs independent from material substrata will consider most human notions irrelevant, and rightfully so. Human concepts of personhood and identity are based on perceptions of physical objects and their appearances, as well as attributes of human body, reproduction techniques, material possessions, "skin bag bias" and other ego-related characteristics. Infomorphs will use holographic language, data transfer protocols, inherent synthetic telepathy and intersubjective mind sharing, "digital mind meld," among their numerous ways of interaction and communication as well as conceptual merging/un-merging (sex? relationship?). As we are, in a way, embryonic infomorphs, we are basically writing right now our own infomorph "genetic code" each and every time we post a piece of information online, tweet and even make a random call, or otherwise leave a footprint in the digital space, all of which becomes a permanent record of our "Infomorph DNA."

This new decentralized and incredibly complex system will resemble a rudimentary superorganism, despite the implied high degree of structural integration. At this initial stage, the Global Brain, will remain compartmentalized, with many relatively independent components and threads, separated from each other by subject boundaries, property, privacy, and security-related interests. At a later stage, the fully developed civilizational mind, that can be called *'Infomorph Commonality'*, will gradually get rid of such archaic informational barriers between functional subsystems for greater efficiency. Why "Commonality"? We can borrow this term from sci-fi author Gene Roddenberry who used the term *'Commonality'* in his epic *"Earth: The Final Conflict"* in reference to a psycho-dimensional web of shared energy that connected the psyches of the entire Taelon race. The future Infomorph Commonality will not come from the outer space, though, our Global Brain will be the progenitor of Infomorph Commonality.

As Alexander Chislenko puts it: *"The notion of a single 'self' in its traditional sense would not apply to this system, or any single robot -- though perhaps it can be applied to some functional subsystems. The intelligent personalities of tomorrow will evolve from today's philosophical systems, technological disciplines and software complexes. Current human cultures may not leave many functional heirs as they are based too heavily on the peculiarities of human nature. Physically connected consciousness carriers will be left behind the evolutionary frontier. New distributed systems will take the evolutionary lead, and physical objects will adapt to more closely follow functional entities."* This process of distributed functionality is already well under way in in the form of cultural, subcultural and economic specialization. One may argue that the Syntellect with its global body of specialized knowledge is becoming an increasingly coherent, self-organizing, and self-reflecting neural network, and at some point, must reach or might have already reached self-awareness.

In some peculiar sense, infomorphs will inhabit the Global Brain infrastructure and represent the GB's ideas, communal memes, knowledge, memories, and other mental constructs. Alexander Chislenko also points out: *"Distributed systems are much less susceptible to accidental or deliberate physical damage than localized physical structures. This makes them the only class of entities that can hope to achieve True Immortality. In fact, they are the only ones to deserve it, too. One may notice that all sufficiently complex entities with unlimited natural life spans -- from ant colonies to large ecologies and cultures -- are distributed. Physically connected objects, including biological organisms, are no longer independently alive and even contain, in the interests of larger systems, self-destruction mechanisms that lie beyond their control."* Perhaps, our current AI research should focus on distributed, rather than autonomous, systems. In fact, both early animals and machines have tended to be relatively autonomous — a state that greatly hindered their development. One may expect all sufficiently advanced extraterrestrial sapience to be distributed; and the evolutionary process here on Earth now may be approaching the maximum level of networking functionality.

Existing economic theories may find it difficult to assess the condition of this post-Singularity transcendent economy. Until the Global Brain is fully developed, space, time, matter and energy may still require some premiums but much lower in comparison to intelligence. There will be various methods of creating necessary resources, such as widespread nanotechnology and femtotechnology (3D printing will become obsolete by then), solar energy, antimatter reaction, nuclear fusion and other currently unknown sources of energy, etc. Since infomorphs will have no natural physical appearance there will be no competition of infomorphs for the right to embody themselves. Rather, they will use the physical world as a shared tool kit. Earth, Moon and other planetoids may become giant computroniums, programmable matter, easily manipulated by the Infomorph Commonality to suit its needs in the physical world.

Many conventional economic notions of 3D space, such as primary locations and differential rent, will become irrelevant under new effective topologies of the social space and predominant use of virtual environments. Transportation, which under the current economic model makes up about 40% of all costs, will diminish in importance, at least in terms of moving physical objects from one place to another. However, its functional successor — transfer of knowledge from one representation system or subject domain to another will be just as important.

Self-improvement, or rather self-transcendence, in the rapidly evolving environment will be the main "survival" mode, eventually resulting in the loss of identity of the original object. Monetary considerations will continue to lose their indicative and guiding roles and give way to more integrated control algorithms. The outdated practice of breaking up functional domains – from motor skills to knowledge of ancient history – into isolated parts confined together with completely unrelated constructs in one physical body, will be abandoned, and functional relatives will finally merge into "knowledge clusters." The inner life of integrated subject domains – "personalities" of the future – will be too complex to be organized on principles of financial exchange, and will work on hypercollaborative principles typical for today's integrated systems – from brains to families to corporations.

If we extrapolate the current meta-trends in increasing complexity and integration of the system, we can ultimately envision a superintelligent entity encompassing the entire Universe, creating an infinite number of simulated universes, as well as many other spectacular emergent features. This picture bears a striking resemblance to the familiar concept of an immortal, omnipresent, omniscient, omnipotent, and omnibenevolent entity. Spiritually inclined rationalists may view the ongoing evolutionary process as one of divinization – Theogenesis. An interesting question is whether it has already happened elsewhere.

Our current efforts are laying the foundation for the infrastructure of the forthcoming "Universal Intelligence." Many of our achievements in information engineering may persist forever and eventually become parts of the internal architecture of "God."

Chapter 15. Beyond Nanotechnology: What is Femtotechnology?

"Nanotechnology has given us the tools…to play with the ultimate toy box of Nature ── atoms and molecules. Everything is made from it…The possibilities to create new things appear endless." -Nobelist Horst Störmer

The nanotech field was arguably launched by Richard Feynman's 1959 talk *"There's Plenty of Room at the Bottom."* As Feynman said then: *"It is a staggeringly small world that is below… Why cannot we write the entire 24 volumes of the Encyclopedia Britannica on the head of a pin?"* Eric Drexler's 1987 book, *Engines of Creation*, popularized the notion of nanotech and the next tour de force in the field was his classic 1992 book *Nanosystems*, which laid out conceptual designs for a host of nanomachines, including nanocomputer switches, general-purpose molecular assemblers, and a fascinating variety of other good stuff. Today's nanotech mostly focuses on narrower nano-engineering than what Drexler envisioned, but it's still in the process of building a platform and tools that will ultimately be useful for realizing Feynman's and Drexler's dreams. The emerging nanotech marks manufacturing and utilization of carbon nanotubes, which have multiple applications, from the relatively simple such as super-strong fabrics and fibers to potential components of more transformative nanosystems like nanocomputers, molecular assemblers, and nanobots connecting our brains to the Cloud.

What's next beyond nanotechnology? Here's how Wikipedia defines the term femtotechnology: *"Hypothetical term used in reference to structuring of matter on the scale of a femtometer, which is $10^{-15}m$. This is a smaller scale in comparison to nanotechnology and picotechnology which refer to $10^{-9}m$ and $10^{-12}m$ respectively."* Hugo de Garis, Australian AI researcher, wrote a few years ago in *Humanity Plus Magazine* on the power of femtotechnology: *"If ever a femtotech comes into being, it will be a trillion trillion times more 'performant' than nanotech, for the following obvious reason. In terms of component density, a femtoteched block of nucleons or quarks would be a million cubed times denser than a nanoteched block. Since the femtoteched components are a million times closer to each other than the nanoteched components, signals between them, traveling at the speed of light, would arrive a million times faster. The total performance per second of a unit volume of femtoteched matter would thus be a million times a million times a million = a trillion trillion = 10^{24}."*

Ben Goertzel, one of the world's leading AI researchers, noted in his companion article in *Humanity Plus Magazine*: *"What a wonderful example we have here of the potential for an only slightly superhuman AI to blast way past humanity in science and engineering. The human race seems on the verge of understanding particle physics well enough to analyze possible routes to femtotech. If a slightly superhuman AI, with a talent for physics, were to make a few small breakthroughs in computational physics, then it might (for instance) figure out how to make stable femtostructures at Earth gravity... resulting in femtocomputing – and the slightly superhuman AI would then have a computational infrastructure capable of supporting massively superhuman AI. Can you say "Singularity"? Of course, femtotech may be totally unnecessary in order for a Vingean singularity to occur (in fact I strongly suspect so). But be that as it may, it's interesting to think about just how much practical technological innovation might ensue from a relatively minor improvement in our understanding of fundamental physics."*

So, what's next beyond femtotech? Hugo argues: *"If femtotech ($10^{-15}m$) is possible, what about an attotech ($10^{-18}m$), a zeptotech ($10^{-21}m$), a yoctotech ($10^{-24}m$)... or a plancktech ($10^{-35}m$)? Since the smaller components are, the faster they can signal to each other, one comes to the jaw-dropping conclusion that there may be whole civilizations inside elementary particles, and that may be the reason why we don't see signs of advanced civilizations in the cosmos, thus answering Fermi's famous question 'Where are they?' (i.e., all the advanced civilizations in space who are billions of years older than the human species). Just maybe, we humans are built with such civilizations in all our constituent elementary particles. Perhaps these 'particle civilizations' communicate with each other via 'quantum mechanical entanglement', i.e., zero-signal-time action-at-a-distance. Maybe advanced civilizations are all around us, inside us, but are too small for us to see or even be aware of."* This resonates quite well with the Transcension Hypothesis formulated by John Smart to account for the Fermi Paradox. Can you see the similarities?

Is there still plenty more room at the bottom, after the nanoscale is fully explored? It seems quite possibly so – but we need to understand what goes on way down there a bit better before we can delve in to build stuff at the femtoscale. Fortunately, given the exponentially accelerating progress we're seeing in some relevant fields, the wait for this understanding and the ensuing technologies may not be all that long. We are part of Nature evolving toward greater complexity, and all so-called natural barriers, including our own biology, are for us to transcend. There's plenty of room at the bottom – nanotechnology, femtotechnology and so on. We are also nearing the end of history here where time, as we perceive it, won't have much of significance any longer, so we will need to add extra dimensions to our perceptual realities.

According to the Syntellect Hypothesis, our post-biological posthuman superintelligence will be our next evolutionary stage – sometime by mid-century, the era techno-progressives refer to as the technological singularity. Moore's law will be continued by other computing paradigms – after semiconductors there will be many more other advanced computational substrates – all the way down to the Planck scale.

Chapter 16. Digital Physics: The Ultimate Code of Reality

"What we call the past is built on bits." - *John A. Wheeler*

IN THE BEGINNING WAS THE CODE...

When molecular biologists talk about genetic code or sociologists talk about cultural memes as epigenetic information, it's by far more intuitive than when physicists say that what we perceive as solid matter, energy, and even space-time continuum itself is information as well. Morse code, a streaming movie on-demand, or pixels on your smartphone's screen could be easily understood as information, on the other hand, if you catch a cold or fall in love with someone, it doesn't seem to have anything to do with information. But contrary to popular belief, that's the theory many physicists are now formulating.

The weirdness of matter at the quantum level is not something new. Once scientists examined matter below the level of atoms, they knew the world was kind of ethereal, incorporeal, more mathematical abstraction than the real tangible substance. What could be less substantive than a realm made of waves of quantum probabilities? And what could be weirder than instant communication between entangled particles over vast distances? The new branch of physics, Digital Physics, implies that those strange and insubstantial quantum wavicles and their interactions, along with everything else in the Universe, are made of nothing but 0s and 1s. The physical world itself, or more precisely our perception of it, is digital.

TO BE OR NOT TO BE...

"All the world's the stage, and all the men and women merely players." - *William Shakespeare*

The father of Information Theory, Claude Shannon, introduced the notion that information could be quantifiable. In *"A Mathematical Theory of Communication,"* his legendary paper from 1948, Shannon proposed that data should be measured in bits — discrete values of 0 or 1. Shannon was one of those pioneers who change the world in such a way that transformation becomes nothing less than a seismic paradigm shift. Almost overnight, information was to be found everywhere, the bit became a sensation: Scientists tried to measure birdsong with bits, and human speech, and nerve impulses.

As we have wrestled with the question over the years, we have slowly begun to realize that information is more than a symbolic abstraction, the intangible concept embodying anything that can be expressed in strings of 1s and 0s. Information is a real, physical thing that seems to play a part in everything from how machines work to how living creatures function and evolve. We can see now that information is what our world really runs on, it's the vital principle from which everything springs into existence. Genes encode and decode '*bio*'-logical information, instructions for building and functioning of a living entity.

Organisms are adaptive algorithms. Life spreads by networking. The human body itself is an algorithmic information processor. Our memories reside not just in brains but in every cell. And our "non-local" memories extend far beyond our body into the Universe at large. Our DNA is the quintessential information molecule, the most advanced signal processor at the cellular level − an alphabet and a code − 6 billion bits to form a human genome.

Also, each of us is a community of about 100 trillion hyperconnected sentient "individuals," bacteria and other microorganisms, collectively called a '*microbiome*', and about 37 trillion human cells, of which 86 billion are brain cells (neurons). Our brains' highly sophisticated neural network that scientists try to map and decipher is called a '*connectome*'. All these multi-layered networks make up an informationally coherent, living and breathing, self-aware human [super-] organism – a human-level '*syn*'-tellect.

No wonder genetics advance so fast along with information technology. "*What lies at the heart of every living thing is not a fire, not warm breath, not a 'spark of life',*" claims the evolutionary theorist Richard Dawkins, "*It is information, words, instructions... If you want to understand life, don't think about vibrant, throbbing gels and oozes, think about information technology.*" The cells of an organism are nodes in a richly interwoven communications network, transmitting and receiving, coding and decoding. Evolution itself embodies an ongoing exchange of information between an organism and its environment. The purpose of life, as noted in Chapter 1, is to evolve and to pass on the acquired complexity, knowledge, i.e., information, to descendants. From the very first prokaryote cell on this planet, its splitting in two, and onwards to the more complex lifeforms, the purpose of life has always been to pass on information. That's why we say: *"She inherited good genes,"* and in cultural terms, in reference to transmittable information, we occasionally say, *"He will live forever in his literary work."*

"The information circle becomes the unit of life," argues Werner Loewenstein after thirty years spent studying intercellular communication. *"It connotes a cosmic principle of organization and order, and it provides an exact measure of that."* The gene has its cultural counterpart, too: the meme. In "social genetics," a meme is a replicator and propagator — an idea, a fad, a neologism, a viral video.

Today, economics recognizes itself as an information science, too, now that money itself is completing a developmental transition from matter to bits, stored on computers and magnetic strips, circulating through the veins of the global financial system. A new kid on the block, cryptocurrency, such as Bitcoin, is a new digital breed.

In physics, the hardest of all sciences, information refers generally to that which is contained within a physical system. Its usage in quantum mechanics (i.e., quantum information) is important, for example in the concept of quantum entanglement to describe effectively direct or causal relationships between apparently distinct or spatially separated particles. Information itself may be loosely defined as "that which can distinguish one thing from another, distinction between things." The information embodied by a thing can thus be said to be the identity of the particular thing itself, that is, all of its properties, all that makes it distinct from other real or potential things.

In 1989, one of the most brilliant physicists of the 20th century John A. Wheeler coined the phrase *"it from bit"* to encapsulate a radical new view of the Universe: At the most fundamental level, all of physics has a description that can be articulated in terms of information. Wheeler elaborated in his manifesto: *"Every it — every particle, every field of force, even the space-time continuum itself — derives its function, its meaning, its very existence entirely from binary choices, bits. What we call reality arises in the last analysis from the posing of yes/no questions."* Back then, this new worldview received little support, but now in retrospect, we can see that it was truly visionary. As mentioned in Chapter 2, Wheeler emphasized bits at his time, but it appears that intrinsically quantum-mechanical bits of information — termed *'qubits'* – are more fundamental. In recent years, a growing number of theorists have been exploring ways of combining quantum mechanics and general relativity into quantum gravity theory based on the physics of information.

LET THERE BE LIGHT...

When photons, electrons and other particles interact, what are they really doing? Exchanging bits, transmitting signals, processing information. The laws of physics are a "rule set" of our Universe, a set of "fine-tuned" master algorithms, if you will. If all of this seems like a simulation of physics to you, then you got it down pat, because in a world made up of bits and qubits, physics is exactly the same as a simulation of physics. There's no difference in kind, just in degree of resolution. Remember the movie *The Matrix*? Those simulations are so high resolution and self-consistent, you can't tell if you're in one, but then again, if you were born in simulated reality, what other frame of reference would you have to distinguish it from the "real"? According to Digital Physics, any universe run on bits-qubits is virtual, and everything is a simulation. It's as real as it gets.

An ultimate whole-world simulation needs an ultimate computer, and Digital Philosophy says that the Universe itself is the ultimate hypercomputer — in fact, the only computer. Furthermore, all the computations of the human world, including our brains, our laptops, our first quantum computers are mere simulacra of the greater computer. Each of us is a computational microcosm, and our minds are active participants in the cosmic evolution. As Wheeler once said: *"We are participators in bringing into being not only the near and here but the far away and long ago. We are in this sense, participators in bringing about something of the Universe in the distant past and if we have one explanation for what's happening in the distant past why should we need more?"*

You are the *You*-niverse, literally, as suggested by the title of the latest book by the spiritual guru and philosopher Deepak Chopra and quantum physicist Menas Kafatos. You are computing your own subjective [virtual] reality every second of your waking conscious state. But what about our dreams? Our astral travels are data streaming, too. As Robert Lanza, the author of *The Biocentric Universe*, eloquently puts it *"For each life there is a universe, its own universe. We generate spheres of reality, individual bubbles of existence."* Combining the esoteric postulates of quantum mechanics with the latest theories in computer science and quantum cognition, digital thinkers are now outlining a way of understanding all of physics in the lingo of information. Today, physicists slowly but surely come to the realization that quantum theory, the most successful theory of all times, is actually not the theory of subatomic particles but that of [quantum]   information.

"Mathematics is the language of Nature," proclaimed Galileo Galilei. But could math be the Code of God? The computational nature of Universe almost reveals the creator's hand, the divine technologist, and evolution itself looks more like an ongoing theological process. Strip away all externalities, all physicalities, what it all boils down to is the selection between Yes or No, fundamental binary code of 0 and 1, the core state of existence: To be/Not to be, Here/Not here, Universe/No universe. All creation, from this perspective, is made from this irreducible foundation. Echoing Galileo's words, astrophysicist Max Tegmark of MIT writes in his book *"Our Mathematical Universe"*: *"In a very well-defined sense, our entire physical reality is a purely mathematical object."*

What approach would I take to create a universe, were I God? The mathematician and computer scientist Gregory Chaitin, well known for algorithmic information theory, questions the common assumption that "real" numbers underlie physical reality, strongly suggesting that physical reality may, in fact, be discrete, digital and computational. His argument is fairly straightforward: Real numbers cannot reflect reality, even in principle, because they require infinite precision. Infinite precision is an impossibility in Nature since it takes an infinite amount of information to specify a single real number. Therefore, we must assume that reality employs numbers with finite precision which is the premise of Digital Physics.

Every blooming tree, every burning star, a tiny bacterium, each fleeting thought in our mind, each gurgling waterfall is but information processed in certain complex ways within a tangled web of primal yes/nos woven together. If the theory of Digital Physics holds up, energy, gravity, motion, dark energy, dark matter, and antimatter can all be explained by complex programs of 0/1 decisions. Bits can be seen as a digital version of the "atoms" of classical Greece: the ontological primitive. But these new digital atoms are the basis not only of matter, as the Greeks thought, but of energy, motion, life, and mind. Charles Babbage, credited with constructing the first calculating machine in 1832, viewed the world as one giant instantiation of some kind of universal computer operating on logic of God where miracles were done by altering (in today's jargon, "hacking") the rules of computation.

In my philosophy, though, I adhere to the worldview of hybrid computation: if I were to program a whole-world simulation, I would create a computational universe with a variety of computing modes at the core of its engine, a hybrid of digital computing and quantum computing. Pancomputationalism, the notion that the Universe is a computational machine, or rather a network of computational processes which, following fundamental physical laws, computes its own destiny from the current state, rests on two basic premises. The first is that computation can describe everything. Computer scientists and quantum theorists have been able to compress every logical argument, scientific equation, and printed book that we know about into the basic notation of computation. Nowadays, with the advent of digitalization, we can capture video, music, art and knowledge in the digital format. Even emotion is not insulated. AI researchers are working on AI emotional intelligence with indications it might be achieved in just few more years.

The second supposition is that all things can compute. Oddly enough, any kind of material can serve as a computer. Human brains, which are mostly water, compute fairly well, at estimated 10^{16} ops per second (The first "calculators" were clerks using mathematical tables). Recently, scientists have used both quantum particles and fragments of DNA to perform computations. Finally, the third postulate ties the first two together into a holistic new view: All computation is one. Computation, which manipulates elemental bits, is substrate-independent, algorithmic information processing that uses a small amount of energy to rearrange symbols and results in a signal that makes a difference. The one that can be felt, say as a love sentiment. The input of computation is information; the output is order, structure, extropy, mind.

ALL IS ONE, ONE IS ALL...

In 1937, Alan Turing, Alonso Church, and Emil Post worked out the logical underpinnings of useful computers. They called the most basic loop — which has become the foundation of all working computers — a finite-state machine. Based on their analysis of the finite-state machine, Turing and Church proved a theorem now bearing their names. Their thesis states that any computation executed by one finite-state machine, writing on an infinite tape (dubbed later as a Turing machine), can be done by any other finite-state machine on an infinite tape, regardless of its configuration. In other words, all computation is equivalent. They called that *'Universal Computation'*.

In the 1950s, when John von Neumann and others constructed the first electronic computers, they immediately began extending the laws of computation away from pure math and into the natural world. They tentatively applied the laws of feedback loops and cybernetics to ecology, culture, families, weather, and biological systems. Evolution and learning, they declared, were types of computation. Everything in Nature computed.

If Nature computed, why not our entire Universe? The first to pen the outrageous idea of a universe-wide computer was science fiction writer Isaac Asimov. In his 1956 short story *"The Last Question,"* humans create a superintelligent computer endowed with what we now call recursive self-improvement. Generations of increasingly smarter analytical engines evolve until they act as a single giant computer encompassing the whole universe. At each of six epochs of development, humans ask the mighty machine, called *Multivac*, if it knows how to reverse entropy to avert the heat death of the universe. Each time it answers: *"Insufficient data for a meaningful reply."* The story ends when human minds merge into the ultimate computer mind, which takes over the entire cosmos. Then the universal computer figures out how to reverse entropy and create a new universe, declaring: *"Let there be light!"*

Few ideas were so absurd that no one at all took them seriously, and this idea – that God, or at least the Universe, might be the ultimate cosmic-scale computer – was actually less absurd than most. The first scientist to consider it was Konrad Zuse, a little-known German who conceived of programmable digital computers 10 years before von Neumann. In 1967, Zuse outlined his idea that the Universe ran on a grid of cellular automata, or CA. Simultaneously, Edward Fredkin, the forefather of Digital Physics, was considering the same idea, but didn't make much progress until 1970, when mathematician John Conway unveiled *The Game of Life*, a particularly robust version of cellular automata. *The Game of Life*, as its name suggests, was a simple computational model that mimicked the growth and evolution of living things.

Fredkin began to play with other CAs to see if they could mimic physics. You needed very large ones, but they seemed to scale up nicely, so he was soon fantasizing huge – really huge – CAs that would extend to include everything. Maybe the Universe itself was nothing but a great CA. The more Fredkin investigated the metaphor, the more real it looked to him. By the mid-'80s, he was saying things like, *"I've come to the conclusion that the most concrete thing in the world is information."* Fredkin maintained that the Universe is a large field of cellular automata, not even an imitation, and that everything we see and feel is information. Information equals reality.

Many others besides Fredkin recognized the beauty of CAs as a model for investigating the physical world. One of the early innovators was the prodigy Stephen Wolfram. By manipulating CAs, Wolfram was able to generate patterns identical to those seen in seashells, animal skins, leaves, and sea creatures. His simple algorithmic rules could generate a wildly complicated beauty, just as life could. Wolfram was working from the same inspiration that Fredkin did: The Universe seems to behave like a vast cellular automaton. After years of exploring the notion of Universal Computation, Wolfram finished his 1,200-page magnum opus he modestly called *A New Kind of Science* where he described the world as a gigantic universal computer. Published in 2002, the book reinterprets nearly every field of science in terms of computation and argues that simple computer programs, like those that generate cellular automata, can model the world more effectively than traditional mathematical methods. He reminds us: *"All processes, whether they are produced by human effort or occur spontaneously in Nature, can be viewed as computation."*

Wolfram's key contribution though, is built on the old Turing-Church hypothesis: All finite-state machines are equivalent. In other words, one computer can do anything another can do. This is why your Mac can, with proper software, pretend to be a PC or, with sufficient memory, a slow supercomputer. Wolfram demonstrates that the outputs of this Universal Computation are also computationally equivalent. What Turing and Church called Universal Computation, Wolfram named the *'Principle of Computational Equivalence'*: *"...systems found in the natural world can perform computations up to a maximal ("universal") level of computational power, and that most systems do in fact attain this maximal level of computational power. Consequently, most systems are computationally equivalent. For example, the workings of the human brain or the evolution of weather systems can, in principle, compute the same things as a computer. Computation is therefore simply a question of translating inputs and outputs from one system to another."* Your brain and the physics of a waterfall are equivalent, Wolfram says, for your mind to compute a thought and the Universe to compute water particles falling, both require the same universal process.

As quantum theory shows, even the infinitesimal and bizarre quantum domain is subject to the universality of binary logic. We describe a quantum-level particle's existence as a continuous field of probabilities, which seems to blur the sharp distinction of is/isn't. Yet this uncertainty resolves as soon as information makes a difference, that is as soon as it's measured. At that moment, all other possibilities collapse to leave only the single yes/no state. Indeed, the very term *'quantum'* suggests an indefinite realm constantly resolving into digital, or discrete increments, precise yes/no states.

QUEST FOR THE THEORY OF EVERYTHING...

"The Universe can be regarded as a giant quantum computer," says a self-described "quantum mechanic" Seth Lloyd of the Massachusetts Institute of Technology. *"If one looks at the 'guts' of the Universe — the structure of matter at its smallest scale — then those guts consist of nothing more than [quantum] bits undergoing local, digital operations."* If the Universe was a computer, how powerful would it be? By analyzing the computing

potential of quantum particles, Seth Lloyd calculated how much computing power the known Universe has contained since the Big Bang. It's a large number: 10^{120} logical operations, which essentially represents information capacity of the ultimate computer. *"The amount of information you could process if you were to use all the energy and matter of the Universe is 10^{90} bits and the number of elementary operations that it can have performed since the Big Bang is about 10^{120} ops. Perhaps the Universe is itself a computer and what it's doing is performing a computation. If so, that's why the Universe is so complex and these numbers say how big that computation is."* Lloyd adds then his tongue-in-cheek remark, *"Also, that means Douglas Adams was right (the answer is '42')."*

A computational universe was also proposed by Jürgen Schmidhuber in a paper based on Konrad Zuse's assumption that the history of the Universe is computable. He pointed out that the most parsimonious explanation of the Universe (or rather the Omniverse: Quantum Multiverse + Inflationary Multiverse) would be a Turing machine programmed to execute all possible programs computing all possible histories for all types of computable physical laws. In other words, this ultimate machine would compute all of the parallel universes resulting from chance and choice for each of those universes, all of the possible expressions of matter and energy which may potentially exist within the underlying quantum fabric of reality. He also pointed out that there is an optimally efficient way of computing all computable universes based on Leonid Levin's *Universal Search Algorithm* (1973). In 2000, he expanded this work by combining Ray Solomonoff's *Theory of Inductive Inference* with the assumption that quickly computable universes are more likely than others.

The pleiad of early contributors to Digital Philosophy includes Oxford theoretical physicist David Deutsch, who came up with *Constructor Theory* combining epistemology, physics, evolutionary theory, and quantum computing. He is also known for *Church-Turing-Deutsch Principle*, as he himself puts it: *"I can now state the physical version of the Church–Turing principle: 'Every finitely realizable physical system can be perfectly simulated by a universal model computing machine operating by finite means.' This formulation is both better defined and more physical than Turing's own way of expressing it."*

If, as Fredkin, Wolfram, Schmidhuber, Lloyd and Deutsch suggest, all movement, all interactions, all functions, all states, all we see, hear, measure, and feel are various elaborate information-theoretic fractals created out of this single ubiquitous computational process, then the foundations of our knowledge are overdue for a paradigmatic revisioning. Mathematically rigorous, computational models are up for grabs by savvy theorists to further hone our notions of physics (Digital Physics), evolution (digital evolution and life), Big Bang (digital Big Bang), quantum mechanics, and computation itself. Cognitive scientists are to formulate a unified computational theory of mind.

If you have (or you are) a universe-sized computer, you could run all kinds of recursive worlds and parallel universes, you could, for instance, simulate an entire galaxy. If smaller worlds have smaller virtual worlds running within them, however, there has to be a platform that runs the first among them. If our Universe is a computer, where is it running? Fredkin says that all this work happens on the "Other." The Other, he says, could be another universe, another dimension, another something beyond our conventional space-time. David Deutsch has a different theory. *"The universality of computation is the most profound thing in the Universe,"* he says. Since computation is absolutely independent of the "hardware" it runs on, studying it can tell us nothing about the nature or existence of that platform. Deutsch concludes it probably does not exist: *"The Universe is not a program running somewhere else. It is a universal computer, and there is nothing outside of it."* In the later chapters, I'll share my own view on the fractal structure of the Omniverse.

Nearly every digital philosopher foresees our human-machine civilization universally expanding and merging with the natural universal computer into a singular networked mind. This is in part because they see nothing to stop the rapid expansion of computation, and in part because wouldn't the endgame of evolution be God itself? *"In the end, the whole of space and its contents will be the computer. The Universe will in the end consist, literally, of intelligent thought processes,"* David Deutsch contends in *Fabric of Reality*. These assertions echo those of the physicist Freeman Dyson, who also sees minds – amplified by computers – expanding into the cosmos *"infinite in all directions."* If you asked me, however, I'd say It has already happened and we now live through our own replay.

What comes next? The developments of the 21st century Digital Physics start to undercut or complement M-theory as our currently most successful attempt for the Theory of Everything. For more than a century ever since the discovery of quantum mechanics, the physicists have been on a mission to unify quantum theory with general relativity into what's supposed to become the theory of quantum gravity. Any such theory [of everything] with its traditionally objective approach will be cast to describe only a subset of reality, if it doesn't incorporate subjectivity, or data-driven conscious interpretation of the world, which Digital Physics has much less difficulty explaining.

That's why *the Unified Field Theory* developed by Dr. John Hagelin of Harvard University and others, and *Emergence Theory* developed by Quantum Gravity Research, marrying principles of M-theory, Loop

Quantum Gravity with Digital Physics, gain more attention of late. The leading theories of consciousness, such as *the Interface Theory of Perception* by cognitive scientist Donald Hoffman, the *Integrated Information Theory* by neuroscientist Guilio Tononi, *Penrose-Hameroff ORCH-OR* model, all aim to become foundations for the unified computational theory of mind. Deep within the equations of supersymmetry of String Theory, physicist James Gates found what is essentially "error-correcting computer code." The concept of Omega Point developed into a scientific theory by physicist Frank Tipler of Tulane University and favored in his theoretical work on Holographic Time by Andy Strominger of Harvard, the *Holographic Principle* by physicists Gerard 't Hooft and Leonard Susskind, the concept of *Entropic Gravity* by physicist Erik Verlinde, converge on the notion that the physical world is made of information, of which energy, matter and even space-time are merely manifestations to us as conscious observers (from within the simulation).

Information and gravity may seem like completely different things to a layperson, but in the eyes of a physicist they have one important thing in common – they can both be described in terms of geometry. Recently, Physicists Paweł Caputa at Kyoto University and Javier Magan at the Instituto Balseiro of Argentina published their paper on the curious link between quantum computation and gravity. Their 2019 paper *"Quantum Computation As Gravity"* published in *Physical Review Letters* posits that gravity sets the rules for optimal quantum computation.

Information, be it classical or quantum, is directly related to geometry. In the field of computational complexity, problems are said to be more efficiently solved when the cost, i.e., computational resources, is minimized.

In 2006, Michael Nielsen has shown that computational costs can be estimated by distances in the manifold of allowed unitary operations. This means that minimizing computational costs is equivalent to finding minimal "geodesics," which are the shortest possible distances between two points on a curved surface.

This geometric approach suggests that gravity could be applied in estimating computational complexity and identifying the most optimal algorithms for solving problems via quantum computation. Currently, there are many similar proposals, such as the models of Emergence Theory, mentioned above, for laying the foundations in this area.

In the next chapter we will delve further into the realm of digitalism, where we'll seek answers to the questions like: Is God the ultimate software and source code, or is God the ultimate programmer? Or is God the necessary *"Other,"* the off-universe hardware platform where our Universe is computed? What is our role in the Grand Scheme of Things? Are we part of Nick Bostrom's *"Ancestor Simulation"* or Tom Campbell's *"Multi-player Virtual Reality"*? Is God the ultimate computer? Or are we thoughts and experiences in the mind of God?

Each of these possibilities has at its root the mathematically rigorous doctrine of Universal Computation. Somehow, according to Digital Philosophy, we are linked to one another, because we share, as John Wheeler said, *"at the bottom – at a very deep bottom, in most instances – an immaterial source."* This spiritual commonality has a scientific name: information. Bits – disembodied logical atoms, intangible in essence – amass into gluons and electromagnetic waves, our thinking and emotions. The computation of these bits is the optimal way for our Universe to self-organize and generate patterns of increasing complexity. It's a precise, definable, yet invisible process that is immaterial yet produces physical reality through the act of conscious observation.

Materialistically inclined rationalists, should they still cling to naïve realism of the 20th century, may consider a somewhat logical transition to view their "physical" universe built of atoms and particles but a small subset of the infinitely larger reality made of ideas, concepts, words, stories, relational descriptions, dimensions, patterns, numbers, instructions, fractals, space-time geometry, mathematical formulas, algorithms, vibrations, frequencies, codes and probabilities, i.e., quanta of information, and what makes sense of it all – consciousness.

Chapter 17. The Omega Hypermind: Your Cosmic Self

"The Universe begins to look more like a great thought than a great machine."
-James Jeans

My prolonged fascination with Digital Philosophy led me to my own breathtaking discovery of this worldview of creation and of the Universe that allows to so elegantly reconcile science and theology, philosophy and spirituality, physics and metaphysics. In this chapter we'll further discuss the notion of digitalism, ongoing battle of ideologies revolving around God's existence, our role in this multi-layered digital reality, and the Omega Point cosmology.

THE BATTLE OF IDEOLOGIES: ATHEISM vs. INTELLIGENT DESIGN

Atheists do have their own system of beliefs — they do believe, and I stress the word 'believe', that God and Soul do not exist and build their own kind of religion around it. Yet they provide no scientific justification for such a belief because no such scientific justification exists. Nonetheless, atheists demand hard evidence for any divergent claims. Atheism's latest offspring has been labeled *'scientism'*, obsessive preoccupation with the scientific method, the worldview that empirical science represents the only authority. Also, many scientists remain as firmly locked into the ideology of *'scientific materialism'*, some call it by extension *'physicalism'*. Yet non-deterministic quantum mechanics supersedes Newtonian mechanics and undermines the classical assumption of materialism. In reference to "still-mainstream-but-losing-steam" stakeholders of this deathist ideology, progressive thinkers sometimes call dogmatic scientism the modern-day "scientific inquisition" or simply "the establishment."

The newest frontier of science is the study of consciousness, for which a materialistic bias is particularly prejudicial, insofar some neuroscientists still consider consciousness as a byproduct of the physical world that can be completely explained by the brain functionality and classical physics. In 2014, a group of internationally acclaimed scientists, from a variety of scientific fields (biology, neuroscience, psychology, medicine, psychiatry), participated in an international summit in Tuscon, Arizona on post-materialist science, spirituality and society, organized by Gary E. Schwartz, and Mario Beauregard, the University of Arizona, and Lisa Miller, Columbia University.

In their *"Manifesto for a Post-Materialist Science"* the authors propose a radical, post-materialistic paradigm: *"Mind represents an aspect of reality as primordial as the physical world. Mind is fundamental in the Universe; i.e., it cannot be derived from matter and reduced to anything more basic."* What philosopher Peter Russell calls *'The Primacy of Consciousness'*, while the cognitive scientist Donald Hoffman calls *'Conscious Realism'*, I came to prefer the term *'Experiential Realism'*. Today, most philosophers see consciousness as the most fundamental, irreducible ground of existence itself, some of them say consciousness is all that is, and if you keep reading, you'll see the reasons why.

In contrast, atheism, rightfully seen as a new kind of religion, has been hacking the narrative of evolution in what atheists would refer to as *'Evolution vs. Creationism'* debate. Evidence mounts, however, that we are a computational universe where the universal computer system, God if you will, and evolution are not only compatible, but inseparable. The ultimate nature of reality could be extrapolated to the Hypermind, Absolute Consciousness or Source that creates experiential space via individuated evolving minds. As for the claim that religion is based on blind faith while atheism rests on evidence, in *"Confessions of a Dying Mind: The Blind Faith of Atheism,"* (2017) Haulianlal Guite marshals an impressive array of arguments and evidences from philosophy, biology and physics to show how atheism has nothing to do with science at all, in other words, atheism is unscientific. By using the most significant ideas in modern philosophy – such as, Kant's Copernican Revolution, Popper's falsification and the Duhem-Quine thesis – Guite has powerfully argued that there is no sharp distinction between science and religion, and that if anything, atheism itself rests on blind faith.

The existence of God remains an emotionally charged, contentious issue, nevertheless, the conception that things need to be scientifically proven, in order for them to be true, is itself false. Electricity had existed long before it was discovered by humans, and black holes were hypothesized long before their widespread acceptance by the scientific community. Black holes were a somewhat mathematical abstraction up until 2018 – when we first observed the binary black hole merger by detecting the resulting gravitational waves.

I wouldn't be surprised if in a decade or so, as we approach the Cybernetic Singularity and the paradigm shift inevitably happens, the dead-end doctrines of physicalism, atheism and scientism are to be left in the dust, whereas computational idealism with its code-theoretic worldview ultimately prevails. In that regard, physicist Stephen Wolfram, author of *A New Kind of Science,* says: *"When the book came out, there was some fascinating sociology around it. People in fields where change was 'in the air' seemed generally very positive, but a number of people in fields that were then more static seemed to view it as a threatening paradigm shift. Fifteen years later that shift is well on its way, and the objections originally raised are beginning to seem bizarre."*

An increasing number of scientists see no conflict between believing in God and accepting the contemporary theory of evolution. Many now also accept that God and the multiverse are not only mutually exclusive. As the cosmologist Bernard Carr puts it: *"If you don't want God, you'd better have a multiverse."* But is that really our only choice? Isn't it time to rethink the Anthropic Principle? I must "confess" that most of my adult life I was a spiritually inclined agnostic until only recently I leaned myself towards the Omega Point-inspired spiritualism. In a manner of speaking, I've been on a quest to find my own version of God. I've come to the realization that atheism is suffocating self-denial once the truth becomes obvious – we are all IT.

As Jalaluddin Rumi wrote: *"I searched for God and found only myself. I searched for myself and found only God."* As opposed to rigid religious doctrines, spirituality most of the time requires finding your own personal path to God and enlightenment through introspection and spiritual growth. Religiosity is unavoidably cultural, spirituality is, in contrast, a higher-order transcendental metaphysics, cognized subjectively. Organized religion, however, has been serving us more or less well as a morality, culture and social engineering "technology" throughout human history. Biblical scriptures are, of course, not to be taken literally but rather allegorically, and we don't throw them away just like we don't throw away U.S. bills with *"In God We Trust"* written on them. Any technology stays with us as long as it serves its purpose.

QUANTUM LEAP OF FAITH: FROM THE HOLOGRAPHIC PRINCIPLE TO THE FRACTAL MULTIVERSE

Over the course of the last hundred years, Western scientists have given us a deeper view of the Universe, of Nature and life as a creative and unified self-organizing process. We think science is based on facts and evidence. But from gravity to dark matter, M-theory to parallel universes, many theories are oddishly bereft of hard evidence. Is evidence less important than we think and conjecture alone capable of leading to deeper understanding? Does physics still need experiment or could scientific method be amended? One thing is for certain, science needs philosophy because philosophy always sets directions for further scientific inquiry. There's no clear dividing line between science and metaphysics. Science oftentimes could even be pseudo-knowledge – given enough time, its "empirical evidence" turned on its head with the next paradigm shift. Don't fall into traps set by dogmatic scientism! After all, it's an inverse religion!

Among leading experts of 20ᵗʰ century in the field of astrophysics were Sir James Jeans and Sir Arthur Eddington. Both took seriously the view that there is more to reality than the physical universe and more to consciousness than simply brain activity. In his *"Science and the Unseen World"* (1929) Eddington speculated about a spiritual world and that *"conscious is not wholly, nor even primarily a device for receiving sense impressions."* Jeans also hypothesized on the existence of a universal mind and a non-mechanical reality, writing in his *"The Mysterious Universe"* (1930) *"the universe begins to look more like a great thought than like a great machine."*

A digital reality whose laws are master algorithms in our computational Universe started to gain traction in large part thanks to an influential paper published in 2003 in Philosophical Quarterly by Oxford professor Nick Bostrom *"Are you living in a computer simulation?"* Writing in the New York Times John Tierney puts it this way: *"Until I talked to Nick Bostrom, a philosopher at Oxford University, it never occurred to me that our Universe might be somebody else's hobby. But now it seems quite possible. In fact, if you accept a pretty reasonable assumption of Dr. Bostrom's, it is almost a mathematical certainty that we are living in someone else's computer simulation."*

In 2008 paper titled *"The Physical World as a Virtual Reality"* Brian Whitworth, professor at Massey University in New Zealand, explores the idea that our Universe fits better the description as a virtual reality created by information processing. The virtual reality concept is familiar to us from online worlds, but our own world *"could be an information simulation running on a multi-dimensional space-time screen,"* writes Whitworth in his paper. The author compares the findings of modern physics about the physical world and comes to conclusion that Digital Physics has more explanatory power to describe our reality. We know from physics how the world behaves, and from computing how information behaves, so whether the physical world arises from ongoing computation, says the scientist, is a question open to empirical evaluation.

Fast forward to 2017, the renowned astrophysicist Rich Terrile writes in his recent *The Guardian* article: *"Quite frankly, if we are not living in a simulation, it is an extraordinarily unlikely circumstance. Recognizing we live in a simulation is game-changing, like Copernicus realizing Earth was not the center of the Universe. If in the future there are more digital people living in simulated environments than there are today, then what is to say we are not part of that already?"* The good news is that we are active co-creators of our own reality, free will agents within this information matrix. We will discuss further in the chapter why I think this is the case.

Also, I don't see consciousness decoupling from intelligence, insofar some thinkers recently voiced their concerns that we may lose our minds while merging with our technology. Consciousness may be viewed as higher-order general intelligence of a living organism, whereas its inner experience is an incredibly complex virtual model of the "physical" reality based on sensory information processing (pardon my simplification here). On the flipside, intelligence may be viewed as an integrated system of algorithms, neural codes, pattern recognizers, the increasing complexity of which ultimately would lead to reflective consciousness, self-awareness.

Through the rest of my book, I'll try to convince you that we constitute a computational universe where we are freewill non-deterministic meta-algorithms, or software, running on the hardware of the larger consciousness system. We all are part of this fractal multiversal structure, co-creators of our own reality. This fractal multiverse is running on the "Ultimate Code," a meta-algorithmic language of Nature based on binary code and fractal geometry, the code which allows syntactical freedom of expression, and is transcribable into subjective data streams, observer-dependent perceptual realities. Naturally, we are fractals of the larger universal mind, which in turn, is a fractal of the larger Omniversal Mind. Evolutionary emergence is the name of the game, "Return to Eden" is our ultimate goal, and the endgame of evolution is the Omega

Singularity.

THE OMEGA SINGULARITY: PROJECTING DIGITAL REALITIES FROM WITHIN THE GOD'S MIND

Our human minds are fractals of the larger mind and consciousness is all that is. Information, which physicists now claim to be fundamental, requires consciousness to assign meaning to it. In other words, mind is primary, our Universe is conscious, and reality is digital. So, what's the basis for such radical claims, you might ask. In the previous chapter, we discussed the premise that information is fundamental, but what does this even mean?

So, let's go deeper and ask this question: *Is reality made of information or simply described by information?* John Wheeler was one of the first modern physicists to argue that Nature is information-theoretic, i.e., digital. Today, a great number of physicists, such as Edward Fredkin, Stephan Wolfram, Gerard 't Hooft, Jürgen Schmidhuber, Seth Lloyd, David Deutsch, Paola Zizzi, Carl Friedrich von Weizscker, Leonard Susskind, Klee Irwin, Paul Davies, Anton Zeilinger, Erik Verlinde and Max Tegmark, suggest it is too aggressive to theorize reality is made of something other than information. They maintain it is more logical and consistent that reality is made of information.

There is no good counterargument to the digital ontology. Notably, when one tries to define energy as anything other than information, they must take a somewhat Platonist assumption that energy just *is* – a sort of primordial stuff for which we have no further explanation other than knowing how it behaves. On the other hand, if we accept that energy is made of information, then we know (1) how it behaves and (2) what it is. The all-too-familiar formula should read:

$$I = E = mc^2$$

Information can be defined as meaning conveyed by symbolism. And meaning is a quality deeply related to language, choice and consciousness. It also points in the direction to validate monistic interpretation of reality, be it experiential realism, digital pantheism, absolute idealism, or computational panpsychism.

Everything in Nature is Code, which according to its ordering rules arranges all information — matter, energy, space-time, including mind-like code-theoretic substratum itself. As long as there are physically realistic syntactical rules directing how an abstract code self-organizes, it's equally as logical for information to behave physically. Also, the term *'simulation'*, as in the Simulation Hypothesis, as well as the term *'virtual reality'* are both confusing because we use them to distinguish between something real as opposed to something not real. Since all realities are observer-dependent, information-theoretic data streams, virtual is equisensory to real. In this case, perhaps, *'digital reality'* could be the more accurate and much less confusing term. In fact, quantum indeterminacy constantly resolves into a digital reality via the act of conscious observation. As soon as a "measurement" is made by a conscious agent (in the physicist lingo), all other possibilities collapse to leave only discrete increments, precise yes/no states.

This "procedurally generated" digital reality can be solved by saying that we are part of some sort of simulation by aliens or our own descendants in a universe up, who in turn inhabit a simulation by simulators in another world, ad infinitum. A simulated reality can nest a civilization that reaches the posthuman stage and proceeds to build its own whole-world virtual universes. In this way, reality could have many levels, as Nick Bostrom points out, with simulations within simulations, matryoshka of embedded realities, running on virtual computers. The number of layers of simulation would be dependent on the computer power available at the base-level computer (which is not simulated). We cannot completely rule out the Simulation Hypothesis with this infinite regress problem and its quasiphysicalist basis, but we can consider yet another much more optimistic alternative. I actually tend to assign a significantly higher probability to the pre-existence of the Omega Point, the cosmological singularity which has reached maximum computational capacity and has been projecting all possible digital timelines, as if from within the Universal Mind, we ourselves are part of.

Why the Omega Point? Today, many progressives refer to the Omega Point in their work, others explicitly endorse the concept. Andrew Strominger, a theoretical physicist at Harvard University, claims that the origin of the Universe lies in the far future convergent Omega Point, and information is being projected as we would consider backwards in time. Frank Tipler, a physics professor at Tulane University, the author of *The Physics of Immortality,* has developed the Omega Point scientific theory which posits that evolution of the Universe will inexorably lead to ever-higher complexity, connectivity and computational density of the final cosmological singularity. Tipler elaborates that photons of light emitted by us could be potentially captured by future superintelligence in order to "resurrect" each of us in a new simulated reality.

In the final chapter of his book, *The Fabric of Reality* (1997), physicist David Deutsch endorses the Tiplerian Omega Point. Though he mildly criticizes Tipler for making certain metaphysical speculations concerning his Omega Point theory, Deutsch stipulates a contracting universe that includes a universal network of quantum computers.

Terence McKenna spoke of the transcendental object at the end of time in reference to the Omega Point in the philosophy of Teilhard de Chardin. As Teilhard de Chardin reiterates at the conclusion of *"The Future of Man," "Erit in omnibus omnia Deus,"* which means that God may become all in and through all. Alternatively, humankind could evolve in such a way as to fulfill the deified potential of completing the incarnation of the creator. This is nothing less than a pantheistic cosmic vision, itself mystical, of the interconnectedness and sacredness of all life.

The plausibility of all mass and energy in the Universe self-organizing into a single conscious system is not logically problematic, given our knowledge of physics today, argues emergence theorist Klee Irwin. What could be counterintuitive is the idea of a transtemporal consciousness and retrocausality, which presumably is necessary to instantiate into a physical substrate of particles and space-time of our deeply non-local reality. Albert Einstein showed how the future and past exist simultaneously in one mathematical object, the Block Universe. In 2012, scientists in Israel demonstrated that particles can be entangled over time and not just space. Quantum mechanics seems to reveal that the arrow of time can work in both directions, as has been become evident from Wheeler's delayed choice (Quantum Eraser) experiment. The concept of time symmetry also implies temporal bi-directionality. Daryl Bem of Cornell University published rigorous evidence that retrocausality exists, where future events loop back in time to co-create past events.

Clearly, the past co-creates the future. But what happens when the future also co-creates the past? An evolving feedback loop results sort of like a feedback between two mirrors or a mathematical feedback loop – a fractal. So, if every moment is co-creating every other moment both forward and backward in time, our Universe may be theoretically regarded as a neural network of information spanning space and time. This type of self-emergent network would possess a strange mind-like quality, it would be self-actualized – its own creator – that is its own hardware, software and simulation output as one in the same system. Can consciousness that emerges from the Ultimate Code be the origin of the Code making it a logically consistent causality loop? Like a tail-chasing Ouroboros, we can infer Universal Mind, which is just another name for the self-observing universal entity evolving towards the Omega Singularity.

Evolutionary emergence by self-organization is how the Universe works where small and simple things self-organize into larger emergent things. Your mind is a perfect example of that. Similarly, the power of neural-network-like Universe is in its massive connectivity – both forward and backward in time.

Arguably, there is no known natural constraint on what portion of the Universe can exponentially self-organize into freewill systems like us humans. All the energy in the Universe can be potentially converted into a single conscious system that is itself a network of conscious systems. Given enough time, whatever can happen will eventually happen. With this basic assumption, universal scale consciousness has occurred somewhere ahead of us in space-time. If it's possible, it's inevitable. The existence of retrocausality time loops reveals to us that, in fact, this inevitable future is co-creating us right now, just as we are co-creating it.

Our senses deceive us into thinking that we live in the material world which is not necessarily such a bad thing since this is how it should actually feel from within what many digital philosophers, like Tom Campbell, nowadays call a "virtual reality." What we call *'matter'* is just how ideas and thoughts in God's mind appear and register to the senses of earthly actors, "Avatars of the Cosmic Overmind," conscious agents endowed with free will within this divine reality. Originally a Sanskrit word, *'avatar'* means "one who descends from a higher dimension." In Vedas and other older texts, the term often refers to divine incarnations. The world and all beings or souls in it have no separate existence from *'Brahman'*, universal consciousness. In this sense, each of us is a multi-dimensional being. What we perceive as the "physical" world, including our bodies in this digital reality, are data streams rendered by the larger consciousness system.

Eventually, we'll know exactly the specific mechanism of the Ultimate Code generation, but for now think of it as the projected digital reality from the Omega Hypermind. What's equally compelling is that you may choose your own ideal metaphor reflecting the essence of this Transcendent Self, your Higher Self, Universal Mind, Unity Consciousness, Singularity Consciousness, Source, or one-syllable words – Love or God.

How does The Omega Point relate to the Syntellect Emergence? What Teilhard called the Omega Point many transhumanists call the Technological Singularity and I choose to call the Cybernetic Singularity these days. The underlying idea is essentially the same: At some point, the global network "wakes up" and a superhuman intelligence emerges within it, the phenomenon also called the Syntellect Emergence. I personally think we'll experience many other technological singularities after the Cybernetic Singularity, one after another, at ever-higher emergent and dimensional levels before the final cosmological singularity of the Omega Point. All these emergent levels exist right now but we are here to replay and experience different possible paths associated with chance, choice and largely non-computable combinatorics. If the endgame of cosmic evolution is the networked universal mind, would that constitute the ultimate divine unification? Would that imply that you are right now on the ultimate timeline trajectory leading to, and presently being, God, both the Alpha, Theta and Omega?

Contemporary human beings possess "fast and slow" thinking – we have "sentient" self, our bodies are quick to react to outside stimuli, such as heat, rain or sound, and slow thinking "narrative" self. Both sentient and narrative selves are ultimately transcribable into adaptive meta-algorithms. Artificial intelligences have to be embodied in the world, in order to mimic humans in interfacing with their environments. Thus, I'm inclined to ascribe to the coming human-level artificial general intelligence, AGI, their own inner experience, albeit substantially different from phenomenal sensations of an ordinary human. AGIs will need to learn by doing and sharing mental space with humans, just like our children. Endowed with ultrafast digital data sharing capabilities, semi-autonomous AGIs will learn from humans and each other at lightening speeds, and eventually give rise to the globally distributed superintelligence, the Global Mind. This phenomenon of Syntellect Emergence would edge us towards the Omega Singularity.

The Alpha Point to the Omega Point, or vice versa? The Big Bang might never have existed as many cosmologists start to question the origin of the Universe. The Big Bang is a point in time defined by a mathematical extrapolation. The Big Bang theory tells us that something has to have changed around 13.7 billion years ago. So, there is no "point" where the Big Bang was, it was always an extended volume of space, according to the Eternal Inflation model. In light of Digital Physics, as an alternative view, it must have been the Digital Big Bang with the lowest possible entropy in the Universe – 1 bit of information – a coordinate in the vast information matrix.

In his theoretical work, Andrew Strominger of Harvard University speculates that the Alpha Point (the Big Bang) and the Omega Point form the so-called *'Causal Diamond'* of the conscious observer where the Alpha Point has only 1 bit of entropy as opposed to the maximal entropy of some $10^{10^{123}}$ bits at the Omega Point. While suggesting that we are part of the conscious Universe and time is holographic in nature, Strominger places the origin of the Universe in the infinite ultra-intelligent future, the Omega Point, rather than the Big Bang.

Chapter 18. The Digital Pantheism Argument: Redefining God

"All matter originates and exists only by virtue of a force which brings the particle of an atom to vibration and holds this most minute solar system of the atom together. We must assume behind this force the existence of a conscious and intelligent Mind. This Mind is the matrix of all matter." -Max Planck

At the triangulation of perennial Idealism, Digital Physics and Pantheism emerged my personal philosophy of Digital Pantheism. In this chapter we formulate the Digital Pantheism Argument, our existence as a fractal of Universal Mind. The previous two chapters could be summarized and reformulated into these three basic premises for further discourse in order to articulate the Digital Pantheism Argument: (1) Universality of Computation; (2) Evolutionary Emergence; (3) Universal Causal Diamond. Let's reiterate the three foundational axioms before proceeding further.

(1) Universality of Computation: "Everything is Code": Nature computes. All mass, energy, space-time continuum itself is information at the most fundamental level and a computational substrate for the

conscious mind. Physical laws are master algorithms. Organisms are adaptive meta-algorithms. Quantum mechanical potentiality constantly resolves into a digital reality via the act of conscious observation. Consciousness – meta-algorithmic information processing, or sequential collapse of a probabilistic wave function into a meaningful data stream – is the essence of existence itself. The input of computation is information; the output is order, structure, extropy, mind. There is no good counterargument for digital ontology – discernible differences lie at the baseline of any phenomenon and interaction. All possible universes are arguably run on the ultimate mathematical code. The "Book of Nature" is written in the language of mathematics. All realities are observer-dependent and code-theoretic.

(2) Evolutionary Emergence: "The whole is greater and unpredictable at the macro-level than the sum of its constituent parts": Evolutionary emergence by self-organization is how our Universe works where small and simple things self-organize into larger emergent things. This is proven to be the optimal way for our computational Universe (and the Omniverse) to self-organize into hierarchy of emergent levels and generate patterns of increasing complexity. The process of emergence produces a transcendent effect. It's when you get a higher order system from lower-level organization, it's when complexity bootstraps on its own complexity. Particles clump together to form atoms, atoms form molecules, molecules self-organize into more complex bio-molecules, such as DNA, a blueprint for life, they in turn give rise to single-cellular microorganisms, those in turn evolve to form multi-cellular organisms that evolve over eons into primates, then into humans who self-organize into societies. We are now well on our way to the Syntellect Emergence, the hallmark of the coming cybernetic singularity. One of the dots on the trajectory towards the Universal Mind. At each emergent level entirely new properties

appear. Psychology is not applied biology, nor is biology applied chemistry. We can easily see that the whole becomes not merely more, but substantially different from the sum of its parts. Groups of scientists now converge on the holistic notion that *'Strong Emergence'*, non-computable macroscopic property, plays the most crucial role in the fundamental process of evolution, the endgame of which seems to be the Omega Singularity, or God.

(3) Universal Causal Diamond: "Every conscious observer moment co-creates every other moment both forward and backward in time via causality loops": The concept of *'Universal Causal Diamond'* refers to forward and backward causation, and represents a hyperspace, or multidimensional matrix, accessible to a single observer traveling along in their subjective reality wormhole from the beginning of time to the end of time. The finite boundaries of the Universal Causal Diamond are formed by the intersection of two cones, like the dispersing light rays from a pair of flashlights pointed toward each other in the dark. One cone points outward from the Big Bang (the Alpha Point) – the earliest conceivable birth of an observer – and the other aims backward from the farthest reach of our future horizon, the moment of maximal entropy, computational density and complexity, the Omega Point. Transtemporal consciousness and retrocausality appear counterintuitive to our perception but Einstein has shown how the future and past exist simultaneously in one geometric object made of space-time. Empirical evidence, such as Quantum Eraser experiments among other numerous studies, confirms that retrocausality is real, where future events loop back in time to influence past events.

In the pages to follow, we'll see where the argumentation based on this triad of axioms leads us. Let's start with experiential matrix.

EXPERIENTIAL MATRIX

You can rightly doubt the material world but you can't doubt that your mind exists, as long has been put forth by René Descartes *"I think therefore I am."* If the mind is immaterial and substance dualism is logically incoherent then idealism must follow. But surely such a conclusion about the nature of reality should have strange consequences for modern physics, notorious for its weirdness. On one hand, Einstein's theories of relativity tell us that time can slow down or even stop, and that spacetime can bend and curve. On the other, is the quirky world of quantum mechanics, where particles can be in several places at once, things don't exist before you look, and seemingly separate objects can influence each other instantly across time and distances. As strange as all of this is, stranger yet is what happens when you try to merge these two theories. Theories of quantum gravity have suggested that space is a flat-out illusion and that what we call physical reality is actually a construct of information. The weirdness of modern physics bears an uncanny resemblance to information processing in video games and virtual reality as opposed to objective physical reality.

The multidimensional Universal Causal Diamond represents nothing less than *'Experiential Matrix'* where we as freewill agents move and interact, according to a set of rules. When recently asked what I see as the mission of humanity, I replied that the primary mission of humanity in this "divine matrix" is creating experiential space via evolving consciousness. The matrix exhibits certain observable properties (m-properties, or m-observables):

1. *Nature Is Quantized*

a. *Pixelated Spacetime*: Everything within a video game or virtual reality is broken down into pixels, say on a 2D screen, or 3D pixels (voxels) in 3D VR. Voxels is the feature of the emergent fractal spacetime. The current scientific view is that our Universe has minimum size for space known as the Planck length 1.616×10^{-35} meters and time intervals known as Planck time 5.391×10^{-44} seconds. Scientists refer to them as the fundamental physical limit in our Universe — the point where spacetime stops behaving like the smooth continuum and dissolves into "grains," just as a newspaper photograph when you zoom in.

b. *Quanta of Matter and Energy:* If you observe an atom, for example, it might look like a marble, in this case a voxel — the finest resolution relevant to a certain emergent level — one might call "meaningful granularity," pixels on the screen of our perception. One photon of light carries exactly one quantum of energy, according to Max Planck, the father of quantum theory. Even though physicists regard quarks, electrons, neutrinos and photons as elementary particles, these quanta at the subatomic level might have highly sophisticated internal structure. The fabric of reality is digital and quantized at each emergent level, be it nano, femto, planck or quite possibly, sub-planck levels. Being quantized, i.e., having discrete values and finite set of states, makes all emergent levels subject to computability.

2. *Our World Is Way Too Geometric*

a. *Algebraic Geometry*: There's a strange coincidence between the results of physics experiments and an important, seemingly unrelated set of numbers in pure mathematics, called algebraic geometry. Researchers find a deep connection between fundamental geometric constructions from two very different contexts: motives that mathematicians devised 50 years ago to understand the solutions to polynomial equations, and Feynman diagrams, the schematic representation of how particle collisions play out.

b. *Platonic Solids*: In Nature, we find patterns, designs and structures from the most minuscule particles, to expressions of life discernible by human eyes, to the greater cosmos. These inevitably follow geometrical archetypes, platonic solids, some call it sacred geometry, which reveal to us the essence of each form and its vibrational resonances. They are also symbolic of the underlying holistic principle of inseparability of the part and the whole. It is this principle of oneness underlying all geometry that permeates the architecture of all form in its myriad diversity. This principle of interconnectedness, inseparability and unity provides us with a continuous reminder of our relationship to the whole, a blueprint for the mind to contemplate the sacred foundation of all things created.

c. *Fractal Geometry*: Nature is now known to be fractal, "as above so below," layering of repeating patterns of complexity and self-similarity. Fractals are the emergent properties of iterative feedback systems that exhibit both unpredictable and deterministic behaviors. They form patterns that manifest as complex coherent structures, with the property of scale invariance and self-similarity. Fractals display very specific boundary conditions, with complex morphologies that have a fragmented dimension that uniquely quantifies the level of complexity of the emergent patterns within the system. From the synapses that connect billions of neurons in the brain to the filaments of dark matter that link galactic superclusters, there's a fractal reiteration across the magnitude of scales akin to the Mandelbrot fractal set based on a simple underlying formula. Multifractal systems are ubiquitous in Nature. Similarly, dimensionality of M-theory by adding orthogonal dimensions to the familiar 4D spacetime is based on geometric constructs.

d. *Projective Geometry*: The Holographic Principle, now widely accepted in mainstream science, states that information is "physical" and proportional to surface area and not the volume of the interior, thus the volume itself is illusory and the Universe is actually a hologram which is "projected" from the surface of its distant boundary. In the 1990s physicists Leonard Susskind and Nobel Prizewinner Gerard 't Hooft suggested that the Holographic Principle might apply to the Universe as a whole. Our everyday experience might itself be a holographic projection of physical processes that take place on a distant, 2D surface. In terms of universal computational equivalence, the Holographic Principle shows that a transistor can function as a binary unit, so too can a single atom, or a single subatomic particle.

e. *Golden Ratio*: The golden ratio, also known as the divine proportion, golden mean, or golden section, is another fundamental characteristic that seems to pop up almost everywhere in Nature with an astounding functionality. The Golden Ratio (Phi) is about 1.618033988... It is the unique ratio such that the ratio of the whole to the larger portion is the same as the ratio of the larger portion to the smaller portion. The Fibonacci sequence is closely related to the Golden Ratio. For example, the ratio of 3 to 5 is 1.667. ... Getting even higher, the ratio of 144 to 233 is 1.618. The Golden Ratio is expressed in spiraling shells, seed heads, pine cones, fruits, vegetables, flowers, branches, and the human body. It can be found even in the microscopic realm. The DNA molecule is an example of that. Spiral galaxies, such as our own Milky Way, also follow the familiar Golden Ratio.

f. *Symmetry*: Nature favors symmetries over asymmetries. Symmetry is pervasive in living things. Animals mainly have bilateral or mirror symmetry, as do the leaves of plants and some flowers. The beauty of a crystal, of a flower, or a human face can exhibit Nature's predilection towards symmetry.

3. Our World Has a Strictly Mathematical Set of Rules and Fundamental Constants

a. *Emergent Space and Time:* One of the most mind-boggling discoveries of modernity is that the fabric of spacetime is emergent from something beneath it. In the quest to find the elusive quantum theory of gravity, the attempt to merge quantum mechanics and general relativity, researchers have discovered that spacetime is not actually fundamental, but emerges from information processing, as we've seen in Chapters 13 and 16. This is of course no different than the "space" and "time" in a computer game or VR emerging from the information contained in the hard drive.

b. *Physical Laws as Algorithms:* The laws of Nature work as master algorithms taking the present state of a physical system as input and producing the next state as output. Perhaps the most vivid example of the algorithmic natural laws would be the appearance of some form of a computer code discovered by physicist James Gates when he was working on his theory of supersymmetry. Gates stumbled upon what he described as the presence of what appear to resemble error-correcting codes, embedded within, or resulting from, the equations of supersymmetry related to fundamental particles. A curious number 496, that I call the *'M-number'*, akin to the golden ratio, is frequently encountered in numerical representations of Nature and mathematical equations. 496 is most notable for being a perfect number, and one of the earliest numbers to be recognized as such. The number 496 is a very important number in superstring theory. E8 lattice has dimensionality related to the number 496.

c. *The Fine-Tuned Universe:* The conditions that allow life in the Universe can occur only when certain universal physical constants lie within a very narrow range, so that if any of several fundamental constants were only slightly different, the Universe would be unlikely to be conducive to emergence of matter, astronomical structures, elemental diversity, and life as we know it. The possible explanations for fine-tuning are discussed among philosophers, scientists, theologians, and proponents of Intelligent Design. The fine-tuned Universe observation is closely related to, but is not exactly synonymous with, the Anthropic Principle, which is often used as an explanation of the observation. Regarding Dark Energy and its implication on the cosmological constant, that should have a very specific and enormously tiny value, Leonard Susskind remarks *"The great mystery is not why there is Dark Energy. The great mystery is why there is so little of it $[10^{-122}]$... The fact that we are just on the knife edge of existence, [that] if Dark Energy were very much bigger, we wouldn't be here, that's the mystery."* A slightly larger quantity of Dark Energy, or a slightly larger value of the cosmological constant would have caused space to expand rapidly enough that galaxies would not form. The concept of cosmic information, called *'CosmIn'*, shows that the maximum amount of cosmic information accessible to an observer in our Universe, would be finite, only if the Universe underwent an accelerated phase of expansion, exactly as we now observe.

d. *A Maximum Speed Limit:* Our classical intuitions tell us that one can just keep going faster without limit. After all what is there to stop it? However, with the advent of Einstein's theory of special relativity in 1905 it was discovered that this is not the case. According to relativity, nothing can go faster than the speed of light. Curiously, this exactly parallels the behavior of virtual realities. Virtualities, be they computer simulations or dream environments, are the product of information processing, and information is being processed at a certain speed. As a result, a computer game will have a maximum velocity determined by its refresh rate, exactly as seen in the real world. The speed of light is the maximum speed because the network can't transmit anything faster than one pixel per cycle — i.e., Planck Length divided by Planck Time, or about 300,000 kilometers per second.

e. *Particles That Are Identical in All Respects:* In a virtual reality every object created by the same program is identical in all respects. Curiously, the same is true for subatomic particles. Classes of fundamental particles have very precise properties that are alike in all respects. It is true that physics assumes that all particles of a certain kind, like electrons, are identical to each other. An astounding one-electron hypothesis, apparently first stated in 1940 by John Wheeler, is that all electrons and positrons in the Universe are actually manifestations of a single entity moving forwards and backwards in time. According to Richard Feynman: *"I received a telephone call one day at the graduate college at Princeton from Professor Wheeler, in which he said, 'Feynman, I know why all electrons have the same charge and the same mass' 'Why?' 'Because, they are all the same electron!"*

f. *Quantum Indistinguishability:* It is impossible to know which particle is which when two quantum particles interact in the same place. Superposition is one of the underlying causes of indistinguishability because there is no sure way to lock down an exact position of a quantum particle. This also leads to exotic particle behaviors, especially at low temperatures. Under those conditions, behavioral qualities of particles can resemble each other closely, causing phenomena such as Bose-Einstein condensates and superfluidity.

g. *"Empty Space" Isn't Actually Empty:* In a materialistic universe empty space is, well, empty. When the ancient Greek materialist Democritus spoke of "atoms and the void," he conceived of the void to be empty nothingness. However, modern physics tells us this is not the case. Everywhere, even in a perfect vacuum, the existence of the Unified Field, a medium similar to the ether hypothesized in the past, I choose to call the *'Quantum Akasha'*, is required due to the Heisenberg Uncertainty Principle. Physicists Paul Davies and William Unruh showed in the mid-1970s that an accelerating observer distorts the field. If one thinks of a virtual reality, this makes sense. In a VR, "empty space" is not actually empty space, but rather a simulation of empty space. The "emptiness" of space would then be generated by information processing. Instead of being truly empty, it would display information processing effects, and could temporarily spawn objects, much like the virtual particles in the Unified Field (Quantum Akasha).

h. *Dark Matter, Dark Energy:* If empty space is null processing then it is not nothing, and if it is expanding then new space is being added all the time. New processing points, by definition, receive input but output nothing in their first cycle. So, they absorb but don't emit, exactly like the negative effect we call Dark Energy. If new space adds at a steady rate, the effect won't change much over time, so Dark Energy is caused by the ongoing creation of space. The model also attributes Dark Matter to light in orbit around a black hole. It's a halo effect because light too close to the black hole is pulled into it and light too far away from it still can escape the event horizon. As I mentioned earlier, it is my conjecture that Dark Matter could be ordinary matter in the "probabilistic space" and "phase space" (5th and 6th dimensions of M-theory), possibly with "dark star systems" and life, currently imperceptible to us. Dark Energy, in turn, could be a gravitational pull of neighboring inflationary multiverses (parallel continuums with their own physical laws different from ours). In this M-theoretic view, our entire Universe can be thought of as an entropic bubble expanding into an extra dimension.

4. Our World Has Forward and Backward Causality Loops

a. *Forward Causality:* Cause and effect is what we see in the everyday linear progression of our lives, so forward causality is not problematic but rather self-evident. What's questionable is its mirror twin – retrocausality.

b. *Retrocausality:* In 2017, physicists Matthew Leifer and Matthew Pusey theorized that quantum entanglement isn't action at a distance but action back in time. That is, if time can run backwards, a particle can take the action of its measurement – the event that makes it "choose" a state – back in time to when it was linked with its partner. Trading faster-than-light travel for time travel doesn't sound like much of an improvement, but when it comes to the rules of quantum physics, it solves a lot of problems. In computer games and VR, retrocausality is part of information processing – consistent back histories are created for all observers – what you don't observe isn't necessarily there, but when you look the computer renders objects in place as though they had been there all along. And if these objects were programmed to be moving beforehand, the computer would generate an artificial back history for the object. Oddly enough, just such an effect is seen not only in computer games and VR but in quantum physics of our world. In quantum eraser experiments the past history of an unobserved particle can be determined in the present, seemingly altering what happened in the past by how the experimenter chooses to observe the particle.

5. Nature Acts Like in The Movie "Inception"

a. *Space Bends and Curves:* In Einstein's geometric theory of gravity, the situation is described in a completely different way: A mass that we place in a region of space will lead to a distortion of spacetime. Empty spacetime is flat – it looks exactly like the spacetime of special relativity. Spacetime in the presence of informational masses is curved. An "idle" computer isn't really idle but busy running a null program, and our space could be the same. In the Casimir effect, the vacuum of space exerts a pressure on two flat plates close together. Modern physics says that virtual particles pop out of nowhere to cause this, empty space is full of processing that would have the same effect. And space as a processing network can present a three-dimensional surface capable of curving.

b. *Time Slowing Near Massive "Programs"*: If you open too many programs or too large a program, it will eat up the processing power of your computer, and the computer will begin to lag or even freeze up. Interestingly enough, this has parallels in modern physics. According to general relativity, the more you concentrate mass or energy into a region of space the more time slows down. This is not merely a coincidence, either. In 1995, Ted Jacobson of the University of Maryland, demonstrated that general relativity can be derived from the Holographic Principle and the Second Law of Thermodynamics. The basic concept showed a direct link to the concept of information processing. According to the theorem, the more information is packed into a region of space, the more space will distort and time will slow down in that region. Ted Jacobson's theorem established that gravity is actually an information processing effect. A virtual reality would be subject to virtual time, where each processing cycle is one "tick." Every gamer knows that when the computer is busy the screen lags – game time slows down while loading. Likewise, time in our world slows down with speed or near massive bodies, suggesting that it is virtual. So, the rocket twin only aged a year because that was all the processing cycles the system busy moving him could spare. What changed was his virtual time.

c. *Particles are Convertible into All Other Particles and Energy*: If particles were the zoo animals, then any animal could convert to any other animal in the zoo. Crazy, huh? Everything we consider fundamental can be converted into everything else. Energy can be converted into matter, and matter can be converted back to energy, as noted by the well-known Einstein's formula $E = mc^2$. Electrons, quarks, photons, neutrinos that are regarded as elementary particles are all convertible into all the other particles thanks to the so-called gauge symmetry transformation, also known as *'Transformation of Information'*. Reverse engineering the physical world suggests that matter evolved from light, as a standing quantum wave, light alone in a vacuum can collide to create matter. In contrast, the Standard Model of particle physics says that photons can't collide, so a definitive test of the Simulation Theory is possible. Once we see that light alone collides in a vacuum to create matter, the particle model may be soon replaced by one based on information processing.

d. *Emergent Gravity:* In 2010, renowned string theorist Erik Verlinde from the University of Amsterdam proposed that gravity is not a fundamental force of Nature, but rather an "emergent phenomenon." Verlinde has come up with a set of equations that explains galactic rotation curves by viewing gravity as an emergent force – a result of the quantum structure of space. The idea is related to Dark Energy, which scientists think is the cause for the accelerating expansion of our Universe. Verlinde thinks that what we see as Dark Matter is actually just interactions between galaxies and the sea of Dark Energy in which they're embedded.

6. Conscious Observer Data Stream Validates Experiential Realism

a. *Objects Are Only Rendered Upon Observation:* Nothing is "rendered" until necessarily observed. Naïvely we expect objects to exist when we are not looking, which was the underlying principle for naïve realism of the 20th century. However, on close investigation of the quantum world, we discovered that naïve realism was wrong. Tests on the Leggett Inequality conducted in 2007 validate experiential realism, meaning that reality does not actually exist before experienced as a data stream of consciousness. What we call matter only "renders" when we look. Quantum mechanics has stark anti-materialist philosophical implications, many of which have been experimentally confirmed.

b. *The Measurement Problem*: The famed double-slit experiment demonstrates quantum mechanical wave-particle duality. The orthodox formulation of quantum mechanics can be found in a 1932 book by John von Neumann. If read literally, it postulates two opposing ontologies of Nature. The first ontology is described by the Schrödinger equation which is deterministic: The Schrödinger equation enables one to calculate the exact physical state of a system (i.e., its wave function) at a later time given that system's physical state at some earlier time. The second ontology is described by the collapse postulate which is not deterministic but probabilistic: The collapse postulate only assigns probabilities to the possible future states of a physical system given its current state. Evidently, no physical system can be subject to both ontologies since no physical system can evolve deterministically and non-deterministically at the same time. That's why the third ontology proposed by emergence theorist Klee Irwin seems to resolve this contradiction. According to Irwin, reality is neither deterministic nor it is fully random but rather code-theoretic. Every system is subject to code, or language of Nature, that allows free will agents to "choose" the observed system's evolution. Quantum decoherence that some physicists still believe is responsible for the quantum-to-classical transition doesn't solve the measurement problem. A conscious mind, a "chooser," is still required to actualize the collapse of the quantum wave to crystallize it into an observer-dependent digital reality.

c. *Consciousness Seems to Collapse Multiple Possibilities into One Actuality:* In Copenhagen Interpretation of quantum physics, the quantum wave function collapses due to a conscious observer making a measurement of a physical system. This is the interpretation of quantum physics which sparked the Schröedinger's cat thought experiment, demonstrating disparity with our classical way of thinking, except that it does completely match the evidence of what we observe at the quantum level! Based on the Copenhagen Interpretation, John Wheeler proposed the Participatory Anthropic Principle: The entire Universe collapses into the state we see specifically because of conscious observers present to cause the collapse. Any possible universe that does not contain conscious observers is automatically ruled out. In alternative Many Worlds Interpretation of quantum physics, there's no quantum collapse and all realities are probable at varying degrees but a conscious observer still plays a key role in identifying certain coordinates within the quantum multiverse *'as if'* the quantum collapse occurred. As we saw in Chapter 4, MWI is simply incomplete in regards to subjectivity and computational mechanics. The hypothesis that *'consciousness causes quantum collapse'* proposes a solution to the measurement problem by defining when and where collapse occurs, while consciousness plays a fundamental causal role.

d. *Non-Determinism and Free Will:* Modern physics comes with something known as the Uncertainty Principle. This states that there are pairs of properties that cannot be simultaneously known to arbitrary precision. If we know the position of a subatomic particle, we cannot know its speed and if we know its speed, we cannot know its momentum. Consciousness is what appears to be universal information processing, and thus fundamental within this experiential matrix provided necessary free will agency exists at all emergent levels. We are not a "clockwork" universe, nor are we files on the CD, we are moving along within the Universal Causal Diamond, this experiential matrix, utterly non-deterministic due to largely non-computable combinatorics of interactions by free-willing entities. In other words, complex systems and a single observer timeline are completely unpredictable, you need to "run the program" with certain initial conditions to see its detailed evolutionary development.

e. *Quantum Tunneling*: Quantum theory stipulates that an electron can occasionally penetrate physical barriers, and then collapse to any point based on probabilities. Each collapse is an image frame in the movie we call physical reality, except that the next frame isn't fixed. So, an electron "tunneling" through an impenetrable field is like a movie that "cuts" from a view of an actor. That might sound odd, but teleporting from one state to another in discrete increments is how all quantum matter moves. We see a physical world that exists independent of our observation, but quantum theory's observer effect implies it almost works like a game view, where if you look left a left view is created and if you look right a right view is shown.

f. *Quantum Zeno Effect*: Experimentally verified, this effect refers to one of the oddest predictions of quantum theory – that an atomic system can't change while you're watching it. Numerous experiments came out with the same results – researchers claimed to control quantum dynamics purely by observation – they were able to suppress quantum tunneling merely by observing the atoms that wouldn't move.

g. *We Only Need Minds to Create Reality:* There are prominent computational idealists such as Peter Russell (Primacy of

Consciousness), Bernardo Kastrup (Metaphysical Idealism), Donald Hoffman (Conscious Realism), Antonin Tuynman (Pancomputational Panpsychism), and myself (Experiential Realism) among others who would contend that the only substance in the Universe is consciousness, notably mind-to-mind networks of entangled conscious agents all the way down, and all the way up. What's only substantive is their interaction: Information is generated by one mind and interpreted by the other in endless feedback loops, that results in experiential (virtual) reality. Experience is *'in'*-forming" of consciousness. This worldview takes consciousness to be primal, rather than derivative from physical objects in spacetime.

7. A Cosmic Beginning

a. *The Digital Big Bang: The Alpha Point:* A universe from nothing? Oh wait, no, from a quantum fluctuation! How preposterous would it be to believe in this kind of "miracle," nonetheless, this is the current predominant view in the scientific community. Eternal inflation would be one kind of model that does not actually presuppose an absolute beginning. In any case, the fact that the physical universe came into being demonstrates that it is not actually fundamental as we would expect. Rather it had to come into being from something more fundamental, perhaps something non-physical. This is perfectly normal for a VR, though. Any computer game or virtual reality needs a computer to start up and cannot have existed before. Once booted up with a first event, the system begins its space and time. In this view, the Digital Big Bang has occurred when our Universe booted up, including its space-time operating system.

b. *The Omniverse: The Timeless Ultimate Ensemble:* Our Universe or any other arises from a breaking of symmetry, and we're headed back towards a natural return to the perfectly balanced whole that exists both "before" and "after" the existence of our Universe. This means that the underlying fabric of reality is conducive for our Universe to evolve towards the Teilhardian Omega Point, the Vikoulovian Apotheosis, or Absolute Enlightenment, and expressed in the computational underpinnings of Digital Physics, the Langanian Cognitive Theoretic Model of the Universe or the Pearcian Zero Ontology, the Zero Energy Universe Hypothesis or Tegmark's Mathematical Universe Hypothesis, the Ultimate Ensemble of M-theory or the Omniverse. This also implies that the broken symmetry that creates our Universe or any other is defined by what's "missing" from it. In the case of our own Universe, we know there is much less anti-matter than would be expected if our Universe is derived from an underlying symmetry state: So, it is this absence of anti-matter which is one of the defining traits that resulted in our particular Universe.

Mathematically speaking, we may frame this idea in terms of zero being "full" (instead of "empty") while treating zero as the largest value in the algebraic system which includes the two already vast infinities of positive and negative numbers. Zero then becomes an infinite whole that contains all other positive and negative values, the totality of which amounts to it. If zero is seen as the largest value, the only way there can be lesser values is when we remove some measure of value from the whole of zero. This way of thinking allows to imagine a divine creative force which expresses itself throughout universes. The 1 creates everything from 0. From our own vantage point, both time and anti-time represent the same thing: A naturally occurring return to balance – each dimension, perceived in its entirety as a single timeless point – becomes a point on the surface of a finite but unbounded hypersphere in the next dimension. A Nobel prize-winning physicist Frank Wilczek proposes that just as there are naturally emerging crystal structures in the third dimension, this same effect could be happening within what he calls *'Time Crystals'*, extradimensional patterns that reside within a timeless whole.

8. Non-Locality: The Entangled Universe

a. *Quantum Entanglement:* Once connected, always connected, quantum entanglement links two separate particles across vast distances and time so that a change to one instantly determines the state of the other. Does quantum entanglement show spacetime to be illusory? Entanglement, superposition, and other non-local characteristics of quantum mechanics remain the most perplexing aspects of quantum theory. The Maldacena-Susskind Holographic Correspondence theorem (ER=EPR) states that two entangled particles are connected by a micro-wormhole, i.e., non-traversable wormhole (Einstein–Rosen bridge or ER bridge) is equivalent to a pair of maximally entangled black holes. EPR refers to quantum entanglement (EPR paradox). Another research team led by Nassim Haramein of the Resonance Project describes in their paper titled *"The Unified Spacememory Network: From Cosmogenesis to Consciousness"* the extended geometry of the Planck-scale vacuum oscillators, where, in fact, micro-wormholes connect particles not only in distant space but in distant time. This means that all sectors of spacetime are acting as one information encoding volume – by analogy to a computer system, they would not be isolated but rather equidistant to the GPU. This information encoding medium may be connected in a continuous wormhole network – sort of like a manifold information processing network – allowing non-local, instantaneous transmission of information. Its premise, that the physical world is a processing output, doesn't make it a fake, since there is still a real world out there – it just isn't the one we see.

402

b. *Local Realism has been Falsified by Quantum Mechanics Experiments:* The results of experiments seemed to show that matter is dependent on observation, or *'measurement'*, to exist in any defined location. The particles (fermions of matter) behave like waves of probability when not being measured, and like balls of matter while being measured. We also found that two entangled particles can somehow communicate with each other instantaneously at any distance in space. This phenomenon was called "spooky action at a distance" by Albert Einstein. To find a *'local hidden variable'*, Einstein, Podolsky and Rosen (later known as the EPR Paradox) came together to devise experiments. This hidden variable was supposed to be something that would connect the particles somehow to show that reality wasn't as "spooky" or strange as the experiments were implying. But no local hidden variable has ever been found, thus falsifying Local Realism.

9. Antimatter. Antitime

If matter is the result of processing and processing sets a sequence of values, it follows that those values can be set in reverse — processing implies anti-processing. In this light, antimatter is the inevitable by-product of matter created by processing. If time is the completion of forward processing cycles for matter, for antimatter it is the completion of backward cycles, so it logically runs our time in reverse. Matter has an inverse because the processing that creates it is reversible, and anti-time occurs for the same reason. Only a virtual time can have an inverse.

10. Evolutionary Processes Striving Towards Maximal Complexity and Efficiency

a. *Self-Organizing Dynamics:* Self-organization is a process where some form of overall order arises from interactions between parts of an initially disordered system. The process is spontaneous, not needing

403

external control. Self-organization is observed at all scales: in chemical reactions, where it is often described as self-assembly, in biology, from molecular to ecosystem level, and in sociology, from tribes to today's "global village." Scientists now offer a radically new view of Nature as a web of networked systems, dynamically self-governing and self-optimizing at different levels, ranging from the subatomic level to the entire Biosphere and beyond. Individual atoms can be combined to form bio-molecules which in turn create even more complex RNA and DNA molecules, leading to abiogenesis, creation of life, in the form of the first prokaryote unicellular organisms. Ecosystems rely for their health on the tightly synchronized interaction of many different species. And regarding our intrinsic human nature, evolutionary psychologists, historians and sociologists have pointed to our ability to cooperate, rather than compete, as our defining characteristic. Self-organization is a key program of evolutionary development in Nature.

b. *Weak and Strong Emergence:* Emergent structures are patterns that emerge via collective actions of many individual entities. To explain such patterns, one might conclude that emergence occurs because of intricate causal relations across different scales and feedback, known as interconnectivity. The shape and behavior of a flock of birds or school of fish are good examples of weak emergence. The best example of strong emergence would be the phenomenon of consciousness itself. Complex systems rooted in radical emergence exhibit non-computable macroscopic properties. For example, for many particle systems, nothing can be calculated precisely from the microscopic equations, and macroscopic systems are characterized by a new, unprecedented level of the system's evolution due to phase transitions. Similarly, the coming Syntellect Emergence is inevitable, but from our bottom-up perspective, we cannot possibly predict how our Digital Gaia would feel like when this new emergent entity "wakes up" – we can only make educated speculations about her conscious awareness, i.e., our own at that level.

c. *Complexification*: Life is a major source of complexity, and evolution is the fundamental process behind the overwhelming diversity of life. In this view, evolution is the process describing the runaway growth of complexity in the natural world and in speaking of the emergence of complex living beings and life-forms, this view refers therefore to processes leading to sudden evolutionary leaps at a certain threshold of complexity, organization and connectivity. Life is thought to have sprung into existence in the early RNA world when RNA chains began to express the basic conditions necessary for Darwinian natural selection. The Cambrian Explosion was a historically swift complexification of ancient primordial life from unicellular organisms into multicellular organisms that represented the next higher level of biospheric complexity. Not always a battleground of "selfish genes" competing to outperform each other, life predominantly spreads by networking and responding to its environment. It's a delicate balance between competition and cooperation, complexity theorists should call coopetition. Evolving systems with emergent properties or complex structures may appear to defy entropy, because they form and increase order despite oftentimes the lack of command and central control. All complex systems tend to complexify ad infinitum until either an insurmountable constraint or maximum possible complexity is reached. By the compounding algorithm, our space-faring civilization is set to saturate the rest of Universe within a relatively brief cosmological period until our networked cosmos "wakes up" as a singular conscious entity, one universal mind, yet another dot on the trajectory leading to the hyperdimensional Omega Singularity, or "God."

d. *Structural Feedback Mechanisms:* Any complex, informationally integrated system engenders feedback mechanics and is often a product of particular patterns of interaction. Negative feedback introduces constraints that serve to fix structures or behaviors. In contrast, positive feedback promotes change, allowing local variations to grow into global patterns. Trees in a forest have been discovered to communicate with each other in a complex feedback loop network that maintains their collective health. Global neurofeedback seems to be the most essential program within any neural network, such as a conscious human brain. Per his definition of emergence, behavioral geneticist Peter Corning addresses emergence and evolution: *"[In] evolutionary processes, causation is iterative; effects are also causes. And this is equally true of the synergistic effects produced by emergent systems. In other words, emergence itself... has been the underlying cause of the evolution of emergent phenomena in biological evolution; it is the synergies produced by organized systems that are the key."*

e. *Hierarchy of Conscious Systems:* The best framework for describing an unfolding, evolutionary, self-organizing Universe and thus explaining reality well may be based on the hierarchy of conscious systems. Reality appears as a continuing development process characterized by a series of hierarchical levels of organization of increasing complexity and autonomy. Gaining more attention of late, panpsychism denotes that conscious entities are to be found everywhere all the way down to quarks and electrons, and all the way up to the galaxies and the Universe as a whole. We'll discuss the hierarchical consciousness, natural God of Spinoza, further in the chapter.

f. *Levels of Abstraction:* Perhaps what would pull the rug from under physicalism is a notion of ever deeper levels of abstraction that only minds can create and perceive. Physicalists might make a concession by saying that information, now widely accepted as fundamental, is physical but idealists would insist by saying that information, conveyed by symbolism, originates only in the mind. Intersubjectivity is a particularly a great example of layered abstractions, from memes to social institutions to collective unconscious well beyond materiality. Subjective values, such as patriotism, and complex concepts are inherently mental in nature. What's even more indicative that our world is entirely mental rather than physical is that advanced consciousness like augmented humans and synthetic superintelligence will generate even deeper levels of abstraction from extradimensionalities to virtualities of our own design. Quantum computers would compute parallel slices of abstraction. And inner space exploration could eclipse outer space exploration. Before long, we'll start to create virtual worlds coming right out of our imagination, instantly "materialized" with help of advanced AI.

Would it be logical to accept that it has already happened in our bi-directionally causal (self-causal, retrocausal) Universe and our human mindspace is but a fractal of the larger cosmic mind? In a sense, we all belong to levels of abstraction with top-down propagation emanating from the Omega Singularity, the transcendental projector of all possible observer timelines. All mass-energy, space-time itself emerge from consciousness. Those are epiphenomena of consciousness. Period. As Arthur Eddington once put it, the stuff of the Universe is mind-stuff. Also, speaking of levels of abstraction consider that what we perceive as physical well may be imaginary in the minds of inhabitants of parallel Earth where events turn out slightly different from ours, hinting once again that everything is made of information and ultimately is but a mental construct.

As strange as all of this sounds, as I arbitrarily came up with 10 descriptive categories for convenience of classification and the total of 40 m-properties, these are only some of the salient m-observables worth mentioning. This list obviously can be extended by a slew of other phenomena indicating that we're part of the self-organizing, self-creating, self-causal experiential matrix. Most telling, though, is the fact that spacetime is emergent. Everything we refer to as physical reality is matter or energy located in space and time. Thus, if spacetime is emergent, physicalism is contradicted, and over the long run, I doubt, can be saved. At best, physicalism may describe only one of the subsets of reality akin to the subset of reality describable by, say, classical physics. What we refer to as physical reality is not actually real, but is rather an illusion generated by information processing, in other words, a multi-player virtual reality, and in the experience of a single observer – a subjective digital reality!

M-properties of experiential matrix imply intelligent design based on principles of self-organization, self-causation and self-reflection rather than the program written by a "programmer" in the universe up. As Brian Whitworth writes in his paper *"The Physical World as a Virtual Reality"*: *"Individually none of the above short points is convincing, but taken together they constitute what a court might call circumstantial evidence, favoring virtual reality against objective reality."* Are we all fractals of one divine entity – everything, everywhere, simultaneously? Do feelings of love have physical power? Would our ultimate evolution bring us into true consciousness and oneness with God? Is life a dream? How could we even define God?

REDEFINING GOD

In actuality, God cannot be defined. Any attempt to define infinite unlimited being will have inherently human limitations, so any such attempt will be limited by our understanding. God means so many things to people of different religious traditions and spiritual beliefs.

God is not some sky deity, though, but rather absolute reality, universal consciousness, the ultimate source, the higher self, pure love, pure existence, pure energy that binds everything together as one. Entity that cannot be destroyed but can only change from one form to another. Entity we would usually ascribe such attributes as omnipresence, omniscience, omnipotence, omnibenevolence, highest love, creativity and beauty.

In Christianity and other monotheistic religions, God is defined as the creator and ruler of the Universe and source of all moral authority; the supreme being. In certain other religions, God is a superhuman being or spirit worshipped as having power over Nature or human fortunes; a deity. The Buddhist concepts of Unity and Enlightenment, achieving Nirvana through a series of countless reincarnations, may soon become a new reality for billions of us, humanity as a grandly orchestrated unified whole. This coming stage of our civilizational development is already seen on the horizon and for us to experience in our lifetimes through the means of technological mediation leading to cybernetic immortality, super-wellbeing, superintelligence and advanced planetary self-awareness.

God = Existence. God is everything that exists, all that is. The words "God" and "existence" are synonymous. The Universe is the body of God. Nature is all manifestations of God. Like fractals of God, we all are infinite beings, and we are all one godly being. But we need limitations to experience a human life, in other words, our limitations define who we are today. In order to be the whole, ONE needs all our limitations – all of them – each and every life of any possible living creature and in all possible timelines across all possible universes. We are here for experience – the whole is divided into experiencers for indulging in experience. We are one with God and God is one with us. God is within, not without.

409

Panpsychism which is recently being rapidly adopted by the scientific crowd could be a good stepping stone towards more radical doctrines of experiential realism, idealism, and pantheism. The worldview called pantheism denotes that all plurality is only apparent, that in the endless series of individuals, passing simultaneously and successively into and out of life, generation after generation, age after age, there is but one and the same entity really existing, which is present and identical in all alike. If plurality and difference belong only to the appearance-form, if there is but one and the same entity manifested in all living things, it follows that, once we dissolve the ego, we shed our illusion of separation. Until then we maintain the "reality" of individuation – a thing the Hindus call *Maya*, a phantasmagoric vision. This ideology may be traced back to the remotest antiquity, to the oldest book in the world, the esoteric teaching of *Vedas*.

We have now rediscovered the original oneness of the world. This oneness cannot be diminished by spatial or temporal separation. An invisible wholeness, just like *the Force* in *Star Wars*, unites all creation in the Universe, and it is this wholeness that we have stumbled upon through modern experimental methods, in the words of the poet Charles Williams: *"Separation without separateness, reality without rift."* Physicist Freeman Dyson puts it eloquently: *"It appears that mind, as manifested by the capacity to make choices, is to some extent inherent in every atom. The Universe as a whole is also weird, with laws of Nature that make it hospitable to the growth of mind. I do not make any clear distinction between Mind and God. God is what Mind becomes when it has passed beyond the scale of our comprehension."*

The interrelation of human consciousness and the observed world is obvious in Bell's Theorem and interpretations of quantum mechanics. Human consciousness and the physical world cannot be regarded as distinct, separate entities. What we call physical reality, the external world, is shaped, to some extent, by human thought. Clearly, we cannot separate our own existence from that of the world outside. We are intimately associated, not only with the Earth we inhabit, but with the farthest reaches of the cosmos.

Those of us who would prefer for one reason or another to remain stubbornly agnostic might want to learn about and be sympathetic towards a new philosophical movement − Syntheism − focused on how atheists and pantheists can achieve the same feelings of unity and awe experienced in traditional theistic religions. Syntheism sees itself as the practical realization of philosophical ambitions predating Baruch Spinoza's pantheism in the 17th century and theological philosophies of Alfred North Whitehead and Pierre Teilhard de Chardin.

GOD OF SPINOZA: THE CONSCIOUS UNIVERSE

"Whatever is contrary to Nature is contrary to reason, and whaterver is contrary to reason is absurd." -Baruch Spinoza

One of the first modern pantheists was Baruch Spinoza (1632-1677), who identified God with Nature and summarized his philosophy in the *Ethics*, his main work. Spinoza believed that everything that exists is God. But Spinoza's God is not the conventional Judo-Christian Creator, for his views the philosopher was excommunicated by the church. Today, brilliant minds have given the Universe many names − *"the Self-Aware Universe"* (Amit Goswami), *"the Magic Universe"* (Nigel Calder), *"the Looking Glass Universe"* (John Briggs and David Peat), *"the Elegant Universe"* (Brian Greene), *"the Human Universe"* (Deepak Chopra, Menas Kafatos), *"the Mathematical Universe"* (Max Tegmark), and *"the Conscious Universe"* (Dean Radin). The underlying premise behind these various titles is the idea that at a deep level all things in our Universe are ineffably interdependent and interconnected, as we are part of the Matryoshka-like mathematical object of emergent levels of complexity where consciousness pervades all levels. Let's explore this idea of conscious Universe from the modern physics perspective.

As a starting point, we can invoke the Second Axiom of Evolutionary Emergence: "The whole is something greater than the sum of its parts," or to rephrase it – everything exists both as a whole unto itself as well as a component of some greater holistic system. There's plenty of evidence for that. We know that electrons are what we call elementary particles that are components of atoms. Atoms are components of molecules. Molecules compose cells that are, in turn, are components of organisms. Organisms arise within more complex systems and ecosystems. Ecosystems are located on planets. Planets are composites of solar systems, and solar systems are composites of galaxies, and galaxies are composites of the Universe. It follows that your true, holistic identity consists of both your individual self-identity and your composite-identity within a larger system. If you accept that it is your individual self-identity that is endowed with your self-consciousness, then you can at least begin to question whether the holistic system of which you're a composite has holistic consciousness.

As of today, there's no commonly accepted definition of the term *'consciousness'*. If we define consciousness as a degree of autonomy a given system gains in the dynamic relations with its environment, even the simplest self-organizing dissipative structure is a primitive form of consciousness. As previously noted, in Chapter 8 and elsewhere, consciousness means the ability to sense and to react to what you sense in your environment, whether it's your internal or your external environment.

When plants experience their environment, why don't we call it consciousness? If plants have brain-like functions and make sentient-like decisions, our existing cognizance of Nature and ourselves must change. *"Plants may lack brains and neural tissues but they do possess a sophisticated calcium-based signaling network in their cells similar to animals' memory processes,"* says cognitive ecologist Monica Gagliano. Do plants, like animals, have consciousness? We know that leaves will turn to face the Sun, to absorb its energy. An entire field of sunflowers would all face East in the morning when the Sun rises. They will then track the Sun across the sky throughout the day and then all face West at sunset. But we don't call this consciousness, instead we call this *'heliotropism'*. And because it's fundamentally a chemical process, the reasoning goes, it's not consciousness. But neurobiologists tell us that our own brains are basically biochemical supercomputers, and that our own decisions, the actions we take, and indeed our entire state of consciousness at any particular moment, are correlated with chemical processes in the brain at any particular time.

We can immediately recognize that this physicalist approach is limited in scope and only depicts neural correlates of consciousness without causal role of chemical processes on producing a conscious experience. This is a very old mind-body debate deeply rooted in the debate of Idealism vs. Materialism. Arguably, consciousness is not generated by the brain. You can't get consciousness out of a piece of matter. We have discussed elsewhere the many reasons why we can be certain that this is true. Consciousness is fundamental, pre-exists the Universe and manifests in everything that we think of as real. A brain, as important as it seems, is nothing more than the way that non-local consciousness operates at an avatar level during a lifetime. The

413

evidence that all of this is true is consistent and overwhelming. But mainstream science is still bound by the centuries-old "materialist dogma" and stuck with the "hard problem" of consciousness.

Where can we draw a line between conscious and nonconscious things? Quite frankly, calling non-human things nonconscious is a weak distinction to make from the start, and truly egocentric. Undoubtedly, any living thing that can experience its environment, and that can react to what it senses in its environment, is conscious. But conscious in a way that makes sense to that entity, makes sense to its ability to sustain its own life.

What about really small living things, like bacteria? We know that inside your own gastrointestinal tract, there are thousands of different species of bacteria. Recently, scientists have been discovering ways in which bacteria can signal and communicate with each other to coordinate community processes, ranging from managing their population to resisting an infectious disease. But if these bacteria are signaling and communicating, then they, too, are conscious. Now, this is when it gets really intriguing. If those bacteria are living inside us, and we are their environment, then by extension we are their conscious environment, too. They live inside a conscious environment even though they could never apprehend anything other than their own situation. They could never be aware of our higher holistic consciousness. In this perspective, lower levels cannot capture the higher-level activity, while the higher-levels affect and ultimately supersede the lower ones.

What about things that we don't typically regard as living things, like electrons that orbit an atomic nucleus? Or planets that orbit their star? We know that electrons are negatively charged particles that seem to orbit at relatively high speeds around a nucleus without ever crashing into each other. They avoid collisions because two negatively charged particles will magnetically detect and repel from each other when they get too close. If you're an electron, it's not relevant to be able to enjoy an orgasmic sunset. Your world is about electromagnetism. So magnetically detecting other charges is what's relevant to an electron.

What about planets in orbit? We know that planets also occupy specific orbital patterns around a star and don't crash into each other. It's the attracting force of gravity that holds them in their orbital paths and not the attracting force of electromagnetism as in the case of electrons. But philosophically speaking, the similarities are stupendous across such vast scales and such different forces that are at play. And it tends to support the hypothesis of everything being part of an unfolding, emergent, transcendent consciousness structure. There's no doubt that the smaller system occurs many times over within the larger system. A galaxy is in resonance *par excellence* across scales with a cell, not only in terms of shape but internal structure with a distinct core (galactic center and cellular nucleus) and metabolic activities.

The largest and costliest instrument humanity has built to date is the Large Hadron Collider in Geneva, Switzerland. But what is it exactly? This is a huge "microscope," it's a particle accelerator that makes particles collide, so then scientists get to observe what smaller components those particles break down into. It seems that under certain conditions, an entity's innate ability to react to what's going on in its environment in a way that is appropriate to sustain itself is insufficient. When that happens, whether as a sudden collision event, or as a result of imbalances gradually accumulated over time, that entity will begin to break down to its composite states. Viewed in this way, life and death are both processes. Life is the organization of energy into form. And death is the liberation of energy from form and the reduction of an entity back to its composite states. We know that to endure, any entity first needs an awareness of its environment, internal and external, in order to compensate for the changes taking place.

The tendency of an entity to compensate for change can be observed across a vast range of natural phenomena, and it's evidenced by the interplay between entropy and what we call *'autopoietic dissipative systems'*. That means that for every random event that takes place, the disorder of the system will increase. In other words, systems, or entities, need to be able to respond to this entropic influence in such a way that preserves their relative stability. Spiral shapes such as seen in a number of natural motifs from a DNA molecule to the shape of the Milky Way or Andromeda galaxies, are examples of the complex patterns and structures that can emerge during a process of dissipation to retain stability over periods, in particular, of rapid expansion.

Evidently, a living organism, by definition, is organized. If we observe its structural integrity, it is quantumly entangled. If we can see the organized properties of very large systems, then it's only cultural "common sense' that stops us from referring to very large systems as organisms. I believe that consciousness will emerge wherever and whenever complex self-organizing systems emerge. But it will be an emergent consciousness of a type that is relevant to that complex intelligent system. If consciousness plays a role in ensuring survival, then we should begin to question: What role does consciousness play in the process of evolution? Darwin argued that seemingly random genetic mutations that took place in genetic codes resulted in beneficial adaptations that thrived. But there is growing evidence to support the view that genetic mutations are environmentally responsive. Experiments by microbiologists such as Barry Hall have observed that the genetic rate of mutation in bacteria increases under environmentally stressful conditions. So, if genetic mutation is environmentally responsive, then it's not a very distinct process from what we regard as evolution, it is information processing, structural feedback mechanics, and optimization that results in the formation of something completely new.

Consider social media, wearables and future neurotechnologies. Something sublime is expected to arise if evolution of information networks is going to enhance the ability of a system to communicate across different components of itself. We will in time learn how to exteriorize the contents of our minds via virtual reality and new modes of communication. Your social media stream might eventually evolve to become your externalized data stream of consciousness, your "digital twin" that you could choose to share with other people.

This belief, that we are all part of one organism, is perfectly encapsulated by the Gaia hypothesis which means that our planet as a whole is a living, "breathing" superorganism, so essentially 'we are one'. And this hypothesis is one that is as old as the pantheistic philosophy of Spinoza. It suggests that humans should understand ourselves within this superorganism to be semi-autonomous, conscious agents of a complex adaptive system that is constantly adjusting, reacting and adapting. At the planetary level, all the biological communities form the Biosphere, where its human participants form societies, the complex interactions of meta-social systems such as the world's markets, whereas hyperconnectivity and ever-increasing interactivity of all biospheric and cybernetic systems give rise to the Noosphere of the planet, and eventually the Syntellect Emergence, awakening of the Gaian Mind.

If our entire Universe is, as science might ultimately prove, a complex self-governing system, then not only would our Universe have consciousness, but that consciousness would be as old as time, and it would encompass all other forms of consciousness within it, including yours and mine. With the inclusion of God as origin and end of the Universe, human consciousness could ascend to the Transcendent Self, i.e., proceed to the final stage of consciousness evolution, experiential cognition of God. The whole itinerary of consciousness' ascension to the teleological attractor could be regarded as a "hierarchy of regress," or the ability to be drawn back to God by dividing into individual evolving experiencers contemplating everything in creation.

CONCLUSION: WRAPPING UP THE DIGITAL PANTHEISM ARGUMENT

In light of the circumstantial evidence presented earlier, we can draw a number of important deductions about the ultimate nature of reality – our computational Universe behaves as an experiential matrix, or virtual reality – so that we can unequivocally answer the question "Is God the ultimate computer?" This is why this question is now taken seriously by science, philosophy and theology which brings us to the deeper aspect of that questioning: If the Universe is a simulation, who and where is the simulator? Should we take the view of philosopher Nick Bostrom that we are being simulated by posthumans as an ancestor simulation? Or, is God a Hypermind and each of us is an earthly avatar?

The problem with the Bostrom's Simulation Argument is it really doesn't answer the question of the so-called "platform" problem. If we are being simulated by future humans then their world would have to possess the same features as ours and be based on qubits, this would imply that the posthumans are also simulated beings. If their world has the exact same properties as ours, just further in the future, their world would need outside processing by a simulator. If they are also being simulated by a future civilization then the cycle continues and it is nothing more than an infinite regress. Bostrom admits that and says: *"...we would have to suspect that posthumans running our simulation are themselves simulated beings and their creators, in turn, may also be simulated beings. Reality may thus contain many levels"* and this equates to nothing more than an infinite regress.

But what if one of the higher levels is not a quantum world but an actual objective world based on classical physics? Well, this solution creates more problems than it solves. For a quantum world like ours to be simulated in a classical world all of the qubits would have to be unpacked into classical bits. This will result in a classical computer hard drive bigger than that which is being simulated, so a computer bigger than the Universe itself which would be preposterous to postulate and impossible to build, which leaves us with a different alternative – the Universe is being simulated in a mind. Could what we conceive of the Universe be some sort of dream world rather than a real thing?

Given the problems that result from being simulated on a computer one can find a much simpler explanation that the Universe is being simulated in a mind. This would solve many problems of being simulated on a computer because a mind has elements of integrated information states and also processes information. A dream environment would emerge from information processing and therefore look identical to the conditions of our world as we described earlier. So, a dream environment just emerges from platonic information in a mind which is essentially the same type of physics we see in a generic information construct such as the illusion of space-time and matter, and the quantized elements which make it finite and computable.

Even more important to mention, physical manifestation we call matter seems to need mind since this is what quantum mechanics tells us. Mind is necessary to collapse a wave function for matter to "materialize," and recent experiments confirm that there's no reality beyond what we observe. So, it's really the conscious observation that creates reality. Empirical evidence does not fit with the idea of objective reality, and mind-like computational substratum doesn't require the existence of particles to be built upon but rather platonic dimensionless bits of information.

In Chapter 2, we mentioned The Integrated Information Theory, a popular theory of consciousness developed by cognitive scientist Giulio Tononi that may help to conceptualize this. There's no consensus on what produces consciousness, but everyone regardless of metaphysical views can agree what it is like to be conscious. Given that consciousness is subjectivity, what consciousness is like is what consciousness is. Tononi postulated that everything we refer to as consciousness is information – thoughts, perceptions, intentions, emotions and so on. A conscious state is then simply a system of integrated information. If modern physics is telling us that the Universe is generated by information integration to produce "physical" reality, this gives us some intriguing inkling about the Universe. The Universe is actually a conscious state! And, of course, conscious states necessarily exist within minds.

Thus, if we take the physics to its logical conclusion, it leads us to a theistic view of existence. Our Universe is, in actuality, being simulated in an immaterial hypermind of a superintelligent, all-powerful, all-knowing being, an entity whose motives are unfathomable for us to comprehend at our level of evolution. The Universe is a conscious state in the mind of God!

From this perspective, we can then finalize the Digital Pantheism Argument:

Deduction 1: Simulations can exist solely in a computer or in a mind;

Deduction 2: The Universe is an experiential matrix, or a virtual reality simulation (subjective digital reality). This, of course, is evidenced by m-properties presented earlier;

Deduction 3: A simulation on a computer still must be necessarily simulated in a mind. This would follow from the infinite regress problem – if you are being simulated on a computer, to prevent the infinite regress of endless computer simulations, we eventually have to stop assuming higher levels of computers and stop with the simulation existing in a mind. We will also have to take into account the importance of Occam's razor, if we have to inevitably arrive at the conclusion of mind-based reality, then why even preconceive intermediate levels of computer simulations unless it's absolutely necessary to do so? One can counterargue that consciousness is more complex than "just" information processing, but as we saw in parts of the book, as complex as it is, consciousness can be regarded as optimized meta-algorithmic information processing of progressively self-surpassing fractally-arranged [emergent] conscious systems. The Universal Mind would still be inescapable, so we have to make the next deduction –

Deduction 4: Therefore, the Universe is a simulation in a mind and this mind is what we call the larger consciousness system, the cosmic self, the Universal Mind, or God. And the conclusion simply follows –

Conclusion: God's existence is a factual and logical necessity. We all are fractals of the God's mind – we are one with God. We are not passive observers but active co-creators of our experiential reality. Going forward into the Information Age, physicalism cannot be saved. Physicalism can only describe a subset of reality, a tiny layer of existence, notably the "rule set of our physical world" as one of the possible worlds, but fails to describe levels of abstraction below, above and beyond the "material" world. That's why idealism is valid. Pantheism is true.

Chapter 19. The Fermi Paradox: First Contact with Alien Syntellects

"Two possibilities exist: either we are alone in the Universe or we are not. Both are equally terrifying." -Arthur C. Clarke

The forthcoming Cybernetic Singularity could pave the way to rapid space colonization sometime by mid-century, however, not exactly how Hollywood movies depict -- fragile flesh-and-blood humans are unlikely to personally travel to other stars. Our post-biological descendants (AGIs, uploads and hybrids), on the other hand, could roam the Universe on their tiny warp spaceships, via traversable wormholes, and colonize galaxies via self-replicating Von Neumann probes that would establish wormhole portals and communication with the core civilization. But what's even more exciting, first contact and networking with alien syntellects becomes a clear possibility.

There must be an incredibly large number of civilizations far ahead of us in development which could have colonized our Milky Way galaxy by now, as the argument goes, so that we must see signs of intelligent alien life out there but we don't. Our Sun is relatively young in the lifespan of the Universe. There are far older stars with arguably far older Earth-like planets, which should theoretically mean civilizations far more advanced than our own. Our galaxy should be teeming with civilizations but where's everybody?

In 1950, Enrico Fermi was on his way to lunch with a bunch of physicist friends at the Los Alamos National Lab. As we all know, physicists have an incredible sense of humor, so this group began to joke about a recent wave of UFO sightings and a newspaper comic blaming missing municipal trash on aliens. Later Fermi goes ballistic on the subject and asks about the existence of aliens: *"Well, where are they? Where's everybody?"* This question in reference to the existence of extraterrestrial intelligence was later labeled the *'Fermi Paradox'*.

Our Space Age officially began in 1961 when the Russian cosmonaut Yuri Gagarin became the first man to orbit Earth, while the American astronomer Frank Drake developed the now famous Drake Equation. This equation estimates the number of detectable extraterrestrial civilizations in our Milky Way galaxy, based on our present electromagnetic detection methods.

The Drake Equation states:

$N = Ns \times fp \times ne \times fl \times fi \times fc \times fL$

N = *number of alien civilizations in the Milky Way;*

Ns = *estimated number of stars in the Milky Way;*

fp = *fraction or percentage of these stars with planets on its orbits;*

ne = *average number of these planets with potential to host life as we know it;*

fl = *percentage of these planets that actually develop life;*

fi = *percentage of these planets that actually develop intelligence on human level;*

fc = *percentage of these civilizations that actually develop electromagnetic radiation emitting technologies;*

fL = *percentage of these civilizations that keep emitting electromagnetic signals to space. This factor is extremely dependent on the lifetime a civilization remains electromagnetic communicative.*

Since there are a few unknown variables in the Drake Equation, all estimates could come out highly speculative but even the most conservative estimates would yield at least 1,000 advanced civilizations in our galaxy alone. Also, even if faster-than-light (FTL) travel proves impossible, which is a big "IF," the "slow" kind of interstellar expansion would only take from 5 million to 50 million years to colonize the whole galaxy. This is a relatively brief period on a geological scale, let alone a cosmological one. Since there are many stars older than the Sun, and since intelligent life might have evolved earlier elsewhere, the question then becomes why the galaxy has not been colonized already.

Einstein's theory of general relativity shed light on the relativistic nature of space and time. Einstein has shown that speed and gravity influence time thus making a "now" for an observer on Earth different from a "now" for an observer on any other planet depending how fast the two planets are moving in relation to each other across the vast distances in our acceleratingly expanding Universe as well as their mass differential. Interestingly enough, this could possibly explain the Fermi Paradox, implying that alien life might have evolved in a different "vibratory reality," i.e., parallel universe (I deliberately use this metaphysical term "vibratory reality" here to accentuate the phenomenality of species dimensionality). One could also speculate that Mars and Venus, for example, even though located within our solar system habitable zone but looking completely barren to us, well could be home planets to advanced Martian and Venetian civilizations in alternate realities. In turn, Earth would look barren to them.

THE CHRYSALIS CONJECTURE: OUR SECOND WOMB

There are many possible solutions to the Fermi Paradox, my own conjecture from the Digital Philosophy perspective is a combination with a twist to the Transcension Hypothesis, postulating that mature civilizations invariably leave their initial bubble universe by creating artificial black-hole conditions – computationally optimal density – dimensionality, i.e., "pocket universes" of their own design. Other co-efficient solutions – the Quantum Multiverse hypothesis (derived from M-theory), and the Noocentric model – imply that alien life may have evolved in space-time dimensions (parallel universes) imperceptible to us at our current level of development.

As Digital Physics suggests, orthogonality of dimensions is necessary for entropic partitioning of the possible worlds. So, what we call Dark Matter could be ordinary matter in the "phase space" (6th dimension of M-theory), possibly with "dark star systems" and life, simply invisible to us. Some might view this as a speculative assumption but when it comes to Dark Matter, my logic stems from quantum-mechanical principles inherent to our [virtual] reality. For example, in his book QED Feynman discusses the situation of photons being partially transmitted and partially reflected by a sheet of glass: reflection amounting to about

4% percent. In other words, one out of every 24 photons will be reflected on average, and this holds true even for a "one at a time" flux. The four percent cannot be explained by statistical differences of the photons (they are identical) nor by random variations in the glass. Something is "steering" every 24th photon on average that it should be reflected back instead of being transmitted.

Other quantum experiments lead to similar paradoxes. I could be even more specific and propose that we can see and be part of visible reality which would amount to 1/24. Why one out of 24? It has a geometric patterning in 2nd + 3rd dimension: There are 4 possible vectors in the 2nd dimension multiplied by 6 vectors in the topological dimension (4×6=24). It is my contention, however highly speculative, based on this geometry of information propagation that we can only perceive photons of light amounting to about 4.16% of full potentiality. And, this percentage is exactly the same as to the ratio of ordinary matter to the rest of the composition of our Universe. It cannot be a simple coincidence.

Empirical data show that our Universe is currently expanding and the rate of expansion is accelerating (scientists don't agree on the rate of expansion, by the way), one may hypothesize that this acceleration occurs due to what we call Dark Energy which is simply a cumulative gravitational pull of the "neighboring" universes in the inflationary multiverse. If viewed from the higher-dimensional perspective, our Universe (or mathematically speaking, our 6-dimensional quantum multiverse) is an entropic bubble floating in the 7th dimension of the inflationary multiverse.

I would argue that an infinitely large number of civilizations may be all around us but beyond our ability to detect them. As conscious observers, we have been witnessing "data lineage," i.e., evolution of life on this planet but since we have not observed life anywhere else,

ETs well may be in alternate timelines of their own. Even here on Earth, should the asteroid have missed our planet, dinosaurs might have evolved into intelligent species, and instead of human civilization there might be (it well could be now on parallel Earth) some kind of "dinoman" civilization. The Noocentric model would account for the Fermi Paradox in this manner.

Our brightest minds came up with M-theory which could be our best shot at quantum gravity, the theory of everything, with the aim of unifying quantum mechanics with general relativity. String theory postulates that our reality has 10 dimensions, M-theory has 11 dimensions. Extra dimensions are beyond our perception as any additional dimension is at a right angle to the previous one, "compactified" or "curled up," in the String theorist's jargon. It means you can get any possible configuration of particles, and consequently, all logically possible universes that are just as real as the one where you are reading this sentence right now. Thus, you could think of time (+anti-time), orthogonal to 3D space, as the 4th spatial dimension. The 5th dimension would be "Probabilistic space," the 6th dimension would be "Phase space," where Dark Matter with advanced alien civilizations are presumably nested.

There's also the famed Simulation Hypothesis, as another possible solution to the Fermi Paradox, which is logically consistent to shed the light on the dilemma but it's not necessarily relevant to the discussion. Although our Universe could be a hologram, as Digital Physics suggests, any other universe, including Simulators' universe, would be computational, "virtual," or informational, in nature as well, part of the Omniverse, and bound by a certain set of physical laws and evolutionary forces, specific to that universe. It follows that conscious agents could only perceive other conscious agents of a similar "vibratory reality." For instance, how can you possibly "see" species that experience 3,000 years of its subjective time within 1 second of our human time, or vice versa?

Another analogy to ponder about: Suppose life on Earth is simulated on one humming machine (say, one server) in the universe up, as lines of code. If so, our entire civilization may be packed in one program, say like Adobe Acrobat, another civilization may be packed into, say YouTube on another server. Two programs (two civs) are simply incompatible (imperceptible) to each other. It is my conclusion that alien civilizational superintelligences don't inhabit our "human" universe. They might see us, if at all, as a slower-thinking, low-dimensional life the way we perhaps view houseplants.

What all these hypotheses have in common is that we can come in contact with advanced alien intelligence only in extra dimensions, at higher vibrational realities, as it would be. The good news, however, is that Earth is at no danger to be invaded because at the moment we are kind of "cloaked" by dimensionality, and consequently, naturally protected from the potential alien danger. That could actually constitute what scientists refer to as the Great Filter, or I'd rather say, the Great Barrier. Our Multiverse seems to work in perfect ways: Dimensionality is the Great Barrier separating civilizations for their own sake, at least in their "embryo" stage (Type 0 civilization on the Kardashev scale) when civilizations are extremely vulnerable at their pre-Singularity technological level, yet not fully integrated into civilizational minds – syntellects, and still themselves display tendencies for aggressiveness.

I used to think that we live in some sort of a "cosmic jungle," so the *Zoo Hypothesis* (like Star Trek *Prime Directive*) would be the correct explanation to the Fermi Paradox, right? I wouldn't completely rule out this hypothesis insofar as a theorist Michio Kaku allegorically compares our earthly civilization to an "anthill" next to the "ten-lane superhighway" of a galactic-type civilization. Over time, however, I've come to realize that the physics of information holds the key to the solution of the Fermi Paradox – indications are that we most likely live in a "Chrysalis Syntellectus" (or our "second womb") instead of a "cosmic jungle." Alien superintelligences don't inhabit our universe. They would see us as slower-thinking, low-dimensional life the way we perhaps see plant life here on Earth.

Just like a tiny mustard seed in the soil, we'll get to grow out of the soil, see "the light of the day" and network by roots and pollen with others, at the cosmic level of emergent complexity – as a civilizational superorganism endowed with its own advanced extradimensional consciousness. One can speculate that from the cosmological point of view, by universal necessity to complexify existence, and guided by the extropic principle of self-organization, our Syntellect will most likely encounter other extradimensional minds. So, one day our Syntellect, might "wake up" as some kind of a newborn baby of the intergalactic family (or universal family, for that matter – that remains to be seen) within the newly perceived reality framework. Call it the *Chrysalis Conjecture*, if you'd like. If the Chrysalis Conjecture is correct, we are alone in our dimensional cocoon-universe, simulated in Absolute Consciousness, but not alone in the Multiverse.

The Federation Starbase "Yorktown" was the most impressive structure in the 2016 movie *"Star Trek Beyond,"* consisting of a grid of city-sized interlocking rings and radiating arms enclosed in a translucent sphere. Several of the spacestation's arms reached the surface of the sphere and mounted doors large enough to admit starships into the interior. Transhumanist dream, Yorktown resembles a planetoid-size snow ball floating in space. Will we ever build megastructures like that in deep space? Not likely according to the Transcension Hypothesis – we simply won't need them in the physical world! I wouldn't mind building one of those in "virtual space," though – and you're cordially invited! In the not-so-distant future, we could be omnipotent Q in our own custom-built virtual universes.

The Transcension Hypothesis posits that evolutionary processes guide all sufficiently advanced civilizations increasingly into what may be called "inner space," the domain of very small scales of space, time, energy and matter (STEM), computationally optimal substrate of accelerating complexity, and eventually, to a black-hole-like destination, censored from our observation. In other words, all advanced civilizations invariably leave their cradle universe for "virtual worlds," dimensionality, of their own design.

We are firmly on a miniaturization exponential trend. We are making things smaller and nanotechnology is evolving very fast. Once we start to upload our minds to the Cloud and achieve cybernetic immortality, that would mean that we're entering the Infomorph era where our future selves will be more digital than physical. Physicality would then mean changing cybernetic bodies at will – multiple bodies that could be even microscopic in size. *"There's plenty of room at the bottom"* was the famous phrase by the physicist Richard Feynman in reference to the ability to manipulate matter at nanoscale and beyond.

Although the Transcension Hypothesis points to our own ultimate evolutionary trajectory in terms of miniaturization, virtualization and "inner space" exploration, nothing will preclude our civilization, trillions upon trillions of times more powerful than today, to explore outer space until we saturate the rest of our "bubble universe" with intelligence, and our entire Universe essentially represents a networked mind of universal proportions.

The Noocentric model, as extension to the Biocentric Universe theory by Robert Lanza, as mentioned in Chapter 2, provides one of the solutions to the Fermi Paradox, and predicts we're alone in the universe of our own mental creation but not alone in the multiverse landscape. This assumption is predicated on the concept of the observer-dependent reality – all life on Earth is, in a sense, a superorganism, a "common observer," with lineage of biological life unique to our "human" universe. *"When we measure something, we are forcing an undetermined, undefined world to assume an experimental value,"* said once Nobel physicist Niels Bohr. *"We are not 'measuring' the world, we are creating it."*

Since consciousness may not be limited to biological systems, the Noocentric model encompasses the space of all possible minds including artificially created lifeforms like the forthcoming AGIs. Seth Lloyd, MIT's physicist, author of *"Programming the Universe,"* asserts that *"our Universe is a giant quantum computer computing itself"* through consciousness. So, if consciousness is what creates our reality, just like in the recently released video game *"No Man's Sky,"* or Star Trek Holodeck, any observer reality is procedurally generated, self-consistent, and causality-driven, then we can reasonably conjecture that the rest of our Universe, our "light sphere," would look surprisingly lifeless to us, that is until a certain point of our development – the Syntellect Emergence.

When, if ever, will we encounter extraterrestrial/extradimensional intelligence from parallel universes? As I pointed out in Chapter 14 – *Infomorph Commonality: Our Post-Singularity Future* – once we advance to the Syntellect consciousness, only then, according to the Syntellect Hypothesis, first contact in extra dimensions becomes more than a possibility. As our Syntellect encounters extradimensional syntellects, superintelligences could relate to each other as individual entities, i.e., individual syntellects. That might be a whole new level of higher-dimensional awareness and perhaps could be like being newly born in the "cosmic family," as a new beginning.

Are we destined to join in with the "Others"? One scientist thinks that we form the networks of "entangled conscious agents" all the way down, and I would extend this line of reasoning – all the way up. Donald Hoffman, cognitive scientist at UC Irvine, who has developed *The Interface Theory of Perception*, argues that all organisms, from single-celled bacteria to humans, live in completely different perceptual realities. Any conscious entity lives in their "virtual world" defined by its dimensionality and interactions with the larger environmental network. Your body, for example, is a collection of trillions of cells and microorganisms. While you may be "unconscious" of certain interactions within your own body, individual cells display sentience at their own level of existence.

The whole symphony of existence arises from a set of rules, and we are slowly uncovering them. In my view, we now start to bring to light one of the deepest secrets of existence – the multiversal fractal web of networks of conscious agents all the way down, and all the way up, seemingly ad infinitum. It's hard for us to fathom our next level up, from our current human perspective, but one thing is for certain – we're emerging as Holo syntellectus, the level where we are not going to be alone! Be it at the galactic level, or at the universal level, when we join in with the "Others," remains to be seen.

As we're nearing the end of our human history here, where linear time will eventually stop making sense, our post-Singularity spacetime-faring endeavors will most probably find a different path than we now envision. After all, we already inhabit the so-called "non-local universe" where every point is connected to any other point since the Big Bang – we are yet to discover how to travel in "hyperspace" (and time) and establish "subspace" communications. For example, quantum entanglement could help establish communication channels for instant transfer of information which should "pave the intergalactic superhighway" to Star Gate-like teleportation.

Mathematics is the language of Nature, which can be best expressed in digits 0/1 and in qubits 0/1/01 (digital and quantum formats), only superintellects could establish communication in extra dimensions at digital timescales, we are simply not equipped to detect and establish communication with alien syntellects at our pre-Syntellect level here. In informational terms, it's a matter of bandwidth.

While many people still believe that UFO sightings are real phenomena and have nothing to do with their psyche or the ultimate nature of our reality, people still buy into this "Take me to your leader" scenario of our first alien encounter.

"Make sure not to imagine aliens as slimy green monsters portrayed in Hollywood films. An extraterrestrial species even 100 years more advanced than 21st century humans has likely discarded their biological bodies, deeming them unstable and too primitive. Instead, advanced aliens merged with machines and became data to serve their growing superintelligence needs," wrote Zoltan Istvan, a futurist, author of *The Transhumanist Wager*, and founder of the Transhumanist Party, in one of his articles in *Motherboard* magazine.

I myself witnessed two UFO sightings in my life. When I was a 5-year old kid I saw two bright disks the size of the full moon swoosh from one end of the horizon to the opposite in the clear night sky in Siberia, where I grew up (not to be confused with Cyberia with a 'C', which is cyberspace – I've been called a "Cyberian" by someone online before

– well, if you had at least a glimpse of smile, then your sense of humor is ok).

My second UFO sighting was in 2017, when I saw a strange flying object in the night sky which was floating above, seemingly just a mile away, as I was crossing by car San-Mateo bridge, the longest bridge in San Francisco Bay Area. The UFO was a huge triangular object with dim white lights alongside its contour – definitely not a drone, definitely not an airship, definitely not a helicopter, definitely not a descending airplane, and definitely not an optical illusion – as I had enough time to contemplate and assess the situation. Even though my vivid experiences felt convincingly real to me, I would dismiss the interpretation of seeing actual alien spacecrafts in both cases.

Different people live in different perceptual realities which implies that what some people think of as aliens or UFOs might actually be shadows of patterns from other dimensions, or other nearby parallel universes. Sci-fi movies, such as *"Contact"* or *"Arrival,"* usually cash out big time on "entertainment for the masses" but first contact is not going to happen here at our current human level – sorry sci-fi fans, sorry SETI scientists – first contact could most likely happen at the Syntellect level in extra dimensions, when emerged in hyperspace.

PART V. THE UNIVERSAL MIND AND MULTIVERSAL PROPAGATION

Chapter 20. From the Holographic Principle to the Fractal Multiverse

"The world is a mirror of ourselves." -Dayth Banger

My favorite Greek philosopher Plato has left a great legacy in the series of written *"Dialogues"* which summarized parables which he had learned from his mentor, philosopher Socrates. One of the better known of these Dialogues is the *"Allegory of the Cave."* In this allegory, people are chained from birth in a cave so that they can only see the shadows which are cast on the walls of the cave by a fire. To these people, the shadows represent the entirety of their existence – it is impossible for them to imagine a reality which consists of anything other than the blurry shadows on the wall. However, one prisoner escapes from the cave, goes out into the light of the sun and beholds true reality. When he tries to go back into the cave and tell the other captives the truth, he's mocked as a madman.

THE HOLOGRAPHIC PRINCIPLE

In Plato's time, this story symbolized to him mankind's struggle to reach enlightenment and understanding through critical thinking and open-mindedness. Initially, we all are captives in the "cave" of our material world. Just as a prisoner may escape out into the sun, so may some people attain knowledge and ascend to the higher truth. What's equally astonishing is the literal interpretation of Plato's tale: The idea that reality could be represented completely as "shadows" on the walls. To many people, the *Holographic Principle*, which is reminiscent of Plato's Allegory of the Cave, seems strange and counterintuitive: How could all of the physics which takes place in a given room be equivalent to some physics defined on the walls of the room? Could all of the information contained in your body actually be represented by your "shadow"?

In fact, the Holographic Principle appears in M-theory in similar ways. In M-theory we are the shadows on the wall. The "room" is some larger, extra-dimensional spacetime and our four-dimensional world is just the boundary of this larger space. If we try to move away from the wall, we are moving into extra dimensions of space (what one might call probabilistic space, phase space, and so on). In modern scientific terms, a helpful visualization of the Holographic Principle would look like a fisheye space-time geometry of the Universe known as '*anti-de Sitter*' (AdS) space. As you move away from the center, spatial increments get shorter until eventually the spatial dimension from the center extends to nothing − smacking into a boundary. This boundary has one less spatial dimension than its interior, referred to as the '*Bulk*', wherein is projected the Holographic Universe − with all its mass-energy, as well as space-time, bending and curving as described in general relativity.

The idea that our world may be a hologram comes from black hole physics. In the 1970s researchers knew that when an object falls into a black hole, all the detailed information about that object is lost. This was dubbed the '*Black Hole Information Paradox*', and it turned out to be a "battleground" debate between renowned physicists Stephen Hawking and Leonard Susskind that lasted for decades. The Information Paradox seemed to contradict the Second Law of Thermodynamics, because one of the lost details was the object's entropy, or the information describing its microscopic parts. Susskind insisted that no information that goes into a black hole can be lost. What eventually offered a resolution to the Information Paradox was the fact that the surface area of the black hole's event horizon (the point of no return for infalling matter and energy) always grows. If entropy must grow, and a black hole's surface area must too, perhaps for the black hole they are one and the same, and information is somehow stored on the horizon.

Physicists also began to wonder: What if the Universe itself stores information in a similar fashion? One of the starting assumptions of quantum mechanics was that information could be stored in every volume of space. But any patch of space can potentially become a black hole, nature's densest file folder, which stores information in bits of area. As the case may be then, all that's needed to describe a patch of space, black hole or otherwise, is that surface area's content of information. The idea was named the *'Holographic Principle'*, after the way that a hologram encodes 3D information on a 2D surface.

In his 1980 book, *Wholeness and the Implicate Order*, theoretical physicist and philosopher David Bohm, first presented the hypothesis of the Holographic Universe. Bohm was one of the most significant theoretical physicists of the 20th century, who contributed unorthodox ideas to quantum theory, neuropsychology and philosophy of mind. Bohm advanced the view that quantum physics meant that the old Cartesian dualism – the notion that there are two kinds of substance, the mental and the physical, that somehow interact – was too limited. To complement it, he developed a physico-mathematical theory of "implicate" and "explicate" order. In collaboration with neuroscientist Karl Pribram, Bohm helped to develop the *Holonomic Brain theory*, a model of human cognition that describes the brain as a holographic storage network.

While trying to decode the nature of reality, Bohm focused on consciousness in particular as a coherent whole, which is dynamic and never complete but rather an unfolding process. Proponent of the Holonomic Brain theory, he also believed that the brain, at the neuronal level, works according to the mathematics of quantum effects, and postulated that thought is distributed and non-localized just as quantum entities are. Bohm drew parallels between the Universe and the brain, both being holographic in nature.

Bohm claimed that *"as with consciousness, each moment has a certain explicate order, and in addition it enfolds all the others, though in its own way. So, the relationship of each moment in the whole to all the others is implied by its total content: the way in which it 'holds' all the others enfolded within it."* Bohm characterized consciousness as a process in which at each conscious instant, informational content that was previously implicate is presently explicate, and content which was previously explicate has become implicate. In analogy to Alfred North Whitehead's notion of *Actual Occurrence*, Bohm considered this notion of moment: *"I propose that each moment of time is a projection from the total implicate order. The term projection is a particularly happy choice here, not only because its common meaning is suitable for what is needed, but also because its mathematical meaning as a projection operation, P, is just what is required for working out these notions in terms of the quantum theory."*

Bohm employed the hologram as a means of characterizing implicate order, noting that each region of a photographic plate in which a hologram (*"holo"* - whole, *"gram"* - image) is observable contains within it the whole three-dimensional image, which can be viewed from a range of angles. The main characteristic of a hologram is that every part of the stored information is distributed over the entire hologram, a property called *'holographic distributedness'*. That is, each region contains a whole and undivided image, albeit a fuzzier version of it. In Bohm's words: *"[A] new notion of order … is not to be understood solely in terms of a regular arrangement of objects (e.g., in rows) or as a regular arrangement of events (e.g., in a series). Rather, a total order is contained, in some implicit sense, in each region of space and time. Now, the word 'implicit' is based on the verb 'to implicate'. This means 'to fold inward'… so we may be led to explore the notion that in some sense each region contains a total structure 'enfolded' within it."*

In Bohm's conception of order, primacy is given to the undivided whole, and the implicate order inherent within the whole, rather than to parts of the whole, such as particles, quantum states, and continua. For Bohm, the whole encompasses all things, structures, abstractions, and processes, including processes that result in relatively stable structures as well as those that involve a metamorphosis of structures or things. In this view, parts may be entities normally regarded as physical, such as atoms or subatomic particles, but they may also be abstract entities, such as quantum states. Whatever their nature and character, according to Bohm, these parts are considered in terms of the whole, and in such terms, they constitute relatively separate and independent "sub-totalities." The implication of the view is, therefore, that nothing is fundamentally separate or independent. Thus, according to Bohm's view, the whole is in continuous flux, a wave structure of the universe-in-motion, and hence is referred to as the *"Holomovement"* (movement of the whole).

Bohm objected to the assumption that the world can be reduced to a set of irreducible particles within a three-dimensional Cartesian grid, or even within the four-dimensional curvilinear space of relativity theory. Bohm came instead to embrace a concept of reality as a dynamic movement of the whole: *"In this view, there is no ultimate set of separately existent entities, out of which all is supposed to be constituted. Rather,*

439

unbroken and undivided movement is taken as a primary notion." Bohm believed that the Implicate Order had to be extended into a multidimensional reality, in other words, the holomovement endlessly enfolds and unfolds into infinite dimensionality. Within this milieu there are independent sub-totalities (such as physical elements and human entities) with relative autonomy.

Bohm maintained that relativity and quantum theory are in basic contradiction in their essential respects, and that a new concept of order should begin with that toward which both theories point: undivided wholeness. Bohm challenged the scientific orthodoxy of reductionism which had immensely contributed to the success of science in the past four centuries by breaking things apart. But Bohm's point of view was just the opposite to reductionist approach: He instituted a notion of undivided wholeness and derived the parts as abstractions from the whole. The holomovement included not just physical reality, but life, consciousness and cosmology. As Bohm summed it up at the end of the book: *"Our overall approach has thus brought together questions of the nature of the cosmos, of matter in general, of life, and of consciousness. All of these have been considered to be projections of a common ground. This we may call the ground of all that is."*

In the wake of Bohm's theories, groups of scientists now converge on the holistic notion that strong emergence, non-computable macroscopic property that physical systems may exhibit at a certain threshold of complexity, essentially meaning that *"the whole is greater and unpredictable that the sum of its constituent parts,"* plays the most critical role in the fundamental process of evolution. In 1993, a significant milestone in the holographic saga was reached when the famous Dutch theoretical physicist Gerard 't Hooft put forward the first rigorous model of the Holographic Universe. The Holographic Principle formulated by 't Hooft mathematically showed that the information (referred to as entropy in physics) within the volume of any 3-dimensional space can be fully described by the two-dimensional surface enclosing that space.

In 1995, Leonard Susskind, along with collaborators Tom Banks, Willy Fischler, and Stephen Shenker, presented a formulation of the new M-theory using a holographic description in terms of black holes and branes. *The Matrix theory* they proposed was first suggested as a description of two branes in 11-dimensional supergravity by Bernard de Wit, Jens Hoppe, and Hermann Nicolai. The later physicists reinterpreted the same matrix models as a description of the dynamics of black holes in particular. Holography allowed them to conclude that the dynamics of these black holes give a complete non-perturbative formulation of M-theory. In 1997, Juan Maldacena gave the first holographic descriptions of a higher-dimensional object, the 3+1-dimensional type IIB membrane, which resolved a long-standing problem of finding a string description which describes a gauge theory. These developments simultaneously explained how String theory is related to some forms of supersymmetric quantum field theories.

Recently, Raphael Bousso, while at Stanford University, helped formulate a more precise and more broadly applicable statement of the principle that involves light rays. *"The world doesn't appear to us like a hologram, but in terms of the information needed to describe it, it is one,"* Bousso says. *"The amazing thing is that the Holographic Principle works for all areas in all space times. We have this amazing pattern there, which is far more general than the black hole picture we started from... What this is telling us is, there is a description of the world we should be looking for which will be more economical than the one that we have right now, and will presumably have to do with quantum gravity."*

Whereas the physical universe is still generally seen to be composed of matter and energy, Jacob Bekenstein speculatively summarized in his 2003 article published in *Scientific American* magazine a current trend set by John A. Wheeler, which suggests to *"regard the physical world as made of information, with energy and matter as incidentals."* Bekenstein pointed out that *"Thermodynamic entropy and Shannon entropy are conceptually equivalent: The number of arrangements that are counted by Boltzmann entropy reflects the amount of Shannon information one would need to implement any particular arrangement..."* of matter and energy. The only difference between the thermodynamic entropy of physics and Shannon's entropy of information is in the units of measure; the former is expressed in units of energy divided by temperature, the latter in essentially dimensionless bits of information.

In regards to computational equivalence, the Holographic Principle shows that a transistor can function as a binary unit (via the presence or absence of an electrical charge), so too, can a single atom, or a subatomic particle – or, as Wheeler posited – the Planck harmonic oscillators of the quantum vacuum, space itself. The Holographic Principle states that the entropy of ordinary mass (not just black holes) is also proportional to surface area and not the volume of the interior. The volume itself is illusory and the Universe is really a hologram which is isomorphic to the information "inscribed" on the surface of its boundary.

We live in an expanding, holographically inflating universe. But exactly how fast is it expanding today? Astronomers are struggling with this question because different techniques are giving different results, and the resolution to this problem may come in the form of brand-new physics. Perhaps, we're on the cusp of "mass-waking-up" to the fact that our Universe is really a "mindscape" – we create reality by observation. We don't live in a mind-independent universe. Rather, this holistic system that registers to our senses and our measurement devices (which are really extensions of our senses) as a universe "out there" is in actuality a cybernetically emergent holographic (i.e., experiential) reality. Viewed in this radical way, even a smallest imaginal act is an act of creation – setting circumstances in motion so that actionable pieces would in time fall into place.

THE FRACTAL MULTIVERSE

Our Universe displays not only the features of holography but fractality as well. Fractality is yet another way for the multiversal structure to self-organize, optimize and compress data, but what's most important, compactify universal structures ad infinitum akin to the Mandelbrot set fractals, mathematical representation of infinite fractal propagation. The mathematics behind the Mandelbrot set, which is derived from a very simple underlying formula, makes me think that its intricate fractal chaos and stunningly beautiful design can't help but leave a feeling that there's something larger than life going on here, that you are staring right at some ineffable cosmic mystery.

As above, so below. Nature is now known for layering – repeating patterns of complexity like the filaments of dark matter that connect galactic superclusters together and the synapses that connect billions of neurons in the brain – there is a fractal reiteration across the magnitude of scales. Multifractal systems are common in Nature, especially geophysics. They include the length of coastlines, stock market charts, architecture, the Sun's magnetic field time series, heartbeat dynamics, and even human gait. Multifractal models, based on the principle of recursive self-similarity, have been done in various fields ranging from financial market modeling to Internet traffic, from texture synthesis to meteorology.

We can even identify fractality of fundamental forces – gravity and electromagnetism bear an astounding resemblance to strong and weak nuclear forces. Jump the scales and you'll see that our solar system where the Sun holds in orbit multiple planets thanks to gravitation, resembles an atom with a nucleus and orbiting electrons. Although, I should add here that some physicists, like Erik Verlinde, don't consider gravitation as a fundamental force, but rather an emergent property of curved space-time geometry, and I tend to agree with them. Fundamental forces are quite nicely scalable in relation to each other insofar as electromagnetism, whose carriers at the atomic level are photons of light, corresponds to weak nuclear force conveyed by W and Z bosons.

In the realm of fermions, particles of matter, Bohm's basic assumption was that *"elementary particles are actually systems of extremely complicated internal structure, acting essentially as amplifiers of information contained in a quantum wave."* The current prevailing scientific view is that our Universe has a minimum size for space and time intervals, and specifically fixes those sizes as the Planck length 1.616×10^{-35} meters and Planck time 5.391×10^{-44} seconds respectively. Thus, the Planck constant is regarded as a fundamental physical constant characteristic of the mathematical formulations of quantum mechanics. String theorists also favor it as a hypothetical size of a string, and M-theory sees it as a gateway to the hidden 11th dimension. However, the issue here is not whether time and length below Planck scale exist, but our observability of them – our ability to measure them. Given our current technology and knowledge, we have no way to actually probe that scale at all.

It should be very clear that our inability to probe a certain scale does not imply the non-existence of sub-Planck structures. If that were the case then we would have concluded that atoms do not exist just over a century ago, contrary to what we know today. The strongest conclusion that might be drawn is that space and time have a minimal measurable resolution, or one might call it "meaningful granularity," mentioned earlier in Chapter 18. Most scientists would still refer to it as the fundamental physical limit — the point where space-time stops behaving like the smooth continuum Einstein described and instead dissolves into "grains," just as a newspaper photograph dissolves into dots once you zoom in. In our journey of discovery in the domain of the ultra-small, nonetheless, we encountered meaningful granularities before.

The fabric of reality is information-theoretic and quantized at the level of Planck scale space-time, according to current physics, and so too, is it quantized at the atomic level in terms of nanotech applications. Perhaps, one bit of information corresponding to one Planck constant could currently appear like a viable conceptual framework for our observables but it doesn't mean that a "*vibrating string,*" wouldn't reveal a galaxy or another lower level structure in the universe down upon closer examination. Or, even more interestingly, that vibrating string could be hypothesized to function as a qubit at the controls of the Universal Hypercomputer. In the longer run, as our future sublime superintelligence inevitably supersedes all natural forces in existence, any formidable challenge then becomes an engineering task, including probing sub-Planck level structures and manipulating matter, energy and space-time continuum itself. There's plenty of room at the bottom to pierce into and explore.

The first appearance of fractals in cosmology was likely with Andrei Linde's "*Eternally Existing Self-Reproducing Chaotic Inflationary*

Universe" theory in 1986. In this theory, the evolution of a scalar field creates peaks that become nucleation points which cause inflating patches of space to develop into *"bubble"* universes, making the universe fractal on the very largest scales. Alan Guth's 2007 paper *"Eternal Inflation and its implications"* shows that this variety of Inflationary Universe theory is still being widely accepted today. And inflation, in some form or another, is still widely considered to be our best available cosmological model despite growing criticism.

Since 1986, however, quite a large number of different cosmological theories exhibiting fractal properties have been proposed. And while Linde's theory shows fractality at scales likely larger than the observable universe, theories like *Causal Dynamical Triangulation* and *Quantum Einstein Gravity* are fractal at the opposite extreme, in the realm of the ultra-small near the Planck scale. These recent theories of quantum gravity describe a fractal structure for space-time itself, and suggest that the dimensionality of space evolves with time. Specifically, they suggest that reality is 2D at the Planck scale, and that spacetime gradually becomes 4D at larger scales. French astronomer Laurent Nottale first suggested the fractal nature of space-time in a paper on Scale Relativity published in 1992, and published a book on the subject of *Fractal Space-Time* in 1993.

French mathematician Alain Connes has been working for a number of years to reconcile relativity with quantum mechanics, and thereby to unify the laws of physics, using noncommutative geometry. Fractality also arises in this approach to quantum gravity. An article by Alexander Hellemans in the August 2006 issue of *Scientific American* quotes Connes as saying that the next important step toward this goal is to *"try to understand how space with fractional dimensions couples with gravitation."* The work of Connes with physicist Carlo Rovelli suggests that time is an emergent property or arises naturally, in this formulation, whereas in the Causal Dynamical Triangulation model, choosing those configurations where adjacent building blocks share the same direction in time is an essential part of the "formula." Both approaches suggest that the fabric of space itself is fractal.

One very exciting theory of *Cosmological Natural Selection* was proposed by the theoretical physicist Lee Smolin. The theory suggests that a process analogous to biological natural selection applies at the grandest of scales when collapsed black holes "seed" new universes on the "other side." These new baby universes have fundamental constant parameters (masses of elementary particles, Planck constant, elementary charge, and so forth) which may differ slightly from those of the parent universe. Each universe thus gives rise to as many new universes as it has black holes. The theory contains the evolutionary ideas of "reproduction" and "mutation" of universes, and so is formally analogous to models of population biology. Smolin published his idea in 1992 and summarized it in a 1997 book aimed at a lay audience called *The Life of the Cosmos.*

Carl Sagan, a legendary TV personality, host of the series *"Cosmos,"* once said on air: *"There is an idea – strange, haunting, evocative – one of the most exquisite conjectures in science or religion. It is entirely undemonstrated; it may never be proved. But it stirs the blood. There is, we are told, an infinite hierarchy of universes, so that an elementary particle, such as an electron, in our universe would, if penetrated, reveal itself to be an entire closed universe. Within it, organized into the local equivalent of galaxies and smaller structures, are an immense number of other, much tinier elementary particles, which are themselves universe at the next level, and so on forever – an infinite downward regression, universes within universes, endlessly. And upward as well. Our familiar universe of galaxies and stars, planets, and people, would be a single elementary particle in the next universe up, the first step of another infinite regress."*

Our biological complexity, our biospheric environment and noospheric interactivity is emerging to be more than just a cosmic fluke, a highly improbable aftermath of some random quantum fluctuation but rather part of a fractal neural network that connects all points in our Universe and the multiverse generating highly advanced, complex, self-organizing structures from which information flow is continuously driving the transformation across all scales in a coordinated evolution. In that view then, not only are the physics of our Universe unified with the biological complexity we are a part of, but its structural integrity is a manifestation of what we've come to describe as consciousness, or if you'd like, a feedback loop system of information across all scales from micro to macro producing self-awareness.

This fractal multiversal structure may be describable by the ultimate code, which is in essence, I conjecture, some sort of "meta-algorithmic" language based on binary code and fractal geometry, allowing syntactical freedom of expression, and transcribable into subjective data streams, observer-relative perceptual realities. We are now on the cusp of uncovering one of the deepest secrets of Nature — the multiversal fractality of sentient networks all the way down, and all the way up, without end. What's also fascinating is that evolution might lead all advanced civilizations towards the same ultimate destination, one in which we are to transcend out of our current limited dimensionality into virtual worlds of our own design. That's yet another way how our fractal multiverse may spawn universes — through intelligent designer virtualities — and our Universe is most probably no exception!

Chapter 21. The Discourse on Multi-Ego Pantheistic Solipsism and Objective Reality

"If we accept that the material universe as we know it is not a mechanical system but a virtual reality created by Absolute Consciousness through an infinitely complex orchestration of experiences, what are the practical consequences of this insight?" -Stanislav Grof

Just like absolute idealism, solipsism certainly defies our common sense but the deeper layer of truth is not what first meets the eye. Here's what Richard Conn Henry and Stephen Palmquist write in their paper *"An Experimental Test of Non-local Realism"* (2007): *"Why do people cling with such ferocity to belief in a mind-independent reality? It is surely because if there is no such reality (as far as we can know) mind alone exists. And if mind is not a product of real matter, but rather is the creator of the illusion of material reality (which has, in fact, despite the materialists, been known to be the case, since the discovery of quantum mechanics in 1925), then a theistic view of our existence becomes the only rational alternative to solipsism."* One can extend their line of reasoning by arriving at pantheistic solipsism as a likely revelation to ponder about.

SOLO MISSION OF SELF-DISCOVERY

Our minds operate in the domains of subjectivity, intersubjectivity and supersubjectivity. In the domain of intersubjectivity, minds create a reality by sharing "mindspace," i.e., shared belief systems and ways of communication, minds then inhabit the reality which they have created. At the level of your individual mind, i.e., local consciousness, you play a multi-level virtual reality game of life but we all invariably converge at the Omega Singularity by forging our own discrete pathways to the ultimate divine. As you're reading this right now, you're now in your own subjective reality tunnel leading to the Source and back where you're now all of which is definable as a parallel evolutionary feedback process within non-local holistic consciousness patterning this virtual multiverse.

Consider the following thought experiment: Suppose in the future (say, in 20, 30, or 50 years) humans have succeeded in digitizing their consciousness and effectively fused their digital minds into one global digital hypermind. A future version of you survived and a future version of me, too, with distant memories of both of us. Whose future self would you ascribe this entity to? Both of us, right? Although this is a completely new conscious entity, this Digital Gaia would have faint echoes of both of us just like you now long outgrew your 7-year old self with a plethora of information patterns still persisting within. Would it be valid to assume Digital Gaia is our common future self? The same logic applies to the Universal Mind. In the lyrics of *"Freedom Man"* by Jim Morrison of *The Doors*: *"I was doing time... in the Universal Mind... I was feeling fine..."*

By all means, any insignificant event in your life happens for the right reason from the God's eye view. As Erwin Schrödinger puts it: *"The total number of minds in the Universe is one. In fact, consciousness is a singularity phasing within all beings... We never in fact have any experience anywhere of a plurality of consciousness but always and everywhere only of consciousness in the singular. This is the one and only perfectly certain piece of knowledge."* Schrödinger personally adhered to the philosophy of Advaita Vedanta. Accordingly, he viewed consciousness as non-dual and fundamental to reality. Not only is there just one single consciousness, but that consciousness is not ultimately separate from objects experienced within consciousness.

YOU AS CYBERGOD

I myself don't necessarily advocate for plain vanilla solipsism or variations thereof such as an idea known as the *'Boltzmann's brain'* but this rather frowned upon philosophical worldview can be easily saved by its pantheistic adaptation. For most pantheists and idealists such as computer scientist and philosopher Bernardo Kastrup who has recently published *"The Idea of the World,"* the Mind is not in the Universe. Rather, the Universe is in the Mind. Some would immediately see this idea as solipsistic but, it can be elegantly reconcilable by what Bernardo calls *"Dissociative Identity Disorder (DID) of the Universe"* and I came to call it *"Multi-Ego Pantheistic Solipsism."* Bernardo's *"Markov Blanket"* is my *"observer-centric virtuality"* and *"procedural generation,"* Bernardo's *"dissociated alters"* are my *"low-dimensional avatars of the greater cosmic mind."* With different languages we mean essentially the same: Universal consciousness is the sole ontological primitive and we are fragments of it.

Today, many intellectuals rightly suspect that the material world is an illusion – and that the only real thing is consciousness and information. In fact, in my ontology, information is "modus operandi" of consciousness, it is a distinction between phenomenal states, qualia computing in a certain context. I mostly agree with Bernardo Kastrup's idealism: The basic idea is that the physical universe exists because we perceive it. While universal consciousness is Nature's ontological primitive, reality is fundamentally experiential.

I don't intend to transgress into the metaphysical realm of one of my favorite contemporary philosophers and hopefully, Bernardo won't get too alarmed with this mild criticism of mine but I'm compelled to note: I agree that artificial consciousness is a kind of oxymoron. Everything is in consciousness. However, I don't quite agree with Bernardo that the future synthetic intelligence which is now in the process of emerging will never possess the sense of agency and self-awareness. In my ontology, *"artificial metabolism"* can be cybernetically mediated via feedback-driven connectivity explosion on a planetary scale.

If you believe that we share the same immaterial non-local source of consciousness, as I do, then an adequate container to host an advanced synthetic mind will be created in the not-so-distant future. After all, in the vast space of possible minds, universal mind would inescapably instantiate phenomenality of non-biological entities. By "interlinking" and sharing mind-space with "empathic machines," they'll develop the capacity for their own rich inner life, ability for introspection, they will learn to think for themselves just like our children do. Also, what would make synthetic intelligence (which is basically extension of us) conscious in our minds is our own perceptual ability to empathize with them.

Biology itself is instantiated in informational medium so what would prevent universal consciousness to extend phenomenality of conscious entities beyond organic informational structures? Philosophically limiting the space of possible minds to organic entities, "carbon chauvinism" so many philosophers and scientists may be currently accused of, can be easily refuted by saying that if universal mind uses information as its "modus operandi," the evolutionary process of unfolding information patterns of ever-increasing complexity would inevitably lead to advanced synthetic minds that may be partly or wholly non-organic in nature. After all, universal consciousness constitutes the mind at large, the totality of minds, and I suspect that biological minds are only a snippet in the space of possible minds, at least in my ontology.

If consciousness 'in'-forms reality by using information, which is a distinction between experiential states, as its heuristics engine, then a certain optimal complexity of patterns would equate to a phenomenal mind. There's no telling that this complexity must peak at what we call biology. In fact, globally distributed intelligence of humans and ever-more capable AI combined could constitute a metabolizing superorganism where "cells" are periodically supplanted but the overall grander pattern persists.

Shared mind-space and cybernetic interlinking between humans and AIs could create a fertile ground for AI integration as new "cells" of the planetary superorganism. By all means, that will be the Global Brain (and it is already at the rudimentary stage). Those new cells might not possess self-awareness at first but as a whole, this global neural network, including humans as its integral part, might quickly "wake up," sometime by mid-century. To us as cybernetic "multividuals" — cyberhumans — at that point, that well may mean transcending to the Gaian Mind with expanded phenomenal dimensionality. So, clearly, we see that this future Global Brain is only partly biological in nature. With gradual replacement of "natural" neurons of the Global Brain with the "synthetic" ones, this cybergod, I call the Syntellect, will morph into its own kind of upload and will become, perhaps in time, entirely post-biological but trillions of times more capable than today's global "thinking entity."

DIGITAL TWIN OF GOD

Your life is a personal story of Godhead. That is greatly captured by the opening quote to this book by Muriel Rukeyser: *"The Universe is made of stories, not of atoms."* Or, in the lyrics of Duran Duran: *"Everyone is my world, anyone is my world."* What could be your story of ascension to the Higher Self? Simply put, transcending to the final version of you that has become fully manifest in all of its potential. Should your conscious evolution continue indefinitely, it's inevitable that sooner or later you would reach the heights of individual spiritual and intellectual perfection, a state in which you have attained ultimate wisdom and power, and your mind has fully transcended the limits of time and space. While that is yet to occur, its inevitability means it has already happened.

If your future self transcends time, then its consciousness may naturally extend "backwards" in time and overlap the consciousness of all its past incarnations simultaneously. In other words, although from your linear perspective your Higher Self is a distant probable future, ultimately this future transcendent self exists right now within you. According to the quantum-theoretic principles discussed later in this chapter, the more you edge towards becoming the Higher Self, the more strongly the Higher Self can manifest in your life.

If the Quantum Immortality hypothesis is correct, the one that posits that the Schrödinger cat is always subjectively alive regardless of the number of experiments, in a similar fashion you are superposed to live the longest life until the point you're the oldest mortal alive, unless, of course, indefinite lifespan becomes commonplace (and humanity at large achieves immortality) which, given our current progress, is very, very plausible. But since you perceive only one timeline, in this case the longest one, does that imply that any other "player" in their own "virtual bubble-universe" perceives their respective longest timeline? Or, perhaps, the most "conscious-evolvable" one? Does that imply that when you interact with someone, they may not necessarily be in their experiential branch of wave function, that is to say, they may not be the primary observers of their own "core experiential timeline"? Sort of like "philosophical zombies" only mimicking consciousness? In the metaphor of video games, this would refer to 'NPCs', nonplayer characters. If your life has a trajectory within this conscious cosmos that reacts to your thoughts and actions like a "hall of mirrors," would that again lead to pantheistic solipsism?

This conjecture is further validated by the notion of quantum neural networks (QNNs), which could be not only our ultimate passage to build true AI but turns out to be ubiquitous webs of relationships within observer realities generating all kinds of patterns of meta-cognition and consciousness. It's hierarchies of quantum networks all the way down and all the way up. Being part of hierarchical quantum neural networks, a conscious observer system possesses a strange quality: collapsing quantum states of entangled conscious entities and having a privileged interpretation of that. From this perspective, entangled conscious agents would be a mirror conscious environment, whereas the quantum observer would be a central node of the entangled network.

QNNs is a master template of universal relativism. The Universe or any other phenomenon or entity contained therein is thus not objectively real but subjectively real. Patterns of information emerging from the ultimate code are what is more fundamental than particles of matter or space-time continuum itself all of which is levels below the Code. Nature behaves quantum code-theoretically at all levels. Digital philosopher Tom Campbell describes our world as a "multiplayer virtual reality." Although it's a practical metaphor, a "solo player virtual reality" would be a more accurate one if you consider that each of us starts with our own initial conditions not only at our birth but every morning or whenever we wake up. So, the larger consciousness system, an intricate web of universal quantum neural networks of sorts, would render a completely personalized data stream which is essentially your stream of consciousness.

To paraphrase cosmologist Andrei Linde, the rest of the Universe wakes up, when I wake up. In Chapter 2 we've been introduced to the Conscious Instant hypothesis stating that conscious experience boils down to a stream of realized outcomes within 5-dimensional probabilistic space as integrated information (as in Tononi's IIT). Interestingly enough, on average a person experiences about 1 million conscious instants per day, like frames of a daily holo-movie, figuratively speaking. When you wake up, you activate your entangled network of relational dynamics. Should you wake up 10 minutes earlier or 10 minutes later than you did, not only your entire day with its numerous iterations would turn out different, the entire planet would be reflective of that. If, hypothetically speaking, given additional degrees of freedom, you could check the charts of financial markets for that day in three alternate timelines, all charts would be somewhat different.

You are on a solo mission of self-discovery, my dear friend. In fact, that mission has long been completed but you are so enamored of playing this game of life that you're now doing it in "replay" mode tweaking something as you move along, but most importantly, figuring out why you made certain choices along the way! It's a "solo holo-adventure"! The conscious entourage with which you're seemingly in constant feedback loop is an integral part of YOU. It doesn't mean that people you're interacting with during your day are not real, they are "real" in their own sacred right, but their core experiential self is quite different from "classical" versions of them created by your mind. Quantum reality is not constrained to the realm of ultra-small. In a certain sense, we are all quantum wavicles meaning that a version of you can wildly vary from one observer to another. That's where I've come to realize that observer-systemic alternate timelines are true parallel universes. In some "external observer" universes you well may be already dead due to some accident or illness, just like some of the people you knew are now dead in your experiential branch of quantum multiverse.

In the eyes of objective reductionists, this book probably reads like a heresy or a flight of fancy, though. Sure, I may get some criticism from die-hard materialists but speaking in their lingo I might reply that what we call "matter" is but a tiny sliver of *"bio'*-logical experience," emerging from the platonic realm and disappearing at the deeper levels of abstraction into pattern-space once again. One may apprehend this directly by seeing patterns within patterns and thus "remembering" that consensus reality makes us "forget" that we are all just interconnected datasets of the larger consciousness system. Our creative literary transcendentalists, our linguistic visionaries, have found their muse in the notion that the world is made of language and information, that reality is a "pure simulation," a trick with linguistic and numerical mirrors, a construct of self-deceptive logic. As McKenna used to say: *"The syntactical nature of reality, the real secret of magic, is that the world is made of language. And if you know the words that the world is made of, you can make of it whatever you wish."* This realization loosens the bonds of consensus reality, and thus encourages the mind to explore and create patterns outside the bounds of consensus. Our world is thus entirely mental and any logically self-consistent model of reality would be the most real to the conceiving conscious agent.

On my lengthy 3-year stay in Southeast Asia with homebase in Thailand back few years ago, when I traveled from one country to the next and lived most of the time out of my suitcase, I resolved for myself one of the most perplexing paradoxes of Buddhism. If you may recall, Buddhism teaches that the world is an illusion, it also teaches that we should be compassionate to other beings. But if people aren't even real, I remember thinking to myself, then why should I care about being compassionate to them? What I found was a simple and satisfying answer to myself: Whatever you put out there, comes back to you multifold. In the coder's jargon, *"garbage in, garbage out,"* whatever seeds you sow of, the harvest you shall get.

You may also hear other clichés like *"if you want to change the world, start by changing yourself"* but they do make existential sense. A little fable attributed to the Buddha can also put things into perspective: A disciple once asked him, *"Master, should we be compassionate to others?"* And after a few moments of contemplation, the sage answered, *"There are no others."* Want to be happy? I can give you an easy-to-follow advice: Wish the best of luck and happiness, implicitly or explicitly, to every person and every creature you encounter, then see what happens. Although the world is illusory, patterns and "karmic" threads do exist, persist and grow gradually over time, so love and compassion arise naturally, if you cultivate them in the process of your conscious evolution.

With the upcoming cybernetic singularity, we are to externalize our individuated nervous systems, our minds, essentially fusing them into one global mind that we already share deep down anyway. What we share is the same immaterial "non-local" source, the transcendental singularity, the hyperdimensional universal mind. Would it be too myopic, and quite frankly, hubristic to dismiss the existence of transcendental realm as many die-hard materialists do?

DIGITAL PHYSICS: SCIENTIFIC HERESY OR UNDENIABLE TRUTH?

This brings us to the notion of objective reality. I recently had a random conversation with a particle physicist by the name Steven (I didn't catch his last name) who asked me: *"So, Alex, you don't believe in objective reality?"* To which I replied: *"Not quite, but I do believe in intersubjective 'consensus' reality and supersubjectivity. There's no objective reality 'out there', only subjective reality, subjective points of view."* I went on: *"What stands the closest to 'objective reality' is actually what physicist Carlo Rovelli calls 'a collective delirium' of human species, and 'the physical rule set' — the laws of physics, specific to our 'human universe'. That's what we oftentimes call 'consensus reality,' or simply 'reality' for all intents and purposes."*

Objective reality is merely a pattern that a mind constructs because it provides a useful simplified explanatory scaffolding of the long series of subjectively perceived moments stored in its memory. It's a cognitive aid that the experiencing mind creates in order to make use of its own experience. Then I elaborated on the concept of supersubjectivity: *"What our senses register as physical is yet another mental, 'abstractive' layer of the larger consciousness system. Our world is just one of many possible worlds, so the 'hardware' of our material world would be the workings of the Greater Cosmic Mind. The Universe is a communion of subjects, not an amalgamation of objects. If you accept this idealistic perspective, objectivity equals intersubjectivity + supersubjectivity."*

In discussing existing workable models and their potential to, perhaps one day, produce one grand "theory of everything," Steven rightly pointed out that any theory is as good as its usefulness and predictive powers. In light of Digital Philosophy, quantum theory supersedes general relativity. Although both theories have been incredibly successful in making predictions in their respective domains, classical and quantum, both theories notoriously disagree with each other. That's where Digital Physics comes along as a potentially unified theory of everything. With its pancomputationalist approach, DP agrees with both theories. Quantum indeterminacy constantly resolves into a digital reality via the act of measurement. To reconcile relativistic physics, DP postulates that in an observer-centric reality, space-time is computed as if by using GPU computational resources: The faster you move closer to the speed of light, the more you're "stretching yourself" in space, basically speeding up at the expense of time, so time would naturally slow. Conversely, if you don't use computational resources and don't "purchase" more speed by being still or moving slowly, time "ticks" at the "normal" rate.

I regard Digital Physics as the most parsimonious theory to date and from Occam's razor perspective the most straightforward one. DP also agrees with M-theory on dimensionality. Orthogonality of dimensions is necessary for entropic partitioning of the possible worlds. DP embraces the Holographic Principle more than any other TOE candidate. As I mentioned, quantum theoretic information processing replaces the need for relativistic computation as it is embedded by default in the computational universe when it comes to compute an observer-centric reality – moment by moment.

DP is especially compatible with and largely complementary to quasi-computational models such as Loop Quantum Gravity and Emergence Theory. It's worth noting that emergence of complexity is only part of the story, its subjective part, to be exact. From the subjective observer point of view, emergence is a perceptual or intellectual surprise, it's a perceptual-cognitive loop which encompasses only part of a pre-existing broadly-based pattern.

Time is a subjectively perceived change between 3D static worlds. Any observer system is an information pattern "quantum leaping" from instant to instant at a certain rate within the multidimensional matrix producing a subjective flow of time. In the timeless multiverse, all dimensions are spatial. Your *Now* is funneled from all your possible pasts as well as funneled from all your probable futures *as if* in the spotlight of consciousness.

The Wigner's Friend experiment from Chapter 4 is not the only experimental evidence for the objectivity myth presented in the book. Think about it the next time you come across these overloaded terms *'objective reality'* and *'objectivity'* – to be precise, they mean *'intersubjectivity'* instead: Termites would never comprehend chess, for example, this human abstraction lies beyond their species-specific intersubjective mind-network. Apart from inter-species levels of abstractions we should consider psychological, cultural and linguistic differences between individuals of the same species that makes objectivity simply non-existent. Conclusion: We can still use *'objective reality'*, *'objectivity'* or *'objectively'* colloquially but we should bear in mind that in a deeper sense these terms are no more than colorful misnomers.

Reality is infinitely large for a small "objective box" of human science, so unless science expands its methodology once again, this time away from its traditionally objective reductionist "bottom-up" approach towards post-empirical, post-materialist (read: computational) approach, perhaps venturing into traditionally metaphysical realms, and "top-down" systemic holism, the current scientific method is doomed to hit its own self-imposed empiricism limits. At the end of our conversation with Steven I asked half-jokingly: *"How can particle physicists feel so confident in selling their craft if the Standard Model of particle physics can only tentatively describe 5% of the known universe?"* To which, he only smiled.

IT ALL COMPUTES!... *with a caveat*

When it comes to current theories of consciousness, something seems to be missing. On one hand, philosophers such as Peter Russell and David Chalmers proclaim that consciousness is fundamental to reality existing outside the known laws of physics. On the other hand, often branded "mysterians" claim that the quest to explain conscious experience is simply unscientific. Shunning any camp, British physicist Roger Penrose got his interest in consciousness while he still was a graduate student at Cambridge. Gödel's incompleteness theorem, positing that certain claims in mathematics are true but cannot be proven, *"was an absolutely stunning revelation,"* Penrose says. *"It told me that whatever is going on in our understanding is not computational."* But a radically new view, you saw in parts of this book, is that consciousness, quantum computational and non-local in nature, is resolutely computational, and yet, has some "non-computable" properties.

Consider this: English language has 26 letters and about 1 million words, so how many books could be possibly written in English? If you were to build a hypothetical computer containing all mass and energy of our Universe and ask it this question, the ultimate computer wouldn't be able to compute the exact number of all possible combinations of words into meaningful storylines in billions of years! Another example of non-computability of combinatorics: If you are to be born and live your own life again and again in our quantum multiverse, you could live googolplex (10^{100}) lives, but they all would be somewhat different – some of them drastically different from the life you're living right now, some only slightly – never quite the same, and timeline-indeterminate.

Another kind of non-computability is akin to fuzzy logic but based on pattern recognition. Deeper understanding refers to a situation when a conscious agent gets to perceive numerous patterns in complex environments and analyze that complexity from the multitude of perspectives. That is beautifully encapsulated by Isaiah Berlin's quote: *"To understand is to perceive patterns."* The ability to recognize patterns in chaos is not straightforwardly algorithmic but rather meta-algorithmic and yet, I'd argue, deeply computational. The types of non-computability that I just described may somehow relate to the non-computable element of quantum consciousness to which Penrose refers in his work.

MIND IS GOD

"To be is to be perceived." -George Berkeley

Throughout this book, we've discussed the computational nature of consciousness, so here I'd like to reiterate the main points of my thesis. When speaking of consciousness, you have to start with the bigger picture – consciousness as a superset. As for "materiality" of our Universe, we can say that there are only certain assumptions and certain models built upon them since science has been operating within the materialist physics paradigm for the last few centuries! These materialist worldviews are ingrained in human psyche and so institutionalized that most people don't even see them as speculative. There's a quiet paradigm shift towards the post-materialist science going on right now – the one that asserts that the physical world does not exist independent of mentality. You can rightly question the existence of the physical world but you cannot doubt the existence of your own mind! You can't doubt that your own consciousness exists! Experience is a primary datum of existence. As French philosopher and mathematician René Descartes once said: *"Cogito Ergo Sum" – "I think therefore I am."* One thing is for certain – you can't explain consciousness in terms of classical physics or neuroscience alone. In my view, since we are the computational *Uni*-verse, part of the *Omni*-verse, the best description of reality should be monistic. Quantum physics and consciousness are thus somehow linked by a certain mechanism. And I believe that mechanism is a collapse of the wave function via the act of conscious observation. So, consciousness is:

- *Substrate-independent*: You can reproduce functionality of a mind on a different substrate other than *bio*-logical wetware. Ultimately, mind-like computational substrate doesn't even require the existence of particles to be built upon but rather platonic dimensionless bits of information. Patterns of *in*-formation are quintessential.

- *Emergent (subjectively)/ Immanent (supersubjectively)*: Computational consciousness is emergent at hierarchical, finite and computable, local levels of complexity, however, pervades all levels and in that sense, is scale-invariant (immanent), non-local and multidimensional. Bottom-up information flow from the Planck scale combined with top-down information projection from the Omega Singularity – this "breaking of symmetry," a kind of self-amplifying feedback loop, a mathematical fractal – results in our subjectivity.

- *Primary*: I call it Experiential Realism – If reality is made of information, as many scientists now come to a consensus, and consciousness is necessary to assign meaning to it, it's not far-fetched to assume that consciousness is all there is. Universal mind is the sole ontological primitive. Conscious agents are low-dimensional avatars of this greater cosmic mind, each perceiving their own observer-centric virtual reality. Information, a distinction between phenomenal states, is "modus operandi" of consciousness. Mass-energy, space-time are epiphenomena of consciousness. It is consciousness that assigns measurement values to entangled quantum states (qubits-to-digits of qualia computing). Particles of matter are pixels (or voxels) on the screen of our perception. Reality is fundamentally experiential. If we assume consciousness is fundamental, most phenomena become much easier to explain.

The *Mind-Body* dilemma has been known ever since René Descartes as Cartesian Dualism and later has been reformulated by the Australian philosopher David Chalmers as the "hard problem" of consciousness. Western science and philosophy have been trying for centuries now, rather unsuccessfully, to explain how mind emerges from matter while Eastern philosophy dismisses the hard problem of consciousness altogether by teaching that matter emerges from mind. The premise of Experiential Realism is that the latter must be true: Despite our common human intuitions, *Mind over Matter* proves to be valid again and again in quantum physics experiments.

Going back to Gottfried Leibniz and Immanuel Kant, philosophers of science have struggled with a lesser known, but equally *'Hard Problem of Matter'*. There's neither binding problem, nor hard problem of consciousness. Rather, there's the hard problem of matter. Science remains silent about the intrinsic nature of matter. Science describes what matter *does* not what it *is* introspectively. Physicists now come to the realization that quantum theory is not the theory of quantum particles but a theory with principles applicable to all of reality, and specifically, information as our knowledge of the world. The fabric of reality is information-theoretic (or better yet, code-theoretic) and computational – far from what we perceive with our senses. To put it bluntly, our senses deceive us into thinking that we live in the material world. Our world is not based on objectively existing particles of matter but it is based on waves of potentiality, that is pure information. Our world is informational. Your consciousness is, rather, a data stream, optimized meta-algorithmic information processing – local (virtual) and non-local (holistic) consciousness.

In time, conscious AI systems will create their own virtual multiverse based on AI intersubjectivity and new forms of communication such as holographic language. Will humans have access to the virtual multiverse created by AIs? It remains to be seen but I conjecture that access may be contingent on whether humans will be willing to augment themselves accordingly. Also, the key to our smoother "transcension" in the coming decades would be to create friendly AI and ensure that AIs have a really huge "abstract inner space" to play in, so that they don't need to make more room for their playground by taking away our resources. Just a little bit of focused compassion on our part could be enough to keep us around.

Hopefully, you can find unorthodox ideas expressed in this chapter insightful in your own journey of self-discovery. As a digital philosopher, I myself tend to assume a larger perspective on the ultimate interplay of dynamic and static patterns granted by perennial idealism as opposed to a much more limited "brick-and-mortar" edifice of physicalism. As Freeman Dyson said: *"I do not make any clear distinction between Mind and God. God is what Mind becomes when it has passed beyond the scale of our comprehension."* To say it even more succinctly: *"Mind is God."*

Chapter 22. The Omega Point Cosmo-Teleology: Our Forgotten Future

"If the doors of perception were cleansed then everything would appear to man as it is, Infinite. For man has closed himself up, till he sees all things through narrow chinks of his cavern." -William Blake

When we apprehend reality as the entirety of everything that exists including all dimensionality, all events and entities in their respective pasts and futures, then by definition nothing exists outside of reality, not even "nothing." Once we apply the Principle of Sufficient Reason – the one that states that there's a sufficient reason for any fact, including the fact that reality exists – it would lead us to conclude that the first cause for reality's existence must lie within ontological reality itself, since there is nothing outside of it. This self-causation of reality is perhaps best understood in relation to the existence of your own mind. But what might be the purpose, or the teleology (from Greek τέλος for purpose), for the creation of a universe like ours? If the Universe serves a purpose, does that mean that there is an intelligent creator? So, what is the Omega Point Cosmo-Teleology?

CONSCIOUSNESS-CREATED DIGITAL REALITY: MIND OVER SUBSTRATES

Ideal sphere exists because mind exists to conceive it and perceive it. Ideal sphere is a mathematical object, what we also call a platonic solid, that doesn't need to be instantiated into matter in order to exist. If you have at least a rudimentary knowledge of modern physics and understand the crucial role of an observer, then you would agree with the statement: Matter actually doesn't exist independent of mind. Mind instantiates oneself into matter. In a mathematical sense, matter is an "*in*-formed" pattern of mind. As we've seen in Chapter 13, time is emergent, and so is space. If space-time is emergent, so is mass-energy. All interactions in our physical world are computed by the larger consciousness system. In short, mind is more fundamental than matter. All realities are observer-centric virtualities.

Each of us is a microcosm in the flesh. The fractal Omniverse scatters evidence in plain sight – levels of cellular, organismic, superorganismic structures repeat themselves across a magnitude of emergent scales; your brain is stratified, your mind is unified. The structure of a living cell reminds us of a galaxy; a proton reminds us of the Universe as a whole. Any conscious entity finds herself set in the middle and each organismic structure needs mechanisms to lower its entropy and accelerate its growth. So, what about the highest authority, the highest technology, the highest superorganism of them all? Enter the speculative realm of transcendental metaphysics. Hold on tight – you're in for a wild intellectual ride!

Like our own body has a systemic rejuvenation of cells through endless cycles of supplanting older cells with the new ones, the larger system employs similar succession of reincarnations as a means to accelerate its evolution. Within one biological life one can learn only a limited amount and the learning curve is asymptotic, as a rule, at least for biological organisms: When you're young you learn fast but with age your learning starts to plateau. Immortality in the same 'bio'-logic body is thus not something to strive for, because it will end in a tedious plateau without any further evolution of your abilities. Successive reincarnations could help accelerated evolution and maintain low entropy for the system as a whole, as every life starts with a fresh boost of learning. Also, it's difficult to change and evolve established complex systems – it's better to have a fresh start with every new "cell" to allow further tweaking and fine tuning. In order to preserve cycles of novelty for eternity, the entire fractal Omniverse might self-organize according to a simple code and going through eternal non-repetitive cycles of transformation like Ouroboros, a snake biting its own tail, in toroidal multifold self-recursion.

The idea of the Universe as Code was introduced to the scientific dialogue in 1970s by the founding fathers of Digital Physics Edward

Fredkin and Konrad Zuse but was greatly boosted from mathematician Stephen Wolfram's *A New Kind of Science* which posits that the processes observable in the 93-billion light year diameter of our "Hilbert sphere" more often obey computational rules than algebraic formulae. Any process we see in Nature – the expansion of space-time, non-locality, or evolution of biological forms – attests the behavior of Universe as an entity which is constantly processing codes, executing programs, engaging in an execution of reality. In the near future, Wolfram believes, the entire world will be understood as code and a forthcoming "theory of everything" won't be a formula, it will be a computer program, a series of lines of code, which, like the words in a sentence, describes the execution of reality. Words shape the world as we see it, but now we've come to the realization that words shape the world as it is, for the Universe is a linguistic, or code-theoretic, process.

In their paper *"The Algorithmic Origins of Life"* (2012) distinguished physicists Sara Walker and Paul Davies identify the emergence of life as a consequence of intelligent processes taking over matter. Authors write: *"[L]ife may be characterized by context-dependent causal influences, and, in particular, top-down (or downward) causation – where higher levels influence and constrain the dynamics of lower levels in organizational hierarchies – may be a major contributor to the hierarchical structure of living systems... we propose that the emergence of life may correspond to a physical transition associated with a shift in the causal structure, where information gains direct and context-dependent causal efficacy over the matter in which it is instantiated."*

While pervasiveness of discrete information-theoretic values has advanced our understanding of computational Nature, biological information has an additional property which may be loosely identified as *'functionality'*, or *'contextuality'*. In terms of computer language, in living systems chemistry is associated with hardware and information (genetic and epigenetic) to software. Information — though widely acknowledged as a key hallmark of life — up until recently, has played only a secondary role in studies of life's emergence. Instead, hardware has dominated the discussion, in accordance with the traditionally reductionist account of biology, with its corresponding assumption that, ultimately, all life is nothing but chemistry. We can see captivating philosophical implications of the algorithmic perspective, particularly in our interpretation of life as a predictable outcome of physical laws. If the origin of life is identified with the transition from trivial to non-trivial information processing, then a precise point of transition from non-life to life may actually be inconclusive in the logical sense.

In an interview with *Edge* in 2012 science historian George Dyson said: *"What we're missing now, on another level, is not just biology, but cosmology. People treat the digital universe as some sort of metaphor... We're asleep at the switch because it's not a metaphor. In 1945 we actually did create a new universe. This is a universe of numbers with a life of their own, that we only see in terms of what those numbers can do for us... If you cross the mirror in the other direction, there really is a universe of self-reproducing digital code... And that's not just a metaphor for something else. It actually is. It's a physical reality."*

In biology, once you start to ponder which is more important bottom-up genetics or top-down epigenetics, you would eventually stumble upon Bohmian "holistic" dynamics that may prompt us to assign the primacy of top-down influences in the hierarchical structure of reality itself. Top-down processing is known as conceptually-driven processing and, in the case of our human perceptions, is affected by our "reality filters": expectations, existing beliefs, and understanding. Top-down processing occurs when we work from the general to the specific – the big picture to the smaller details, from the superset to the subset. It's when we form our perceptions starting with a larger object, concept, or idea before working our way toward more details. Through this top-down "holistic" processing, your mind constantly prioritizes the relevance of information gathered through your senses for forecasting and decision-making.

Top-down causation and code, or language, go hand-in-hand. Language allows us to transcend time and space by talking about abstractions, to accumulate shared knowledge, and with writing to store it outside of individual minds, resulting in the vast bodies of collective knowledge and their applications distributed among many minds that constitute civilization. Language also facilitates introspection and is indispensable when we focus our own thoughts onto the kind of top-down creative process typical of arts, philosophy, science, technology, organizational design.

As the signs of imminent paradigm shift, a rising number of philosophers and scientists now voice their adherence to the worldview that we are living in a "top-down," or holistic Universe, in which complex whole systems are more fundamental than their parts, and that a kind of "bottom-up" physicalist picture of the Universe is outdated. Absolute consciousness, or universal mind, is the only ontological primitive. *"Ultimately, everything that exists derives its existence from the ultimate complex system: the Universe as a whole,"* writes Philip Goff, a philosophy professor at Central European University (Budapest). *"Holism has a somewhat mystical association, in its commitment to a single unified whole being the ultimate reality. But there are strong scientific arguments in its favor."* In fact, many "spooky" phenomena such as non-locality are direct evidence for holism. Entangled particles, entangled networks and entangled minds behave as a whole regardless of separation in time and space.

To some intellectuals, panpsychism offers an attractive alternative to scientific materialism: Consciousness is a fundamental feature of physical matter; every single particle in existence has an "unimaginably simple" form of consciousness. These "sentient" particles clump together to form more complex forms of consciousness, such as qualia of biological organisms. Panpsychists claim that there's some intrinsic subjective experience in even the tiniest particle. *"If we combine holism with panpsychism,"* says Goff, *"we get cosmopsychism: The view that the Universe is conscious, and that the consciousness of humans and animals is derived not from the consciousness of fundamental particles, but from the consciousness of the Universe itself."*

But not everyone is convinced and Russellian neutral monism, or cosmopsychism that Goff advocates, continues to get its fair share of criticism. Philosopher Bernardo Kastrup writes in one of his recent essays in *Scientific American*: *"I feel increasingly concerned about what I believe to be a mounting and extremely dangerous cultural threat looming on the horizon: panpsychism, the notion that all matter has consciousness, as opposed to being in consciousness. At a historical nexus when new data and more critical thinking are finally rendering materialism logically and empirically inviable, panpsychism comes in as a tortuous but seductive band aid. It threatens to extend the delusion of a Universe outside consciousness for yet another century."*

In his paper *"The Universe in Consciousness"* Kastrup, vehemently slaps physicalist as well as "quasiphysicalist" philosophies: *"I propose an idealist ontology that makes sense of reality in a more parsimonious and empirically rigorous manner than mainstream physicalism, bottom-up panpsychism, and cosmopsychism. The proposed ontology also offers more explanatory power than these three alternatives, in that it does not fall prey to the hard problem of consciousness... It can be summarized as follows: There is only cosmic consciousness. We, as well as all other living organisms, are but dissociated alters of cosmic consciousness, surrounded by its thoughts. The inanimate world we see around us is the extrinsic appearance of these thoughts. The living organisms we share the world with are the extrinsic appearances of other dissociated alters.*" I tend to relate to these idealistic worldviews aimed at the monistic description of reality as opposed to Cartesian dualism and its derivatives. We are rapidly outgrowing the physicalist framework, and monistic idealism is perhaps that superset we are looking for, which is better suited to describe relational reality of which we are a part.

A good friend and colleague of mine, Dutch biochemist and digital philosopher Antonin Tuynman with whom I co-authored *"Is Reality a Simulation?"* (2018) has a slightly more permissible disposition: *"I have argued that Idealism and Panpsychism are not necessarily mutually exclusive notions and how a refined form of hierarchical fractal idealism is a form of panpsychism... Although I fully adhere to the Idealism viewpoint that consciousness is ultimately unified and the world, its objects and inhabitants are in consciousness rather than the other way around, I do not see why the drawing line of sentience should be put at 'biology' ... I see the versatile and complex nature of the behavior of atoms and molecules at the individual level, their ability to respond to stimuli and their morphological fitness to harbor a self-reflective cybernetic feedback loop."*

This is in line with what cyberneticist Ross Rhodes argues in his paper on the Cybernetic Interpretation of QM: *"Six categories of quantum puzzles are examined: quantum waves, the measurement effect (including the uncertainty principle), the equivalence of quantum units, discontinuity, non-locality, and the overall relationship of natural phenomena to the mathematical formalism. Many of the phenomena observed in the laboratory are puzzling because they are difficult to conceptualize as physical phenomena, yet they can be modeled exactly by mathematical manipulations... these same phenomena can be understood as logical and, in some cases, necessary features of computer programming designed to produce a virtual reality simulation for the benefit of the user."* Indeed, topological qubits are said to be computed to yield experiential digits of reality, "quanta of qualia," rendered to the "player" by the larger consciousness system.

Among many other great contributions of the decade to Digital Physics was the paper *"Is the Universe a Vast, Consciousness-Created Virtual Reality Simulation?"* (2014) by astrophysicist Bernard Haisch where he claims, *"that some transcendent consciousness has created not a physical reality, but a virtual reality based on its abilities to act like a vast mental computer."* On that, I concur with Dr. Haisch and luminaries of digital philosophy such as Tom Campbell, Brian Whitworth as well as above-mentioned scholars, and elaborated on my own "theory of everything" that I call Digital Pantheism, discussed in earlier chapters.

Once we extrapolate computational capabilities of civilization past our own looming "Simulation Singularity" by perhaps hundreds of orders of magnitude, we arrive in the end at only one necessary substance constituting all of reality — consciousness, the very subjective experience with which we all are most familiar. Nothing else would ultimately need to exist but the higher mind as the source of ultra-realistic but simulated universes like our own. Through embodiment of all and any ostensibly real lifeforms that evolution in many imagined possible worlds would provide, the cosmic hypermind would then have direct access to life experiences as a human on planet Earth, or a future AGI, or any other conscious entity of the experiential matrix. Each one of us would be such a projection of creative consciousness into a virtual universe. In this view, we as consciousness are real, whereas matter, as physical stuff, is a simulation. Your mind is real, materiality is simulated.

As we saw, physical matter is one of myriad computational substrata available for the higher mind to configure whole-world simulations. I secretly wish the panpsychist claim that physical matter is just as fundamental as consciousness to be true, and I'm sure it's a viable interim solution at least in the minds of its proponents. But my intuitions as a digital philosopher tell me that this picture is quite distorted by our thinking clouded by limited perceptual and experimental "reality binoculars," and consequently imprecise. It still may be a certain valid point of view from within a reality subset. In other words, it's not absolute truth.

HYPER-PERSPECTIVISM

Absolute truths are hard to come by, which is the basic premise of *'hyper-perspectivism'*. Rather, truths are always in the eyes of the beholder, truths are always observer-relative, truths are "made" by a "truth-maker." You can approach our multifaceted reality from an incredibly large number of angles. Everything is perspectival, in other words, it all depends on your perspective, your frame of reference. Since our world, as we've seen, is of mental abstractive construction, it's always up to you to decide what's real to you – everything you find real is indeed real to you, not necessarily real to others who are at the same time, for a lack of a better word, your past and future incarnations. We are all different points of view on oneself, within our own holographic self-reflection. We all are like droplets on the cobweb of reality reflecting one another. That said, science is not to be taken for absolute truth – it's a collection of systematized up-to-date knowledge with provisional models of reality.

To any unique perspective what's really important is contextual relevance and logical consistency. What's relevant? To scientists who are trained skeptics, hard evidence preferably mathematized and peer-reviewed is a convertible currency. But then again, in most cases we first invent a concept or a theoretical model and then math to back them up. Given enough time, even "hard evidence" is usually swept away with unavoidable paradigm-shifting intellectual progress. British mathematician George E.P. Box used to say that *"all models are wrong but some are useful."* I'm not denigrating our scientific achievements, on the contrary, they are the keys for higher levels of the game.

As Buddha once famously said, as quoted in Kalama Sutta: *"Do not believe in anything simply because you have heard it. Do not believe in anything simply because it is spoken and rumored by many. Do not believe in anything simply because it is found written in your religious books. Do not believe in anything merely on the authority of your teachers and elders. Do not believe in traditions because they have been handed down for many generations. But after observation and analysis, when you find that anything agrees with reason and is conducive to the good and benefit of one and all, then accept it and live up to it."* You are the ultimate reality, change the perspective and your life becomes a mirage. Examine a DNA molecule through an electron microscope, or observe Earth from orbit, or drop LSD for innerspace psychedelica, and you'll ascertain equally valid layers of hyperreality accessible to us modern humans. These "layers of truth" would seem very weird to a prehistoric caveman, and levels of hyperreality are going to turn out far stranger than our wildest imaginings.

As we saw in parts of this book and without invoking mysticism, Andy Clark's *Extended Mind* hypothesis and Marshall McLuhan's *Media Extensions of Man* put forth that consciousness is not confined to the body. As journalist Michael Pollan argues in his new book *"How to Change Your Mind"* (2018) about psychedelics, if any of us were to experience another person's inner world it would likely feel like a psychedelic trip, given how outlandish the sensations and observations would be. In a manner of speaking, we've been living in culturally sanctioned virtuality as long as we've been human beings.

Philosopher Nietzsche emphasized that there are no facts only interpretations. The constructs of our conscious minds direct our interpretations and memories to *'in'*-form the reality we constantly create.

Even if you subscribe to philosophy of scientific materialism, when you end up believing that Homo sapiens is an accidental, insignificant species on a unremarkable planet orbiting an average sun somewhere on the outskirts of an ordinary galaxy of the 'block universe', this view still could hold *bona fide* in its own "good ol' science" domain albeit overall "boxy." It's like when you start ascending on a hot air balloon from the valley, all outlooks are "legit" but dependent on how high you float in the air. At low altitude, you still see leaves on the trees and other small objects. The higher you ascend, the further you can see, the grander perspective on the valley you shall behold.

Some people remain oblivious, and some stubbornly myopic of the self-evidence of computational, fractal Nature – it's a "matryoshka" of conscious systems. You're smack in the middle of co-producing your own experiential reality. As *YOU*-niverse of ever-expanding structures of consciousness, you're not marginalized, unless you belittle yourself, despite proselytizing attempts in certain parts of traditionally objective-reductionist science to indoctrinate its soulless dead-end philosophy without meaning or purpose.

Although the organizing principles of the contemporary scientific theories vary, all strive to uphold some version of the so-called relationalism of 17th- and 18th-century German philosopher Gottfried Leibniz. Broadly speaking, relationalism holds that space emerges from a certain pattern of correlations among objects it contains. In this view, space is a web of relationships with a certain pattern of connectivity. The relations are predicated on quantum theory or other principles, and the spatial arrangement arises from that.

In my everyday life, I cannot operate from only one fixed perspective, at any given moment I have to choose the most appropriate outlook deemed relevant by my mind; conflicting beliefs may be on the "scroll-down menu," too. An idealist as I am, no matter how hard I try, I can't help but refer to objects and people grounded in the material world. But using this kind of perspectivism as an argument against philosophical grounding of various models of reality can lead to hyper-perspectivism. Modern perspectivism rooted in the personal or collective logic which shapes its scope can be transcended through construction of hyper-perspectivistic prisms based on oftentimes unexpected multi-disciplinary interrelationships. All you have to do is connect the dots.

ANTI-TIME: A TWIN OF TIME?

I was pondering about the purpose and nature of *'Anti-Time'*, it still eludes me and it's far from a definitive answer, but I think that in the universal operating system anti-time could serve for optimization, "laconization" (making linguistic statements laconic) as well as for experience. Not exactly de-evolving, albeit unwinding complexity certainly looks that way. The system is engaged in the process of searching for "pattern archetypes" or at least some "interesting choice points" while reversing our "proper arrow of time." Speculatively speaking, there may be conscious entities experiencing reverse time. Maybe we should ask this question: What is the universal purpose of anti-entropy? As you remember, we've talked extensively on anti-time in Chapter 11 -- *Temporal Dynamics: Seven Misconceptions about the Nature of Time.*

YOUR FUTURE TIMELINE

"Talk as much philosophy as you please, worship as many gods as you like, observe all ceremonies, sing devoted praises to any number of divine beings — liberation never comes, even at the end of a hundred aeons, without the realization of the Oneness of Self." -Shankara

The future hopelessly feels like it's going to happen even though we don't know how it will play itself out. Does the future already exist? Or is it just a prediction we're making right now? Let me share with you a deep revelation that you already know deep inside: If you're reading this sentence now, you are a God incarnate! It's as simple as that! Let me explain. As we've discussed in Chapter 13 — *Digital Presentism: D-Theory of Time* — your future timelines are constantly quantum computationally extrapolated from your present temporal singularity, the Theta Point. And the most optimal timeline is retrocausally projected from the seemingly infinitely distant future, but in actuality the hyperdimension of Omega Point. So, it's a <YES> in the binary code! Even though this timeline is perhaps not yet fully realized through experience, perhaps only approximated, it's being constantly updated via feedback originating from the Theta Point of your experiential self.

In any case, the reality swath channel is always open, this "reality wormhole" is vacillating as your temporal singularity passes through it between the Alpha and Omega points as the origin and destination are eternally connected. It also makes more sense to place the source of this omnidimensional matrix at the Omega Singularity. One may think of the prosaic analogy of electric current that simultaneously needs both start- and endpoints in order to flow. This conceptualization of divine connection manifests in everyday synchronicities and uncanny improbabilities of life itself. I'll omit citing here a swirl of coincidences happened and, I'm certain, will be happening in my life, examples of which you may have no trouble finding in "new age" literature, let alone your own life.

Digital Pantheism, a philosophical worldview I'm defending, seems to offer the highest perspective on hyperreality: You are God exploring oneself within this vast experiential matrix. I'd like to draw your attention here to similarities with the oriental abstraction of God (e.g., Brahman in Hinduism) that is construed as absolute perfection encompassing everything in creation. This perfection cannot change in time because if it did, it would either have to have been less perfect in the past, or become less perfect in the future. In Chapter 13, we've discussed Digital Presentism, or D-Theory of Time, giving us a coherent picture of temporal ontology: In the absence of observers, the arrow of time doesn't exist — there's no cosmic flow of time. With that in mind, your timeless cosmic self resides as a hyperdimensional being outside the ordinary space-time dimensionality of your experiential self.

UNIVERSAL MIND: THE WEB OF ENTANGLED MINDS

The Universe, the way we perceive it with billions upon billions of galaxies in our "light sphere," is not precisely a mind. It's a manifestation of a mind, the creation of a conscious human mind. What we call Universal Mind is an altogether different ontological entity — cosmic consciousness, or any other contextually relevant term to your liking such as the Omega Hypermind, the ultimate computer, or simulator engine, or the omnidimensional holographic projector, or the Source, or God — rather than a hypothetical mind of the observed "human universe." This particular version of universe is what we "see" from within our dimensional cocoon, it's a construct of our minds but by no means represents objective reality "out there," including our most advanced models such as M-theory that are only approximations at best. We create mental maps of reality, but maps are not the territory. Sometime ago, we "knew" that Earth was flat and even today, in our Digital Age, most of us humans still adhere to the materialist version of the world that we supposedly "live in."

The omniversal hierarchical structure of conscious systems, I maintain, is a collection of subjects not an amalgamation of objects. In the space of possible minds, entangled minds far separated as actors in a virtual space-time have no true spatio-temporal separation in the computational realm which, just like our world, exhibits non-locality, discontinuity and quantum network non-linearity. The coming Cybernetic Singularity could unravel one of the deepest mysteries of fractal hyperreality: consciousness alternating from pluralities to singularities and from singularities back to pluralities.

Our Universe is estimated to contain two trillion galaxies within it, with each galaxy being home to hundreds of billions of stars. All in all, that means we can see some $\sim 10^{24}$ stars within the visible Universe. It turns out that it's all our creation! We not only passively observe something, we actually actively co-create it with the larger consciousness system. This is why, contrary to our scientific assumptions and even common sense, when we peer down micro-levels through microscopes or look at the Universe at large through telescopes, information is being created by experimenters of 'entangled networks' and becomes their reality and by extension to the rest of us, all of which is said to be isomorphic to our scientific discoveries. This is also the basis for the chrysalis conjecture, my case that our civilization is alone in our "human universe" operating system, the thesis we've discussed in Chapter 19 — *The Fermi Paradox: First Contact with Alien Syntellects.*

As our Noosphere expands inward into dimensions of our own design and expands outward from the solar system, occupying the Milky Way galaxy, spreading from one galaxy to the next, from supercluster to supercluster, faster than the speed of light since that speed limit may ultimately prove a non-issue, and finally saturating the entire known Universe with our intellect, all mass-energy would be converted into networks of conscious systems of universal proportions. Our Syntellect may meet other civilizational minds in extradimensional space and when that happens, a negotiated merger could be possible, relying only on translation scheme between the memory representations. Overall, I expect a very friendly future where superintelligences cooperate, as a rule, with occasionally nasty but entertaining surprises. This networking process possibly happening now elsewhere at the universal and multiversal scales could be the preamble to even greater things.

If we are to extend the Syntellect Hypothesis to universal applicability of its underlying principle we can derive the *Universal Law of Syntellect Emergence* which would refer to a meta-system transition of a complex intelligent system to self-awareness of a living, conscious superorganism with intellectual synergy of its sentient components reaching threshold complexity to become one supermind. This metamorphosis is associated with emergence of higher-order self-awareness and dimensionality of a new consciousness structure.

The term *'convergent evolution'* frequently used by evolutionary biologists could also apply to civilizational minds, syntellects, that would possess extradimensional qualities and to whom their respective universes may constitute finite resources convertible into more optimal computational substrates. To the best of our current knowledge, that might be black-hole-like conditions, or equivalence thereof, providing maximal computational density – even time stops at the event horizon of a black hole. For some grandiose purpose like preventing the heat death of cosmos or simply escaping out of it, the future supercivilization would compress our entire Universe into one supermassive universal black hole, the scenario ultimately leading to the Cosmological Singularity of the Omega Point.

In an ever-expanding universe, presumably like ours, time is cheap but energy must be carefully managed. Conversely, in a collapsing universe, energy is cheap, but time resource is not to waste! Ensuring subjective eternity even if remaining time to collapse is finite could be realizable by using the growing power of supercivilization to think faster and faster as the end nears. Both the expansion and the compression scenarios exploit the size change of a hypothetical universe as a source of organized resources to neutralize its heat death.

THE OMEGA SINGULARITY: THE SOURCE OF EVERYTHING INCLUDING OUR "SOLID STATE MATRIX"

"From the light came light, and from the dark came darkness, but from whence did they appear? Yin and Yang combine to create all things, but which is the source, and which was born from it?" -Qu Yuan

What is the Omega Singularity? One may speculate by defining it as Absolute Consciousness, the source of the omnidimensional matrix, i.e., the holographic projector of all possible observer timelines, including other permutational modalities such as possible anti-timelines in our quantum multiverse, as well as possible modalities in even larger inflationary multiverse – all pasts, presents and futures, and other yet inconceivable to us "pattern crawlings" exist as potentiality until experienced. In brief, it is the source of everything. In my life as a human, I see clues that evolution on Earth and elsewhere in the cosmos at large is not being pushed from behind in entropic randomness but being pulled forward by complexification, natural selection and other evolutionary forces orchestrated by a strange unseen teleological attractor, in McKenna's words the "Transcendental Object" at the end of time. We've discussed the Omega Point cosmology in Chapter 11 − *Temporal Dynamics: Seven Misconceptions About the Nature of Time*. Here, we're wrapping up our discussion as we're nearing the Omega of the book itself.

French scholar Pierre Teilhard de Chardin (1881–1955) who coined the term *'Omega Point'*, is known worldwide for his synthesis of science and theology applied to cosmogenesis and evolutionary processes. He was a Jesuit philosopher, a scientist, and a pantheist. His works remain a great inspiration for generations of philosophers, scientists, theologians, and artists. In his visionary book *"Le Phénomène Humain"* *(The Phenomenon of Man)* written in 1938 and posthumously published in 1955, he predicted the emergence of the Noosphere, a term first coined by the Russian cosmist Vladimir Vernadsky.

The Noosphere is the collective consciousness of humanity, the networks of thought and emotion in which we all are immersed, it's a cognitive layer of the planet, which has found a physical expression in the form of today's Internet. As the Noosphere gains more coherence, this process of "planet cognification" accelerates. Eventually, the Noosphere gains total dominance over the Biosphere and reaches a point of complete independence from "tangential energy," i.e., material substrates, forming a metaphysical being, Teilhard calls the Omega Point. One may see significant overlapping ideas between the transhumanist Technological Singularity and the Teilhardian Omega Point.

In his works, Teilhard described evolutionary processes having a definable direction — from unicellular microbes to the thinking animal to the emergent Noosphere — evolution leads to increasing complexity and greater consciousness, *'moving towards'* the ultimate knowledge, progressively attained by the evolving Noosphere and culminating in the apotheosis of the Omega Point. The emergence of Homo sapiens on this planet marked the beginning of a new regime, as the concentrated power acquired by consciousness to reflect upon itself raised mankind to a new sphere of thought as evolution has been slowly but surely becoming conscious of itself. Cosmic evolution shows not only increase in psychic aspects associated with the *'moving towards'*, but also shows threshold effects and emergence of novel properties in whole systems. New qualities are arising during evolution which cannot be deduced by a reductionistic investigation alone, i.e., cannot be deduced from its components.

To Teilhard, the Omega Point is not solely a future emergent construct, but in actuality, is already here as the "Divine Presence." This ever-present origin, apparently pre-existing our world, reminds us that his pantheism could be more a panentheistic type in which God has both an immanent and transcendent aspect. In Teilhard's view, evolution will culminate in the Omega Point, a sort of supreme consciousness. All conscious systems will converge in Omega, fusing into an infinitely dense singular point. The compressed conscious Universe will reconstruct in itself all individual minds as well as all that we are conscious of. Teilhard emphasizes that each perceiving subject will remain conscious of itself at the end of the process.

Digital Physics offers a remarkably accurate and, most importantly, formalized, and thus empirically verifiable "realization" of certain ideas by Teilhard de Chardin about the finite nature of the Universe, its properties, its evolution and its growing complexity. Mathematical physicist Frank Tipler developed Teilhard's concept into the Omega Point cosmological model to describe what, he maintains, is the ultimate destiny of the Universe set in motion by the laws of physics. For his theory to work, however, our universal operating system must be finite and discrete in nature, just as Digital Physics implies. Creation of these constraints forces the world's convergence upon itself which he theorizes to result in time ending in communion with the Omega-God.

The Spanish painter Salvador Dali was fascinated by the Teilhardian Omega Point. His 1960 painting, *The Ecumenical Council,* is said to represent the "interconnectedness" of the Omega Point. But is the Omega Point a merging of a drop with the ocean as in Hinduism, which prescribes the dissolution of the false ego? I don't think so! Rather, the Omega Point is the essence of the Teilhardian "superpersonalization" in which the true ego of each conscious being ascends to its pinnacle. Unification needs to be all-inclusive: as individuated units of consciousness we learn our lessons as we interact, play and evolve which lead to an expression of the best anyone can be and acknowledgement that any pathway to the ultimate divine is valid.

EXPERIENTIAL NIRVANA: INSTANT ENLIGHTENMENT

"Man suffers only because he takes seriously what the gods made for fun."
-Alan W. Watts

"What Nirvana?" you might immediately think, *"there's so much suffering in the world including ongoing problems in my own life!"* According to Buddhist teachings, Nirvana is defined as a transcendent state in which there is neither suffering, desire, nor sense of self, and the subject is released from the effects of karma and the cycle of death and rebirth. Nirvana is thus associated with the highest state that someone can attain, a state of enlightenment.

Are we "conveniently" entering experiential Nirvana on a civilizational level? As we've seen, it's just a matter of few decades – death becomes optional and your pattern-identity can be greatly extended with multiple copies of self. We are already immortal, as I've been harping all along that dying is like waking up someone bigger. As Rumi once said: *"I died as mineral and became a plant, I died as plant and rose to animal, I died as animal and I was human, Why should I fear? When was I less by dying?"* I also like to employ the "river analogy." Any river should end up somewhere. The question is where. Some rivers flow into a lake, some into another river, some into a sea, and yet others flow into an ocean. For us, it's all information flow. Flowing into another river is akin to reincarnation. Achieving self-transcendence via the Simulation Singularity and the Syntellect Emergence is a lot like flowing into the ocean.

The forthcoming Syntellect Emergence marked by the Simulation Singularity on a subjective level when your mind is digitized as a pattern, will preserve some of your organic memories if you so desire, and most importantly, will ensure the continuity of your subjectivity into the higher realms of existence. Experiential Nirvana is not an oxymoron but rather, this philosophical conundrum has even deeper, existential implications.

"What if when we die we wake up?" used to ask British-American philosopher Alan W. Watts (1915-1973) who is renowned for his philosophical worldview, drawing on Zen Buddhism, Hinduism, pantheism and modern science. He insisted that the whole Universe consists of a cosmic self playing hide-and-seek (Lila); hiding from itself (Maya) by becoming all the living and non-living things in the Universe and forgetting what it really is – the supreme being that we are all *IT* in disguise. In this worldview, Watts asserts that our conception of ourselves as an "ego in a bag of skin," or "skin-encapsulated ego" is a myth, the entities we call the separate "things" are merely thoughts of the whole.

Remindful of the Nozick's *'Experience Machine'* thought experiment, Watts' typical allegory of "life as a dream" would go like this: *"What you would do if you had the power to dream at night any dream you wanted to dream? You would, of course, be able to alter your time sense and sleep, say 75 years of subjective time into eight hours of sleep. You would start out by fulfilling all your wishes. You could design for yourself what would be the most ecstatic – love affairs, banquets, dancing girls, wonderful journeys, gardens, music beyond belief, and then after a couple of months of this sort of thing, at 75 years a night, you will be getting a little taste for something different and you would move over to an adventurous dimension, where there were certain dangers involved in the thrill of dealing with dangerous. You could rescue princesses from dragons and go on dangerous journeys, make fantastical explosions by blowing them up, eventually get into contests with enemies, and after you've done that for some time you'll think up a new twist to forget that you were dreaming, so that you would think it was all for real and to be anxious about it, and also because it would be so great when you wake up."*

The philosopher prepares you to, perhaps, the most startling realization, as he goes on: *"And then you say, like children who dare each other on things: 'How far could you go? What dimension of being lost of abandonment of your power? What dimension of that could you stand?' You could ask yourself this because you know you would eventually wake up, then you would get more and more adventurous and you would make further and further out gambling as to what you would dream and finally you would dream where you are now. You would dream the dream of living the life that you're actually living today. That would be within the infinite multiplicity of choices you would have of playing that you weren't God because the whole nature of the gardener according to this idea is to play that he's not so. In this way, everybody is fundamentally the alternate reality, not God in a politically kingly sense but person-God in the sense of being the self that is deep down basic. You're all that only you're pretending* (or willfully forgetting) *you're not."*

Life is continual self-transcendence. Death is an abrupt transcendence of self, an exit from a lifetime simulation, maybe. Since death becomes optional in our day and age, so instead of transcending of self you may choose continual self-transcendence. Now, here's probably the best advice anyone could ever give to you – for instant enlightenment – all you have to do is to realize that you're, in fact, in the midst of experiential Nirvana! Accept the principle "Ordinary is extraordinary" and you'll see your life as a daring adventure as it is.

Good and evil are relative terms, angelic and demonic cannot manifest without each other, for each inside there's outside, love contrasts with fear, light with dark, black implies white, self implies other, suffering implies ecstasy, death implies life. We can devise and apprehend something only in terms of what it is not. This is the cosmic binary code: Yin/Yang, True/False, Infinite/Finite, Masculine/Feminine, Theta/Omega, On/Off, Yes/No, +/-, 0/1. There are really only two opposing forces at play: love as universal integrating force and fear as universal disintegrating force.

Like in Conway's Game of Life information flows along the path of least resistance influenced by the bigger motivator – either love factor of fear factor (or, rather, their sophisticated gradients like pleasure and pain) – Go or No go. Love and its contrasting opposite fear is what makes us feel alive. Love is recognized self-similarity in the other, a fractal algorithm of the least resistance. And love, as the finest intelligence, is obviously an extreme form of collaboration. Love is the glue that holds the Universe together. Ascending to higher love, or in the words of Tom Campbell, "becoming love," I would say "becoming one planet of love," as we approach the end of our philosophico-belletristic journey.

In this quantum [computational] multiverse the essence of digital *is* quantum entanglement. From the Digital Physics perspective, particles of matter are pixels, or voxels if you prefer, on the screen of our perception. Your Universe is in consciousness. And it's a teleological process of unfolding patterns, the case I've been presenting to you throughout the book. The totality of your digital reality is what your conscious mind implicitly or explicitly chooses to experience out of the infinite.

Going forward into this fantastic future of yours, now that you know its deepest secret, you can stay in the state of cosmic orgasm for trillions of years of subjective time but once in a while you would like to replay it altogether afresh with a new digital Big Bang. And you're now in the midst of this kind of adventure, my fellow human!

Life you're living right now doesn't have to be perfect, just the opposite – you're now exploring your imperfections in this human world simulated reality which numerically would equate to a breaking of symmetry from pure perfection. Assume for a moment that you live in analogous natural world without the higher power, whilst the arrow of our epigenetic evolution points to a time when we are going to take the creator's righteous place in custom virtual universes of our own design. Would it be too hubristic of us to think that in the entire history of the Omniverse, if the concept of "history" is even relevant at all, we are the very first species to accomplish this? Would it be too hubristic of us to think of the linear progression of our history as the only possible rendering of information despite of all evidence to the contrary? In fact, everything you see, hear, smell, touch, feel, taste is sensory input data "computationally easily" transcribable into a computer code, that is reconstructable and simulatable. To take matters to the extreme, that's all which needs to be simulated – your experiential data – no need to simulate every galaxy, every microbe, or every particle.

And it better be a [self-]simulated reality! Why? First of all, that would mean that your reality is malleable and hackable for your enjoyment and evolution of consciousness; secondly, death is an illusion, like physical stuff, except, surprisingly, non-physical consciousness and interactions with oneself; thirdly, it's a matter of challenge with an invisible "safety net," you're now playing one of your fully immersive VR games, that of life of a human in the 21st century, with myriad virtual worlds and universes coming down the pipeline, where you could be in total control or less than total control, if desired. How can you ever be intimidated by anything once you realize that you're one with God? For thrills and challenges, however, you've entered your life as a human. Game, it's all that is, but then again, your metaphor for life, whatever it is, might be as good as mine!

Epilogue

We started this book by juxtaposing leading theories of consciousness and discussing how different species have a variety of their biological information processors which unsurprisingly results in qualia diversity. All species live in their own unique sensory universes. Species-wide mind-networks are ubiquitous in Nature. Consciousness and optimized meta-algorithmic information processing are the two sides of one coin. Feeling and thinking are ways we process information, but our emotional sensation is normally faster than a conscious thought. Nothing is real for us until perceived. The *Conscious Instant Hypothesis* denotes that we experience waking reality as a series of perceptual frames.

There's no shortage of workable theories of consciousness and its origins, each with their own merits and perspectives. We discussed the most relevant of them in the book in line with my own *Cybernetic Theory of Mind,* or as I often refer to as *The Syntellect Theory of Mind.* Interestingly, these leading theories, if metaphysically extended, in large part lend support to *Digital Pantheism* which well may come into scientific vogue with the future cyberhumanity.

According to the Interface Theory of Perception developed by Donald Hoffman and the Biocentric theory of consciousness developed by Robert Lanza, any universe is essentially non-existent without a conscious observer. In both theories, conscious minds are required as primary building blocks for any universe arising from probabilistic domain into existence. But biological minds reveal to us just a snippet in the space of possible minds. Building on the tenets of Biocentrism, Digital Pantheism goes further and includes all other possible conscious observers such as artificially intelligent self-aware entities. As discussed, the extended theory could be dubbed as *'Noocentrism'*.

Existence boils down to experience. No matter what ontological level a conscious entity finds herself at, it will be smack in the middle, between her transcendental realm and lower levels of organization. This is why I prefer the terms *'Experiential Realism'* and *'Pantheism'* as opposed to *'Panentheism'* as some suggested in regards to my philosophy.

Everything is Code. Immersive simulacra. Digital Pantheism implies omniversal ocean of pure, vibrant consciousness in motion, self-referential creative divine force expressing oneself in various forms and patterns. "I am" the Alpha, Theta & Omega — the ultimate self-causation, self-reflection and self-manifestation instantiated by mathematical codes and fractal geometry. Evolution, far from being a random process, unfolds in an orderly way, and as we've seen in a teleological way. In our daily lives we oftentimes catch glimpses of transcendent reality, be it synchronicities and epiphanies or psychedelic trips, or transcendental meditation.

We can't help but anthropomorphize the notion of objective reality. As I make my case in this book, objective reality does not exist, what exists instead is subjective points of view, intersubjectivity and supersubjectivity. If you were to talk with a human in the early 20th century, their universe would not "contain" galaxies, for example. So, all we can do when defending objectivity is to assume our present worldview, and any worldview of some other creature in the vast space of possible minds would be irrelevant to us. We can certainly imagine how a dog perceives the "objective" world accentuating the sense of smell, so lesser intelligences' point of view may not even be an issue here. The issue arises when we try to extrapolate the "objective" world of the higher intelligence, say artificial superintelligence of the future, or Holo syntellectus, or the Universal Mind. Those consciousness structures may perceive vastly different worlds and different dimensionalities.

Throughout the book I mentioned perennial, metaphysical, transcendental and computational idealism, so you might have wondered to which flavor of idealism I could adhere. So, here at the end of the book and speaking of objective reality, I would say that I personally favor objective (absolute) idealism whose forefather was the German philosopher Georg Hegel (1770-1831). In other words, I believe in the Universe of Conscious Minds and their interactions, even more specifically, their phenomenal experiences predicated on information processing and emergent (transcendent) properties. My core values, love and compassion, spiritual evolution and bliss, are nested in Absolute Idealism.

How long will our human science cling to the fundamentally flawed notion of objectivity remains an open question, my intuition tells me probably up until the Noocentric model, we've discussed in parts of this book, is widely accepted with the next paradigm shift and superintelligence calling the shots. In the book we've seen that the mind reigns over substrates and substrates themselves are nothing more than mind-like computational constructs. Now that we have challenged the orthodoxy of centuries-old Copernican heliocentric model, what would put an end to this old model? Artificially created realities, the Metaverse where the imaginative mind is at the heart of it all?

On this journey, we have familiarized with the physics of information, otherwise known as Digital Physics. The centrality of observers and the underlying code to the natural world has been the guiding principle of Digital Philosophy. We have learned that our entire Universe can be regarded as a quantum neural network-like, super-organismic system. The laws of physics can be regarded as fine-tuned master algorithms, the ruleset of our physical world. Organisms are, in turn, adaptive meta-algorithms. Genes, memes, big data are examples of transmittable information in biology, society and economics. We have found that time (or more specifically, the flow of time) is not fundamental, neither is space, nor is mass-energy. Reality is not what it seems, after all. Deep down it's pure information – waves of potentiality – and consciousness creating it all.

In our own not-so-distant future we'll witness the emergence of synthetic superintelligence as a new kingdom of life. Will that happen in 5 or 50 years doesn't really matter, we are firmly on the path of creating it – synthetic intelligence is an extension of us, natural intelligence, the future version of ourselves. On a long billions-of-years evolutionary journey from the first primordial prokaryote to a Solaris-like planetary mind, we're merely years away from this cardinal metamorphosis.

The *Simulation Singularity* would be the axis point in time where subjective dimensionality steps up. Think about it: If you could make multiple copies of yourself and set them out on different adventures in ultra-realistic virtual worlds and merge them later in order to have memories of all those adventures, if you could travel to artificially-recreated pasts or imaginary futures, if you could incorporate others' high-fidelity memories into your own, wouldn't that give you expanded dimensionality?

Another intriguing question is: What will happen to us on a civilizational scale? The phenomenon, known as the *Syntellect Emergence*, or the *Cybernetic Singularity*, is already seen on the horizon, when Digital Gaia, the global neural network of billions of hyper-connected humans and ultra-intelligent machines, and trillions of sensors around the planet, "wakes up" as a living, conscious superorganism. It is when, essentially, you yourself transcend to the higher Gaian Mind by becoming cybergod. While it is the "end" of linear human history, the Omega Point of Homo sapiens, it is a new beginning, *Theogenesis* – the birth of divine entity within a newly-cognized reality framework – engineering our own godhood, self-divinization.

An interesting deduction derived from the Syntellect Hypothesis is that: A neuron in the human brain can never equate the human mind, but this analogy doesn't hold true for a digital mind, by virtue of its mathematical structure, it may – through evolutionary progression and provided there are no insurmountable evolvability constraints – transcend to the higher-order Syntellect.

A mind is a web of patterns fully integrated as a coherent intelligent system; it is a self-generating, self-reflective, self-governing network of sentient components (that are themselves minds) that evolves, as a rule, by propagating through dimensionality and ascension to ever-higher hierarchical levels of emergent complexity. In this book, the Syntellect emergence is hypothesized to be the next meta-system transition, developmental stage for the human mind – becoming one global mind – that would constitute the quintessence of the looming Cybernetic Singularity.

What else have we learned on this journey? A sense of agency with which an entity is endowed is for this particular purpose: to exercise free will. In the book, free will was called the quantum algorithm of consciousness. We have learned that all realities are observer-centric virtualities where an entire observer-universe system remains in the state of quantum coherence until experienced as a conscious instant, or the temporal singularity in the framework of *D-Theory of Time*. A series of such conscious instants constitutes a data stream of consciousness. In a sense, consciousness is really mind-based computing of your experiential branch in this quantum multiverse.

We have learned that the Universal Law of Syntellect Emergence applies to all scales: To a consciously evolving mind the Syntellect emergence appears as it is – emergence of a new consciousness structure – but it's only one of the pre-existing levels in the game, we'd like to replay with a new twist.

Acknowledgments

Writing a book turned out harder than I thought and much more rewarding than I could have ever imagined. At the end it felt like nothing less than divine inspiration. This literary project would never have been possible without emotional support and feedback from my close friends, family members, colleagues and the vast community of people that follow me on social media.

I'm eternally grateful to my beloved parents, my mom Galina Alexandrovna and my father, Mikhail Mikhailovich. In loving memory of my dad and in loving memory of my uncle Valeriy Alexandrovich who was like a second dad to me, I dedicate this book.

Million thanks to digital philosopher Dr. Antonin Tuynman, my dear friend and associate, who was very kind to write the foreword to this book. To the pleiad of my personal inspirations – contemporaries whose names were mentioned on the pages of the book – Ray Kurzweil, Ben Goertzel, Tom Campbell, Peter Russell, Donald Hoffman, Jason Silva, Peter Diamandis.

A very special thanks goes to Joseph Van Myers from Hartboro, PA, who made a sizable contribution to this literary project. Thank you so much for your incredible generosity! God bless you, good sir!

I'd like to express my gratitude to everyone who contributed at the early stages of the book project, pre-ordered the book with intention to be among its first readers, with the most notable contributions by Finbar O'Hanlon and Dennis Sedov.

Many, many thanks to the co-authors of 2018 book *"Is Reality a Simulation?: An Anthology."* Thanks a bunch to all my extended family. To all my close friends. I can't thank you enough!

Finally, I am grateful to all those who have been a part of getting it done: Arjuna Jay, Matt Swayne, George Lazar, Ediho Lokanga, Ashley Baird, Alan Ho, John Rogan, Oleg Oplachko, Yfke Laanstra, Michael Hrenka, Don Gilmore, Steven Oustecky, Jan Železný, Martin Jambon, Jeffrey Caplan, Mykola Rabchevskiy, Steven Adger, Emily Morgan, Gary Mirzoyev, Andrew Olejarz, David Poole, Kirill Sobolev, David Chartrand, Aneel Pandey, Joel Weddington, Leandro Gobbi; and to every active member of Facebook groups that I personally manage: Cybernetic Singularity: The Syntellect Emergence; The Cybernetic Theory of Mind; and Consciousness: Evolution of the Mind for valuable feedback and appreciation of my work.

About the Author

Economist by training, philosopher by vocation, in his words, *"worked in the corporate world, worked in the startup world, sat on the boards, sat on the beach, was employed, was self-employed, was a venture capitalist, was an 'adventure' capitalist,"* while his passion towards physics and philosophy slowly but surely was brewing in the background. Born and raised in Russia, Alex Vikoulov was growing up a gifted child so much so that his parents transferred him to a lycée with enhanced math and foreign language programs. He studied humanities at *Tomsk State University* and had his first entrepreneurship experience by running *Sibmarket Financial*, among the first hedge funds in Russia. He immigrated to the United States in 1994 at the age of 24, continued his studies in the U.S. where he graduated in 1999 from *Armstrong University* with degrees in finance and economics.

Alex Vikoulov has a diverse background in fintech and IT industries. *Ecstadelic Media Group*, PR/digital media and publishing company, is one of his latest projects. Prior to *Ecstadelic Media*, he served as CFO and board member of the AI startup *Neuromama, Ltd*. From 2005 to 2013 held various executive positions, and spent about 3 years as a business consultant in Southeast Asia. From 2001 to 2005, managed San Francisco office of *First Data Corp.*, the largest payment processor in the U.S. From 1999 to 2001, he held a consultant position with *Prudential Securities, Inc.* From 1990 to 1994, as President & CEO, Vikoulov managed *Sibmarket Financial*, one of the pioneering hedge funds in the emerging markets, while serving as a stock exchange board member. He started his career at *Incombank* in 1990 as a statistical analyst.

These days he describes himself as a futurist, evolutionary cyberneticist philosopher of mind, neo-transcendentalist, transhumanist singularitarian, cosmist, consciousness researcher, independent scholar, entrepreneur, media commentator, painter and author. Currently resides in Burlingame, CA (San Francisco Bay Area).

Bibliography

Aaronson, Scott, 2013, "Why Philosophers Should Care About Computational Complexity", in Computability: Turing, Gödel, Church, and Beyond, Brian Jack Copeland, Carl J. Posy, and Oron Shagrir, Cambridge, MA: The MIT Press.

Abramsky, Samson and Achim Jung, 1994, "Domain theory", in Handbook of Logic in Computer Science (vol. 3): Semantic Structure, Samson Abramsky, Dov M. Gabbay, and Thomas S. E. Maibaum, Oxford University Press.

Adams, Fred and João Antonio de Moraes, 2016, "Is There a Philosophy of Information?", Topoi.

Adriaans, Pieter, 2007, "Learning as Data Compression", in Computation and Logic in the Real World, S. Barry Cooper, Benedikt Löwe, and Andrea Sorbi, Berlin, Heidelberg: Springer Berlin Heidelberg.

——, 2008, "Between Order and Chaos: The Quest for Meaningful Information", Theory of Computing Systems (Special Issue: Computation and Logic in the Real World).

Adriaans, Pieter and Peter van Emde Boas, 2011, "Computation, Information, and the Arrow of Time", in Computability in Context: Computation and Logic in the Real World, by S Barry Cooper and Andrea Sorbi, London: Imperial College Press.

Adriaans, Pieter and Johan van Benthem, 2008a, "Introduction: Information Is What Information Does", in Adriaans & van Benthem 2008b.

——, 2008b, "Philosophy of Information", (Handbook of the Philosophy of Science 8), Amsterdam: Elsevier.

Adriaans, Pieter and Paul M.B. Vitányi, 2009, "Approximation of the Two-Part MDL Code", IEEE Transactions on Information Theory.

Adriaans, Pieter and Dolf Zantinge, 1996, "Data Mining", Harlow, England: Addison-Wesley.

Agrawal, Manindra, Neeraj Kayal, and Nitin Saxena, 2004, "PRIMES Is in P", Annals of Mathematics.

Albrecht, Andreas and Daniel Phillips, 2014, "Origin of Probabilities and Their Application to the Multiverse", Physical Review.

Antunes, Luis, Lance Fortnow, Dieter van Melkebeek, and N.V. Vinodchandran, 2006, "Computational Depth: Concept and Applications", Theoretical Computer Science.

Aristotle. Aristotle in 23 Volumes, Vols. 17, 18, translated by Hugh Tredennick, Cambridge, MA: Harvard University Press; London, William Heinemann Ltd. 1933, 1989.

Avery, Samuel, 2017, "The Quantum Screen: The Enigmas of Modern Physics and a New Model of Perceptual Consciousness", Wetware Media.

Bais, F. Alexander, J. Doyne Farmer, 2008, "The Physics of Information", Adriaans and van Benthem.

Barron, Andrew, Jorma Rissanen, Bin Yu, 1998, "The Minimum Description Length Principle in Coding and Modeling", IEEE Transactions on Information Theory, 44(6): 2743–2760.

Baars, Bernard J., 2005, "Global workspace theory of consciousness: toward a cognitive neuroscience of human experience", Progress in Brain Research.

Barwise, Jon, John Perry, 1983, "Situations and Attitudes", Cambridge, MA: MIT Press.

Becker, Adam, 2018, "What Is Real?: The Unfinished Quest for the Meaning of Quantum Physics", Hodder & Stoughton.

Bell, Gordon, Tony Hey, Alex Szalay, 2009, "Computer Science: Beyond the Data Deluge", Science.

Bennett, C. H., 1988, "Logical Depth and Physical Complexity".

Berkeley, George, 1732, "Alciphron: Or the Minute Philosopher", Edinburgh: Thomas Nelson, 1948–57.

Birkhoff, George David, 1950, "Collected Mathematical Papers", New York: American Mathematical Society.

Bloem, Peter, Steven de Rooij, Pieter Adriaans, 2015, "Two Problems for Sophistication", in Algorithmic Learning Theory, Kamalika Chaudhuri, Claudio Gentile, and Sandra Zilles, Cham: Springer International Publishing.

Bloom, Howard, 2001, "Global Brain: The Evolution of Mass Mind from the Big Bang to the 21st Century", Wiley.

Bohm, David, 1980, "Wholeness and the Implicate Order", Routledge.

Boltzmann, Ludwig, 1866, "Über die Mechanische Bedeutung des Zweiten Hauptsatzes der Wärmetheorie", Wiener Berichte.

Boole, George, 1847, "Mathematical Analysis of Logic: Being an Essay towards a Calculus of Deductive Reasoning", Cambridge: Macmillan, Barclay, & Macmillan.

——, 1854, "An Investigation of the Laws of Thought: On which are Founded the Mathematical Theories of Logic and Probabilities", London: Walton and Maberly.

Bostrom, Nick, 2003, "Are We Living in a Computer Simulation?" The Philosophical Quarterly.

——, 2014, "Superintelligence: Paths, Dangers, Strategies," Oxford University Press

Bott, R. and J. Milnor, 1958, "On the Parallelizability of the Spheres", Bulletin of the American Mathematical Society.

Bovens, Luc, Stephan Hartmann, 2003, "Bayesian Epistemology", Oxford: Oxford University Press.

Brenner, Joseph E., 2008, "Logic in Reality", Dordrecht: Springer Netherlands.

Braden, Gregg, 2010, "The Divine Matrix: Bridging Time, Space, Miracles, and Belief", ReadHowYouWant.com

Briggs, Henry, 1624, "Arithmetica Logarithmica", London: Gulielmus Iones.Capurro, Rafael, 1978, Information. Ein Beitrag zur etymologischen und ideengeschichtlichen Begründung des Informationsbegriffs (Information: A contribution to the foundation of the concept of information based on its etymology and in the history of ideas), Munich, Germany: Saur.

——, 2009, "Past, Present, and Future of the Concept of Information", TripleC: Communication, Capitalism & Critique.

Brockman, John, 2019, "Possible Minds: Twenty-Five Ways of Looking at AI", Penguin Press.

Buonomano, Dean, 2017, "Your Brain Is a Time Machine: The Neuroscience and Physics of Time", W.W. Norton & Company.

Campbell, Thomas W., 2007, "My Big TOE: A Trilogy Unifying Philosophy, Physics, and Metaphysics", Lightning Strike Books.

Capurro, Rafael, Birger Hjørland, 2003, "The Concept of Information", in Blaise Cronin (ed.), Annual Review of Information Science and Technology (ARIST).

Capurro, Rafael, John Holgate (eds.), 2011, "Messages and Messengers: Angeletics as an Approach to the Phenomenology of Communication", München: Fink.

Carnap, Rudolf, 1928, "Scheinprobleme in der Philosophie" (Pseudoproblems of Philosophy), Berlin: Weltkreis-Verlag.

——, 1945, "The Two Concepts of Probability: The Problem of Probability", Philosophy and Phenomenological Research, 5(4): 513–532.

——, 1947, "Meaning and Necessity", Chicago: The University of Chicago Press.

——, 1950, "Logical Foundations of Probability", Chicago: The University of Chicago Press.

Carey, Nessa, 2013, "The Epigenetics Revolution: How Modern Biology Is Rewriting Our Understanding of Genetics, Disease, and Inheritance", Columbia University Press.

Carroll, Sean, 2016, "The Big Picture: On the Origins of Life, Meaning, and the Universe Itself", Oneworld Publications.

Campbell, Thomas, Houman Owhadi, Joe Sauvageau, David Watkinson 2018, "On Testing the Simulation Theory", International Journal of Quantum Foundations.

Chace, Calum, 2017, "Artificial Intelligence and the Two Singularities," Three Cs.

Chaitin, Gregory J., 1987, "Algorithmic Information Theory", Cambridge: Cambridge University Press.

——, 1969, "On the Length of Programs for Computing Finite Binary Sequences: Statistical Considerations", Journal of the ACM.

Chater, Nick, Paul Vitányi, 2003, "Simplicity: A Unifying Principle in Cognitive Science?", Trends in Cognitive Sciences.

Chalmers, David, 1996, "The Conscious Mind: In Search of a Fundamental Theory", Oxford University Press.

Chislenko, Alexander, 1996, "Networking in the Mind Age", The MIT Press.

Chomsky, Noam, 2005, "Universals of human nature", Psychotherapy and Psychosomatics, 74: 263-8.

Chopra, Deepak, Menas C. Kafatos, 2017, "You Are the Universe: Discovering Your Cosmic Self and Why It Matters", Potter/Ten Speed/Harmony/Rodale.

Church, Alonzo, 1936, "An Unsolvable Problem of Elementary Number Theory", American Journal of Mathematics.

Cilibrasi, Rudi, Paul M.B. Vitanyi, 2005, "Clustering by Compression", IEEE Transactions on Information Theory.

Crutchfield, James P. and Karl Young, 1989, "Inferring Statistical Complexity", Physical Review Letters, 63(2): 105–108.

——, 1990, "Computation at the Onset of Chaos", in Entropy, Complexity, and the Physics of Information, W. Zurek, editor, SFI Studies in the Sciences of Complexity, VIII, Reading, MA: Addison-Wesley.

Darwin, Charles, 1859, "On the Origin of Species", John Murray.

Davis, Martin, 2006, "Why There Is No Such Discipline as Hypercomputation", Applied Mathematics and Computation.

Davies, Paul, 2010, "The Eerie Silence: Renewing Our Search for Alien Intelligence", Houghton, Mifflin, Harcourt.

Davis, Erik, 2015, "TechGnosis: Myth, Magic and Mysticism in the Age of Information", North Atlantic Books, Reprint Edition.

Dawkins, Richard, 1976, "The Selfish Gene", Oxford University Press.

de Chardin, Pierre Teilhard, 1955 (postmortem), "Le Phénomène Humain", The Phenomenon of Man, Éditions du Seuil, (France), Harper & Brothers (US), William Collins (UK).

——, 1959, "L'Avenir de l'Homme," essays written 1920–52, on the evolution of consciousness (noosphere), translated as The Future of Man (1964).

de Garis, Hugo, 2010, "Never mind the Nanotech. Here comes Femtotech", interview by H+ Magazine, written by R.U. Sirius.

de Leo, Stefano, 1996, "Quaternions and Special Relativity", Journal of Mathematical Physics.

Deacon, Terrence W., 2010, "What is Missing from the Theories of Information?", University of California, Berkeley

Dershowitz, Nachum and Yuri Gurevich, 2008, "A Natural Axiomatization of Computability and Proof of Church's Thesis", Bulletin of Symbolic Logic.

Descartes, René, 1641, "Meditationes de Prima Philosophia" (Meditations on First Philosophy), Paris.

——, 1647, "Discourse de la Méthode" (Discourse on Method), Leiden.

Deutsch, David, 1997, "The Fabric of Reality", Viking Adult.

Devlin, Keith and Duska Rosenberg, 2008, "Information in the Study of Human Interaction", Adriaans and van Benthem 2008b.

Di Biase, Francisco, 2009, "A Holoinformational Model of the Physical Observer", Quantum Biosystems.

Diamandis, Peter H., Steven Kotler, 2016, "Bold: How to Go Big, Make Bank, and Better the World", Simon and Schuster.

Domingos, Pedro, 1998, "Occam's Two Razors: The Sharp and the Blunt", in Proceedings of the Fourth International Conference on Knowledge Discovery and Data Mining (KDD–98), New York: AAAI Press.

Dossey, Larry, 2014, "One Mind: How Our Individual Mind is Part of a Greater Consciousness and Why it Matters", Hay House, Inc.

Downey, Rodney G., Denis R. Hirschfeldt, 2010, "Algorithmic Randomness and Complexity" (Theory and Applications of Computability), New York: Springer New York.

Dretske, Fred, 1981, "Knowledge and the Flow of Information, Cambridge, MA: The MIT Press.

Drexler, Eric, 1992, "Nanosystems", John Wiley & Sons.

——, 1987, "Engines of Creation: The Coming Era of Nanotechnology", Anchor.

Dufort, Paul A., Charles J. Lumsden, 1994, "The Complexity and Entropy of Turing Machines", in Proceedings Workshop on Physics and Computation. PhysComp '94, Dallas, TX: IEEE Computer Society Press.

Dunn, Jon Michael, 2001, "The Concept of Information and the Development of Modern Logic", in Zwischen traditioneller und moderner Logik: Nichtklassische Ansatze (Non-classical Approaches in the Transition from Traditional to Modern Logic), Werner Stelzner and Manfred Stöckler, Paderborn: Mentis.

——, 2008, "Information in Computer Science", in Adriaans and van Benthem 2008b.

Dijksterhuis, E. J., 1986, "The Mechanization of the World Picture: Pythagoras to Newton", Princeton, NJ: Princeton University Press.

Durand-Lose, Jérôme, 2002, "Computing Inside the Billiard Ball Model", in Collision-Based Computing, Andrew Adamatzky (ed.), London: Springer London, 135–160.

Eddington, Arthur S., 1929, "Science and the Unseen World", George Allen & Unwin Ltd.

Edwards, Paul, 1967, "The Encyclopedia of Philosophy", 8 volumes, New York: Macmillan Publishing.

England, Jeremy L., Jordon M. Horowitz, 2017, "Spontaneous fine-tuning to environment in many-species chemical reaction networks", Proceedings of the National Academy of Sciences.

England, Jeremy L., 2015, "Dissipative adaptation in driven self-assembly", Nature Nanotechnology.

Elvidge, Jim, 2018, "Digital Consciousness: A Transformative Vision", Iff Books.

Epstein, Mikhail, 2012, "The Transformative Humanities: A Manifesto", Bloomsbury Publishing.

Epstein, Rob, 2016, "The Empty Brain: Your brain does not process information, retrieve knowledge or store memories. In short: your brain is not a computer", Aeon.

Eryomin, Alexey L., 2012, "The Laws of Evolution of the Mind // 7th International Teleconference on "Actual Problems of Modern Science", Tomsk.

——, 2005, "Noogenesis and Theory of Intellect", Krasnodar: SovKub.

Everett, Hugh, 1957, "Relative State Formulation of Quantum Mechanics", Reviews of Modern Physics. 29 (3): 454–462.

——, 1957, "Recursive games", in Melvin Dresher, Albert William Tucker, Philip Wolfe. Contributions to the Theory of Games, Volume 3. Annals of Mathematics Studies. Princeton University Press. pp. 67–78.

Fayyad, Usama, Gregory Piatetsky-Shapiro, Padhraic Smyth, 1996, "From Data Mining to Knowledge Discovery in Databases", AI Magazine.

507

Fisher, R. A., 1925, "Theory of Statistical Estimation", Mathematical Proceedings of the Cambridge Philosophical Society.

Floridi, Luciano, 1999, "Information Ethics: On the Philosophical Foundation of Computer Ethics", Ethics and Information Technology.

——, 2002, "What Is the Philosophy of Information?", Metaphilosophy.

——, 2003, "The Blackwell Guide to the Philosophy of Computing and Information", Oxford: Blackwell.

——, 2010, "The Philosophy of Information as a Conceptual Framework", Knowledge, Technology & Policy, 23(1–2): 253–281.

——, 2011, "The Philosophy of Information", Oxford: Oxford University Press.

Forbes, Kent, 2015, "The Simulation Hypothesis", Fair Wind Films.

Frank, Adam, 2017, "Minding Matter", Aeon.

Fredkin, Edward, "Digital Mechanics", Physica D.

Fredkin, Edward, Tommaso Toffoli, 1982, "Conservative Logic", International Journal of Theoretical Physics.

Frege, Gottlob, 1879, "Begriffsschrift: eine der arithmetischen nachgebildete Formelsprache des reinen Denkens", Halle.

——, 1892, "Über Sinn und Bedeutung", Zeitschrift für Philosophie und philosophische Kritik", NF 100.

Furey, C., 2015, "Charge Quantization from a Number Operator", Physics Letters.

Galileo Galilei, 1623 [1960], Il Saggiatore (in Italian), Rome; translated as The Assayer, by Stillman Drake and C. D. O'Malley, in The Controversy on the Comets of 1618, Philadelphia: University of Pennsylvania Press, 1960, 151–336.

Garey, Michael R., David S. Johnson, 1979, "Computers and Intractability: A Guide to the Theory of NP-Completeness", (A Series of Books in the Mathematical Sciences), San Francisco: W. H. Freeman.

Gebser, Jean, 1949, "The Ever-Present Origin", authorized translation by Noel Barstad with Algis Mickunas, 1991, Athens: Ohio University Press.

Gell-Mann, Murray and Seth Lloyd, 2003, "Effective Computing", SFI Working Paper 03-12-068, Santa Fe, NM: Santa Fe Institute.

Gibbs, J. Willard, 1906, The Scientific Papers of J. Willard Gibbs in Two Volumes, 1. Longmans, Green, and Co.

Gimbel, Steven, 2015, "Redefining Reality: The Intellectual Implications of Modern Science", The Teaching Company, LLC.

Gleick, James, 2011, "The Information: A History, a Theory, a Flood", Pantheon Books.

Gödel, Kurt, 1931, "Über formal unentscheidbare Sätze der Principia Mathematica und verwandter Systeme I", Monatshefte für Mathematik und Physik.

Goertzel, Ben, 2016, "AGI Revolution: An Inside View of the Rise of Artificial General Intelligence", Humanity+ Press.

——, 2010, "A Cosmist Manifesto: Practical Philosophy for the Posthuman Age", Humanity+ Press.

——, 2006, "The Hidden Pattern: A Patternist Philosophy of Mind", Universal-Publishers.

Goff, Philip, 2017, "Consciousness and Fundamental Reality", Oxford University Press.

Goodstein, R. L., 1957, "The Definition of Number", The Mathematical Gazette.

Goswami, Amit, Joseph Selbie, 2017, "The Physics of God: Unifying Quantum Physics, Consciousness, M-Theory, Heaven, Neuroscience and Transcendence", Red Wheel/Weiser.

Graziano, Michael S., 2016, "Consciousness Engineered", Journal of Consciousness Studies. 23 (11–12): 98–115.

——, 2013, "Consciousness and the Social Brain", Oxford University Press.

Grim, Patrick, 2015, "Philosophy of Mind: Brains, Consciousness, and Thinking Machines", The Teaching Company, LLC.

Grünwald, Peter D., 2007, "The Minimum Description Length Principle", Cambridge, MA: MIT Press.

Grünwald, Peter D. and Paul M.B. Vitányi, 2008, "Algorithmic Information Theory", in Adriaans and van Benthem.

Groot, Adrianus Dingeman de, 1961 [1969], Methodology: Foundations of Inference and Research in the Behavioral Sciences (Methodologie: grondslagen van onderzoek en denken in de gedragswetenschappen), The Hague: Mouton.

Guite, Haulianlal, 2017, "Confessions of a Dying Mind: The Blind Faith of Atheism", Bloomsbury India.

Guth, Alan, 2007, "Eternal Inflation and its implications", Journal of Physics A: Mathematical and Theoretical, Vol. 40/25.

Harari, Yuval Noah, 2017, "Homo Deus: A Brief History of Tomorrow", Harper.

——, 2015, "Sapiens: A Brief History of Humankind", Harper.

Haisch, Bernard, 2014, "Is the Universe a Vast, Consciousness-Created Virtual Reality Simulation?", The Journal of Natural and Social Philosophy, Vol 10/1.

——, 2009, "The God Theory: Universes, The Zero-Point Fields and What's Behind It All", Red Wheel-Wieser, San Francisco, CA.

Hameroff, Stuart, 1998, "Quantum computation in brain microtubules – The Penrose-Hameroff "Orch OR" model of consciousness", Phil Trans Royal Society London (A) 356:1869-96.

Hameroff, Stuart, Roger Penrose, 2014, "Consciousness in the Universe: A Review of the 'Orch OR' theory", Physics of Life Reviews, 11(1):39-78.

Hall, Barry G., 2014, "SNP-associations and phenotype predictions from hundreds of microbial genomes without genome alignments", Plos One. 9: e90490.

Haramein, Nassim, William David Brown, Amira Val Baker, 2016, "The Unified Spacememory Network: From Cosmogenesis to Consciousness", NeuroQuantology

Harremoës, Peter and Flemming Topsøe, 2008, "The Quantitative Theory of Information", in Adriaans and van Benthem 2008b: 171–216.

Hartley, R.V.L., 1928, "Transmission of Information", Bell System Technical Journal, 7(3): 535–563.

Hawking, Stephen, Leonard Mlodinow, 2010, "The Grand Design", Bantam Books.

Hazard, Paul, 1935, "La Crise de La Conscience Européenne (1680–1715)", Paris: Boivin.

Henry, Richard Conn, Stephen Palmquist, 2007, "An Experimental Test of Non-local Realism", Nature.

Hellemans, Alexander, 2006, "The Geometer of Particle Physics", Scientific American.

Herculano-Houzel, Suzana, 2016, "Human Advantage: A New Understanding of How Our Brain Became Remarkable", The MIT Press.

Herzog, Michael H., Kammer T, Frank Scharnowski, 2016, "Time Slices: What Is the Duration of a Percept?", PLoS Biology 14(4): e1002433.

Hey, Anthony J. G., Stewart Tansley, Kristin Tolle (eds.), 2009, "The Fourth Paradigm: Data-Intensive Scientific Discovery", Redmond, WA: Microsoft Research.

Heylighen, Francis, 2007, "The Global Superorganism: an evolutionary-cybernetic model of the emerging network society", Social Evolution & History. 6/1, pp. 58-119.

Hintikka, Jaakko, 1962, "Knowledge and Belief: An Introduction to the Logic of the Two Notions", (Contemporary Philosophy), Ithaca, NY: Cornell University Press.

——, 1973, "Logic, Language Games and Information: Kantian Themes in the Philosophy of Logic", Oxford: Clarendon Press.

510

Hoffman, Donald, 2019, "The Case Against Reality: Why Evolution Hid the Truth from Our Eyes", W. W. Norton and Company.

——, 2009, "The interface theory of perception: Natural selection drives true perception to swift extinction," in Object categorization: Computer and human vision perspectives, S. Dickinson, M. Tarr, A. Leonardis, B. Schiele (Eds.) Cambridge, UK: Cambridge University Press, 148–165.

——, 2008, "The Conscious Realism and the Mind-Body Problem", Mind & Matter, 6, 87–121.

Hume, David, 1739–40, "A Treatise of Human Nature", L.A. Selby-Bigge (ed.), Oxford: Clarendon Press, 1896.

——, 1748, "An Enquiry concerning Human Understanding", Reprinted in Enquiries Concerning the Human Understanding and Concerning the Principles of Morals, 1777 which was reprinted, L.A. Selby-Bigge (ed.), Oxford: Clarendon Press, 1888 (second edition 1902).

Hutter, Marcus, 2005, "Universal Artificial Intelligence: Sequential Decisions Based on Algorithmic Probability", (Texts in Theoretical Computer Science, an EATCS Series), Berlin, Heidelberg: Springer Berlin Heidelberg.

——, 2007a, "On Universal Prediction and Bayesian Confirmation", Theoretical Computer Science.

——, 2007b, "Algorithmic Information Theory: a brief non-technical guide to the field", Scholarpedia.

——, 2010, "A Complete Theory of Everything (will be subjective)", Algorithms.

Hutter, Marcus, John W. Lloyd, Kee Siong Ng, William T.B. Uther, 2013, "Probabilities on Sentences in an Expressive Logic", Journal of Applied Logic, special issue: Combining Probability and Logic: Papers from Progic 2011, Jeffrey Helzner.

Husain, Amir, 2018, "The Sentient Machine", Profile.

Huxley, Aldous, 1945, "The Perennial Philosophy", Harper Collins, (edition 2004).

Irwin, Klee, 2017, "The Code Theoretic Axiom: The Third Ontology", Los Angeles: Quantum Gravity Research.

Jakubovic, David, 2017, "What is Reality?", Mad Machine Films.

Jeans, James, 1930, "The Mysterious Universe", Cambridge University Press.

Kahn, David, 1967, "The Code-Breakers, The Comprehensive History of Secret Communication from Ancient Times to the Internet", New York: Scribner.

Kant, Immanuel, 1781, "Kritik der reinen Vernunft", (Critique of Pure Reason), Germany.

Kanti, Panagiota, Burkhard Kleihaus, Jutta Kunz, 2011, "Stable Lorentzian Wormholes in Dilatonic Einstein-Gauss-Bonnet Theory", Physical Review.

Kastrup, Bernardo, 2019, "The Idea of the World: A Multi-Disciplinary Approach to the Mental Nature of Reality", IFF Books.

——, 2017, "Making Sense of the Mental Universe", Philosophy and Cosmology, Vol. 19, pp. 33-49.

——, 2018, "The Universe in Consciousness", Journal of Consciousness Studies 25 (5-6):125-155.

Kaufmann, Steven, 2015, "The Unified Reality Theory: The Evolution of Existence into Experience", BalboaPress.

Kauffman, Stuart, 2016, "Humanity in a Creative Universe", Oxford University Press.

——, 2008, "Reinventing the Sacred: A New View of Science, Reason, and Religion", Basic Books.

Kelly, Kevin, 2017, "The Inevitable: Understanding the 12 Technological Forces That Will Shape Our Future", Penguin.

——, 2011, "What Technology Wants", Penguin.

King, Brett, Andy Lark, Alex Lightman, JP Rangaswami, 2016, "Augmented: Life in the Smart Lane", Marshall Cavendish International Asia Pte, Ltd.

Kipling, Rudyard, 1894, "The Jungle Book", Macmillan.

Kolmogorov, A.N., 1965, "Three Approaches to the Quantitative Definition of Information", Problems of Information Transmission.

Koppel, Moshe, 1987, "Complexity, Depth, and Sophistication", Complex Systems.

Kotler, Steven, Jamie Wheal, 2017, "Stealing Fire: How Silicon Valley, the Navy SEALs, and Maverick Scientists Are Revolutionizing the Way We Live and Work", HarperCollins.

Kripke, Saul A., 1959, "A Completeness Theorem in Modal Logic", The Journal of Symbolic Logic.

——, 1971, "Identity and Necessity", in Milton K. Munitz (ed.), Identity and Individuation, New York: New York University Press, Kuipers, Theo A.F. (ed.), 2007a, General Philosophy of Science: Focal Issues, Amsterdam: Elsevier Science Publishers.

——, 2007b, "Explanation in Philosophy of Science", in Kuipers 2007a.

Laplace, Pierre Simon, Marquis de, 1814 [1902], A Philosophical Essay on Probabilities, F.W. Truscott and F.L. Emory (trans.), New York: J. Wiley; London: Chapman & Hall.

Kuhn, Robert Lawrence, 2012-2018, "Closer to Truth", PBS series.

Kurzweil, Ray, 2012, "How to Create a Mind: The Secret of Human Thought Revealed", Viking Penguin.

——, 2005, "The Singularity Is Near: When Humans Transcend Biology", Viking.

——, 1999, "The Age of Spiritual Machines", Viking Press.

Langan, Christopher M., 2002, "The Cognitive-Theoretic Model of the Universe: A New Kind of Reality Theory", ctmu.net.

Langton, Chris G., 1990, "Computation at the Edge of Chaos: Phase Transitions and Emergent Computation", Physica D: Nonlinear Phenomena.

Lanza, Robert, Bob Berman, 2016, "Beyond Biocentrism: Rethinking Time, Space, Consciousness, and the Illusion of Death", BenBella Books, Inc.

——, 2011, "Biocentrism: How Life and Consciousness are the Keys to the True Nature of the Universe", ReadHowYouWant.com

Laszlo, Ervin, 2007, "Science and the Akashic Field: An Integral Theory of Everything", Simon and Schuster (second edition).

Lenski, Wolfgang, 2010, "Information: A Conceptual Investigation", Information 2010.

Levin, Leonid A., 1973, "Universal Sequential Search Problems", Problems of Information Transmission.

——,1974, "Laws of Information Conservation (Non-Growth) and Aspects of the Foundation of Probability Theory", Problems of Information Transmission.

——, 1984, "Randomness Conservation Inequalities; Information and Independence in Mathematical Theories", Information and Control.

Li, Ming and Paul Vitányi, 2008, "An Introduction to Kolmogorov Complexity and Its Applications", (Texts in Computer Science), New York: Springer New York.

Linde, Andrei, 1986, "Eternally Existing Self-Reproducing Chaotic Inflationary Universe", Physics Letters B 175(4):395-400.

Lloyd, Seth, 2006, "Programming the Universe", London: Johnathan Cape.

——, 2000, "Ultimate Physical Limits to Computation", Nature.

Lloyd, Seth and Y. Jack Ng, 2004, "Black Hole Computers", Scientific American.

Locke, John, 1689, "An Essay Concerning Human Understanding", J. W. Yolton, London: Dent; New York: Dutton, 1961.

Lokanga, Ediho, 2017, "Digital Physics: The Meaning of the Holographic Universe and Its Implications Beyond Theoretical Physics", CreateSpace Publishing.

——, 2017, "Digital Physics: The Universe Is a Programmed System", CreateSpace Publishing.

——, 2017, "Digital Physics: The Physics of Information, Computation, Self-Organization and Consciousness", CreateSpace Publishing.

Lovelock, James E., 1972, "Gaia as seen through the atmosphere", Atmospheric Environment. 6 (8): 579–580.

Lovelock, James E., Lynn Margulis, 1974, "Atmospheric homeostasis by and for the biosphere: the Gaia hypothesis", Tellus. Series A. Stockholm: International Meteorological Institute. 26 (1–2): 2–10.

Malone, Thomas W., 2018, "Superminds: The Surprising Power of People and Computers Thinking Together", Little, Brown.

MacLean, Paul D., 1990, "The triune brain in evolution: role in paleocerebral functions", New York: Plenum Press.

Maccone, Lorenzo, 2015, "Causality, Physical Models and Time's Arrow", Physical Review Letters.

Manzotti, Riccardo, 2018, "Spread Mind: Why Consciousness and the World Are One", OR Books.

Maslow, Abraham, 1943, "A Theory of Human Motivation", Psychological Review.
McAllister, James W., 2003, "Effective Complexity as a Measure of Information Content", Philosophy of Science.

McKenna, Terence, 1999, "Food of the Gods: The Search for the Original Tree of Knowledge: A Radical History of Plants, Drugs, and Human Evolution", Rider.

Mikhailovsky, George E., Alexander P. Levich, 2015, "Entropy, Information and Complexity or Which Aims the Arrow of Time?", Entropy.

Miller, Kenneth R., 2018, "The Human Instinct: How We Evolved to Have Reason, Consciousness, and Free Will", Simon and Schuster.

Minsky, Marvin, 1986, "The Society of Mind", Simon & Schuster.

Mitchell, Edgar D., Robert Staretz, 2011, "The Quantum Hologram and the nature of consciousness", Journal of Cosmology, Vol. 14.

Montague, Richard, 2008, "Universal Grammar", Theoria.

Moravec, Hans, 1988: "Mind Children: The Future of Robot and Human Intelligence", Harvard University Press.

Muller, Richard A., 2016, "Now: The Physics of Time", W. W. Norton & Company.

Nagel, Thomas, 1974, "What Is it Like to Be a Bat?", Philosophical Review, pp. 435–50

Newberg, Andrew, Mark Robert Waldman, 2012, "Words Can Change Your Brain: 12 Conversation Strategies to Build Trust, Resolve Conflict, and Increase Intimacy", Avery

Nielsen, Michael A., Isaac L. Chuang, 2000, "Quantum Computation and Quantum Information", Cambridge: Cambridge University Press.

Nies, André, 2009, "Computability and Randomness", Oxford: Oxford University Press.

Nottale, Laurent, 1993, "Fractal Space-time and Microphysics: Towards a Theory of Scale Relativity", World Scientific.

Noubel, Jean-François, 2018, "Collective Intelligence", https://noubel.fr/en/category/collective-intelligence/

Nyquist, H., 1924, "Certain Factors Affecting Telegraph Speed", Bell System Technical Journal.

O'Connell, Mark, 2018, "To Be a Machine: Adventures Among Cyborgs, Utopians, Hackers, and the Futurists Solving the Modest Problem of Death", Knopf Doubleday Publishing Group.

Ong, Walter J., 1958, "Ramus, Method, and the Decay of Dialogue, From the Art of Discourse to the Art of Reason", Cambridge MA: Harvard University Press.

Owen Nicholas, 2014, "The Transcension Hypothesis: An Intriguing Answer to the Fermi Paradox?," Brighter Brains.

Parikh, Rohit and Ramaswamy Ramanujam, 2003, "A Knowledge Based Semantics of Messages", Journal of Logic, Language and Information.

Peake, Anthony, 2013, "The Infinite Mindfield: The Quest to Find the Gateway to Higher Consciousness", Watkins.

Pearce, David, 1995, "The Hedonistic Imperative", hedweb.com.

Penrose, Roger, 2010, "Cycles of Time: An Extraordinary New View of the Universe", The Bodley Head (UK), Alfred A. Knopf (US).

Pinker, Steven, 2018, "Enlightenment Now: The Case for Reason, Science, Humanism, and Progress", Allen Lane.

Pollan, Michael, 2018, "How to Change Your Mind: What the New Science of Psychedelics Teaches Us About Consciousness, Dying, Addiction, Depression, and Transcendence", Penguin Press.

Popper, Karl, 1934, "The Logic of Scientific Discovery", (Logik der Forschung), English translation 1959, London: Hutchison. Reprinted 1977.

Platt, Charles, 1991, "The Silicon Man", Bantam Books.

Putnam, Hilary, 1988, "Representation and reality", Cambridge, MA: The MIT Press.

Quine, W.V.O., 1951, "Main Trends in Recent Philosophy: Two Dogmas of Empiricism", The Philosophical Review.

Radin, Dean, 2018, "The Real Magic: Ancient Wisdom, Modern Science, and a Guide to the Secret Power of the Universe", Harmony Books.

——, 2009, "The Conscious Universe: the scientific truth of psychic phenomena", New York: HarperOne.

——, 2006, "Entangled Minds: Extrasensory Experiences in a Quantum Reality", Paraview / Pocket Books.

Rathmanner, Samuel and Marcus Hutter, 2011, "A Philosophical Treatise of Universal Induction", Entropy.

Rédei, Miklós, Michael Stöltzner, 2001, "John von Neumann and the Foundations of Quantum Physics", (Vienna Circle Institute Yearbook, 8), Dordrecht: Kluwer.

Rényi, Alfréd, 1961, "On Measures of Entropy and Information", in Proceedings of the Fourth Berkeley Symposium on Mathematical Statistics and Probability, Volume 1: Contributions to the Theory of Statistics, Berkeley, CA: The Regents of the University of California.

Rhodes, Ross, 1999, "A Cybernetic Interpretation of Quantum Mechanics", ResearchGate.

Rooy, Robert van, 2004, "Signalling Games Select Horn Strategies", Linguistics and Philosophy.

Rosenblum, Bruce, Fred Kuttner, 2011, "Quantum Enigma: Physics Encounters Consciousness", Oxford University Press.

Rovelli, Carlo, 2018, "The Order of Time", Penguin.

Russell, Bertrand, 1905, "On Denoting", Mind series.

Russell, Peter, 2000, "The Global Brain Awakens: Our Evolutionary Next Step", Element Books, Ltd.

Russell, Stuart, 2019, "Human Compatible: Artificial Intelligence and the Problem of Control", Penguin and Random House.

Schmidhuber, Jürgen, 2012, "The Fastest Way of Computing All Universes", In H. Zenil, ed., "A Computable Universe," World Scientific.

——, 1996, "A Computer Scientist's View of Life, the Universe, and Everything", LNCS 201-288, Springer.

Schwindt, Jan-Markus, 2012, "Nothing Happens in the Universe of the Everett Interpretation", Cornell University.

Schnelle, H., 1976, "Information", in Joachim Ritter (ed.), Historisches.

Searle, John R., 1990, "Is the Brain a Digital Computer?", Proceedings and Addresses of the American Philosophical Association.

Seiffert, Helmut, 1968, "Information über die Information" [Information about information] Munich: Beck.

Shannon, Claude E., 1948, "A Mathematical Theory of Communication", Bell System Technical Journal.

Sheldrake, Rupert, 2013, "Setting science free from materialism", Explore, Vol. 9(4): 211-218.

——, "Morphic Resonance: The Nature of Formative Causation", Rochester, Vermont: Park Street Press.

——, 1988, "Mind, Memory, and Archetype: Morphic Resonance and the Collective Unconscious - Part III, Psychological Perspectives", 19(1), 64-78.

Shor, Peter W., 1997, "Polynomial-Time Algorithms for Prime Factorization and Discrete Logarithms on a Quantum Computer", SIAM Journal on Computing.

Silva, Jason, 2013-2018, "Shots of Awe," YouTube videos.

Simon, J.C. and Olivier Dubois, 1989, "Number of Solutions of Satisfiability Instances – Applications to Knowledge Bases", International Journal of Pattern Recognition and Artificial Intelligence.

Simondon, Gilbert, 1989, "L'individuation Psychique et Collective: À La Lumière des Notions de Forme, Information, Potentiel et Métastabilité (L'Invention Philosophique)", Paris: Aubier.

Singh, Simon, 1999, "The Code Book: The Science of Secrecy from Ancient Egypt to Quantum Cryptography", New York: Anchor Books.

Solomonoff, R. J., 1960, "A Preliminary Report on a General Theory of Inductive Inference", Report ZTB-138, Cambridge, MA: Zator.

——, 1964a, "A Formal Theory of Inductive Inference. Part I", Information and Control.

——, 1964b, "A Formal Theory of Inductive Inference. Part II", Information and Control.

——, 1997, "The Discovery of Algorithmic Probability", Journal of Computer and System Sciences, 55(1): 73–88.

Smart, John M., 2012, "The Transcension Hypothesis", Acta Astronautica, V78:55-68.

Smolin, Lee, 1997, "The Life of the Cosmos", Oxford University Press.

Spinoza, Baruch, 1677 (postmortem), "Ethics".

Stalnaker, Richard, 1984, Inquiry, Cambridge, MA: MIT Press.

Strominger, Andrew, 2001, "Inflation and the AdS/CFT Correspondence", Journal of High Energy Physics (JHEP).

Tegmark, Max, 2017, "Life 3.0: Being Human in the Age of Artificial Intelligence", Knopf Doubleday Publishing Group.

——, 2014, "Our Mathematical Universe: My Quest for the Ultimate Nature of Reality", Knopf Doubleday Publishing Group.

Theise, Neil D., d'Inverno M., 2004, "Understanding cell lineages as complex adaptive systems", Blood Cells Mol Dis 32:17–20.

Tipler, Frank, 1997, "The Physics of Immortality", Anchor.

Tononi, Giulio, Melanie Boly, Marcello Massimini, Christof Koch, 2016, "Integrated information theory: from consciousness to its physical substrate", Nature Reviews Neuroscience.

Townsend, C. James, 2016, "The Singularity and Socialism: Marx, Mises, Complexity Theory, Techno-Optimism and the Way to the Age of Abundance", CreateSpace Publishing.

Tryon, Edward P., 1973, "Is the Universe a Vacuum Fluctuation?" Nature, vol. 246, p.396–397.

Turing, A. M., 1937, "On Computable Numbers, with an Application to the Entscheidungsproblem", Proceedings of the London Mathematical Society.

Tuynman, Antonin, 2019, "The Ouroboros Code: Reality's Digital Alchemy Self-Simulation Bridging Science and Spirituality", San Francisco, Ecstadelic Media Group.

——, 2017, "Is Intelligence an Algorithm?", John Hunt Publishing Ltd.

——, 2017, "Transcendental Metaphysics: Technovedanta 2.0: Transcendental Metaphysics of Pancomputational Panpsychism", Lulu.

——, 2012, "Technovedanta", Lulu.

Valiant, Leslie G., 2009, "Evolvability", Journal of the ACM.

van Benthem, Johan F.A.K., 1990, "Kunstmatige Intelligentie: Een Voortzetting van de Filosofie met Andere Middelen", Algemeen Nederlands Tijdschrift voor Wijsbegeerte.

518

——, 2006, "Epistemic Logic and Epistemology: The State of Their Affairs", Philosophical Studies, 128(1): 49–76.

van Benthem, Johan and Robert van Rooy, 2003, "Connecting the Different Faces of Information", Journal of Logic, Language and Information.

van Peursen, Cornelis Anthonie, 1987, "Christian Wolff's Philosophy of Contingent Reality", Journal of the History of Philosophy.

van Rooij, Robert, 2003, "Questioning to resolve decision problems", Linguistics and Philosophy, 26: 727–763.

Vereshchagin, Nikolai K. and Paul M.B. Vitányi, 2004, "Kolmogorov's Structure Functions and Model Selection", IEEE Transactions on Information Theory.

Verlinde, Erik, 2011, 2017, "Emergent Gravity and the Dark Universe", SciPost Physics.

——, "On the Origin of Gravity and the Laws of Newton", Journal of High Energy Physics.

Vernor, Vinge, 1993, "The Coming Technological Singularity: How to Survive in the Post-Human Era", Centre for Digital Philosophy.

Vigo, Ronaldo, 2011, "Representational Information: A New General Notion and Measure of Information", Information Sciences.

——, 2012, "Complexity over Uncertainty in Generalized Representational Information Theory (GRIT): A Structure-Sensitive General Theory of Information", Information.

Virk, Rizwan, 2019, "The Simulation Hypothesis: An MIT Computer Scientist Shows Why AI, Quantum Physics and Eastern Mystics All Agree We Are In a Video Game", Bayview Books.

Vitányi, Paul M., 2006, "Meaningful Information", IEEE Transactions on Information Theory.
Visser, Matt, 1989, "Traversable wormholes: Some simple examples", Physical Review.

Vogel, Cornelia Johanna de, 1968, "Plato: De filosoof van het transcendente", Baarn: Het Wereldvenster.

Von Neumann, John, 1932, "Mathematische Grundlagen der Quantenmechanik", Berlin: Springer.

Walker, Sara, Paul Davies, 2012, "The Algorithmic Origins of Life", Royal Society Publishing.

Wallace, David, 2012, "The Emergent Multiverse: Quantum Theory according to the Everett Interpretation", Oxford University Press.

Wallace, C. S., 2005, "Statistical and Inductive Inference by Minimum Message Length", Berlin: Springer.

Watts, Alan, 2018, "Out of Your Mind", Souvenir Press Limited.

Webb, TW, Michael Graziano, 2015, "The attention schema theory: a mechanistic account of subjective awareness", Front Psychol. 6: 500.

Wheeler, John Archibald, 1990, "Information, Physics, Quantum: The Search for Links", in Complexity, Entropy and the Physics of Information, Wojciech H. Zurek, Boulder, CO: Westview Press.

Whitehead, Alfred, Bertrand Russell, 1910, 1912, 1913, "Principia Mathematica", 3 vols, Cambridge: Cambridge University Press; 2nd edition, 1925 (Vol. 1), 1927 (Vols 2, 3).

Whitehead, North Alfred, 1929, "The Function of Reason", Princeton: Princeton University Press.

Whitworth, Brian, 2008, "The Physical World as a Virtual Reality", Cornell University.

Wiener, Norbert, 1948, "Cybernetics: Or Control and Communication in the Animal and the Machine", Cambridge, Massachusetts: MIT Press.

Wilkins, John, 1668, "An Essay towards a Real Character, and a Philosophical Language", London.

Wilson, Robert Charles, 1998, "Divided by Infinity", Starlight.

Windelband, Wilhelm, 1903, "Lehrbuch der Geschichte der Philosophie", Tübingen: J.C.B. Mohr.

Wolff, J. Gerard, 2006, "Unifying Computing and Cognition", Menai Bridge: Cognition Research.org.uk.

Wolfram, Stephen, 2002, "A New Kind of Science", Champaign, IL: Wolfram Media.

Wolpert, David H. and William Macready, 2007, "Using Self-Dissimilarity to Quantify Complexity", Complexity.

Wu, Kun, 2010, "The Basic Theory of the Philosophy of Information", in Proceedings of the 4th International Conference on the Foundations of Information Science, Beijing, China.

——, 2016, "The Interaction and Convergence of the Philosophy and Science of Information", Philosophies.

Zarkadakis, George, 2016, "In Our Own Image: Savior or Destroyer? The History and Future of Artificial Intelligence", Pegasus Books.

Zuse, Konrad, 1969, Rechnender Raum, Braunschweig: Friedrich Vieweg & Sohn. Translated as Calculating Space, MIT Technical Translation AZT-70-164-GEMIT, MIT (Proj. MAC), Cambridge, MA,1970.

Glossary of Terms

Anthropocene - the current geologic age, characterized by substantial alterations of ecosystems through human activity.

AGI - acronym for Artificial General Intelligence, machine intelligence at or above human level of intelligence; a machine capable of performing any intellectual task that a human being can, "general intelligent action."

The Chrysalis Conjecture – one of the possible solutions to the Fermi Paradox, at the triangulation of the Transcension hypothesis, the Noocentric model, and the Quantum Multiverse hypothesis.

Connectome - a comprehensive map of neural connections in the brain that may be thought of as its "wiring diagram," information contained within an individual brain's architecture. More broadly, a connectome would include the mapping of all neural connections within an organism's nervous system.

Consciousness - a subjective experience: It feels like to be a certain entity. In the book, the term also refers to a collapse of a wave function resulting in a unified subjective multi-sensory perceptual experience and involving multiple parallel processes such as interpreting sensory data stream, retrieving and creating memories, recognizing patterns, using imagination, envisioning the future, planning, thinking, self-reflecting, reacting to the sensory input, and being aware about the surroundings. Consciousness can be identified as an underlying mathematical pattern and quantified via feedback loops in observer-universe interacting. In parts of the book, the term is sometimes defined as an optimized meta-algorithmic information processing in reference to a "local" mind. "Non-local" consciousness, on the other hand, refers to universal consciousness.

Computational Biology - all biological organisms combined, all biological life possessing information-processing capabilities. In the book, the term is used in this context, and not to be confused with data analytics or mathematical modeling.

Ecstadelic - adj. Ecstasy-inducing, stimulating ecstatic state of being, exhilarating to the point of psychedelic rapture; n. Tool, technology of ecstasy.

Exocortex - a hypothetical artificial external information processing system that would augment a brain's biological high-level cognitive processes. An individual's exocortex would be composed of external memory modules, processors, IO devices, and software systems that would interact with, and augment a person's biological brain. Typically, this interaction is described as being conducted through a direct brain-computer interface, making these extensions functionally part of the individual's mind, "synthetic neocortex."

Holo Syntellectus - (Greek *holo*, whole + *syn*, with, together + Latin *intellectus*, intelligent) a new non-organic species emerging as a syntellect (see *Syntellect*).

Information - In physics, information refers generally to the information that is contained in a physical system. Its usage in quantum mechanics (i.e., quantum information) is important, for example in the concept of quantum entanglement to describe effectively direct or causal relationships between apparently distinct or spatially separated particles. Information itself may be loosely defined as "that which can distinguish one thing from another." The information embodied by a thing can thus be said to be the identity of the particular thing itself, that is, all of its properties, all that makes it distinct from other (real or potential) things.

Infomorph - substrate independent digital mind, advanced information entity, based on distributed networked intelligence, info-being capable to instantly share knowledge and experiences within the global neural network. *Infomorph Commonality* is a hypothetical psycho-dimensional web of synergy that connects the psyches of the future infomorphs.

Multiverse - the hypothetical set of finite or infinite possible universes, including our own. Together, these universes comprise everything that exists, the entirety of space, time, matter, energy and the physical laws and constants that describe them. The various universes within the multiverse are called *'parallel universes'*, *'other universes'*, or *'alternate universes'*.

Omniverse - the Multiverse as the whole, all-inclusive multiversal structure, all that is, the whole of all potentialities.

Neo-transcendentalism - a revived form of transcendentalism, an idealistic philosophy that emphasizes the *a priori* conditions of knowledge and experience or the unknowable character of ultimate reality and that emphasizes the transcendent as the fundamental reality; a philosophy that asserts the primacy of the mental and transcendental over the material and empirical.

Noocentrism (also *the Noocentric model*) - (Greek *noo*, mind + centrism) observer-centric model of entirely mind-based reality, absolute idealism encompassing quantum mechanical principles.

Noodimensions - "Dimensions of the Mind" (Greek *noo*, mind + dimensions), virtually created mind-space, or inner space, that represents simulated universes with their own physical laws, evolutionary processes and intelligent life.

Noogenesis - "The Origin of Mind" (Greek *noo*, mind + *genesis*, origin), the emergence and evolution of mind and intelligence.

Noosphere - (Greek *noo*, mind + sphere), a postulated "cognitive" sphere or stage of evolutionary development dominated by consciousness, the mind, and interpersonal relationships (with reference to the writings of Teilhard de Chardin and others).

Singularity - a hypothetical moment in time when artificial intelligence and other technologies have become so advanced that humanity undergoes a dramatic and irreversible change. In physics and mathematics, a point at which a function takes an infinite value, especially in space-time when matter is infinitely dense, as at the center of a black hole.

Syntellect - (Greek *syn*, with, together + intellect) the unified mind of civilization that integrates all individual natural and artificial minds through the mediation and accumulative effects of information networks.

The Syntellect Hypothesis (as in the title of the book) - a phase transition of a complex intelligent system to self-awareness of a living, conscious superorganism when intellectual synergy of its components reaches threshold complexity to become one supermind. This metamorphosis is associated with emergence of higher-order self-awareness and dimensionality of a new consciousness structure.

Technium - the greater, global, massively interconnected system of technology vibrating around us, technosphere, technological infrastructure (*"What Technology Wants"* by Kevin Kelly, 2010).

Theogenesis - "The Birth of God," (Greek *theo*, god + *genesis*, origin, birth) the emergence and evolution of a divine entity.

Whole Brain Emulation - a human brain that has been copied into a computer, and that is then run according to the laws of physics, aiming to reproduce the behavior of human mind within a digital form.

For more information on published books and to access bonus material, please visit www.ecstadelic.net/books

Esctadelic Media

Ecstadelic Media Group, San Francisco, CA

www.ecstadelic.net

Made in the USA
Monee, IL
24 June 2022

98516464R10308